Lecture Notes in Computer Science 2765

Edited by G. Goos, J. Hartmanis, and J. van Leeuwen

T0238475

Lecture Notes in Computer Science

Edited by G. Goos, J. Hartmanis and J. van Leeuwen

Springer
Berlin
Heidelberg
New York
Hong Kong
London
Milan
Paris
Tokyo

Reidar Conradi   Alf Inge Wang (Eds.)

Empirical Methods and Studies in Software Engineering

Experiences from ESERNET

Springer

Series Editors

Gerhard Goos, Karlsruhe University, Germany
Juris Hartmanis, Cornell University, NY, USA
Jan van Leeuwen, Utrecht University, The Netherlands

Volume Editors

Reidar Conradi
Alf Inge Wang
Norwegian University of Science and Technology
Department of Computer and Information Science
7491 Trondheim, Norway
E-mail: {Reidar.Conradi;Alf.Inge.Wang}@idi.ntnu.no

Cataloging-in-Publication Data applied for

A catalog record for this book is available from the Library of Congress.

Bibliographic information published by Die Deutsche Bibliothek
Die Deutsche Bibliothek lists this publication in the Deutsche Nationalbibliografie;
detailed bibliographic data is available in the Internet at <http://dnb.ddb.de>.

CR Subject Classification (1998): D.2, K.6, K.4, K.3

ISSN 0302-9743
ISBN 3-540-40672-7 Springer-Verlag Berlin Heidelberg New York

Springer-Verlag Berlin Heidelberg New York
a member of BertelsmannSpringer Science+Business Media GmbH

http://www.springer.de

© Springer-Verlag Berlin Heidelberg 2003
Printed in Germany

Typesetting: Camera-ready by author, data conversion by PTP Berlin GmbH
Printed on acid-free paper   SPIN: 10930946   06/3142   5 4 3 2 1 0

Preface

The book *"Empirical Methods and Studies in Software Engineering – Experiences from ESERNET"* is a result of the **ESERNET** project. ESERNET is a thematic network project (2001–2003) in the European Union's 5th Framework Programme under contract number IST-2000-28754; see www.esernet.org. It has the ambition, in cooperation with related activities, to gradually change the mentality of software engineers and their organizations towards *systematic empirical studies*, for the purpose of long-term *learning*. The overall goal is therefore to collect, systematize and disseminate relevant and valid insight. ESERNET is led by IESE in Kaiserslautern (Germany). The project leader is Dieter Rombach, with project manager Christian Bunse. ESERNET has five founding members (contractors):

- Blekinge Institute of Technology (BTH), Sweden: Claes Wohlin and Kennet Henningsson.
- European Software Institute (ESI), Spain: Elixabete Ostolaza and Elisa Gallo.
- Fraunhofer Institute for Experimental Software Engineering (IESE), Germany: Christian Bunse, Andreas Jedlitschka, Markus Nick, and Holger Westing.
- Norwegian University of Science and Technology (NTNU), Norway: Reidar Conradi, Letizia Jaccheri, Tor Stålhane, and Alf Inge Wang.
- The Technical Research Centre of Finland (VTT), Finland: Toni Sandelin and Matias Vierimaa.

Sodalia in Trento (Italy) was originally a partner, but decided to withdraw from the ESERNET consortium due to an internal reorganization activity.

In addition to the contractors, ESERNET has the following 22 participating members, with each contact person indicated:

- DaimlerChrysler AG, Germany: Frank Houdek.
- DELTA Danish Electronics, Light & Acoustics, Denmark: Jørgen Bøegh.
- Engineering Ingegneria Informatica S.p.A., Italy: Stefano de Panfilis.
- Fraunhofer Center for Experimental Software Engineering, Maryland (FC-MD), USA: Victor R. Basili.
- FZI Forschungszentrum Informatik, Germany: Thomas Genssler.
- Lund University, Sweden: Martin Höst.
- MARKET MAKER Software AG, Germany: Martin Verlage.
- methodpark Software AG, Germany: Christian Knuevener.
- Politecnico di Torino, Italy: Maurizio Morisio.
- PSIPENTA Software Systems GmbH, Germany: Torsten Sander.
- Robert Bosch GmbH, Germany: Eberhard Hübner.
- Simula Research Laboratory/University of Oslo, Norway: Dag Sjøberg.
- Softlab, Germany: Wolfgang Koch.
- SOLID Information Technology, Finland: Janne Järvinen.

- Universidad Politécnica de Madrid, Spain: Natalia Juristo.
- Università degli Studi dell'Insubria, Italy: Sandro Morasca.
- Università degli Studi di Bari, Italy: Giuseppe Visaggio.
- Università degli Studi di Roma "Tor Vergata", Italy: Giovanni Cantone.
- University of Calgary, Canada: Yingxu Wang.
- University of Castilla La Mancha, Spain: Mario Piattini.
- University of Kaiserslautern, Germany: Dieter Rombach and Marcus Ciolkowski.
- University of Strathclyde, UK: Marc Roper and Murray Wood.

Of the 22 participating members, 8 are industrial and 2 come from outside Europe. Many of the partners and members already work together.

June 2003   Reidar Conradi and Alf Inge Wang (editors)

Table of Contents

Part IV: Appendix and Author Index

Introduction

Reidar Conradi and Alf Inge Wang (Eds.)

Norwegian University of Science and Technology (NTNU),
NO-7491 Trondheim, Norway
{conradi,alfw}@idi.ntnu.no

1   Motivation

Our societies crucially depend on high-quality software for a large part of their functions and activities. That means that software researchers, managers, and practitioners have to be familiar with *what* software technologies to use for *which* purpose. This again means that we have to systematically study and collect evidence on *what* technologies (UML etc.) will work – or not work – with what effects in *which* contexts (application areas, project models, societal/technological systems etc.).

The field of *software engineering and software technology* is developing very fast. Perhaps as a consequence, there is seldom enough interest or opportunity for systematic investigation of how the underlying technology will actually perform. That is, we constantly introduce new concepts, methods, techniques and tools – or change existing ones – without much scientific reflection. But how can we learn and improve without systematic studies?

Systematic empirical studies in software engineering first of all assume well-proven research methods to plan and carry out investigations, and to collect relevant data. Thereafter comes data analysis – quantitative and/or qualitative – and discussion. Finally comes generalisation for later reuse and learning, and follow-up activities such as changed work practices and dissemination through scientific articles, technical reports and experience bases. In other words, we apply *the scientific method* [1]! Common study types are controlled experiments, case studies, postmortem analyses, and surveys.

Such a study usually starts with some hypotheses to be tested (verified or falsified), based on some previous insight or observations, or some external need. The hypotheses ("goal") will set the premises for what kind of activities and metrics that are relevant. For instance, if the goal is to improve reliability, we may do a case study as part of an existing project. A suitable development activity as part of the study may be to try out (improved) inspection techniques for e.g. UML design artifacts. A partial metrics for this is the number and type of defects in different phases or subsystems, with data coming from previous studies and the recent one. However, a persistent problem in our field is lack of previous data, i.e. no solid "baseline" to compare with.

All this means that there is a need for improved and better qualified empirical methods. But most importantly, there is a need to learn about and to apply such methods in practice, and to spread the results. That is, we should promote *an empirical approach to our field of software engineering*. The present book aims to contribute to this goal. It has six chapters describing different kinds of empirical

R. Conradi and A.I. Wang (Eds.): ESERNET 2001-2003, LNCS 2765, pp. 1–6, 2003.

studies, and methods for performing such studies. For instance, chapter 2 describes the common study types, and chapter 3 describes the ESERNET "template" for planning, performing, analysing, and reporting empirical studies. The book has seven more chapters where actual studies are described and discussed. These studies mainly deal with inspections, testing, object-oriented techniques, and component-based software engineering.

2   ESERNET, Experimental Software Engineering Research NETwork

ESERNET has been a thematic network project in 2001-03 in the European Union's 5th Framework Programme under contract number IST-2000-28754, see www.esernet.org. It has the ambition, in cooperation with related activities, to gradually change the mentality of software engineers and their organisations towards *systematic empirical studies*, for the purpose of long-term *learning*. The overall goal is therefore to collect, systematise and disseminate reliable insight. This type of knowledge will serve as a scientific base for assessing, understanding, changing, innovating, and using software technologies. This task assumes a joint effort between academia, technology providers, software developers, and possibly end-users. One step in this direction is the current ESERNET Method and Experience Book to convey the insights from the ESERNET project. The target audience of the book is software engineers and managers, and corresponding researchers, teachers and students.

ESERNET is lead by IESE in Kaiserslautern (Germany). The project responsible is Prof. Dieter Rombach, with project manager Dr. Christian Bunse. ESERNET has p.t. four other founding members: VTT Electronics in Oulu (Finland), NTNU in Trondheim (Norway), Blekinge Institute of Technology or BTH in Ronneby (Sweden), and ESI in Bilbao (Spain). Sodalia in Trento (Italy) was a sixth founding member, but has later withdrawn. Per June 2003, ESERNET has 27 participating members (including the five founding members). Of these, 8 are industrial and 2 come from outside Europe. Many of the partners and members already worked together before the project.

ESERNET has actively cooperated with and brought synergy to many other initiatives and projects in software engineering, as illustrated by Fig. 1 below.

In Fig. 1, SW means software and SE means Software Engineering. ISERN is the International Software Engineering Research Network, established in 1992, see www.iese.fhg.de/ISERN. PROFES, PERFECT, REBOOT, CORONET, and CLARIFI have been EU-supported software engineering projects in the 1990s (see www.cordis.lu). PROFIT is a Norwegian industrial project on software process improvement (SPI) in 1999–2003 (www.geomatikk.no/profit). VASIE stands for Value Added Software Information for Europe, and is an information and experience base for EU-projects maintained by ESI in Bilbao, see www.esi.es/VASIE/vasie.html. ESPINODEs and ESSI/PIEs encompass over 400 small EU-projects on SPI for Small- and Medium-sized Enterprises (SMEs), many registered by VASIE. Lastly, to promote exchange of ideas and results, ESERNET has supported a researcher exchange program among its members.

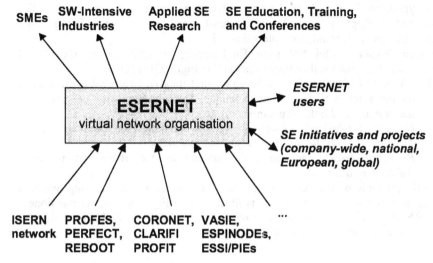

Fig. 1. ESERNET and related initiatives and projects

3 ESERNET Goals, Workpackages, Results, and Empirical Studies

The actual project **goals** are:
- Establish an infrastructure for a collaboration network.
- Evaluate software engineering practices and package the gained experience for reuse.
- Use Experimental Software Engineering (ESE) methods to facilitate the systematic introduction of new practices.
- Accelerate community-wide learning in software engineering.
- Foster collaboration and exchange within and between industry and research.
- Create synergy from existing projects, networks, and organisations.
- Initially focus on inspections, testing, object-oriented technologies, and Component-Based Software Engineering (CBSE).

ESERNET **results and deliverables** include internal reports, four open public workshops, a web portal (via the mentioned www.esernet.org) with relevant links and including a knowledge base of performed empirical studies, and of course this method and experience book.

ESERNET has applied especially four kinds of **empirical studies:** *post-mortems* and partly *surveys* (often in industry), *controlled experiments* (e.g. using students), and *industrial studies* (e.g. real case studies in industry). As described in chapter 4, such studies are often done in the following sequence: First, post-mortems or surveys are used to pre-analyse practical experience by using a specific software technology or process. Then, controlled experiments are used to test out more concrete hypotheses about the chosen study object (e.g. novel inspection techniques), often using university students. Lastly, case studies are used to investigate refined and adapted hypotheses in an industrial setting. Overall methods to support such studies are discussed in chapters 2 and 3, and lessons-learned and recommendations from using two such methods stand in chapters 6 and 7.

The term **Experimental Software Engineering** or **ESE** covers six phased activities, taken from the Quality Improvement Paradigm (QIP) [2]:

1-3. *Characterise/define/plan*: Make an explicit improvement goal and a plan to try out some new process or technique. Extra training may be given and measurements should be planned.

4. *Operate (do)* the study, observe the effects, and collect the specified data.

5. *Analyse/interpret* the results: analyse and generalise.

6. *Present/package:* package and disseminate for reuse, often in a web/experience base.

The QIP principle on project vs. corporate learning, using a double improvement loop each with the above six activities, is illustrated by Fig. 2 below. As mentioned, the ESERNET project is supporting its own experience and knowledge repository to support even cross-corporate learning, see chapter 5.

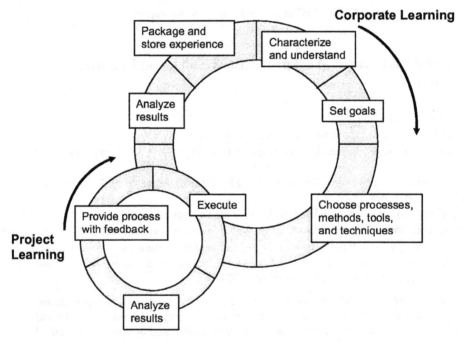

Fig. 2. Project vs. organisational learning in QIP

4   About the Book Content

As mentioned, the book reports on method and experimental work in the project. It is organised in four parts, numbered I–IV.

Part I contains a short **introduction** by the book editors at pages 1–6.

Part II contains **six method chapters, at pages 7–128**. The three first chapters (at pages 7–54) describe general and specific methods for running empirical studies. The next chapter at pages 55–80 deals with supporting an experience and knowledge base for such work. The two following chapters (at pages 81–128) describe experience by using two empirical methods, respectively controlled experiments and surveys. The six method chapters are:

An introduction to "Empirical Research Methods in Software Engineering" by Claes Wohlin, Martin Höst, and Kennet Henningsson from Blekinge Institute of Technology and Lund University (Sweden).

"Challenges and Recommendations when Increasing the Realism of Controlled Software Engineering Experiments" by Dag I. K. Sjøberg, Bente Anda, Erik Arisholm, Tore Dybå, Magne Jørgensen, Amela Karahasanović, and Marek Vokáč from Simula Research Laboratory (Norway).

"Empirical Studies in ESERNET" by Toni Sandelin and Matias Vierimaa from VTT Electronics (Finland) explains empirical studies in the ESERNET project.

A discussion of how to establish, use and maintain "Software Engineering Knowledge Repositories" by Andreas Jedlitschka and Markus Nick from Fraunhofer Institute for Experimental Software Engineering (IESE) in Kaiserslautern (Germany).

A description that explains how to "Using Empirical Studies during Software Courses" by Jeffrey Carver, Letizia Jaccheri, Sandro Morasca, and Forrest Shull from (in order of appearance) University of Maryland (USA), Norwegian University of Science and Technology (Norway), Università degli Studi dell'Insubria (Italy), and Fraunhofer USA Center for Experimental Software Engineering Maryland (USA).

A summary of "Practical Experiences in the Design and Conduct of Surveys in Empirical Software Engineering" by Marcus Ciolkowski, Oliver Laitenberger, Sira Vegas, and Stefan Biffl from (in order of appearance) University of Kaiserslautern (Germany), Droege & Comp. GmbH (Germany), Universidad Politécnica de Madrid (Spain), and TU Wien (Austria).

Part III contains **seven experience chapters, at pages 129–273**. The first chapter at pages 129–141 deals with using two variants of post-mortem analyses in industrial case studies. The four following chapters (at pages 142–232) all report on university experiments with novel inspection techniques and partly testing, applied to either object-oriented designs (in UML) or programs (in Java). The two last chapter in this part (at pages 233–273) report on a university experiment and on an industrial case study with CBSE. Thus, all the topics from the original ESERNET work plan are present. The seven experience chapters are:

A description of a study on "Post Mortem - An Assessment of Two Approaches" by Tor Stålhane, Torgeir Dingsøyr, Geir Kjetil Hanssen, and Nils Brede Moe from Norwegian University of Science (Norway) and Technology and SINTEF (Norway).

"Evaluating Checklist-Based and Use-Case-Driven Reading Techniques as Applied to Software Analysis and Design UML Artifacts" by Giovanni Cantone, Luca Colasanti, Zeiad A. Abdulnabi, Anna Lomartire, and Giuseppe Calavaro from University of Rome at Tor Vergata and Rational Software (Italy).

A description of an experiment with "Effectiveness of Code Reading and Functional Testing with Event-Driven Object-Oriented Software" by Giovanni Cantone, Zeiad A. Abdulnabi, Anna Lomartire, and Giuseppe Calavaro from University of Rome at "Tor Vergata" and Rational Software (Italy).

"Experimentation with Usage-Based Reading" by Thomas Thelin, Magnus Erlansson, Martin Höst, and Claes Wohlin from Lund University and Blekinge Institute of Technology (Sweden).

"Functional Testing, Structural Testing and Code Reading: What Fault Type do they Each Detect?" by Natalia Juristo and Sira Vegas from Universidad Politécnica de Madrid (Spain).

"COTS Products Characterization: Proposal and Empirical Assessment" by Alessandro Bianchi, Danilo Caivano, Reidar Conradi, Letizia Jaccheri, Marco Torchiano, and Giuseppe Visaggio from University of Bari (Italy), Norwegian University of Science and Technology (Norway), Politecnico of Turin (Italy).

A description of a study on "Reuse Based Software Factory" by Manuel Prego from European Software Institute Bilbao (Spain).

Part IV, at pages 274–279 contains an **Appendix** with a glossary, assembled by the book editors and an **Author Index**.

NTNU, Trondheim, 5 June 2003

On behalf of the ESERNET project,
Reidar Conradi and Alf Inge Wang, coordinating editors.

References

[1] Victor R. Basili, "The Experimental Paradigm in Software Engineering", in H. D. Rombach, V. R. Basili, and R. W. Selby (Eds.): Experimental Software Engineering Issues: Critical Assessment and Future Directives, Springer Verlag, Lecture Notes 706 in Computer Science, 1993, 261 p. From International Workshop, Dagstuhl Castle, Germany, Sept. 1992.

[2] Victor R. Basili and Gianluigi Caldiera: "Improving Software Quality by Reusing Knowledge and Experience", Sloan Management Review, 37(1):55–64, Fall 1995.

Empirical Research Methods in Software Engineering

Claes Wohlin[1], Martin Höst[2], and Kennet Henningsson[1]

[1]Dept. of Software Engineering and Computer Science Blekinge Institute of Technology
Box 520, SE–372 25 Ronneby, Sweden
{Claes.Wohlin,Kennet.Henningsson}@bth.se
[2]Dept. of Communication Systems, Lund University
Box 118, SE–221 00 Lund, Sweden
Martin.Host@telecom.lth.se

Abstract. Software engineering is not only about technical solutions. It is to a large extent also concerned with organizational issues, project management and human behaviour. For a discipline like software engineering, empirical methods are crucial, since they allow for incorporating human behaviour into the research approach taken. Empirical methods are common practice in many other disciplines. This chapter provides a motivation for the use of empirical methods in software engineering research. The main motivation is that it is needed from an engineering perspective to allow for informed and well-grounded decision. The chapter continues with a brief introduction to four research methods: controlled experiments, case studies, surveys and post-mortem analyses. These methods are then put into an improvement context. The four methods are presented with the objective to introduce the reader to the methods to a level that it is possible to select the most suitable method at a specific instance. The methods have in common that they all are concerned with quantitative data. However, several of them are also suitable for qualitative data. Finally, it is concluded that the methods are not competing. On the contrary, the different research methods can preferably be used together to obtain more sources of information that hopefully lead to more informed engineering decisions in software engineering.

1 Introduction

To become a true engineering discipline software engineering has to adopt and adapt research methods from other disciplines. Engineering means, among other things, that we should be able to understand, plan, monitor, control, estimate, predict and improve the way we engineer our products. One enabler for doing this is measurement. Software measurement forms the basis, but it is not sufficient. Empirical methods such as controlled experiments, case studies, surveys and post-mortem analyses are needed to help us evaluate and validate the research results. These methods are needed so that it is possible to scientifically state whether something is better than something else. Thus, empirical methods provide one important scientific basis for software engineering. For some type of problems other methods, for example the use of mathematical models for predicting software reliability, is better suited, but in most cases the best method is applying empiricism. The main reason being that software

R. Conradi and A.I. Wang (Eds.): ESERNET 2001-2003, LNCS 2765, pp. 7–23, 2003.

development is human intensive, and hence it does not lend itself to analytical approaches. This means that empirical methods are essential to the researcher.

The empirical methods are however also crucial from an industrial point of view. Companies aspiring to become learning organisations have to consider the following definition of a learning organisation:

"A learning organisation is an organisation skilled at creating, acquiring, and transferring knowledge, and at modifying its behaviour to reflect new knowledge and insights" [1]

Garvin continues with stating that learning organisations are good at five activities: systematic problem solving, experimentation, learning from past experiences, learning from others, and transferring knowledge. This includes relying on scientific methods rather than guesswork. From the perspective of this chapter, the key issue is the application of a scientific method and the use of empirical methods as a vehicle for systematic improvement when engineering software. The quote from Garvin is in-line with the concepts of the Quality Improvement Paradigm and the Experience Factory [2] that are often used in a software engineering context.

In summary, the above means that software engineering researchers and learning organisations both have a need to embrace empirical methods. The main objective of this chapter is to provide an introduction to four empirical research methods and to put them into an engineering context.

The remainder of this chapter is outlined as follows. Four empirical methods are briefly introduced in Section 2 to provide the reader with a reference framework to better understand the differences and similarities between the methods later. In Section 3, the four empirical methods are put into an improvement context before presenting the methods in some more details in Sections 4–7. The chapter is concluded with a short summary in Section 8 and references in Section 9.

2 Overview of Empirical Methods

There are two main types of research paradigms having different approaches to empirical studies. **Qualitative research** is concerned with studying objects in their natural setting. A qualitative researcher attempts to interpret a phenomenon based on explanations that people bring to them [3]. Qualitative research begins with accepting that there is a range of different ways of interpretation. It is concerned with discovering causes noticed by the subjects in the study, and understanding their view of the problem at hand. The subject is the person, which is taking part in a study in order to evaluate an object.

Quantitative research is mainly concerned with quantifying a relationship or to compare two or more groups [4]. The aim is to identify a cause-effect relationship. The quantitative research is often conducted through setting up controlled experiments or collecting data through case studies. Quantitative investigations are appropriate when testing the effect of some manipulation or activity. An advantage is that quantitative data promotes comparisons and statistical analysis. The use of quantitative research methods is dependent on the application of measurement, which is further discussed in [5].

It is possible for qualitative and quantitative research to investigate the same topics but each of them will address a different type of question. For example, a quantitative investigation could be launched to investigate how much a new inspection method decreases the number of faults found in test. To answer questions about the sources of variations between different inspection groups, we need a qualitative investigation.

As mentioned earlier quantitative strategies such as controlled experiments are appropriate when testing the effects of a treatment, while a qualitative study of beliefs and understandings are appropriate to find out *why* the results from a quantitative investigation are as they are. The two approaches should be regarded as complementary rather than competitive.

In general, any empirical study can be mapped to the following main research steps: Definition, Planning, Operation, Analysis & interpretation, Conclusions and Presentation & packaging. The work within the steps differs considerably depending on the type of empirical study. However, instead of trying to present four different research methods according to this general process, we have chosen to highlight the main aspects of interest for the different types of studies.

Depending on the purpose of the evaluation, whether it is techniques, methods or tools, and depending on the conditions for the empirical investigation, there are four major different types of investigations (strategies) that are addressed here:

- **Experiment.** Experiments are sometimes referred to as research-in-the-small [6], since they are concerned with a limited scope and most often are run in a laboratory setting. They are often highly controlled and hence also occasionally referred to as controlled experiment, which is used hereafter. When experimenting, subjects are assigned to different treatments at random. The objective is to manipulate one or more variables and control all other variables at fixed levels. The effect of the manipulation is measured, and based on this a statistical analysis can be performed. In some cases it may be impossible to use true experimentation; we may have to use quasi-experiments. The latter term is often used when it is impossible to perform random assignment of the subjects to the different treatments. An example of a controlled experiment in software engineering is to compare two different methods for inspections. For this type of studies, methods for statistical inference are applied with the purpose of showing with statistical significance that one method is better than the other [7, 8, 9].

- **Case study.** Case study research is sometimes referred to as research-in-the-typical [6]. It is described in this way due to that normally a case study is conducted studying a real project and hence the situation is "typical". Case studies are used for monitoring projects, activities or assignments. Data is collected for a specific purpose throughout the study. Based on the data collection, statistical analyses can be carried out. The case study is normally aimed at tracking a specific attribute or establishing relationships between different attributes. The level of control is lower in a case study than in an experiment. A case study is an observational study while the experiment is a controlled study [10]. A case study may, for example, be aimed at building a model to predict the number of faults in testing. Multivariate statistical analysis is often applied in this type of studies. The analysis methods include linear regression and principal component analysis [11]. Case study research is further discussed in [9, 12, 13, 14].

The following two methods are both concerned with research-in-the-past, although they have different approaches to studying the past.

- **Survey.** The survey is by [6] referred to as research-in-the-large (and past), since it is possible to send a questionnaire to or interview a large number people covering whatever target population we have. Thus, a survey is often an investigation performed in retrospect, when e.g. a tool or technique, has been in use for a while [13]. The primary means of gathering qualitative or quantitative data are interviews or questionnaires. These are done through taking a sample that is representative from the population to be studied. The results from the survey are then analyzed to derive descriptive and explanatory conclusions. They are then generalized to the population from which the sample was taken. Surveys are discussed further in [9, 15].

- **Post-mortem analysis.** This type of analysis is also conducted on the past as indicated by the name. However, it should be interpreted a little broader than as post-mortem. For example, a project does not have to be finished to launch a post-mortem analysis. It would be possible to study any part of a project retrospectively using this type of analysis. Thus, this type of analysis may, in the descriptive way used by [6], be described as being research-in-the-past-and-typical. It can hence be viewed as related to both the survey and the case study. The post-mortem may be conducted by looking at project documentation (archival analysis [9]) or by interviewing people, individually or as a group, who have participated in the object that is being analysed in the post-mortem analysis.

An experiment is a formal, rigorous and controlled investigation. In an experiment the key factors are identified and manipulated. The separation between case studies and experiment can be represented by the notion of a state variable [13]. In an experiment, the state variable can assume different values and the objective is normally to distinguish between two situations, for example, a control situation and the situation under investigation. Examples of a state variable could be, for example, the inspection method or experience of the software developers. In a case study, the state variable only assumes one value, governed by the actual project under study.

Case study research is a technique where key factors that may have any affect on the outcome are identified and then the activity is documented [12, 14]. Case study research is an observational method, i.e. it is done by observation of an on-going project or activity.

Surveys are very common within social sciences where, for example, attitudes are polled to determine how a population will vote in the next election. A survey provides no control of the execution or the measurement, though it is possible to compare it with similar ones, but it is not possible to manipulate variables as in the other investigation methods [15].

Finally, a post-mortem analysis may be viewed as inheriting properties from both surveys and case studies. A post-mortem may contain survey elements, but it is normally concerned with a case. The latter could either be a full software project or a specific targeted activity.

For all four methods, it is important to consider the population of interest. It is from the population that a sample should be found. The sample should preferably be chosen randomly from the population. The sample consists of a number of subjects, for example in many cases individuals participating in a study. The actual population may vary from an ambition to have a general population, as is normally the objective in experiments where we would like to generalize the results, to a more narrow view, which may be the case in post-mortem analyses and case studies.

Some of the research strategies could be classified both as qualitative and quantitative, depending on the design of the investigation, as shown in Table 1. The classification of a survey depends on the design of the questionnaires, i.e. which data is collected and if it is possible to apply any statistical methods. Also, this is true for case studies but the difference is that a survey is done in retrospect while a case study is done while a project is executed. A survey could also be launched before the execution of a project. In the latter case, the survey is based on previous experiences and hence conducted in retrospect to these experiences although the objective is to get some ideas of the outcome of the forthcoming project. A post-mortem is normally conducted close to finish an activity or project. It is important to conduct it close in time to the actual finish so that people are still available and the experiences fresh.

Experiments are purely quantitative since they have a focus on measuring different variables, change them and measure them again. During these investigations quantitative data is collected and then statistical methods are applied. Sections 4–7 give introductions to each empirical strategy, but before this the empirical methods are put into an improvement context in the following section. The introduction to controlled experiments is longer than for the other empirical methods. The main reason being that the procedure for running controlled experiments is more formal, i.e. it is sometimes referred to as a fixed design [9]. The other methods are more flexible and it is hence not possible to describe the actual research process in the same depth. Table 1 indicates this, where the qualitative and quantitative nature of the methods are indicated. Methods with a less fixed design are sometimes referred to as flexible design [9], which also indicates that the design may change during the execution of the study due to events happening during the study.

Table 1. Qualitative vs. quantitative in empirical strategies

Strategy	Qualitative / Quantitative
Experiment	Quantitative
Case study	Both
Survey	Both
Post-mortem	Both

3 Empirical Methods in an Improvement Context

Systematic improvement includes using a generic improvement cycle such as the Quality Improvement Paradigm (QIP) [2]. This improvement cycle is generic in the sense that it can both be viewed as a recommended way to work with improvement of software development, but it may also be used as a framework for conducting empirical studies. For simplicity, it is here primarily viewed as a way of improving software development, and complemented with a simple three steps approach on how the empirical methods can be used as a vehicle for systematic engineering-based improvement.

The QIP consists of six steps that are repeated iteratively:

1. **Characterize.** The objective is to understand the current situation and establish a baseline.
2. **Set goals.** Quantifiable goals are set and given in terms of improvement.
3. **Choose process/method/technique.** Based on the characterization and the goals, the part to improve is identified and a suitable improvement candidate is identified.
4. **Execute.** The study or project is performed and the results are collected for evaluation purposes.
5. **Analyze.** The outcome is studied and future possible improvements are identified.
6. **Package.** The experiences are packaged so that it can form the basis for further improvements.

It is in most cases impossible to start improving directly. The first step is normally to understand the current situation and then improvement opportunities are identified and they need to be evaluated before being introduced into an industrial process as an improvement. Thus, systematic improvement is based on the following steps:

• Understand,

• Evaluate, and

• Improve.

As a scenario, it is possible to imagine that one or both of the two methods looking at the past are used for understanding and baselining, i.e. a survey or a post-mortem analysis may be conducted to get a picture of the current situation. The objectives of a survey and a post-mortem analysis are slightly different as discussed in Section 2. The evaluation step may either be executed using a controlled experiment or a case study. It is most likely a controlled experiment if the identified improvement candidate is evaluated in a laboratory setting and compared with another method, preferably the existing method or a method that may be used for benchmarking. It may be a case study if it is judged that the improvement candidate can be introduced in a pilot project directly. This pilot project ought to be studied and a suitable method is to use a case study. In the actual improvement in an industrial setting (normally initially in one project), it is probably best suited to use a case study approach, which then may be compared with the situation found when creating the understanding. Finally, if the evaluation comes out positive, the improvement is incorporated in the standard software development process.

The above means that the four methods presented here should be viewed as complementary and not competing. They have all their benefits and drawbacks. The scenario above should be viewed as one possible way of using the methods as complementary in improving the way software is engineered.

Next, the four methods are presented in more detail to provide an introduction and understanding of them. The objective is to provide sufficient information so that a researcher intending to conduct an empirical study in software engineering can select an appropriate method given the situation at hand.

4   Controlled Experiments

4.1   Introduction

In an experiment the researcher has control over the study and how the participants carry out the tasks that they are assigned to. This can be compared to a typical case study, see below, where the researcher is more of an observer. The advantage of the experiment is, of course, that the study can be planned and designed to ensure high validity, although the drawback is that the scope of the study often gets smaller. For example, it would be possible to view a complete software development project as a case study, but a typical experiment does not include all activities of such a project.

Experiments are often conducted to compare a number of different techniques, methods, working procedures, etc. For example, an experiment could be carried out with the objective of comparing two different reading techniques for inspections. In this example two groups of people could independently perform a task with one reading technique each. That is, if there are two reading techniques, R1 and R2, and two groups, G1 and G2, then people in group G1 could use technique R1 and people in group G2 could use technique R2. This small example is used in the following subsections to illustrate some of the concepts for controlled experiments.

4.2   Design

Before the experiment can be carried out it must be planned in detail. This plan is often referred to as the design of the experiment.

In an experiment we wish to draw conclusions that are valid for a large population. For example, we wish to investigate whether reading technique R1 is more effective than reading technique R2 in general for any developer, project, organisation, etc. However, it is, of course, impossible to involve every developer in the study. Therefore, a sample of the entire population is used in the experiment. Ideally, it would be possible to randomly choose a sample from the population to include in the study, but this is for obvious reasons mostly impossible. Often, we end up trying to determine to which population we can generalise the results from a certain set of participants.

The main reason for the above is that relation between sample and population is intricate and difficult to handle. In the software engineering domain, it is mostly desirable to sample from all software developers or a subset of them, for example all software designers using a specific programming language. This is for practical reasons impossible. Thus, in the best case it is possible to choose from software developers in the vicinity of the researcher. This means that it is not a true sample from the population, although it may be fairly good. In many cases, it is impossible to have professional developers and students are used, and in particular we have to settle for students in a specific course. The latter is referred to as convenience sampling [9]. This situation leads to that we in most cases must go from subjects to population when the preferred situation is to go from population to subjects through random sampling. This should not necessarily be seen as a failure. It may be a complementary approach. However, it is important to be aware of the difference and also to consider how this affects the statistical analysis, since most statistical methods have developed based on the assumption of a random sample from the population of interest. The challenge of representative samples is also discussed in Chapter 3.

Another important principle of experiments is randomisation. With this we mean that when it is decided which treatment every participant should be subject to, this is done by random. For example, if 20 persons participate in the study where the two reading techniques R1 and R2 are compared, it is decided by random which 10 persons that should use R1 and which 10 persons that should use R2.

In experiments a number of variables are often defined. Two important types of variables are:

- Independent variables: These variables describe the treatments in the experiment. In the above example, the choice of reading technique is an independent variable that can take one of the two values R1 or R2.

- Dependent variables: These variables are studied to investigate whether they are influenced by the independent variables. For example, the number of defects can be a dependent variable that we believe is dependent on whether R1 or R2 is used. The objective of the experiment is to determine if and how much the dependent variables are affected by the independent variables.

The independent and dependent variables are formulated to cover one or several hypotheses that we have with respect to the experiment. For example, we may hypothesize that the number of defects is dependent on the two reading techniques in the example. Hypothesis testing is discussed further in relation to the analysis.

The independent and dependent variables are illustrated in Fig. 1 together with the confounding factors. Confounding factors are variables that may affect the dependent variables without the knowledge of the researcher. It is hence crucial to try to identify the factors that otherwise may affect the outcome in an undesirable way. These factors are closely related to the threats against the validity of the empirical study. Thus, it is important to consider confounding factors and the threats to the study throughout the performance of any empirical study. The threats to empirical studies are discussed in Section 4.4. One objective of the design is to minimise the effect of these factors.

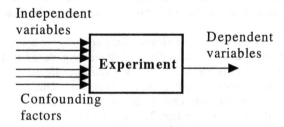

Fig. 1. Variables in an experiment

Often one of several available standard designs is used. Some examples of standard designs are:

- *Standard design 1:* One independent variable with two values: For example, two techniques should be compared and each participant uses one of the techniques.

- *Standard design 2:* One independent variable with two values, paired design: The difference between this design and standard design 1 is that each person in this design is subject to both treatments. The order in which each participant should apply the treatments is decided by random. For example, if the two reading techniques should be evaluated, half of the participants first use R1 and then R2, and the other half first uses R2 and then R1. The reason for using the treatments in different order is that effects of the order should be ruled out.

- *Standard design 3:* One independent variable with more than two values: The difference between this design and standard design 1 is that more than two treatments are compared. For example, three reading techniques may be compared.

- *Standard design 4:* More than one independent variable: With this design more than one aspect can be evaluated in an experiment. For example, both the choice of reading technique and requirements notation may be compared in one experiment.

The designs that are presented here are a summary of some of the most commonly used designs. There are alternatives and more complicated designs. For example, sometimes experiments are carried out as a combination of a pre-study and a main experiment.

4.3   Operation

In the operation of an experiment a number of parts can be included. These include both parts that have to be done when starting the experiment and when actually running the experiment. Three key parts are:

- Commit participants: It is important that every participant is committed to the tasks. There are a number of factors to consider, for example, if the experiment concerns sensitive material, it will be difficult to get committed people.

- Prepare instrumentation: All the material that should be used during the experiment must be prepared. This may include written instructions to the participants, forms that should be used by the participants during the tests, etc. The instrumentation should be developed according to the design of the experiment. In most cases different participants should be given different sets of instructions and forms. In many cases paper-based forms are used during an experiment. It is, however, possible to collect data in a number of other ways, e.g., web-based forms, interviews, etc.

- Execution: The actual execution denotes the part of the experiment where the participants, subject to their treatment, carry out the task that they are assigned to. For example, it may mean that some participants solve a development assignment with one development tool and the other participants solve the same assignment with another tool. During this task the participants use the prepared instrumentation to receive instructions and to record data that can be used later in analysis.

4.4   Analysis and Interpretation

Before actually doing any analysis, it is important to validate that the data is correct, and that the forms etc. have been filled out correctly. This activity may also be sorted under execution of the experiment, and hence be carried out before the actual analysis.

The first part in the actual analysis is normally to apply descriptive statistics. This includes plotting the data in some way to obtain an overview of the data. Part of this analysis is done to identify and handle outliers. An outlier denotes a value that is atypical and unexpected in the data set. They may, for example, be identified through box-plots [16] or scatter-plots. Every outlier must be investigated and handled separately. It may be that the value simply is wrong. Then it may be corrected or discarded. It may also, of course, be the case that the value is correct. In that case it can be included in the analysis or, if the reason for the atypical value can be identified, it may be handled separately.

When we have made sure that the data is correct and received a good understanding of the data from the descriptive statistics then the analysis related to testing one or several hypotheses can start. In most cases the objective here is to decide whether there is an effect of the value of the independent variable(s) on the value of the dependent variable(s). This is in most cases analysed through hypothesis testing. To understand hypothesis testing some important definitions must be understood:

- The null hypothesis H_0 denotes that there is no effect of the independent variable on the dependent variable. The objective of the hypothesis test is to reject this hypothesis with a known significance.
- P(type-I error) = P(reject H_0 I H_0 is true). This probability may also be called the significance of a hypothesis test.
- P(type-II error) = P(not reject H_0 I H_0 is false)
- Power = 1 - P(type-II error) = P(reject H_0 I H_0 is false)

When the test is carried out, a maximum P(type-I error) is first decided. Then a test is used in order to decide whether it is possible to reject the null hypothesis or not. When choosing a test, it must be decided whether to use parametric or non-parametric tests. Generally, there are harder requirements on the data for parametric test. They are, for example, based on that the data is normally distributed. However, parametric tests generally have higher power than non-parametric tests, i.e. less data is needed to obtain significant results when using parametric tests. The difference is not large. It is, of course, impossible to provide any exact figure, but it is in most cases in the order of 10%. For every design there are a number of tests that may be used. Some examples of tests are given in Table 2.

The tests in Table 2 are all described in a number of basic statistical references. More information on parametric tests can be found in [7], and information on the non-parametric tests can be found in, for example, [8, 17].

Before the results are presented it is important to assess how valid the results are. Basically there are four categories of validity concerns, which are discussed in a software engineering context in [18]:

Table 2. Examples of tests

Standard design (see above)	Parametric tests	Non-parametric tests
Standard design 1	t-test	Mann-Whitney
Standard design 2	Paired t-test	Wilcoxon, Sign-test
Standard design 3	ANOVA	Kruskal-Wallis
Standard design 4	ANOVA	

- Internal: The internal validity is concerned with factors that may affect the dependent variables without the researcher's knowledge. An example of an issue is whether the history of the participants affects the result of an experiment. For example, the result may not be the same if the experiment is carried out directly after a complicated fault in the code has caused the participant a lot of problem compared to a more normal situation. A good example of how confounding factors may threaten the internal validity in a study is presented in [19].

- External: The external validity is related to the ability to generalise the results of the experiments. Examples of issues are whether the problem that the participants have been working with is representative and whether the participants are representative of the target population.

- Conclusion: The conclusion validity is concerned with the possibility to draw correct conclusions regarding the relationship between treatments and the outcome of an experiment. Examples of issues to consider are whether the statistical power of the tests is too low, or if the reliability of the measurements is high enough.

- Construct: The construct validity is related to the relationship between the concepts and theories behind the experiment and what is measured and affected. Examples of issues are whether the concepts are defined clearly enough before measurements are defined, and interaction of different treatments when persons are involved in more than one study.

Obviously, it is important to have these validity concerns in mind already when the designing the experiment and in particular when using a specific design type. In the analysis phase it is too late to change the experiment in order to obtain better validity. The different validity threats should also be considered for the other type of empirical studies discussed in the following sections.

When the analysis is completed the next step is to draw conclusions and take actions based on the conclusions.

More in-depth descriptions of controlled experiments in a software engineering context can be found in [18, 20].

5 Case Study

5.1 Introduction

A case study is conducted to investigate a single entity or phenomenon within a specific time space. The researcher collects detailed information on, for example, one single project during a sustained period of time. During the performance of a case study, a variety of different data collection procedures may be applied [4].

If we would like to compare two methods, it may be necessary to organize the study as a case study or an experiment. The choice depends on the scale of the evaluation. An example can be to use a pilot project to evaluate the effects of a change compared to some baseline [6].

Case studies are very suitable for industrial evaluation of software engineering methods and tools because they can avoid scale-up problems. The difference between case studies and experiments is that experiments sample over the variables that are being manipulated, while case studies sample from the variables representing the typical situation. An advantage of case studies is that they are easier to plan but the disadvantages are that the results are difficult to generalize and harder to interpret, i.e. it is possible to show the effects in a typical situation, but it cannot be generalized to every situation [14].

If the effect of a process change is very widespread, a case study is more suitable. The effect of the change can only be assessed at a high level of abstraction because the process change includes smaller and more detailed changes throughout the development process [6]. Also, the effects of the change cannot be identified immediately. For example, if we would like to know if a new design tool increases the reliability, it may be necessary to wait until after delivery of the developed product to assess the effects on operational failures.

Case study research is a standard method used for empirical studies in various sciences such as sociology, medicine and psychology. Within software engineering, case studies should not only be used to evaluate how or why certain phenomena occur, but also to evaluate the differences between, for example, two design methods. This means in other words, to determine "which is best" of the two methods [14]. An example of a case study in software engineering is an investigation if the use of perspective-based reading increases the quality of requirements specifications. A study like this cannot verify that perspective-based reading reduces the number of faults that reaches test, since this requires a reference group that does not use perspective-based techniques.

5.2 Case Study Arrangements

A case study can be applied as a comparative research strategy, comparing the results of using one method or some form of manipulation, to the results of using another approach. To avoid bias and to ensure internal validity, it is necessary to create a solid base for assessing the results of the case study. There are three ways to arrange the study to facilitate this [6].

A comparison of the results of using the new method against a company baseline is one solution. The company should gather data from standard projects and calculate characteristics like average productivity and defect rate. Then it is possible to compare the results from the case study with the figures from the baseline.

A sister project can be chosen as a baseline. The project under study uses the new method and the sister-project the current one. Both projects should have the same characteristics, i.e. the projects must be comparable.

If the method applies to individual product components, it could be applied at random to some components and not to others. This is very similar to an experiment, but since the projects are not drawn at random from the population of all projects, it is not an experiment.

5.3   Confounding Factors and Other Aspects

When performing case studies it is necessary to minimize the effects of confounding factors. A confounding factor is, as it is described in Section 4, a factor that makes it impossible to distinguish the effects from two factors from each other. This is important since we do not have the same control over a case study as in an experiment. For example, it may be difficult to tell if a better result depends on the tool or the experience of the user of the tool. Confounding effects could involve problems with learning how to use a tool or method when trying to assess its benefits, or using very enthusiastic or sceptical staff.

There are both pros and cons with case studies. Case studies are valuable because they incorporate qualities that an experiment cannot visualize, for example, scale, complexity, unpredictability, and dynamism. Some potential problems with case studies are as follow.

A small or simplified case study is seldom a good instrument for discovering software engineering principles and techniques. Increases in scale lead to changes in the type of problems that become most indicative. In other words, the problem may be different in a small case study and in a large case study, although the objective is to study the same issues. For example, in a small case study the main problem may be the actual technique being studied, and in a large case study the major problem may be the amount of people involved and hence also the communication between people.

Researchers are not completely in control of a case study situation. This is good, from one perspective, because unpredictable changes frequently tell them much about the problems being studied. The problem is that we cannot be sure about the effects due to confounding factors.

More information on case study research can be found in, for example, [12, 14].

6 Survey

Surveys are conducted when the use of a technique or tool already has taken place [13] or before it is introduced. It could be seen as a snapshot of the situation to capture the current status. Surveys could, for example, be used for opinion polls and market research.

When performing survey research the interest may be, for example, in studying how a new development process has improved the developer's attitudes towards quality assurance. Then a sample of developers is selected from all the developers at the company. A questionnaire is constructed to obtain information needed for the research. The questionnaires are answered by the sample of developers. The information collected is then arranged into a form that can be handled in a quantitative or qualitative manner.

6.1   Survey Characteristics

Sample surveys are almost never conducted to create an understanding of the particular sample. Instead, the purpose is to understand the population, from which the sample was drawn [15]. For example, by interviewing 25 developers on what they think about a new process, the opinion of the larger population of 100 developers in the company can be predicted. Surveys aim at the development of generalized suggestions.

Surveys have the ability to provide a large number of variables to evaluate, but it is necessary to aim at obtaining the largest amount of understanding from the fewest number of variables since this reduction also eases the analysis work.

It is not necessary to guess which the most relevant variables in the initial design of the study are. The survey format allows the collection of many variables, which in many cases may be quantified and processed by computers. This makes it is possible to construct a variety of explanatory models and then select the one that best fits the purposes of the investigation.

6.2   Survey Purposes

The general objective for conducting a survey is either of the following [15]:

- Descriptive.
- Explanatory.
- Explorative.

Descriptive surveys can be conducted to enable assertions about some population. This could be determining the distribution of certain characteristics or attributes. The concern is not about why the observed distribution exists, rather what it is.

Explanatory surveys aim at making explanatory claims about the population. For example, when studying how developers use a certain inspection technique, we might want to explain why some developers prefer one technique while others prefer another. By examining the relationships between different candidate techniques and several explanatory variables, we may try to explain why developers choose one of the techniques.

Finally, explorative surveys are used as a pre-study to a more thorough investigation to assure that important issues are not foreseen. Creating a loosely structured questionnaire and letting a sample from the population answer it could do this. The information is gathered and analyzed, and the results are used to improve the full investigation. In other words, the explorative survey does not answer the basic research question, but it may provide new possibilities that could be analyzed and should therefore be followed up in the more focused or thorough survey.

6.3   Data Collection

The two most common means for data collection are questionnaires and interviews [15]. Questionnaires could both be provided in paper form or in some electronic form, for example, e-mail or WWW pages. The basic method for data collection through questionnaires is to send out the questionnaire together with instructions on how to fill it in. The responding person answers the questionnaire and then returns it to the researcher.

Letting interviewers handle the questionnaires (by telephone or face-to-face) instead of the respondents themselves, offers a number of advantages:

- Interview surveys typically achieve higher response rates than, for example, mail surveys.

- An interviewer generally decreases the number of "do not know" and "no answer", because he/she can answer questions about the questionnaire.

- It is possible for the interviewer to observe and ask questions.

- The disadvantage is the cost and time, which depend on the size of the sample, and they are also related to the intentions of the investigation.

7 Post-mortem Analysis

Post-mortem analysis is a research method studying the past, but also focusing on the typical situation that has occurred. Thus, a post-mortem analysis is similar to the case study in terms of scope and to the survey in that it looks at the past. The basic idea behind post-mortem analysis is to capture the knowledge and experience from a specific case or activity after it has been finished. [21] identifies two types of post-mortem analysis: a general post-mortem analysis capturing all available information from an activity or a focused post-mortem analysis for a specific activity, for example, cost estimation.

According to [21], post-mortem analysis has mainly been targeted at large software projects to learn form their success or recovery from a failure. An example of such a process is proposed by [22]. The steps are:

1. Project survey.
   The objective is to use a survey to collect information about the project from the participants. The use of a survey ensures that confidentiality can be guaranteed.

2. Collect objective information.
   In the second step, objective information that reveals the health of the project is collected. This includes defect data, person-hours spent and so forth.

3. Debriefing meeting.
   A meeting is held to capture issues that where not covered by the survey. In addition, it provides the project participants with an opportunity to express their view.

4. Project history day.
   The history day is conducted with a selected subset of the people involved to review project events and project data.

5. Publish the results.

Finally, a report is published. The report is focused on the lessons-learned and to use that to guide organisational improvement.

To support small- and medium-sized companies, [21] discusses a lightweight approach to post-mortem analysis, which focuses on a few vital activities and highlights that:

- Post-mortem analyses should be open for participation for all team members and other stakeholders,
- Goals may be used to focus the discussions, but it is not necessary,
- The post-mortem process consists of three main phases: preparation, data collection and analysis. These phases are further discussed in [21].

Post-mortem analyses are a flexible type of analysis method. The actual object to be studied (a whole project or specific activity) and the type of questions posed is very much dependent on the actual situation and the objectives of the analysis.

The referenced articles or the book by Whitten [23] provide more information on post-mortem analysis/review.

Finally, it should be noted that empirical methods also provide positive side effects such knowledge sharing, which is an added-value from conducting an empirical study. This is true for all types of empirical studies. In an experiment, the subjects learn from comparing competing methods or techniques. This is particular true if the subjects are debriefed afterwards in terms of obtaining information about the objective and the outcome of the experiment. In case studies and post-mortem analyses the persons participating obtain a new perspective of their work and they often reflect on their way of working through the participation in the empirical study. Finally, in the survey the learning comes from comparing answers given with the general outcome of the survey. This allows individuals to put their own answers in a more general context.

8 Summary

This chapter has provided a brief overview of four empirical research methods with a primary focus on methods that contain some quantitative part. The four methods are: controlled experiments, case studies, surveys and post-mortem analyses. The main objective has been to introduce them so that people intending to conduct empirical studies can make an appropriate selection of an empirical research method in a software engineering context.

Moreover, the presented methods must be seen as complementary in that they can be applied at different stages in the research process. This means that they can, together in a suitable combination, support each other and hence provide a good basis for sustainable improvement in software development.

References

[1]   D. A. Garvin, "Building a Learning Organization", in Harward Business Review on Knowledge Management, pp. 47–80, Harward Business School Press, Boston, USA, 1998.

[2]   V. R. Basili, G. Caldiera, and H. D. Rombach, "Experience Factory" in Encyclopaedia of Software Engineering, editor John J. Marciniak, John Wiley & Sons, Inc., Hoboken, N.J., USA, 2002.

[3]   N. K. Denzin and Y. S. Lincoln, Handbook of Qualitative Research, Sage Publications, London, UK, 1994.

[4]   J. W. Creswell, Research Design, Qualitative and Quantitative Approaches, Sage Publications, 1994.

[5]   N. Fenton, and S. L. Pfleeger, Software Metrics: A Rigorous & Practical Approach, 2nd edition, International Thomson Computer Press, 1996.

[6]   B. Kitchenham, L. Pickard and S. L. Pfleeger, "Case Studies for Method and Tool Evaluation", IEEE Software, pp. 52–62, July 1995.

[7]   D. C. Montgomery, Design and Analysis of Experiments, 4th edition, John Wiley & Sons, New York, USA, 1997.

[8]   S. Siegel, J. Castellan, Nonparametric Statistics for the Behavioral Sciences, 2nd edition, McGraw-Hill International, New York, USA, 1988.

[9]   C. Robson, Real World Research, 2nd edition, Blackwell, 2002.

[10] M. V. Zelkowitz and D. R. Wallace, "Experimental Models for Validating Technology", IEEE Computer, 31(5), pp. 23–31, 1998.

[11] B. F. J. Manly, Multivariate Statistical Methods – A Primer, Second Edition, Chapman & Hall, London, 1994.

[12] R. E. Stake, The Art of Case Study Research, SAGE Publications, 1995.

[13] S. Pfleeger, "Experimental Design and Analysis in Software Engineering Part 1–5", ACM Sigsoft, Software Engineering Notes, Vol. 19, No. 4, pp. 16–20; Vol. 20, No. 1, pp. 22–26; Vol. 20, No. 2, pp. 14–16; Vol. 20, No. 3, pp. 13–15; and Vol. 20, No. 4, pp. 14–17, 1994–1995.

[14] R. K. Yin, Case Study Research Design and Methods, Sage Publications, Beverly Hills, California, 1994.

[15] E. Babbie, Survey Research Methods, Wadsworth, ISBN 0–524–12672–3, 1990.

[16] J. W. Tukey, Exploratory Data Analysis, Addison-Wesley, 1977.

[17] C. Robson, Design and Statistics in Psychology, 3rd edition, Penguin Books, London, England, 1994.

[18] C. Wohlin, P. Runeson, M. Höst, M. C. Ohlsson, B. Regnell and A. Wesslén, Experimentation in Software Engineering – An Introduction, Kluwer Academic Publishers, Boston, MA, USA, 1999.

[19] C. M. Judd, E. R. Smith and L .H. Kidder, Research Methods in Social Relations, Harcourt Brace Jovanovich College Publishers, Forth Worth, Texas, USA6th Edition, 1991

[20] N. Juristo and A. Moreno, Basics of Software Engineering Experimentation, Kluwer Academic Publishers, Boston, Massachusetts, USA, 2001.

[21] A. Birk, T. Dingsøyr and T. Stålhane, "Postmortem: Never Leave a Project without It", IEEE Software, pp. 43–45, May/June 2002.

[22] B. Collier, T. DeMarco and P. Fearey, "A Defined Process for Project Postmortem Review", IEEE Software, pp. 65–72, July 1996.

[23] N. Whitten, Managing Software Development Projects – Formula for Success, John Wiley and Sons, Inc., New York, USA, 1995.

Challenges and Recommendations When Increasing the Realism of Controlled Software Engineering Experiments

Dag I.K. Sjøberg, Bente Anda, Erik Arisholm, Tore Dybå, Magne Jørgensen,
Amela Karahasanović and Marek Vokáč

Simula Research Laboratory, P.O. Box 134, NO-1325 Lysaker, Norway
Telephone: +47 67 82 83 00
{dagsj,bentea,erika,magnej,amela,marekv}@simula.no

Abstract. An important goal of most empirical software engineering experiments is the transfer of the research results to industrial applications. To convince industry about the validity and applicability of the results of controlled software engineering experiments, the tasks, subjects and the environments should be as realistic as practically possible. Such experiments are, however, more demanding and expensive than experiments involving students, small tasks and pen-and-paper environments. This chapter describes challenges of increasing the realism of controlled experiments and lessons learned from the experiments that have been conducted at Simula Research Laboratory.

Keywords: Empirical software engineering, technology transfer, controlled experiments

1 Introduction

The ultimate criterion for success in an applied discipline such as software engineering (SE) research is the widespread adoption of research results into everyday industrial practice. To achieve this, diffusion of innovation models requires the evidential credibility of software experiments, which depends on both the producer and the receiver of the results. Without a close tie between the experimental situation and the "real", industrial situation, practitioners may perceive the experiment as irrelevant and ignore the results.

Hence, there is an increasing understanding in the software engineering community that realistic empirical studies are needed to develop or improve processes, methods and tools for software development and maintenance [1, 2, 3, 4, 5, 6, 7].

Most of the studies in software engineering that have emphasized realism are case studies. However, a major deficiency of case studies is that many variables vary from one case study to another so that comparing the results to detect cause-effect relationships is difficult [8]. Therefore, controlled experiments should be conducted to *complement* case studies in empirical software engineering.

While the *raison d'être* for experimental research is to establish evidence for causality through *internal* logical rigor and control [9], this is not enough. It is also important to ensure *external* validity [8]. If an experiment lacks external validity, its findings may not be true beyond the experimental setting. An important issue,

R. Conradi and A.I. Wang (Eds.): ESERNET 2001-2003, LNCS 2765, pp. 24–38, 2003.

therefore, is whether the particular features of formal SE experiments are realistic. In particular, it is a challenge to achieve realism regarding experimental subjects, tasks and environment [10].

Controlled experiments in software engineering often involve students solving small pen-and-paper tasks in a classroom setting. A major criticism of such experiments is their lack of realism [11, 12], which may deter technology transfer from the research community to industry. The experiments would be more realistic if they are run on realistic tasks on realistic systems with professionals using their usual development technology in their usual workplace environment [13]. Generally, a weakness of most software engineering research is that one is rarely explicit about the target population regarding tasks, subjects and environments.

During the last couple of years the authors of this chapter have conducted 13 controlled experiments with a total of 800 students and 300 professionals as subjects. The purpose of this chapter is to describe some of the challenges and risks to be encountered when the realism of controlled experiments increases, and to give some recommendations based on our experience.

The remainder of this chapter is organised as follows. Sections 2, 3 and 4 discuss challenges and lessons learned from our attempt of increasing the realism of respectively subjects, tasks and environment of controlled SE experiments. Section 5 addresses the logistics of conducting such experiments. Section 6 concludes.

2 Representative Subjects

A prerequisite for the discussion on realism is that we are conscious about the population we wish to make claims about [14], see also Chapter 2 of this book. Implicit in our discussion is that the interesting population is "representative" software builders doing "representative" tasks in "representative" industrial environments. Nevertheless, it is not trivial defining what "representative" means. For example, there may be many categories of professionals, such as junior, intermediate and senior consultants.

2.1 Target and Sample Population

As in all experimental disciplines involving people, two major challenges are:
- identifying the population about which we wish to make claims and
- selecting subjects who are representative of that population.

The similarity of the subjects of an experiment to the people who will use the technology impacts the ease of the technology transfer [15]. Unfortunately, few papers reporting controlled SE experiments are explicit on the target population. Usually, there is an assumption that the target population is "professional software builders". One should; however, be aware that this group may be very diverse. That is, the performance may differ significantly between various categories of professionals [16].

A common criticism of experiments in software engineering is that most of the subjects are students, which might make it difficult to generalise the results to settings with various kinds of professionals. To simplify the generalisation of experimental results to a realistic setting, one should attempt to sample subjects from the population of professionals that we wish to make claims about. However, students are more accessible and easier to organise, and hiring them is generally inexpensive. Consequently, experiments with students are easier to run than experiments with professionals and the risks are lower.

Student experiments should thus be used to test experimental design and initial hypotheses, before conducting experiments with professionals [17]. Experiments with students might have the goal of gaining an understanding of the basic issues without actually aiming for external validity. Conducting "unrealistic" experiments may be a first step in a technology transfer process, that is, to reduce risks and costs, one should start with a relatively small experiment with students, possibly with small tasks (see Section 3.2) and the use of pen and paper (see Section 4.1), and then increase the scale of realism if the first pilot experiments are promising.

2.2 Background Information about Subjects

Generally, papers describing SE experiments that involve professionals often do not characterise the professionals' competence, experience and educational background, and the authors seldom justify to what extent their subjects are representative of the software engineers who usually perform such tasks. This leads to several problems:

- The results may not be trustworthy, that is, the professionals may not be realistic for the actual experimental tasks. The sample recruited may be biased in some way, for example, a company may only be willing to let the software engineers who are least experienced or least in demand take part in an experiment.
- Comparing results from the original with replicated studies is difficult.
- Successful transfer of the results into industrial practice is less likely.

To generalise from experiments with a given group of subjects, we would need information about the ability and the variations among the subjects and the group of people to which the results will be generalised [18]. For professionals, depending on what we wish to study, it would be relevant to know the variations regarding competence, productivity, education, experience (including domains), age, culture/nationality (?), etc. (Some of this information may be highly controversial and should be carefully considered from an ethical point of view.) A challenge of measuring these attributes is to define good measures that can be used in practice. For example, how do we measure competence and productivity? In practice, we would have to find meaningful substitute measures for those we cannot measure directly. In an experiment on object-oriented (OO) design principles [19], we collected detailed information about:

- age,
- education (number of credits in general, number of credits in computer science),
- general work experience,
- programming experience (OO in general, particular programming languages (Java, C++, etc.),
- knowledge of systems developments methods and tools, and
- subjective description of their own programming skills.

This background information can be used in several ways, for example, to determine

- the target population for which the results are valid, and
- to what extent the results of the treatments depend on the collected background information, e.g., that certain design principles might be easier to understand for experienced professionals than for novices.

It would also be interesting to identify the variations within the same company versus among companies, variations between in-house professionals versus consultants, etc. For example, in-house software development in Nokia, Ericsson, Bosch, etc. may differ from development projects run by consultancy companies. Nevertheless, knowledge about the effect of a certain technology among consultants or even students may still be useful in the lack of knowledge of the effect of the technology in a company's own environment.

2.3 How to Get Subjects?

Both students and professionals are used in SE experiments. For most university researchers it is relatively easy to use students as subjects in experiments. One can organise an experiment as follows:

1. The experiment is considered a compulsory part of a course, either as part of the teaching or as an exercise [20, 21].
2. The experiment is not compulsory; it is voluntary, but is still regarded relevant for the exam [22]. (In practice, students may feel obliged to take part to show their teacher that they are enthusiastic students.)
3. The students are paid, that is, the experiment is not considered as part of the course (but it may still be relevant) [23, 24, 25].

In our research group, we have experienced that the organisation indicated in alternative (3) is usually the easiest one. We then do not have the time constraint of the ordinary classes, the students are motivated and there seems to be few ethical problems [26, 27]. (One might argue that it is unethical if some students have been using a technology that proved better than the technologies being used by others students, that is, some students have learned better technologies than other students. However, when the experiment is voluntary and they are paid, this is hardly a problem). In any case, if practically possible, we inform the students about the results of the experiments.

The lack of professionals in software engineering experiments is due to the conception of high costs and large organisational effort. Warren Harrison [10] puts it this way:

> *Professional programmers are hard to come by and are very expensive. Thus, any study that uses more than a few professional programmers must be very well funded. Further, it is difficult to come by an adequate pool of professional developers in locations that do not have a significant software development industrial base. Even if we can somehow gather a sufficiently large group of professionals, the logistics of organizing the group into a set of experimental subjects can be daunting due to schedule and location issues.*

Norman Fenton claims that "generally, such [formal] experiments are prohibitively expensive and technically infeasible to set up properly" [28]. He then refers to an experiment conducted with MSc students that was criticised for the claim that these students were representative of trainee programmers in industry.

To alleviate these problems, we have applied alternative incentives to conduct experiments with professionals:

- Offer the organisation tailored internal courses and, for example, use the course exercises as experiments.
- Have a part time job in the company and advocate the experiment as useful for the company [29].
- Involve some of the employees in the research and offer them co-authorship of the resulting research paper.
- Offer the organisation a network of people from other organisations with relevant experience.
- Pay the company directly for the hours spent on the experiment [30].

The first and the last alternative have proved most successful. Regarding the last alternative, we thought that it would be most effective to use our personal network to get people to take part in our experiments on their spare time and pay them individually. However, it turned out that a much better approach is to phone the switchboard of a major consultancy company and request a specific service.

This way, one can get a sample of different categories of professionals (junior, intermediate, senior) from different companies as subjects in one experiment. In the OO design experiment [16], 130 professionals from 9 companies took part. They were easy to get. It was considerably more difficult to get subjects to take part in another experiment on design pattern [31], because that experiment was held for a period of three given days, whereas the length of the OO design experiment was only one day, and the day was chosen by the participating companies themselves (within a certain interval).

When we hire people from consultancy companies to take part in our experiments, we are treated professionally like any ordinary customer (although several consultants say that they find our experiments more exciting than most other projects). We agree on a contract and they internally define a project with a project leader, budget, etc. Of course, one must have the resources to do research this way.

3 Realistic Tasks

When conducting controlled experiments in software engineering, one should consider the realism and representativeness of the tasks regarding the, complexity and duration of the involved tasks. Specification, implementation and verification methods also vary considerably between domains, such as accounting software versus flight-control systems. In our opinion, some experimental tasks bear little resemblance to actual tasks in software engineering; others are very similar to actual tasks [32]. In between there is a continuum. Larger development tasks may take months, while many maintenance tasks may take only a couple of hours.

Most experiments in software engineering seem simplified and short-term: "the experimental variable must yield an observable effect in a matter of hours rather than six months or a year" [10]. Such experiments are hardly realistic given the tasks of building and maintaining real, industrial software, particularly since many of the factors we wish to study require significant time before we can obtain meaningful results.

3.1 Collecting Information about "Typical" Tasks

A systematic way to define representative tasks according to a given application area in a given context, is to collect information about the kinds and frequencies of tasks in the actual environment and then create "benchmark tasks", i.e., a set of tasks that is a representative sample of tasks from the population of all tasks. An example use of such benchmark tasks is described in [33]. In that study, the maintenance benchmark tasks were derived from another study of 109 randomly sampled maintenance tasks [34].

In yet another study, we collected information about all the maintenance tasks in a tool vendor company through a Web interface during a period of six months [35].

3.2 Longer Experiments

Generally, to increase the realism of SE experiments, the duration of the experimental tasks should be increased. As far as we have observed, the tasks carried out in student experiments take only up to three-four hours – most of them are shorter to fit with the time schedule of a university class. In the experiment on object-oriented (OO) design principles [16], the subjects spent one day each on five experimental tasks; whereas in the design pattern experiment [31] the subjects spent three days (including a course on design patterns the second day).

We have conducted one longer-term (35 hours), one-subject explorative study [36], that is, an "N=1 Experiment" [10]. The longer duration of this study allowed a wider spectrum of tasks to be carried out. The system on which the tasks were performed was also larger in size and complexity than usual in most experiments. Another positive effect of the longer duration was that the pressure from the experimental situation put on the subject was less, that is, more realistic, than what we have experienced in the controlled experiments we have run. In the student experiments, most students felt as if they were in an exam situation. "How did I do?" they asked after the experiment.

Another example of an experiment with high realism of tasks is our ongoing study on uncertainty in the estimation of development effort. In that experiment we pay an organization to evaluate three estimation processes. The organization now estimates one third of their incoming projects respectively according to the first, second and third estimation process.

Increasing the duration of the experiments enables more realistic tasks to be carried out. We have tried several means to achieve longer experiments; some of them with success (see Section 4.2). Of course, our tasks may still be small compared with many actual tasks. We are therefore planning an experiment where an application system that is actually needed by Simula Research Laboratory, will be developed by 4–5 different project teams (each consisting of 4–5 persons) from different consultancy companies. It should be possible to develop the system in a couple of months. This would then be a very realistic development task. Of course, the number of subjects (here teams) is too small to conduct hypothesis testing, but we still have some control. Nevertheless, there are many challenges to such an experiment.

3.3 Methodological Challenges Regarding Quality and Time

Time is often a dependent variable in SE experiments. Usually, we want the subjects to solve the tasks with satisfactory quality in as short time as possible, as most software engineering jobs put a relatively high pressure on the tasks to be done. However, if the time pressure put on the participatory subjects is too high, then the task solution quality may be reduced to the point where it becomes meaningless to use the corresponding task times in subsequent statistical analyses. A challenge is therefore to put a realistic time pressure on the subjects. How to best deal with this challenge depends to some extent on the size, duration and location of the experiment. For smaller experiments where the subjects are located in the same physical location (e.g., a classroom), we have applied the following strategies:

- All subjects receive a fixed honorarium for their participation. This eliminates potential problems of subjects speculating in working slowly to get higher payment.

- The subjects work for the same amount of time (e.g., 3 hours), finishing as many tasks as they can. This prevents faster subjects from disturbing the slower subjects. At the finishing time, everyone has to leave.

- The subjects are informed that they are not all given the same tasks. This (combined with the fixed time on the tasks) reduces the chances that the "slow" subjects deliver solutions with inadequate quality (faster than they should) in an attempt to appear smart in front of their peers; most persons would find it embarrassing to be the last to complete the tasks.

- The last task of the experiment is a large task that we a priori do not expect the subjects will be able to complete. This assumption should be tested in a small pilot experiment. Unknown to the subjects, this extra task is not included in the analysis. The extra task puts sufficient time pressure also on the fast subjects. It also reduces threats to validity caused by "ceiling effects", that is, the adverse effect of having too much or too little time towards the end of the experiment, since this extra task is not included in the analysis.

We applied all of these strategies in the pen-and-paper version of the OO design experiment [16]. Since nobody finished the extra task, there was sufficient time pressure. Everyone left at the same time (after three hours). Hence, there was no disturbance and it was fair that everybody received a fixed honorarium. Furthermore, there was no reason to speculate in working slowly (to increase their payment), or to work faster than they should (to look good).

In our more work-intensive experiments, the tasks would typically take one day or more to complete. Furthermore, the experiment may be located in different physical locations, e.g., in their usual work environment (Section 4). In these cases, the fixed honorarium and fixed time strategies seem less appropriate since many subjects will have to be present without doing any sensible work for a longer time and disturbance is less of an issue. In these cases we have applied the following strategies:

- Instead of a "fixed" honorarium, we estimate the work to (say) 5 hours, and then say that the subjects will be paid for those 5 hours independently of how long they would actually need. (Note that we wish the subjects to finish as soon as possible; we would discourage people to speculate in working slowly to get higher payment.) Hence, the subjects who finish early (e.g., 2 hours) are still paid for 5 hours. However, in practice, we tell the subjects when the 5 hours have passed, that they will be paid for additional hours if they finish their tasks.

- The subjects are allowed to leave when they finish.

- As for fixed time, smaller scale "classroom" experiments, the subjects are still informed that they are not all given the same tasks to reduce the chances that they for competitive reasons work "faster" than they should with resulting low quality of the delivered task solutions.

- As for fixed time, smaller scale "classroom" experiments, the experiment should preferably still include an extra, last task not to be included in the analysis. Although the benefit of an extra task is probably not as large as for fixed time, fixed honorarium experiments, our results suggest that the last task nevertheless may exhibit ceiling effects and therefore should not be included in the analysis. The potential benefits of an extra, last task may justify the added duration and costs of the experiment.

We applied these alternative strategies for the professionals participating in the replicated OO design experiment [16]. Our experiences suggest that these strategies work fairly well, although each strategy provides different advantages and disadvantages in terms of threats to validity, practical issues and costs. For example, restrictions imposed by an existing experiment design might make it difficult to include an "extra task", like the experiment reported in [31].

In another experiment on UML design processes with 53 students [37], we combined the strategies described above. The experiment was run in a classroom setting and was scheduled for three hours. However, due to the need for extra time caused by the use of a CASE tool (see Section 4.1); many students had not finished after the three hours. Those students were then encouraged to stay longer and finish their tasks by being offered additional payment. This way, we managed to collect more data points than if everybody had left after the scheduled time.

4   Realistic Environment

While our focus is on controlled experiments, this does not mean that we are only concerned with laboratory, or *in vitro*, experiments. Controlled experiments can also be conducted *in vivo*, in a more realistic environment than is possible in the artificial, sanitized laboratory situation [3]. However, the realistic environment can also be a weakness, because it may be too costly or impossible to manipulate an independent variable or to randomize treatments in real life. Thus, the amount of control varies through a continuum, and prioritizing between the validity types is an optimization problem, given the purpose of the experiment. Nevertheless, external validity is always of extreme importance whenever we wish to generalize from behaviour observed in the laboratory to behaviour outside the laboratory, or when we wish to generalize from one non-laboratory situation to another non-laboratory situation.

4.1 System Development Tools

Even when realistic subjects perform realistic tasks, the tasks may be carried out in an unrealistic manner. The challenge is to configure the experimental environment with an infrastructure of supporting technology (processes, methods, tools, etc.) that resembles an industrial development environment. Traditional pen-and-paper based exercises used in a classroom setting are hardly realistic for dealing with relevant problems of the size and complexity of most contemporary software systems. Recently, we have replicated three experiments where we have replaced pen and paper with professional system development tools:

- In the OO design principle experiment [16], a variety of Java development environments were used (JBuilder, Forte, Visual Age, Visual J++, Visual Café, etc.). This is a replication of the experiment described in [24].

- In the OO design pattern experiment [31], a C++ environment was used. This is a replication of the experiment described in [38].

- In the experiment on UML design processes [37], 27 subjects used a commercially available OO development CASE tool (Tau UML Suite), while 26 subjects used pen and paper. This is a replication of the experiment described in [39].

Our experience from these experiments is that using system development tools requires proper preparation:

- Licences, installations, access rights, etc. must be checked.

- The subjects must be or become familiar with the tools.

- The tools must be checked to demonstrate acceptable performance and stability when many subjects are working simultaneously. In one experiment, several subjects had to give up because the tool crashed.

Other researchers who plan experiments using professional tools should take into account that our results show that the time spent to solve the same tasks took 20-30% longer when using tools than when using pen and paper [16,31,37]. Note also that the variance also increases considerably when tools are used. This may influence the time allocated to the experiment.

Regarding quality, there are, as expected, *fewer syntactical* errors when tools are used. More surprising is that there seem to be *more logical* errors. More analysis is needed to investigate this issue into further depth. In particular, the relationships among the three realism dimensions (subjects, tasks and environment) need to be investigated, for example, regarding scalability: a professional development tool will probably become more useful the larger and more complex the tasks and application system become.

4.2 Experimental Procedure in a Realistic Environment

Many threats to external validity are caused by the artificial setting of the experiment. For example, because the logistics is simpler, a classroom is used instead of the usual work place. Conducting an experiment on the usual work site with professional development tools implies less control of the experiment than we would have in a classroom setting with pen and paper. Thus, there are many challenges when conducting experiments with professionals in industry. We have learned the following lessons:

- Ask for a local project manager of the company who should select subjects according to the specification of the researchers, ensure that the subjects actually turn up, ensure that the necessary tools are installed on the PCs, and carry out all other logistics, accounting, etc.
- Motivate the experiment up-front: inform the subjects about the purpose of the experiment (at a general level) and the procedure (when to take lunch or breaks, that phone calls and other interruptions should be avoided, etc.).
- Ensure that the subjects do not talk with one another in breaks, lunch, etc.
- Assure the subjects that the information about their performance is kept confidential (both *within* company and *outside*).
- Assure the company that its general performance is kept confidential.
- Monitor the experiment, that is, be visible and accessible for questions.
- Give all the subjects a small training exercise to ensure that the PC and tool environment are working properly.
- Assure the company and subjects that they will be informed about the results of the experiment (and do it).
- Provide a proper experiment support environment to help set up and monitor the experiment, and collect and manage the experimental data (see Section 5.2).

5 Supporting the Logistics of Controlled Experiments

Our experience from the experiments we have run with both students and professionals is that all the logistics around the experiments is work intensive and error prone: general information and specific task documents must be printed and distributed, personal information (bank account, etc.) and background information must be collected, all solution documents must be collected and then punched into an electronic form, etc. This may in turn lead to typing errors, lost data [40], and other problems.

We realised that if we were to scale up our experiments, and particularly run experiments with professionals in industry using professional development tools, that is, make our experiments more realistic, we would need electronic tool support. Hence, we searched for suitable tools and found several Web tools developed to support surveys, most of them designed by psychologists (e-Experiment[1], PsychExperiments[2], Survey Pro 3[3], S-Ware WWW Survey Assistant[4], Wextor[5]).

---

[1] http://www-personal.umich.edu/~ederosia/e-exp/
[2] http://www.olemiss.edu/PsychExps/
[3] http://apian.com/survey/spspec.htm
[4] http://or.psychology.dal.ca/~wcs/hidden/home.html
[5] http://www.genpsylab.unizh.ch/wextor/index.html

Those tools basically distribute questionnaires to the respondents who fill them in online. Then the results are stored in a local database or sent via emails to the researchers. However, to conduct the kind of experiments that we were interested in, we needed a more sophisticated tool. Therefore, in collaboration with a software company that develops solutions for Human Resource Management, we developed (and are still extending and improving) the Web-based Simula Experiment Support Environment (SESE). SESE is built on top of the company's standard commercial human resource management system. Fig. 1 illustrates the way SESE supports an experiment:

Step 1:   The researcher defines a new experiment (SESE can manage an arbitrary number of experiments simultaneously) with the required questionnaires, task descriptions, files to be downloaded etc.

Step 2:   The administrator creates a user-id and password for each person that will take part in the experiment, and emails that information to the person.

Step 3:   The user (subject) fills in questionnaires (personal and background information) and downloads task descriptions and other required documents (design models, source code, etc.).

Step 4:   The user carries out the tasks, answers questions along the way and uploads the finished documents. Timestamping is done continuously (when were the task descriptions downloaded and task solutions uploaded, when a break started and stopped, etc.).

Step 5:   When a subject has finished the tasks, his or her results are stored in the (relational) database of SESE. When all the subjects have finished, the researcher can start analysing the data.

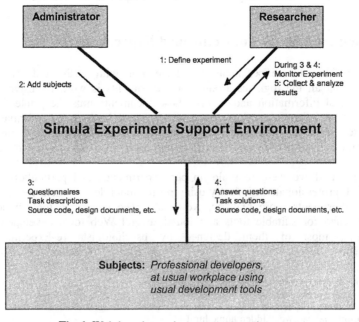

Fig. 1. Web-based experiment support environment

The OO design experiment was run at 10 different sites using SESE via the Web. The experiences from using SESE are positive. SESE enables us to run distributed experiments – both in location and time – instead of only "big-bang" experiments. If acceptable from a methodological point of view, one should avoid "big-bang" experiments to reduce risks. For example, in our design pattern experiment, a fibre cable breakdown far beyond our control forced us to send 44 consultants home and defer the experiment to start on the next day. This accident caused a lot of frustration and a direct loss of 20 000 €. Also in the UML experiment we had serious problems. The day before the experiment, there was a hacker break-in into the computer network of Oslo University where the experiment was to be run. All the 52 000 passwords of the university had to be changed by the systems department and all accounts were closed at the exact same time as our experiment was supposed to start. Fortunately, we managed to get a deal with the systems department to treat the accounts of our subjects as special cases.

Future extensions of SESE may include detailed logging of the way a task is performed or a technology is used. This may include window operations, keystrokes, mouse operations and movements logged with timestamps [41]. SESE and the experiences from using it are more fully described in [42].

6 Summary

This chapter focused on the need for conducting more realistic experiments in software engineering. Using a large experiment on OO design alternatives and other experiments conducted by our research group as examples, we described how increased realism can be achieved, particularly along the dimensions subjects, tasks and environment. A Web-based experiment supporting tool was also described briefly.

We discussed several extra challenges and larger risks that must be taken into account when conducting more realistic experiments. Based on our experiences, we described lessons learned and recommendations for tackling the challenges and reducing the risks, amongst others:

- Be explicit about your target and sample population, possibly divided into sub-populations (e.g., junior, intermediate and senior consultants).
- Record background information about subjects.
- Using professional system development tools in an experiment increases the realism, but requires careful planning, risk analysis and more resources.
- To get subjects to take part in experiments, consider the various kinds of "award" proposed.
- To help tackle the tradeoffs between quality of the tasks to be conducted in an experiment and the time spent on solving them, consider the proposed techniques.
- Apply the described guidelines on the practical conduct of experiments in industry.

We believe that many of the challenges described in this paper also are faced by other researchers conducting controlled software engineering experiments. To increase the knowledge of the empirical software engineering community in this area, we hope that more experiences on how to tackle these challenges will be reported in the literature.

References

[1]   Basili, V.R., Selby, R.W. & Hutchens, D.H. Experimentation in Software Engineering. IEEE Transactions on Software Engineering, Vol. SE-12, No. 7, pp. 733–743, July 1986.

[2]   Rombach, H.D. Basili, V.R. & Selby, R.W. Experimental Software Engineering Issues: Critical Assessment and Future Directions, Dagstuhl Workshop, Germany, Sep. 1992, LNCS 706, Springer Verlag, 1993.

[3]   Basili, V.R. The Role of Experimentation in Software Engineering: Past, Current, and Future, Proceedings of the 18th International Conference on Software Engineering, Berlin, Germany, March 25-29, pp. 442–449, 1996.

[4]   Tichy, W.F. Should Computer Scientists Experiment More? 16 Reasons to Avoid Experimentation, IEEE Computer Vol. 31, No. 5, pp. 32–40, May 1998.

[5]   Zelkowitz, M.V. & Wallace, D.R. Experimental Models for Validating Technology, IEEE Computer, Vol. 31, No. 5; pp. 23–31, May 1998.

[6]   Wohlin, C., Runeson, P., Höst, M., Ohlsson, M.C., Regnell, B. & Wesslén, A. Experimentation in Software Engineering – An Introduction, Kluwer Academic Publishers, Boston, MA, USA, 1999.

[7]   Juristo N. & Moreno, A. Basics of Software Engineering Experimentation, Kluwer Academic Publishers, Boston MA., USA, 2001.

[8]   Shadish, W.R., Cook, T.D. & Campbell, D.T. Experimental and Quasi-Experimental Designs for Generalized Causal Inference, Boston: Houghton Mifflin Company, 2002.

[9]   Montgomery, D. C. Design and Analysis of Experiments, 4th edition, John Wiley & Sons, New York, USA, 1997.

[10] Harrison, W. N=1: An Alternative for Software Engineering Research?, Beg, Borrow, or Steal: Using Multidisciplinary Approaches in Empirical Software Engineering Research, Workshop, 5 June, 2000 at 22nd Int. Conf. on Softw. Eng. (ICSE), Limerick, Ireland, pp. 39–44, 2000.

[11] Potts, C. Software-Engineering Research Revisited, IEEE Software, Vol. 10, No. 5, pp. 19–28, 1993.

[12] Glass, R.L. The Software-Research Crisis, IEEE Software, Vol. 11, No. 6, pp. 42–47, 1994.

[13] Sjøberg, D.I.K., Anda, B., Arisholm, E., Dybå, T., Jørgensen, M., Karahasanovic, A., Koren, E.F. & Vokac M. Conducting Realistic Experiments in Software Engineering, ISESE'2002 (First International Symposium on Empirical Software Engineering), Nara, Japan, October 3–4, 2002, pp. 17–26, IEEE Computer Society.

[14] Kitchenham, B.A., Pfleeger, S.L., Pickard, L.M., Jones, P.W., Hoaglin, D.C. El-Emam, K. & Rosenberg, J. Preliminary Guidelines for Empirical Research in Software Engineering. IEEE Transactions on Software Engineering, Vol. 28, No. 8, pp, 721–734, 2002.

[15] Rogers, E.M. Diffusion of Innovations, Fourth Edition, New York: The Free Press, 1995.

[16] Arisholm, E. & Sjøberg, D.I.K. A Controlled Experiment in Industry to Evaluate the Effect of Responsibility-Driven Design Principles on Software Changeability for Different Categories of Professional, 2003 (in preparation).

[17] Tichy, W.F. Hints for Reviewing Empirical Work in Software Engineering. Empirical Software Engineering, Vol. 5, No. 4, pp. 309–312, 2000.

[18] Basili, V.R., Shull, F. & Lanubile, F. Building Knowledge through Families of Experiments. IEEE Transactions on Software Engineering, Vol. 25, No. 4, pp. 456–473, July 1999.

[19] Arisholm, E. & Sjøberg, D.I.K. A Controlled Experiment in Industry to Evaluate the Effect of Responsibility-Driven Design Principles on Software Changeability for Different Categories of Professionals, 2003 (in preparation).

[20] Anda, B., Sjøberg, D.I.K. & Jørgensen, M. Quality and Understandability in Use Case Models. In J. Lindskov Knudsen (Ed.): ECOOP'2001 (Object-Oriented Programming, 15th European Conf.), Budapest, Hungary, June 18-22, 2001, LNCS 2072 Springer-Verlag, pp. 402–428.

[21] Jørgensen, M. A Review of Studies on Expert Estimation of Software Development Effort, To appear in Journal of Systems and Software. 2004

[22] Jørgensen, M. & Sjøberg, Impact of Software Effort Estimation on Software Work. Journal of Information and Software Technology. Vol. 43, pp. 939–948, 2001.

[23] Anda, B. & Sjøberg, D.I.K. Towards an Inspection Technique for Use Case Models, SEKE'2002 (Fourteenth International Conference on Software Engineering and Knowledge Engineering), Ischia, Italy, July 15–19, pp. 127–134, 2002.

[24] Arisholm, E., Sjøberg, D.I.K. & Jørgensen, M. Assessing the Changeability of two Object-Oriented Design Alternatives – a Controlled Experiment. Empirical Software Engineering, Vol. 6, No. 3, pp. 231–277, Sep. 2001.

[25] Karahasanovic, A. & Sjøberg, D. Visualizing Impacts of Database Schema Changes – A Controlled Experiment, In 2001 IEEE Symposium on Visual/Multimedia Approaches to Programming and Software Engineering, Stresa, Italy, September 5–7, 2001, pp 358–365, IEEE Computer Society, 2001.

[26] Sieber, J.E. Protecting Research Subjects, Employees and Researchers: Implications for Software Engineering. Empirical Software Engineering, Vol. 6, No. 4, 329–341, 2001.

[27] Davis, M. When is a Volunteer Not a Volunteer?, Empirical Software Engineering, Vol. 6, No. 4, pp. 349–352, 2001.

[28] Fenton, N. Conducting and Presenting Empirical Software Engineering, Empirical Software Engineering, Vol. 6, No. 3, pp. 195–200, 2001.

[29] Anda, B. Comparing Effort Estimates Based on Use Case Points with Expert Estimates. In Empirical Assessment in Software Engineering (EASE 2002), Keele, UK, April 8–10, 2002.

[30] Jørgensen, M. & D.I.K. Sjøberg. The Impact of Customer Expectation on Software Development Effort Estimates. Submitted for publication, 2003.

[31] Vokác, M., Tichy, W., Sjøberg, D.I.K., Arisholm, E. & Aldrin, M. A Controlled Experiment Comparing the Maintainability of Programs Designed with and without Design Patterns – a Replication in a real Programming Environment. Submitted for Publication. 2003.

[32] Deligiannis, I.S., Shepperd, M., Webster, S. & Roumeliotis, M., A Review of Experimental Investigations into Object-Oriented Technology. Empirical Software Engineering. Vol. 7, No. 3, pp. 193–232, 2002.

[33] Jørgensen, M. & Bygdås, S. An Empirical Study of the Correlation between Development Efficiency and Software Development Tools. Technical Journal of Norwegian Telecom, Vol. 11, pp. 54–62, 1999.

[34] Jørgensen, M. An Empirical Study of Software Maintenance Tasks. Journal of Software Maintenance, Vol. 7, pp. 27–48, 1995.

[35] Arisholm, E. & Sjøberg, D.I.K. Towards a Framework for Empirical Assessment of Changeability Decay. Journal of Systems and Software, Vol. 53, pp. 3–14, Sep. 2000.

[36] Karahasanovic, A. & Sjøberg, D.I.K. Visualising Impacts of Change in Evolving Object-Oriented Systems: An Explorative Study. Proceedings of the International Workshop on Graph-Based Tools (GraBaTs'02). 2002. Barcelona, Spain, pp. 22–31.

[37] Anda, B. & Sjøberg, D.I.K. Applying Use Cases to Design versus Validate Class Diagrams – A Controlled Experiment Using a Professional Modelling Tool. Simula Research Laboratory Technical Report, No. 2003–01, 2003.

[38] Prechelt, L., Unger B., Tichy, W.F., Brössler, P., & Votta, L.G. A Controlled Experiment in Maintenance Comparing Design Patterns to Simpler Solutions. IEEE Transactions on Software Engineering, Vol. 27, No. 12, pp. 1134–1144, 2001.

[39] Syversen, E., Anda, B. and Sjøberg, D.I.K. An Evaluation of Applying Use Cases to Construct Design versus Validate Design, Hawaii International Conference on System Sciences (HICSS-36), Big Island, Hawaii, January 6–9, 2003.

[40] Briand, L.C., Bunse, C. & Daly, J.W. A Controlled Experiment for Evaluating Quality Guidelines on the Maintainability of Object-Oriented Designs, IEEE Transactions on Software Engineering, Vol. 27, No. 6, pp. 513–530, 2001.

[41] Karahasanovic, A., Sjøberg, D.I.K. & Jørgensen, M. Data Collection in Software Engineering Experiments. Information Resources Management Association Conference, Soft. Eng. Track. 2001. Toronto, Ontario, Canada: Idea Group Publishing, pp. 1027–1028, 2001.

[42] Arisholm, E. Sjøberg, D.I.K., Carelius G.J. & Lindsjørn, Y. A Web-based Support Environment for Software Engineering Experiments, Nordic Journal of Computing Vol. 9, No. 4, pp. 231–247, 2002.

Empirical Studies in ESERNET

Toni Sandelin and Matias Vierimaa

VTT Electronics, P.O.Box 1100, 90571 Oulu, Finland
{Toni.Sandelin,Matias.Vierimaa}@vtt.fi

Abstract. The goal of the ESERNET project has been to combine empirical studies research and their results into a common repository. The main objective of the empirical studies in ESERNET has been to further expand the available empirical knowledge about selected software engineering practices that are relevant for the software industry. The approach selected has been to perform co-ordinated and repeatable empirical studies across varying software development environments. By producing reliable and successful empirical studies, ESERNET has aimed to continue the interest of the companies and academia to further support ESERNET and Experimental Software Engineering (ESE) repository. The ESERNET project created a specific plan for experimental studies that has been used as a basis for empirical studies. The studies followed a common process and produced specified work products. At the end of studies the results were stored to the ESERNET Knowledge Repository for other project participants to evaluate, replicate, utilise and learn. This chapter describes the selected approach.

1 Introduction

The overall objective of the ESERNET project has been to establish a world-leading network of excellence in Experimental Software Engineering (ESE). The results are used for continuous product and process improvement aiming at improving industrial competitiveness and innovation potential. In order to achieve this objective, ESERNET systematically collected experience that enables industry to use best software development practices available. Efficient sharing of empirically founded experiences about best software engineering practices - their benefits as well as their context - is seen as a key issue to success [1]. ESERNET has supported the transfer of research results to industry and it has fostered the exchange of experience between different industrial software companies.

This chapter describes the process used in performing the studies within the ESERNET project. Also the roles, documents and topic areas (i.e. research areas where experimentation has been done) are described. ESERNET members have been performing empirical studies in six research areas: Inspections, Testing, Object-Oriented design, Object-Oriented implementation, Component-based Software Engineering, and Agile methods. A more detailed description of the selected topic areas can be found in Section 3.1.

R. Conradi and A.I. Wang (Eds.): ESERNET 2001-2003, LNCS 2765, pp. 39–54, 2003.

The remainder of this chapter is outlined as follows. Related work of four other initiatives is briefly introduced in Section 2 to provide the reader with a reference framework to better understand work performed in ESERNET project. In Section 3, the topic areas, the ESERNET framework and the process according to which the empirical studies were performed are described. The chapter is concluded with a short summary in Section 4 and references in Section 5.

2   Related Work

Both in Europe and in the US there are quite a few initiatives, with objectives broadly similar to those of the ESERNET project. These initiatives can be considered synergetic with ESERNET network. This section reports on the activities of some of these networks.

2.1   CeBASE (www.cebase.org)

CeBASE is a United States based, National Science Foundation founded Center for Empirically-Based Software Engineering. Partners of CeBASE are University of Maryland College Park, University of Southern California, Fraunhofer Center for Experimental Software Engineering - Maryland, University of Nebraska-Lincoln, and Mississippi State University. CeBASE's objective is to transform software engineering from a set of practices based on anecdotes, hearsay, fashion etc. to an engineering-based discipline [2]. The development processes are selected based on what is known about their effects on products. The selection is done through synthesis, derivation, organization, and dissemination of empirical knowledge on software development and evolution phenomenology. Software development teams need to understand the right models and techniques to support their projects. CeBASE accumulates empirical models in order to provide validated guidelines for selecting techniques and models, to recommend areas for research, and to support software-engineering education. CeBASE was organized to support software organizations in answering questions such as:

- What is the best life-cycle process model to choose for this particular project?
- What is an appropriate balance of effort between inspections and testing in a specific context?
- What are the benefits, if any, to buy a readily available software component instead of developing it?

CeBASE approach is to investigate a spectrum of activities from techniques to life cycle models, mainly focusing on defect reduction and COTS-based development. In the beginning of year 2003, CeBASE has added agile methods as a new topic for their repository of experiment results. The data from the experiments are stored in a national repository of software engineering experiences. The results from the experiments in terms of reports, data and tools are freely available from the web site.

CeBASE brings benefits to:

Industry, in offering a basis for choosing and customizing development strategies, *research*, in engaging in collaboration with industry, in enabling integration of results, packaging and dissemination results, and

education, in offering material for training students on how to select the right SE methods and tools as well as providing realistic artifacts for teaching.

2.2   ISERN (www.iese.fhg.de/ISERN/)

International Software Engineering Research Network (ISERN) is a worldwide network on experimental software engineering founded in 1993. The following partners, many of who are members of ESERNET network as well, initially created ISERN:

- University of Kaiserslautern (Germany)
- University of Maryland College Park (US)
- University of New South Wales, Sydney (Australia)
- Nara Institute of Science and Technology (Japan)
- University of Roma at Tor Vergata (Italy)
- VTT Electronics, Technical Research Centre of Finland (Finland)

Numerous other academic and industrial organizations have joined ISERN since the beginning of its activities. Currently ISERN has more than 30 member organizations that jointly work together in the field of experimental software engineering. Participation to the annual meeting as well as to joint research activities, researcher exchange projects, etc. is open to members only. However, results (e.g., reports) are freely accessible also to non-members.

Joint ISERN activities focus on the following categories:

- Exchange of tools and/or people,
- Further development of experimental infrastructure technologies for model building, experimentation and measurement/assessment approaches,
- Joint experiments,
- Definition and use of a common terminology, and
- Compilation and maintenance of a common annotated bibliography.

ISERN is open to academic and industrial groups who are active in experimental software engineering research and willing to adopt the experimental research framework. There is no membership fee. ISERN members are pairs of organization and a contact person. If the contact person leaves the organization, the organization must reapply for membership. Anyone affiliated with member organizations may participate in ISERN activities. In ISERN, the fact that experimental software engineering research requires the co-operation of industry and academia has been acknowledged. Both industrial and academic groups participate to ISERN.

Researchers in experimental software engineering frequently suffer from the lack of access to industrial data, resources for replicating interesting experimental research results, reuse research results and tools from other environments, and exchange junior researchers in order to broaden their experience. The necessary globalisation requires co-operation with other groups. ISERN provides a common framework for such co-operation in the area of experimental software engineering research.

Companies typically suffer from the inability to affect the direction of software engineering research and, therefore, have problems with identifying, tailoring, and transferring research results into practice. Each industrial ISERN member has its own interests. Expected benefits are the involvement of companies in the setting of research goals, the participation in experiments, the reception of technologies packaged with experience according to their goals, the delegation of personnel to research groups, and the hiring of highly experienced research personnel.

The data from the experiments are documented in various technical reports and articles. These can be accessed at the available ISERN bibliography of technical reports. Other artifacts such as replication packages etc., can be requested from the author/members of ISERN. Since ISERN is a non-profit organization without any funding the web-site is the only source of relevant ISERN material. There is no repository for experiences. When the ESERNET project was planned, one of the key issues was to provide a repository for the experiences for the industrial and academic members of ISERN. In addition, the ESERNET project has organized meetings for all members and by doing that, has given the participants a chance to share knowledge and to initiate joint experiments and research work.

2.3   ViSEK (www.visek.de)

ViSEK (Virtuelles Software-Engineering Kompetenzzentrum, Virtual Software-Engineering Competence Centre) [3] is expected to become a national German network project. The project has started in 2001 and its build up phase will end in 2003. ViSEK has several national partners in Germany, including five Fraunhofer units and several Universities.

Experimental software engineering is part of ViSEK scientific goals but it is not the main focus of the initiative. ViSEK also provides consulting services to organizations willing to co-operate and organizes workshops on software engineering. The work of ViSEK is focused on certain application domains, namely system-engineering, critical systems (automotive, automation domain and medical systems) and e-business systems (e-trading, e-government). The main topics for which ViSEK plans to provide valuable knowledge in the aforementioned domains are component-based software development, project management, software inspection and testing and man-machine interface. The main scientific goals of ViSEK are:

- To build a community for Software-Engineering Know-how,
- Technology transfer, and
- Building a software engineering database of software engineering methods and empirically founded knowledge on applications in specific domains.

All the data collected (experience and lessons learned) will be packaged and will be available through the ViSEK portal. ESERNET and ViSEK have been collaborating in an effort to build a repository that supports needs of both initiatives. Fraunhofer IESE has had an active role in collaboration. The main customers of ViSEK are German SW industries. ViSEK has a clearly defined business model for exploiting the results of the build up phase. During the first phase of ViSEK (phase ending in year 2003), data collection and community building will be actively per-formed. At the same time some marketing strategies are being put in place to find members, partners and customers for the ViSEK results. After the end of the first phase (beginning of year 2004) financing of the initiative will be arranged through customers, German federal states, partners and members. However, the main source of income will be through procurement fees, event fees and advertisements. The ViSEK portal will therefore offer the following services to members:

- Knowledge elements available online, discussion groups, chats, workshops and information events,
- Procurement of experts for know how transfer and consulting, and
- Procurement of SW methods and tool vendors.

2.4   VASIE (http://www.esi.es/VASIE/vasie.html)

The aim of the VASIE project (ESSI Project No 24119) was to provide value-added information for the European software industry and to disseminate the validated ESSI (European System and Software Initiative) Process Improvement Experiments (PIE) results through the web-based repository. The European Commission launched the ESSI program in 1993 and since then about 400 PIEs have been funded by the EC. All ESSI improvement projects have been reviewed, categorized and added continuously to the repository for dissemination [4]. The repository contains results from approximately 250 most useful PIEs. Some of the documentation (i.e. data questionnaires) used in VASIE has been modified for use in the ESERNET project.

3 ESERNET Approach

The main objective of the empirical studies in ESERNET has been to further develop the available empirical knowledge about selected software engineering practices that are relevant for the software industry. The selected approach has been to perform co-ordinated and repeatable empirical studies across varying software development environments. By producing reliable and successful empirical studies, ESERNET has aimed to continue the interest of the companies and academia to further support ESERNET and Experimental Software Engineering (ESE) repository.

ESERNET has taken a phased approach where each selected topic area has been evaluated in three phases, which include (1) post-mortem analysis of existing sources, (2) controlled experiments, and (3) industrial studies. The process has been similar (as described later in Section 3.3) for each type of empirical studies, but in addition, phases support each other.

One challenge of empirical studies has been to plan and divide studies' schedule and contents so that they best supported selected goals. To achieve this, each of the empirical studies has been carefully planned and executed – the planning and performing of the empirical studies themselves has been ESERNET member organisations' task. In addition, ESERNET organised various events (i.e. General Assemblies, Scientific Workshops and Experience Days) related to experiments.

3.1   ESERNET Topic Areas

This section describes the technical topic areas where empirical studies in ESERNET were performed. Inspections and testing are the key techniques for defect detection, which is important in today's software development. Better defect detection techniques result in higher product reliability, faster and better controlled software development, as well as reduced software development cost (mainly because of avoided rework effort). Inspections and testing are also software engineering techniques for which quite many empirical results exist. The results, however, are not yet consolidated and packaged so that they could easily be used throughout the software industry. For this reason, the experience packaging and dissemination efforts are expected to be particularly effective for these techniques. In ESERNET, the defect detection topics are presented in many empirical studies. The studies vary from comparison of different reading techniques to finding a balance between inspection and testing in order to make the whole defect detection activity as effective as possible.

Object-oriented design and implementation are popular techniques and they are commonly being used in industrial software development. To date, there is relatively little empirical knowledge available about these techniques. The empirical work co-ordinated by ESERNET provides important baseline knowledge that can guide the use of object-oriented techniques in industrial software development. Object-oriented design and implementation are useful in demonstrating how Experimental Software Engineering (ESE) can contribute to making relatively new software engineering practices more mature. Quality goals of ESERNET specific empirical studies in object-oriented design and implementation include improving understandability and verifiability of software products by patterns – the objective is to show that systematic refinement and translation of models to code improves the overall quality. Another quality goal is to show that introduction of object-oriented techniques results in better maintainability compared to structured design documents. Empirical studies are also planned to find out which factors have an effect on the quality of object-oriented design documents.

Component-based Software Engineering (CBSE) is an approach that aims to improve productivity and quality of software development. A lot of effort has been put in developing processes, tools and techniques to support CBSE. However, there have been several problems in introducing CBSE in industrial environments. This is true not only for large companies, but especially for small and medium-sized companies. Many companies are also experiencing problems in introducing CBSE techniques in a systematic and cost effective way. In this situation, ESERNET can help in exploring and understanding CBSE at a very early stage of its deployment. CBSE is also in many aspects interrelated with object-oriented design and implementation. The understanding of CBSE through the empirical studies of ESERNET will benefit very much from the investigations of other techniques. The motivation to perform empirical studies in the area of CBSE is to find out whether component-based software engineering practices lead to higher reusability, higher quality and better performance in developing software components in comparison to traditional approaches. Other areas of interest to ESERNET community include, for example, how component providers can meet the requirements of integrator, and how to specify, design and document the components so that they can be sold and reused effectively to several customers.

Agile software development methods have caught the attention of software engineers and researchers worldwide. Scientific research is yet scarce. Despite of this, a number of agile methods have already been proposed. Extreme programming is the most well-known of these agile methods. Agile software development solutions are designed to address three common software engineering problems: often changing product requirements, rapidly evolving technologies and tight time-to-market requirements. While many success reports have been published in recent years, concrete experimental data is still difficult to find. Without convincing data, the potential benefits of agile approaches will not be exploited efficiently in the software engineering community. The empirical body of knowledge collected by the ESERNET regarding agile methods and techniques provides a starting point for industrial partners to evaluate the applicability of these methods in different situations and domains. ESERNET is specifically interested in empirically validated experience data from the application of agile methods or techniques in practical settings. Currently, this type of data is mostly missing.

3.2   ESERNET Framework

This section gives an overview of ESERNET framework that describes services and roles. The ESERNET framework is depicted in Fig. 1. In the ESERNET project, there were two types of members; *Contractors* and *Members*. The first group, the *Contractors*, (i.e. IESE, ESI, BTH, NTNU, and VTT) had a more active role in planning and administration of infrastructures for the project. This included coordination of project, organizing events, coordination of empirical studies and maintenance of the central point of project, the ESERNET Portal. The portal contains tutorials and support material in form of Competence Centre and a repository for the study results. The *Members* had committed to provide the study results for the ESERNET project to be included in the ESERNET Knowledge Repository.

Project Coordinators role was to keep the project running and arrange *General Assemblies, Scientific Workshops* and *Experience Days* – events where the experiences from studies, coaching and personnel exchange were shared among the members. *Study Coordinator* (see Fig. 1) coordinated the empirical studies, coaching and exchange projects. *Repository Administrator* was responsible for the Knowledge Repository infrastructure (i.e. online forms for submitting results, database for results and management of access rights). In the Fig. 1, an *Experiment conductor* is a member of ESERNET who was doing the actual experimentation in his own environment. The ESERNET project offered support for the member organizations performing the studies by offering *Coaching* and *Personnel Exchange* projects. *Coaching* was available for Experimental techniques (ESE methods and the set-up of corporate ESE knowledge repositories) and technical aspects of the experiments (Inspections, testing, object-oriented design, object-oriented implementation, component-based software engineering, and agile methods). The experts within the ESERNET community provided the requested coaching. Another type of supporting activity were the *exchange of personnel* projects. *Personnel Exchange* supported the collaboration among partners in order to further develop ESE methods or knowledge management infrastructures for ESE (i.e. repositories for storing the gained knowledge).

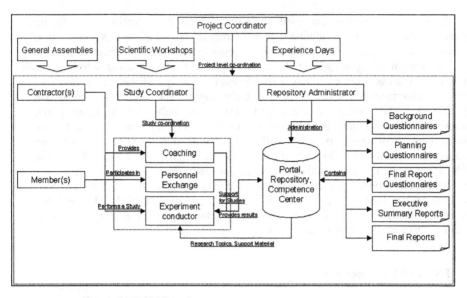

Fig. 1. ESERNET framework; roles, services and work products

The execution of each empirical study was structured according to the widely accepted Quality Improvement Paradigm (QIP) [5]. The Quality Improvement Paradigm is a comprehensive framework for systematically managing improvement by using experiments and measurement. Quality Improvement Paradigm consists of six steps that are repeated iteratively:

- **Characterise.** Understand the current situation and establish a baseline.
- **Set goals.** Quantifiable goals are set and given in terms of improvement.
- **Choose process.** Based on the characterisation and the goals, choose the appropriate processes and supporting methods and tools.
- **Execute.** The study or project is performed and the results are collected for evaluation purposes.
- **Analyze.** The outcome (current practices, possible problems, and findings) is studied and future possible improvements are identified.
- **Package.** The experiences are packaged to build the basis for future improvement projects.

On ESERNET level, it was assured that the results of the empirical studies were reported and packaged in a way that made it easy to reuse and further analyse the results from the individual studies. An essential element in each of these different types of empirical studies was packaging the results in a web-based repository and sharing the knowledge via ESERNET collaboration mechanisms. For these purposes, a set of standardised document templates was defined. Experimentation in general faces two kinds of problems [6]. First, studies need to be replicated so that research community can ensure that the results from a single study are generalizable. However, replicating the study is not possible without complete understanding on how the study was conducted. Second, meta-analysis allows researchers to combine results from several studies to test theories and to ensure generalizability. Again, the conducting of meta-analyses requires understanding the design of the studies analysed. To solve these problems, adequate reporting is needed. In various phases of ESERNET studies, certain documents were created and submitted by the performing party to a co-ordinator of studies. These documents have been available for online-browsing via the ESERNET Internet portal to all ESERNET members. See the Fig. 1 for an overview of work products. A more detailed description of work products and their relation to actual process can be found in next section.

3.3   Process for Conducting Studies

In this section, we describe the different tasks that were conducted during an empirical study in sequence according to the steps of QIP. Because the empirical studies carried out within ESERNET were of different types (post-mortem analyses, controlled experiments or industrial case studies), the steps described were followed to the appropriate extent and adapted to meet the needs of a particular empirical study. For example, when conducting a post-mortem study it was not necessary to fill out the Planning Phase Questionnaire. Before going into details of process, a short explanation of study types is given. *Post-mortem* analysis is conducted on the past as indicated by the name. The post-mortem analysis may be conducted by looking at project documentation or by interviewing people, who have participated in the object that is being analysed in the post-mortem analysis. *Controlled* experiments are sometimes referred to as research-in-the-small [7], since they are concerned with a limited scope and most often are run in a controlled laboratory setting. Case studies study "typical" projects in *industrial* settings. Case studies can be used for monitoring projects and their activities with the aim of, for example, building a model to predict the pass-through time of testing and number of faults found. A *case study* is an observational study while the *experiment* is a controlled study [8]. A more detailed description of various types of empirical studies can be found in Chapter 2 of this book.

The following figure (Fig. 2) presents the ESERNET process according which the empirical studies within ESERNET were performed. Right half of the process picture (labeled as "ESERNET project") depicts the supporting activities and tools ESERNET has provided for the study conducting organizations. ESERNET supported the tasks of all phases by co-ordinating the experiments in ESERNET level and by offering coaching for members whenever needed. Coaching – which means training and guidance related to performing empirical studies and also to technical aspects of ESERNET – was provided by ESERNET and was available to ESERNET members upon request. Additionally, Exchange of Personnel projects provided support in planning and execution of studies. The Competence Centre was created to contain support material for all phases of studies performed – from Characterise to Package. Arrows from right to left describe the type of input that was available in each phase of the process. Small arrows reflect to work products created within an organization conducting an empirical study. Those work products were stored in ESERNET Knowledge Repository. The existing studies in ESERNET Knowledge Repository can be browsed based on recorded goal information. The existing empirical studies may be replicated or a new empirical study can be started based on existing results. The left half of the process picture (labeled as "A Single Empirical Study") presents the process steps of an organization conducting the studies. Next sections describe the process steps – the left half of the picture - in more detail.

3.3.1   Phase 1: Characterise

The aim of the first task within Characterise phase, *Perform Current State Analysis*, (see Fig. 2) is to describe the study environment and to make a current state analysis. The goal is to clarify the needs for empirical studies and also to characterise the environment and its projects. In the beginning of ESERNET project, ESERNET Research Agenda was defined in cooperation with all project members. That agenda worked as a framework plan for forthcoming studies. The problems identified in current state analysis were formulated so that the topics matched topics of ESERNET research plan. Organisations conducting the studies were responsible for the *Selection of empirical study's topic*. Previous research results stored in the ESERNET Knowledge Repository were available so that they could be used to find ideas for new research.

In last task of Characterise phase the conductor of the study *fills the ESERNET Background Questionnaire*. The information gathered with the ESERNET Background Questionnaire is needed to collect general information of the organisation conducting the study (e.g. name and contact information) and the study itself (e.g. name, type, and area) as well as the coaching needs. Background questionnaires served as a preliminary information source for planning purposes. Background questionnaires were filled by all organisations willing to conduct the experiments and submitted to *Study Coordinator*.

The information that was collected using the ESERNET Background Questionnaire was published on the ESERNET WWW-pages, so that other ESERNET partners, who were interested in the same topic that the empirical study covered, could contact the originator and commit their interest in taking part in the empirical study.

3.3.2   Phase 2: Set Goals

The purpose of Set Goals phase is to define where the foundation for the empirical study is laid. The objective and goals of the study must be defined. The *goal is formulated* from the problem to be solved. The goal, constructed as in GQM [9], consists of the following constituents:

> Object of study – what is studied?
> Purpose – What is the intention?
> Quality Focus – Which effect is studied?
> Perspective – From which perspective the object is studied?
> Context – Where is the study conducted?

An example of a typical ESERNET study goal could be: *Analyse the testing process for the purpose of understanding the effect of inspections to defect finding rate from the perspective of process developer in the context of system testing of product X.*

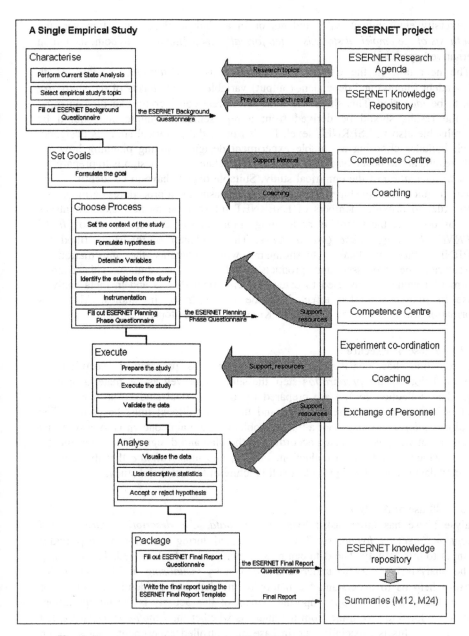

Fig. 2. Process of empirical studies in ESERNET with supporting activities

3.3.3   Phase 3: Choose Process

In Choose Process phase, the organizations conducting the study design their empirical studies in detail. The design activity prepares the performing of the empirical study. First, the *context of the study* is determined in detail. This includes personnel and environment, for example, whether the empirical study is performed in a university environment with students or in an industrial setting. Moreover, the *hypothesis of the empirical study is stated formally*, including a null hypothesis and an alternative hypothesis.

The next task in the Choose Process phase is to *determine variables* (both independent (inputs) and dependent (output) variables. The *subjects* of the study *are* then to be *identified*. This should be done with great consideration keeping in mind that the results should be derived from a representative sample and should be generalisable also in ESERNET level. Furthermore, the empirical study is designed, which includes choosing a suitable experiment design including planning how the study results are to be analysed. An issue closely related to the design is to prepare for the *instrumentation* of the empirical study. Suitable objects have to be identified and prepared, guidelines developed if necessary and measurement procedures defined.

In order to provide members of ESERNET information on new experiments as early as possible, the members performing empirical studies were asked to *fill the ESERNET Planning Phase Questionnaire*. The conductor of the study filled the ESERNET Planning Phase Questionnaire which contains the information to characterise the processes and products involved in the studies. This context information gathered was used to categorise empirical studies and in meta-analysis phase to find factors that affected to the results found in studies. Also, this information was added to the ESERNET Knowledge Repository.

3.3.4   Phase 4: Execute

The execution phase consists in principle of three steps: preparation, execution and data validation. In the *preparation* step, the subjects as well as the material needed (e.g., data collection forms) are prepared for the empirical study. The participants must be informed about the intention and their commitment must be gained. The actual *execution* is normally not a major problem. The main concern is to ensure that the empirical study is conducted according to the plan and design of the experimental studies, which includes data collection. Finally, one must *validate* that the actually collected data is correct and provide a valid picture of the empirical study.

3.3.5   Phase 5: Analyse

Analyse phase has three tasks: *Visualise the data, Use descriptive statistics and Accept or Reject the hypothesis*. The data collected during execution phase provides the input to this activity. The data can now be analysed and interpreted. The first step in the analysis is to try to understand the data by *visualising* it. The *descriptive statistics* help us to understand the nature of the data and to identify abnormal or invalid data points in it. One important aspect of this activity is the interpretation. That is, we have to determine from the analysis whether the *hypothesis was accepted or rejected* – this is especially true in case of controlled experiments, not so often when performing case studies. This forms the basis for decision-making and conclusions concerning how to use the results from the empirical study, which includes motivation for further studies, for example, to conduct an enlarged experiment or a case study.

3.3.6   Phase 6: Package

The last phase is concerned with storing, packaging and presenting the results of empirical studies for the use within the study organisation as well as for ESERNET Knowledge Repository for others to evaluate, replicate, utilise and learn. At the end of the empirical study, the Experiment *Conductors fill out the ESERNET Final Report Questionnaire*. This questionnaire includes information such as the effort, the variables and the results of the study, among other relevant information. This is vital information in order to provide results of studies to wider use. The questionnaire also helped to assure that all relevant data (e.g. the context of the empirical study, the effort spent on the study) were stored and that all the empirical studies produced uniform data.

The questionnaires were stored into ESERNET Knowledge Repository together with Final Reports. The Final Reports, which were written after the ESERNET Final Report Questionnaire was filled out, had to follow a strict structure. A common structure assures that the results of different empirical studies are easier to compare and (like the questionnaire) that all relevant data, such as descriptions of the starting and resulting scenarios and the conducted study in detail, is collected. Last but not least, following a clearly structured approach saves time and money. In contrast to this, an ad hoc approach to reporting the results is usually inefficient and always leaves some room for doubts about the quality of the results gained. To fulfil the requirement of strictly structured Final Reports, a template and a writing guide were created. Several existing guidelines were assessed and combined to find the most suitable format for reports. One source of information was Singer's report how to apply APA style guidelines to report experimental results [6]. The Final Reports include the following information: objectives of the study, the company and project context where the study has been performed, phases, subjects and objects of the study, main results, discussion about the results and their influence. A typical length for the final report is ten pages; additional information is linked if needed.

After the empirical study elements (i.e. Final Report Questionnaire and Final Report) were submitted to ESERNET organisation, the ESERNET experiment co-ordinator appointed a reviewer for the empirical study element. The reviewers were selected based on their expertise in the area of the empirical study. The reviewers checked that the ESERNET Final Report Questionnaire and Final Report document of the empirical study contained consistent information. After finishing the review the empirical study elements found suitable for repository insertion were added into the repository. On ESERNET level, Study Coordinator composed two summary reports from the results reported in the ESERNET Knowledge Repository.

In addition to studies performed within ESERNET, the ESERNET Knowledge Repository contains reported results from empirical studies that have been conducted prior to ESERNET project or that are performed outside of ESERNET. For these studies a lighter reporting format was defined. For reporting these studies, we created a document called Executive Summary Report (ESR). Fig. 3 depicts the layout of the ESR template. The contents is very similar to Background Questionnaire (BGQ, see Section 3.3.1). The only difference is that in the ESR template the Summary section has been added.

The following information was stored from each of the studies: The first section ("1. Organisational Information:") of the Executive Summary Report template

ESERNET Executive Summary Report

1. Organisational Information:	
Name of Organisation:	
Contact Person, Contact information:	

2. Empirical Study Information:
(Please, fill a separate form for each empirical study to be performed in your organisation)

Name of the Study (for identification):	
Purpose of the Study (overall goal and main hypotheses):	
Objects of the Study (material/apparatus: what artifacts and sw/hw were used):	
Subjects of the Study (project/process and human participants):	☐ Project/process (please specify): ☐ Undergraduates ☐ Graduates ☐ Post-Graduates ☐ Professionals ☐ Others (please specify):
Procedure of the Study (process steps incl. "treatment"):	
Main application area of baseline (surrounding) project:	☐ CAD/CAM System ☐ Control System ☐ Decision Support System ☐ EDP (Electronic Data Processing) ☐ Geographic/Technical Information System ☐ Knowledge Based System ☐ Manufacturing/Production System ☐ MIS (Management Information Systems) ☐ Multimedia System ☐ Office Automation System ☐ Process Control System ☐ Real Time System ☐ Safety Critical System ☐ Simulation System ☐ Telecommunication System ☐ Transaction Processing ☐ Other (please specify):
Technical area:	☐ Testing ☐ Inspection ☐ Object Oriented Design ☐ Object Oriented Implementation ☐ Component Based Software Engineering
Type of Study:	☐ Post-Mortem ☐ Controlled ☐ Case Study ☐ Survey
Start date:		End date:	

3. Summary:	
Brief summary of the results, analysis techniques, and main findings:	
Brief discussion of the results/findings:	
Link / reference to the report:	If it is freely available on the web, please use http:// to indicate the URL; otherwise give literature reference.
Thank you for your effort!	-- WP3 Responsible -- Email: toni.sandelin@vtt.fi

Fig. 3. Executive Summary Report (ESR) template

concentrates on gathering organisational information. Basic identification data of the organisation, such as the name of the organisation and its contact person's name, address and other contact information have to be reported here.

The second section ("2. Empirical Study Information:") of the template is concerned with collecting empirical study information. First, the study has to have an identifier that was also used to facilitate the categorization of the ESRs within the ESERNET Knowledge Repository. Second, the purpose of the study has to be stated together with the main goals and hypotheses. Third, the subjects and objects of the study have to be recognized and then the procedure of the study described briefly. Fourth, the main application and technical areas of the study together with the study's type have to be identified and last, the schedule for the study has to be defined by reporting the start and end dates of it.

The third and last section ("3. Summary:") of the form summarises the empirical study's results. First, a brief summary of the results and main findings of the study has to be composed together with a description of the analysis techniques used in the empirical study. Second, the results and findings have to be discussed and reflected. Last, a link to the complete empirical study report (if one exists) can be linked either as a WWW-address or a literature reference so that people interested in the study can read more about it.

4 Conclusion

This chapter has provided an overview of ESERNET project, the related work and ESERNET framework for conducting studies. As a motivation to studies performed, we described the reasons why testing, inspection, object-oriented analysis and design, component-based software engineering, and agile methods were selected as topic areas. We described also the process the organisations performing the empirical studies followed and the work products created during the process. The main objective of this chapter has been to give a picture how the studies in ESERNET were done, why different tasks were included in the process and what kind of information was collected during the studies. The evaluation how well the selected infrastructure worked remains to be performed in the future when more empirical studies have been performed and their results stored in the ESERNET Knowledge Repository.

The common structure used in reporting the result of studies is necessary for comparing the results of separate studies and to make summarizing possible. Common structure – together with online questionnaires – also makes the storing of information into Knowledge Repository possible.

References

[1] B. Boehm, V.R. Basili. "Gaining intellectual control of software development", IEEE Software, May 2000.
[2] CeBASE home page, http://www.cebase.org/www/home/index.htm
[3] ViSEK home page, http://www.visek.de
[4] VASIE home page, http://www.esi.es/VASIE/vasie.html

[5] Victor R. Basili, Gianluigi Caldiera, and H. Dieter Rombach. Experience Factory. In John J. Marciniak, editor, Encyclopedia of Software Engineering, volume 1, pages 469–476. John Wiley & Sons, 1994.

[6] J. Singer, "Using the American Phychological Association (APA) Style Guidelines to Report Experimental Results", Proceedings of Workshop on Empirical Studies in Software Maintenance, Oxford, England. September 1999. pp. 71–75. NRC 44130.

[7] B. Kitchenham, L. Pickard and S. L. Pfleeger, "Case Studies for Method and Tool Evaluation", IEEE Software, pp. 52–62, July 1995.

[8] M. V. Zelkowitz and D. R. Wallace, "Experimental Models for Validating Technology", IEEE Computer, 31(5), pp. 23–31, 1998.

[9] van Solingen, Rini, and Berghout, Egon. The Goal/Question/Metric Method, McGraw Hill, 1999. Japanese Ethnology, Human Organization, Vol. 56, No. 2, pp. 233–237

Software Engineering Knowledge Repositories

Andreas Jedlitschka and Markus Nick

Fraunhofer Institute for Experimental Software Engineering (IESE)
Sauerwiesen 6, D-67661 Kaiserslautern, Germany
Tel: +49 (0) 631-707 260, Fax: +49 (0) 631-707 200
{andreas.jedlitschka,markus.nick}@iese.fraunhofer.de

Abstract. In order to improve the maturity and competitiveness of software intensive organizations, there is a need to efficiently share experiences about best software engineering practices, their benefits as well as their context requirements and boundaries. Such knowledge enables companies to improve faster and at lower cost. Many such experiences exist locally either in individual companies or departments – derived via case studies in projects, or in research organizations – derived via controlled technology experiments. Supporting the extraction of experiences, their packaging for cross-organization reuse, and making them available from a central storage are (some) of the challenges a cross-organization knowledge repository faces. Therefore it has to provide at least a technical infrastructure and organizational support for acquiring, using, maintaining, and evolving relevant knowledge. This chapter describes an empirically validated approach to the design, construction, and evaluation of software engineering repositories, alongside an example of the construction and the evaluation of the ESERNET knowledge repository.

Keywords: Software engineering, knowledge management, experience management, experience factory, experience base, repository.

1 Introduction

To enable companies to improve, in the sense of developing high quality software at lower costs, it has become more and more accepted to have some kind of knowledge management installed. In order to support the collection, central storage, and dissemination of software engineering (SE) knowledge for example, empirical studies on SE techniques and associated experiences, one solution would be a knowledge repository.

According to [1] we adopt the notion of an Experience-based Information System (E_BIS) for such kind of repositories. Based upon the well-known information system concept from business informatics, this covers other notions drawn from the literature (e.g., experience base (system), experience database (system), experience management system, lessons learned repository). An E_BIS is an information system that contains experiences. This abstracts from the actual technology used for implementing the information system and leaves open whether other kinds of knowledge are included as well. In addition, it highlights the importance of

R. Conradi and A.I. Wang (Eds.): ESERNET 2001-2003, LNCS 2765, pp. 55–80, 2003.

experience which, to quote Albert Einstein, "is the only source of knowledge"[1]. The importance of experience for SE has also been demonstrated by the work of Vic Basili and his development of the well-known Experience Factory (EF) approach [2].

An EF is a logical and/or physical infrastructure for continuous learning from experience, and includes – according to our terminology – an $E_b IS$ for the storage and re-use of knowledge. The EF approach was invented in the mid-eighties [3, 4] and initially designed for software organizations. It takes into account the software discipline's experimental, evolutionary, and non-repetitive characteristics [5]. As practice shows, it is important for the support of organizational learning that the project organization and the learning organization are logically separated [6]. This is the main feature of the EF. It is based on the Quality Improvement Paradigm (QIP), which is a goal-oriented learning cycle for experience-based improvement and evaluation of project planning, execution and analysis [2]. The initially focused topics like cost estimation and failure prediction are extended in various directions, including new foci like lessons learned e.g., regarding project management or the applicability of technology (e.g., [7, 8]). These lessons have been learned during "real" projects and not from laboratory experiments (e.g., [9, 5, 10, 11, 12, 13, 14]).

Other approaches to tackle the typical problems of companies investing efforts in SE, like the rapid change of technology, fast growth, time-to-market, and repeated failures (this list can be expanded infinitely), use so-called "Knowledge Brokers". The approaches vary from so-called yellow-page systems pointing to experts, to company organization structures [15]. The common factor in these approaches is their preference of human-based knowledge exchange. This approach dedicates special roles, among others the Knowledge Broker (e.g., [15, 16, 17]) in particular, whose task is to drive the "experience engine" [16]. Some of these have reported that this kind of exchange works until the size of the organization grows [15]. The drawbacks of such approaches, mentioned by the authors themselves, are finding the adequate persons [15] and the heavy reliance on highly experienced staff to act as brokers [16].

In (e.g., [18, 19]) proposals for "lightweight" approaches to acquire experiences can be found. The authors stated that several lightweight elements have to be added to the original EF approach. For them lightweight means: low effort and low cost. One criticism among others is that the separate EF organization is too expensive.

Proposals to start as simple as possible and to grow the scope incrementally have also been presented (e.g., [20, 21]). They have experienced that simple, web-based $E_b ISs$ seem to behave best [20]. Incremental approaches allow detecting strengths and weaknesses early and make it possible to adapt the further development better to the users' (changing) needs [21].

In the $E_b IS$ so-called artifacts, pieces of information that can be processed by a machine or a tool specialized for it, are stored. Artifacts are not restricted to documents (e.g., requirements documents, design documents, code components, test cases, but also executables, process models, quality models, project schedules, personnel allocation plans, organization charts, and documented experience (e.g., in the form of lessons learned)). The artifact has to be enriched with a characterization containing all information necessary to make the decision on whether to utilize the artifact or not. This especially includes the *context*, that describes in which environment the artifact has been, for instance, developed or successfully applied. The context includes information about e.g., organization, project, product, people,

---

[1] Confer, for example, http://www.ournet.md/~hi-tech/einstein_knowledge.html.

and tools used. Since each experience depends heavily on its context, this information is crucial for proper decision-making.

By now many organizations from research and also from industry, have their own proprietary solution of how to deal with experience and the other kinds of knowledge. ESERNET aims at coordinating those activities and building up a framework for cross-organizational exchange of SE experiences[2]. As such, an initiative that aims at a large number of users and participants with different skills, different expectations, strongly varying motivations, and different goals, means that there are a lot of requirements to be synchronized (e.g., researchers, industrial managers, software engineers, students). Despite these difficulties, we have to deal with the challenge that competitive organizations should share experience. According to [10], a major success factor for lessons learned systems, in particular, and knowledge management systems, in general, is the integration of the system into the day-to-day work processes in an organization. For ESERNET, this is beyond the control of the organization, which is building and running the E_bIS. Furthermore, the ESERNET contents aim at supporting a very specific task, the selection and infusion of a new SE technology in a company. Thus, the challenge is to build an E_bIS that is simple enough to make people contribute and complex enough to retrieval a meaningful volume of information. Therefore and to get an initial idea of the usage, the approach for realizing the E_bIS must not be too complicated [20]. Hence, the strategy is to keep the E_bIS implementation simple and clear, so that it is able to attract a broad audience (lesson learned from CBR-PEB [22]).

The remainder of this chapter is structured as follows. First an overview of a generic state-of-the-art methodology for E_bIS development (Section 2) is given. Then in Section 3 the application of this generic method to build up the "ESERNET knowledge repository" is described. In Section 4 we give an overview of the evaluation method for E_bIS and the results of its application to ESERNET. In order to systematically maintain ESERNET, we developed a maintenance strategy consisting of so-called maintenance policies (Section 5). In Section 6, we summarise the chapter and drawn some overall conclusions.

2   A Generic EbIS Buildup Method

In [21] a generic method for the development of an EF/E_bIS[3] is presented. The method is called DISER, a methodology for designing and implementing software engineering repositories. DISER accelerates the design of an effective and efficient management system for SE experience. Using the DISER method, the systematic build up of an E_bIS is performed in three phases, based, in turn upon eight main steps (see Fig. 1). DISER has already been applied in industrial settings, such as telecommunications, banking, and insurance organizations. It has demonstrated its applicability not only to build SE E_bISs, but also for administrative tasks dealing with security engineering [14].

---

[2] For examples of studies that document this need for better and empirically founded software engineering practices refer to [23]

[3] The buildup of an E_bIS always requires a surrounding EF either by (re-)using an existing one (i.e., the E_bIS is extended) or by infusing one into the respective organization. While the DISER methodology considers both, in this document we focus on building up an E_bIS only.

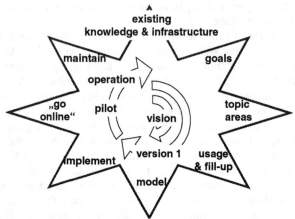

Fig. 1. The 4 phases (arrows) and eight aspects (edges of the star) of the generic E$_b$IS development method

The objective of the *first phase (vision)* is to develop a vision for the E$_b$IS, that demonstrates the idea of how the E$_b$IS can support the organization's business and how it is embedded in the organization. Thus, the emphasis is on how experience could be (re-)used and recorded (experience usage & recording scenarios). This vision has to consider related running activities and systems as well (i.e., the aspect "existing knowledge"). Thus, one part of the vision building is an analysis of the existing E$_b$IS-related measures and activities in order to define the starting point for the E$_b$IS-related improvements. Business goals and related success criteria have to be considered if the sponsor has already pre-defined these. Eventually, the vision integrates existing and new experience management measures and activities.

The *2nd phase (version 1)* has the objective of systematically developing the design of the envisioned E$_b$IS system and building and piloting a first version of the envisioned E$_b$IS. The vision is the starting point for detailed systematic analysis of the goals, relevant subject areas, and reuse & recording scenarios for the E$_b$IS, which are the requirements for the E$_b$IS. The reuse scenarios then include definitions of retrieval goals that state the information requirements of the users in a formal manner. Based on this, the conceptual model and the first version of the system are developed. Phase 2 ends with the "seeding", which is the initial fill-up of the E$_b$IS.

For a small group of the stakeholders the system is made accessible in the *pilot phase (3rd phase)*. This is used to evaluate the question of whether or not the system fulfills the needs of the stakeholders.

After having revised the prototype the system can "go online" for the whole intended organization and *regular use (4th phase)* starts. Although in other software systems we try to minimize maintenance efforts, experience management systems need some more maintenance because of the vivid (? – needs another word) of the content. The circle is thus closed and the system can be further improved.

A development process using DISER creates a schematic, top-down documentation for the implementation concept (i.e., conceptual model and knowledge acquisition plan).

3   ESERNET Repository Build-Up Approach

This section describes Phase 1 and Phase 2 of DISER in the context of building the ESERNET knowledge repository. First we develop the vision for the ESERNET repository (Section 3.1), followed by a description of how the DISER approach was adapted to design and build the repository (Section 3.2).

3.1   Phase 1: Develop a Vision for the ESERNET Repository

This section describes the development of a vision for the repository, that addresses the development of a high-level usage model of the repository, as well as the critical issues that can be identified in this early stage of development.

Based on the short vision statement from the project proposal (Section 3.1.1), we conducted a survey via email among the intended audience to find out more about the specific needs and expectations of the audience, i.e., the user requirements (Section 3.1.2). We consolidated these requirements based on experiences gained in other international and national projects (e.g., ViSEK, PROFES, VASIE, INTER-PROFIT, CeBASE)[4] as well as requirements from the literature (Section 3.1.3).

3.1.1   The Vision Statement for the ESERNET Repository

If an organization wants to improve, certain changes have to be introduced. The introduction of these changes is rarely managed in an appropriate way. This repository offers the possibility to learn about the following:

- new methods, techniques, and tools evaluated in research projects;
- the transfer to industrial environments;
- the applicability of technologies in specific contexts;
- how companies introduced changes (applying the experimental results); and,
- how they have solved their problems and what strategies they have chosen in order to achieve their business goals.

This repository is intended to provide valuable and useful help in the fundamental step of selecting best practices that organizations from research and industry have applied in their own context, and in adopting them to a new situation. It also provides guidance to select new technologies and consider their applicability and limitations depending on the context.

3.1.2   Survey on User Requirements (Needs and Expectations)

To find out more about the specific needs and expectations of the intended audience, a very brief and high-level survey was sent out to the ESERNET members. The intention behind the survey was to find out: (a) the requirements of the users, (b) an idea how the users will use the repository, and (c) an idea why they would use it (cf. [24]). The conclusions from the survey were used for building the repository in Phase 2. Some examples of the conclusions included: Users from research query the

---

[4] www.visek.de, www.iese.fhg.de/profes, www.esi.es/VASIE, www.cebase.org, http://geomatikk.no/profit.

repository to get an idea for research, for conducting new laboratory experiments, for finding empirical studies already performed by others in similar contexts, and for finding references for his work. Users from the software industry will query the repository mainly before and also during the study. The users prime objective when consulting the repository is to know about previous similar studies in order to increase the probability of success in their own study. Additionally, industrial organizations need confidentiality for their data.

3.1.3 Requirements from Former SE Repository Projects

Other projects like ViSEK, have collected similar requirements for their repositories [25]. Additionally, we have collected requirements for improving our own in-house experience management system (Fraunhofer IESE Corporate Information Network - COIN). These requirements are likewise summarized in terms of the requirements for the ESERNET repository.

Many approaches can be found in literature. They span the whole range from solutions more suitable for research-based environments, as well as approaches tailored to the requirements of business. . Some of them provide a very complete set of requirements for E_bIS [21]. Tautz [21] for example, mentioned that, E_bIS covers (at least potentially) a very large knowledge area. Consequently, three practical constraints must be met:

- **Integration of existing information.** When a new experience base is set up, already existing information (e.g., in the form of files or printed documents) must be integrated. For ESERNET this "seeding" is obtained from empirical studies reported in ISERN (International Software Engineering Research Network).
- **Processing of knowledge in different ways.** The information stored in the experience base is utilized in different ways depending on the task to be achieved. This may require specialized tools that operate on a defined subset of the information. Often, some of these specialized tools already exist in the organization when an experience base is introduced and continue to be used.
- **Acquisition Process for Empirical Study Results.** For supporting the members who deliver results (i.e., study report, lessons learned), a uniform method for the collection of the results from different projects and organizations is necessary. This includes templates for reporting the results.

3.2   Phase 2: The DISER-Approach Adapted for the ESERNET Repository

In this section, we apply the second phase of DISER to develop the ESERNET repository. We include a description of how the DISER method was applied. The answers to the survey and the resulting requirements described in Section 3.1 are used as input to the method. Each subsequent section refines the respective DISER step and demonstrates how it is applied.

3.2.1 Set Objectives (Second Step)

This involves defining objectives and associated success criteria for the EB. For this purpose, stakeholders and their interests have to be identified. Following this, their objectives are derived and selected. Furthermore, success criteria are defined for selected objectives (see Section 4 on evaluation). The criteria allow early and simple analysis of the success.

We identified as stakeholders the ESERNET members, the software industry and researchers from the field of software engineering. Based on the survey amongst our stakeholders in Phase 1 and the ESERNET project objectives, we derived the objectives for the repository.

The ESERNET repository principal aim is to disseminate the results of various kinds of empirical studies in software engineering performed either in research or in industry through the WWW. The information contained in the repository describes studies, the results achieved, and the lessons learned.

The design objective of the ESERNET repository is to allow the intended users to navigate through the repository by using a standard web browser. The repository will provide a set of search-alternatives that can be combined to filter the retrieved information according to their needs. Each study is shown as a HTML document that describes the study's objectives and results, the phases followed during the study, lessons learned, and a set of additional information for better comprehension of the whole empirical study.

3.2.2 Set Subject Areas (Third Step)

Due to the expert status of the ESERNET partners, the availability of experienced people and respective materials, the topics of testing, inspections, object-oriented design and implementation, and component-based software engineering are emphasized. The subject areas are confirmed with the ESERNET general assembly and accepted by the European commission (i.e., stakeholder in the sense of intended users and financiers).

3.2.3 Detailed Scenarios (Fourth Step)

A scenario includes descriptions of the organizational context, character profiles for the individuals appearing in the scenario, and a sequence of events.

Two kinds of scenarios are advocated here: how to reuse the contents of an experience base and how to populate the experience base. For the description regarding how to maintain and keep the content of the experience base alive see Section 5.

Identify Reuse Scenarios

Users of the experience base are asked to describe how they would use the repository. The description should include how to locate known artifacts and/or how to search for those which are presently unknown, as well as how they intend to utilize the artifacts. Special attention is paid to critical aspects, e.g., time, quality, and other resources needed. The scenarios are divided into three main parts: (1) Trigger (why does something start?), (2) Actions (which actions are to be performed?), and (3) Expected benefit (why does the user do it this way?).

The retrieval of artifacts in a scenario may be either direct (i.e., the user finds the suitable artifact(s) without expert help) or indirect (i.e., the user finds a contact person in the experience base who in turn suggests suitable artifact(s)).

To give a broader context, first, a basic scenario is described, which reflects the overall ESERNET scenario and the lifecycle of knowledge (cf. [24]). Based on the survey more detailed scenarios can be defined, describing typical situations for industrial organizations. In this section we present one such detailed scenario as an example.

Scenario for the Searcher

Trigger:

A software developing company (W-SOFT) has problems with the quality of their products. The main customer has reported critical failures that occur when the software is used. The product manager wants to have better (e.g., more reliable) products in the future.

Actions:

While searching for a solution, the development manager in charge comes to the ESERNET repository. He (hopefully) finds some studies that have evaluated a suitable SE technology within his context. (retrieval goal: "find applicable technology")Furthermore, he wants to have additional information on selected SE technologies (e.g., lessons learned, success stories etc). (retrieval goal "find additional information on SE technology")

Expected Benefits:

He gets valuable information on SE technologies, their applicability within specific contexts and relevant experience with this technology. Thus, he receives support for his decision.

This and the other scenarios, not described here (cf. [24]), are formalized in retrieval goals. The commonalities are extracted and documented in a template format.

Define Retrieval Goals

The relevant retrieval goals are extracted from the informal descriptions and augmented with a unique name and the informal descriptions from which they were extracted. Retrieval goals are the primary means of rationalizing the experience base schema. They motivate why a particular concept or attribute is necessary. Therefore, it is important that stakeholders agree to support the defined set of retrieval goals.

Based on the survey and the reuse scenarios, the retrieval goals are defined. One such retrieval goal is given in the following.

Retrieval Goal "Retrieve Empirical Studies in Similar Contexts"

Retrieve	empirical study descriptions
for the purpose	of estimating the applicability of a SE technology
from the viewpoin	of a project manager or project member
in the context	of the specific organization

Identify Record Scenarios

The outcomes of this step are record scenarios consisting of potential knowledge sources and informal descriptions of knowledge acquisition, both for existing knowledge and new sources of knowledge. They describe how the repository can be populated.

Existing Sources:

Amongst the ESERNET members much material and experience about empirical studies exist. This is documented in a survey. The ISERN reports are included in the form of seeds. Additionally, links to other collections of empirical studies in SE are available.

New Sources:

If an ESERNET empirical study has been performed, the report and the experience are gathered by means of questionnaires and a report template (cf. Chapter 4 "Empirical Studies in ESERNET" of this book).

Critical aspects are the effort needed for the description of the study and the collection of relevant information. In addition, confidentiality can also be a risk factor, because a company can decide not to share the gained experience at the required level of detail or provide enough context information. Nevertheless, for such an E_bIS it is valuable to store information about the fact that a study has been performed along with the contact person.

3.2.4 Conceptual Model (Fifth Step)

This section describes the conceptual model of the repository at a high level, based on the ideas of Tautz [21] and Birk [26]. In particular, we use Birk's idea of describing the so-called *technology application context (TAC)* for software engineering technologies. A *TAC* is the sum of attributes of a context situation in which a certain SE technology is applied to a certain task (process), that influences the success of technology application with regard to a certain success criterion (product quality). Furthermore, we use Tautz' ideas regarding the general structure and the attachment of lessons learned to the SE technology descriptions. The resulting conceptual model is shown in Fig. 2.

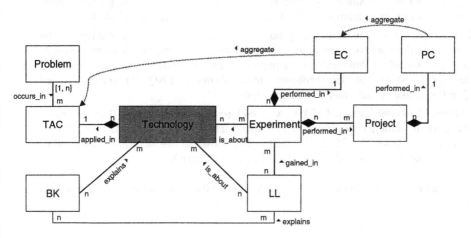

Fig. 2. Entities of the ESERNET repository schema

Entities that belong to the Top Level of the ESERNET repository schema guarantee a minimal and common set of information to describe and characterize the technologies stored in the repository. Fig. 2 depicts the entities and their relations:

- Entity "**Technology**" is the main entity of the ESERNET repository schema. It keeps administrative information like the name (e.g., name: Inspections).

- Entity "**Experiment**" is used to store available documentation about a study related to technologies stored in the repository. Such documentation describes how a certain technology has been applied in a specific context.

- Entity "**Project**" is used to store available project documentation related to empirical studies stored in the repository. Such project documentation can be seen as additional information on how (a set of) studies have been performed in a concrete project.

- Entity "**Project Context (PC)**" is divided from **Project** to support (a) confidentiality, (b) aggregation of context to a higher level, and (c) comparability. It provides information about project context (i.e., the environment). The entity provides a set of attributes needed for minimal characterization of the context. This includes, for example, information on the size of the project team (e.g., 5 persons).

- Entity "**Experiment Context (EC)**" provides aggregated information about the study's context (i.e., the environment) in which the study is running. The context has to be aggregated if it is running in different projects. Thus, different projects have been performed with the same task, but with different PCs. Those PCs will be summarized within the entity EC.

- Entity "**Technology Application Context (TAC)**" is automatically associated/inherited to all technology entries stored in the repository. It provides information about the context (i.e., the environment) in which the technology is empirically validated or is applicable (i.e., it can or has been used). Furthermore, the set of context factors has to be minimal: Only those, relevant for decision support and not subsumed by another context factor in the set (e.g., application domain: automotive, team size: 15-20, Product Quality Attribute: reliability)

- Entity "**Problem**" is used to store problem descriptions that are relevant for a given context. In the context of the repository, one can think of the problems as questions and the stored technologies or experience as answers. Hence, the problem description stored by the Problem entity allows a FAQ (Frequently Asked Questions) like system interface for the repository.

- Entities "**Lessons Learned (LL)**" & "**Background Knowledge (BK)**". Besides the pure technology descriptions and quantitative data, we wanted to provide qualitative data via the ESERNET portal. BK allows to link descriptive material to a technology (e.g., tutorials, literature references, experts).

A more detailed schema description including attribute definitions can be found in [24].

3.3   Architecture of the ESERNET Repository

This section gives a very brief overview on the general architecture of the repository. On the bottom level resides the storage of the repository. It consists of: (a) a database, which contains, besides administrative data (e.g., user data), data about the empirical studies and references to the native artifacts (e.g., reports, process descriptions); and, (b) a hierarchical file system to keep the native artifacts. Their individual location is derived from their characterization (e.g., the technology used, type of study).

The core of the repository is the ESERNET Server. This is responsible for granting access to the ESERNET repository by providing $E_b IS$ tools, e.g., both, navigational and contents-based repository search facilities. The application level provides tools to administer users and contents together with tools for the acquisition of study information (questionnaires). On the client side, no specific tool is necessary. A standard web browser allows the connection to the repository through the ESERNET Server. A more detailed description can be found in [22].

4   Evaluation

The success of an $E_b IS$ or SE repository can be measured in many ways (see, e.g., [27] for overviews and references). There are examples for specific views on evaluation mainly from the knowledge-based system field and related fields. Furthermore, some evaluation work has been done in the area of software reuse (software artifacts), mainly regarding economic success. Many of the economic models for software reuse can also be used for evaluating $E_b IS$ like SE repositories, because these are also about reuse. Other evaluation criteria, most importantly *recall* and *precision*, come from library and information science. Cooper [28] proposes to measure the success of an information system by the "personal utility" of the delivered information to the user. However, as pointed out by Cooper, the ideal measurement of the usefulness as perceived by the user is both practically, and economically impossible.

In the following, we give an overview on the evaluation efforts for the ESERNET repository. Section 4.1 addresses general issues on how to measure the success of an experience base like the ESERNET repository. Section 4.2 gives an overview on our approach to the evaluation of SE repositories, which is based on the Goal-Question-Metric (GQM) method [29]. Section 4.3 gives an overview on the goals for the evaluation. Section 4.4 describes the GQM-based evaluations regarding utility. Section 4.5 summarizes the analysis of the available feedback channels. A summary, lessons learned, and conclusions can be found in Section 4.6.

4.1   Monitoring and Measuring the EB Value (Timeline)

The theoretically correct $E_b IS$ value (in terms of money or effort saved) can be defined as the value of all the query results less the costs for all queries, as well as build-up and maintenance activities. The value of a query result is the value of the retrieved cases in terms of money or effort saved and includes any future use of the retrieved cases that happen without querying the $E_b IS$ [30].

Since operationalization of the theoretically correct value is very difficult in general, practical measurement uses the monitoring of indicators to identify trends regarding the value of an E_bIS [22]. Such indicators are usage, utility as perceived by the stakeholders, and usability. These indicators have certain restrictions and problems, for examplemsability only ensures that the E_bIS is used and, thus, that the E_bIS can have a certain utility. High usage does not guarantee that the users find useful experience cases, but sustained high usage does. Less usage, or none at all, can be explained in terms of insufficient perceived utility or insufficient usability. Measuring sustained usage is required to monitor usage over a longer period of time. This is not necessary when measuring the perceived utility of the retrieved cases. Such a utility measure was also used for an experiment with COIN [21]. Therefore, we use two indicators for the E_bIS value: sustained usage of the E_bIS and perceived usefulness of the retrieved cases.[5]

Using the indicator "sustained usage" in practice requires a "calibration" to determine meaningful time interval sizes for analyzing usage. If the interval size is too small, the number of usages for the interval will rise and fall without real meaning and thus, analysis would be impossible. If the interval size was too large, the study could take very long before we would get meaningful results.

4.2   Our Approach to Evaluating SE Repositories

Our evaluation methodology is based on the Goal-Question-Metric (GQM) method [10] for goal-oriented measurement of SE products and processes. It includes the process, templates, and guidelines for the application of GQM [29]. GQM is an industrial-strength technique that has been successfully used in the field of software engineering, for example, within NASA-SEL, Robert Bosch GmbH, Allianz Lebensversicherungs AG, Digital SPA, Schlumberger RPS[6].

In GQM initiatives, the analysis task of measurement is specified precisely and explicitly by detailed measurement goals, called GQM goals, these reflect the business needs/goals. Relevant measures are derived in a top-down fashion based on the goals via a set of questions and quality/resource models. This refinement is precisely documented in a GQM plan, providing an explicit rationale for the selection of the underlying measures. The data collected is interpreted in a bottom-up fashion considering the limitations and assumptions underlying each measure.

In this section, we give a short overview on the parts of the method that are relevant for ESERNET: The 3-phase quality model showing how evaluation goals, criteria, and metrics for E_bISs evolve over time (Section 4.2.1) as well as the feedback channels (Section 4.2.2).

A detailed, comprehensive description of the our evaluation method can be found in [31]. Parts of the method are described in [22, 27].

---

[5] There are also additional benefits from measuring the perceived usefulness [27], for example, the similarity measures can be tested and validated for the E_bIS under examination.

[6] The CEMP Consortium. *Customized establishment of measurement programs.* Final report, ESSI Project Nr. 10358, Germany, 1996.

4.2.1 3-Phase Quality Model for Meaningful Goals and Metrics over Time

Depending on the maturity level of the E_bIS, the measurement program has to be adapted. Hence, the quality models used for evaluating a single E_bIS have to change over time. Fig. 3 illustrates these changes. In our model, we distinguish three phases for the evaluation of an E_bIS: In the beginning of the usage of the system (i.e., Phase E_A), we use our standard model for measuring indicators about the acceptance of the system. Later, in Phase E_{AS}, application-specific issues can be added for a more detailed evaluation. Phase E_{ASV} extends the measurement program with the aspect of understanding and analysing the economic viability of the E_bIS. These phases are not strictly separated, but may overlap.

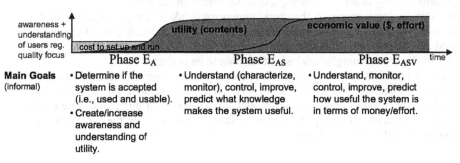

	Phase E_A	Phase E_{AS}	Phase E_{ASV}
Main Goals (informal)	• Determine if the system is accepted (i.e., used and usable). • Create/increase awareness and understanding of utility.	• Understand (characterize, monitor), control, improve, predict what knowledge makes the system useful.	• Understand, monitor, control, improve, predict how useful the system is in terms of money/effort.

Fig. 3. Quality model for the development of goals (and metrics) over time

When the evaluation program was developed (July 2002), the first release of the ESERNET repository was almost finished. Thus, according to the 3-phase model, the ESERNET repository was considered to be in Phase E_A. Therefore, we put the emphasis on Phase E_A in the following. For details on Phases E_{AS} and E_{ASV}, the reader is referred to [31, 20].

Phase E_A focusses on measuring acceptance with simple, "cheap" quality models. The focus on acceptance is meaningful because the acceptance of an E_bIS by the intended users is crucial, since such a system can only yield benefits if it is accepted and used. Because the system tends to be changed relatively often in the beginning, it is very difficult to address the actual quality of the system regarding its contents, retrieval mechanisms, etc. with a measurement program. For this purpose, our standard model addresses two aspects: First, we combine measuring the usage of the E_bIS (e.g., number of queries) and feedback on the utility of the retrieved experiences as stated in Section 4.1. Combining usage and utility allows a picture to be built up regarding acceptance more quickly than just monitoring usage since, in the beginning, usage can also be high because the system is new there is a tendency for people to play with it. Furthermore, the utility feedback helps to better understand what the users are really interested in. Secondly, the coverage is measured by monitoring the number of cases in the EB over time. This is compared to the expected development of the number of cases. Section 4.2.2 gives details on feedback channels regarding collecting and analysing feedback on utility.

4.2.2 Feedback Channels

The feedback channels allow the identification of usefulness problems based on user feedback. They explain causes for a selected number of factors from the cause-effect model from [27] and the respective effects/problems that are experienced by the user. These effects are described using indicators. For each indicator, one or several causes are stated. From the causes, the respective measures for evaluation are derived. For each cause, a respective improvement action is stated. An improvement action can be implemented as: (a) a recommendation from the user interface to the user; or, (b) a maintenance guideline (see Section 5).

For GQM, the cause-indicator pairs provide answers to questions about the indicated problems: if they occur, how often, and under which circumstances.

To select feedback channels, the users' viewpoint is taken or representatives of the users are interviewed. In such an interview, the type of feedback given by users is clarified.. A measurement specialist can now tell what in addition has to be measured in order to allow a meaningful analysis of the data to be collected.

Feedback channels are set up for each retrieval goal or query interface. Details on the feedback channels can be found in [31, 27]. [27] includes an initial list of feedback channels and a generic usage model. An extension of this is integrated into the evaluation method in [31]. This also includes guidelines for the selection and implementation of feedback channels.

4.3   Business Goals and Measurement Goals

Based on the business goals for ESERNET (see [32]), the measurement goals are defined [22]. The focused business goals are as follows:

- **BG1** = Provide a knowledge sharing infrastructure for structuring and packaging.
- **BG2** = Packaging experiences on existing SE practices.

Fig. 4 gives an overview on the identified and selected GQM goals.[7] For BG1, we refined this to Goal 1 on the usability of the questionnaires for entering information on experimental studies in SE. BG2 is reflected by the monitoring of the coverage in Goal 2, i.e., the question if the packaging leads to contents in the repository. This is also related to the standard model for Phase E_A of the 3-Phase Model. Goals 3 and 4 focus on the perceived utility (Section 4.4). This quality focus ("with respect to") is taken from the 3-Phase Model. Goal 3 has to consider the retrieval goal for the analysis as stated in its context. Goal 5 addresses the usage of the system. For the usage, we have to distinguish between usage of the web server itself and of the actual repository.

In the following, we provide details of the utility goals and feedback channels. For the other goals, the reader is referred to [32].

---

[7] The standard GQM templates for goals are used. The so-called quality focus is the item for "with respect to".

Goal 1	Analyze	the questionnaires
	for the purpose of	evaluation
	with respect to	Usability
	from the viewpoint of	a provider of empirical study information
	with the task	filling questionnaire (provide study information)
	in the context of	ESERNET.
Goal 2	Analyze	artifacts in the repository
	for the purpose of	Monitoring
	with respect to	the coverage of an ESERNET technology
	from the viewpoint of	the ESERNET contractors
	in the context of	ESERNET.
Goal 3	Analyze	the retrieved information
	for the purpose of	Characterization
	with respect to	perceived utility
	from the viewpoint of	the user/reader of empirical study information
	in the context of	ESERNET, retrieval goal X.
Goal 4	Analyze	the information in the ESERNET repository
	for the purpose of	Characterization
	with respect to	Utility
	from the viewpoint of	the maintainer
	in the context of	ESERNET, technology.
Goal 5	Analyze	the information in the ESERNET repository
	for the purpose of	Characterization
	with respect to	usage
	from the viewpoint of	Users
	in the context of	ESERNET, retrieval goal X.

Fig. 4. Overview on GQM goals for the ESERNET repository in Phase E_A

4.4   Measuring Perceived Utility

The perceived utility of the user is analysed from two different viewpoints: user and maintainer (E_bIS team). While the viewpoint "users" focuses more on how well the information needs of the users were served by the repository, the viewpoint "maintainer" focuses on understanding which items from the repository served the users best and worst, in order to provide hints for improving the repository and its maintenance.

In general, the perceived utility is measured in accordance with the models presented in [31]. However, there are two slight differences: There are three levels for the rating of the perceived usefulness (☺, ☺, ☹) instead of the binary "useful / not useful".

Goal 3 describes the perceived utility from the viewpoint of the users. The abstraction sheet that was developed in a GQM interview [24], focusses on: (1) the distribution of perceived usefulness per session; (2) the rate of queries without suitable information in query result; (3) the rate of queries without suitable retrieval goal; and, (4) the rate of queries where user could not locate existing information.

Goal 4 analyses the perceived utility from the maintainers' viewpoint. The focus here is not the analysis of the query results, but the identification of "good" and "bad" artifacts. The quality factors are the distribution of perceived utility and usage per item for "top items" and "flop items" as well as the identification of unused items. These three quality factors are analyzed per ESERNET technology and for ESERNET as a whole.

Understanding what users found useful and what they did not find useful supports decisions about acquisition of new artifacts and maintenance of existing artifacts. Less useful artifacts have to be analysed in order to identify the specific problems with the artifacts and to improve or remove these artifacts. Comparing very good with very bad artifacts helps to identify what makes an artifact "good", as well as improving the quality criteria for recording and developing more and/or better guidelines for writing reusable artifacts.

The analyses are performed by technology and not per retrieval goal. The reason for this is that (in ESERNET) decisions on the acquisition of studies are made per technology. Therefore, it is relevant to know how 'good' the knowledge in a technology performs in comparison to other technologies. Furthermore, the technology can be identified for each case because it is stated in the case. In contrast to this, a retrieval goal is not fix for a case.

Both utility goals require metrics for analyses per time interval (Section 4.1). These issues are addressed by GQM plan and measurement plan. The measurement plan for the two utility goals demonstrates that these evaluations can be based on very few and simple data collection procedures. The respective part of the measurement plan mainly consists of the data collection for the rating of pages or items by user using ☺, ☺, ☻. The rating is stored in the database. Query ID, user ID, date&time of query, retrieval goal, record/case ID, and rating are stored. The complete measurement plan can be found in [24].

4.5   Analysis of Feedback Channels Available by the Measurement Plan

The measurement plan is analyzed to check which utility feedback channels are already available from the implementation of the GQM plans for the utility goals.

Table 1 summarizes the results of the analysis and shows which feedback channels with which indication strength are implemented, possible or not available.

For some indicators where "strong" feedback channels are implemented, "weak" feedback channels are also available. However, the analyses will use only the "strong" feedback channels.

4.6   What Did We Learn about SE Repository Evaluation?

The quality models for utility and the evaluation method in general [22, 31] were validated once more. Furthermore, we developed a quality model for the perceived utility analyzed from the viewpoint of the maintainers. Overall, the following lessons were learned:

- Quality focus "coverage" in Phase 1: The development of a more detailed defini-tion then "number of cases per topic/subject area" is a difficult and time-consum ing task. We recommend, using the measure "number of cases per topic/ subject

Table 1. Analysis of feedback channels in ESERNET regarding availability

ESERNET [8]	Indicator	Strength of Indication	Data Collection & Analysis	Required
I	appropriate retrieval goal not available	Strong	respective feedback	
I	type of needed artifact cannot be specified	Strong	respective feedback	
I	not enough useful artifacts	Strong	respective feedback	
P	-"-	weak..strong	• binary: #useful artifacts in result < user expectation • gradual: grade of unfulfillment of user expectation := 100% - #useful artifacts in result / user expectation	user expectation regarding #useful artifacts in query result (per retrieval goal)
n	user cannot decide whether an artifact is useless or should be considered for (viewing and) utilizing	Strong	utility feedback "don't know" for artifact	
i	-"-	Weak	no utility feedback	
n	order in which user views artifact is not the order recommended by the system	Strong	order by user differs from order by similarity	
p	-"-	medium	useful items do not have the highest similarity - i.e., some useless items have higher similarity than useful items	
(i)	user does not select any artifact	Strong	respective feedback	
p	-"-	Medium	#useful artifacts in query result = 0 AND usefulness feedback given for the query	
p	-"-	Weak	no utility feedback for whole result	
N	artifact is not as useful as originally estimated	Strong	collect feedback after utilization of the artifact	feedback loop

area" because it is easy to comprehend and the respective data is easy to collect and analyse. To monitor the trend, one must state the expectations about the number of cases and about the type of trend (e.g., linear).

- An E_bIS measurement specialist has be included in the development of an evaluation program - otherwise a lot of effort for training other people is required.
- Verify GQM plan and measurement program with respect to the mandatory metrics [31] to ensure that meaningful evaluations are possible.

---

[8] i = implemented, p = possible, n = not available.

- The implementation of the data collection procedures has be be checked to ensure that the measurement program is implemented correctly and that some metrics are not discarded. This check is particularly important when the measurement specialist and repository developer(s) are not the same person.

These lessons learned were integrated into the evaluation method [31].

5 Maintenance

In [33], we explained that maintenance of E_bIS such as SE repositories has a certain complexity and is a knowledge-intensive task. Thus, guidance and decision support for maintenance is almost essential to successfully maintain and improve such a system. Due to the variety and number of the knowledge in an E_bIS, maintenance support has to combine human- and computer-based maintenance activities. In [30], we presented the EMSIG framework and an integrated technical solution that operationalizes the support for E_bIS maintenance regarding cases and conceptual model using specific maintenance knowledge. As a jump-start for continuous operation, this maintenance knowledge should be available at the end of the buildup, that is, when the initial acquisition and development of the system and of the knowledge in the "standard" containers (vocabulary, cases, similarity measures, adaptation [34]) has been finished.

Knowledge and information on the quality of the E_bIS and its contents can be acquired and improved using a systematic approach as presented in the previous section). Manually performed maintenance processes (e.g., acquisition of new cases) are described at a coarse-grained level in methodologies such as INRECA [35] or DISER [21]. Automatic or tool-supported maintenance procedures are available, e.g., from case-based reasoning research for very specific knowledge types for certain task and domain types [36, 37]. However, the maintenance knowledge for decision support and specific maintenance tasks is rather acquired "by chance" during continuous operation (so far). Thus, it might take long to learn the required maintenance knowledge for decision support. The problem is that existing methods such as INRECA or DISER only fill the "standard" knowledge containers of E_bIS systems.

Based on DISER, we have developed (within the context of maintenance) the EMSIG framework for maintenance support for E_bIS, which combines human- and computer-based maintenance activities and respective decision support.

For the maintenance of ESERNET, we wanted to validate the part of the maintenance method that addresses the linking of maintenance with evaluation by identifying the "when" component of maintenance, based on the measurement program.

In the following, we give an overview on E_bIS maintenance knowledge types and discuss where authoring support is necessary and/or beneficial (Section 5.1). Then we describe by some examples of how we derived maintenance knowledge from the evaluation plan (Section 5.2). Following this, we describe (Section 5.3), feasible tool support for using this maintenance knowledge for authoring. Finally, we summarize what we learned about experience base maintenance in the ESERNET project (Section 5.4.).

5.1   Overview on EB/CBR Maintenance Knowledge Types

5.1.1. Quality Knowledge

Quality knowledge[9] describes how the quality of the E_bIS is measured and the current status of the system with respect to quality as well as the rationale for the definition of quality [38]. Quality knowledge deals with quality aspects of the E_bIS as a whole, i.e., the E_bIS's contents and conceptual model as well as retrieval mechanisms, usability of the user interface, etc. An example for content-related quality knowledge is a definition of measures for the utility or value of single cases [22]. There are several types of quality knowledge that are related as follows: The measures define what data is collected. The data collection is performed automatically or manually by respective data collection procedures. The collected data is analyzed using predefined models or procedures. The results of the analyses can be used for justifying an E_bIS and as input for decisions about maintenance [22, 30].

5.1.2   Maintenance Process/Procedure Knowledge

Maintenance process and procedure knowledge defines how the actual maintenance activities are performed. The actual maintenance can be performed as a mix of automatically and manually performed activities. For the *automatically* performed activities (*maintenance* procedures), tool support by components of the E_bIS or separate tools is required. The remaining activities have to be performed *manually* (*maintenance processes*). To improve guidance for the maintainers, descriptions of these processes are provided. A maintenance process can have maintenance procedures as automated subprocesses/steps, which use input from, or provide input for manually performed steps.

5.1.3. Maintenance Decision Knowledge

Maintenance Decision Knowledge links the quality knowledge with the maintenance process knowledge. It describes under what circumstances maintenance processes/procedures should be executed or checked for execution. Such maintenance knowledge can be described in an informal manner as *maintenance policies* [37], which define when, why, and how maintenance is performed for an E_bIS. The "why" component addresses not only the reason for maintenance but also the expected benefits of the maintenance operation. These expected benefits should be related to the objectives of the E_bIS or to the general goal of maintenance (i.e., to preserve and improve the E_bIS's value [30]). Since these objectives are typically very high-level, it is not very meaningful to address the E_bIS objectives directly. Instead, we use a refinement of the objectives: the quality criteria from the evaluation program or the recording methods. The "how" component is a combination of maintenance processes and procedures with additional steps as "glue."

---

[9] The term "quality knowledge" was introduced by Menzies [34].

5.2   Deriving Maintenance Decisions Knowledge from the Evaluation Program for ESERNET

We derived a number of maintenance policies from the evaluation program, i.e., from the GQM abstractions sheets and GQM plan for ESERNET.

In general, the triggers can be derived from the evaluation program because this is the link from the maintenance decision knowledge to the quality knowledge, which is described by the evaluation program. For the trigger identification, the quality factors and variation factors from the abstraction sheets are analyzed:

- The quality factors together with the respective baseline define expectations regarding the quality. If there is no well-founded baseline available in the beginning, the first policy has to be defined with the expectation/estimation. After some iterations (Phase 2), the policy is revised to consider the well-founded baseline. The maintenance activity is to check whether the expectations are met sufficiently or not.

- The variation factors and respective analysis model results can be used in three different ways: (1) It can be used directly in a trigger. (2) It can "adjust" a trigger by, e.g., choosing respective values from the baseline. (3) It can be used as background information for human-made decisions when no explicit decision model has been developed yet.

After identifying the triggers, the respective actions are outlined. In a second step, the actual maintenance policies are "compiled", selected, and refined. In particular, the actions are defined, discussed and reviewed by the maintenance personnel.

To document the relation between measurement program and maintenance policies & guidelines, the IDs of the referred questions/criteria/measures/models are stated in the maintenance policies & guidelines.

For ESERNET, we derived five maintenance policies from the goals 1, 2, and 4. Two of these policies have special variants for the beginning of regular use of the ESERNET repository. Goal 3 provides the maintenance guidelines related to the improvement actions for the feedback channels. Here, we simply had to selected the feasible and relevant improvement actions based on the analysis of the available feedback channels in Section 4.2.2. In the following, we present two selected maintenance policies from ESERNET where each is of a different type.

The first maintenance policy deals with the reaction on complaints about bad understandability/comprehensibility of questions in the questionnaire for studies. It has two variants: At the beginning of regular use, we consider every complaint as important since the questionnaire is still new (Fig. 5). Later, when the questionnaire is more established, we react only when there are complaints by more than a certain number of different providers. Before switching to the second variant, when the questionnaire is relatively settled, we have the opportunity to learn about the appropriate number of complaints for the policy. This number then defines the baseline hypothesis for a revised GQM plan and the revised condition in the second variant of the maintenance policy.

Trigger: new complaint about understandability of a question   *[Goal 1, Q4]*
Actions:
- check complaint
- decide about improvement of question
  - criteria: to be learned
- if yes
  - improve/rephrase question
  - ask the provider (who had the understandability problem) if the revised version is better to understand and ask for feedback within 2   weeks
  - if no answer available after 2 weeks: ask again (maximum: 2 times)
  - when answer is available: depending on the answer, update the question

Expected benefits:
- better understandability of questions in questionnaire
- therefore: better completeness of study descriptions

Fig. 5. ESERNET maintenance policy derived from quality factor (variant for Phase 1)

Trigger: periodical,
    >40 queries in last period where no suitable artifact is found
    in the query result *[Goal 3, Q2]*
Actions:
- Make a survey among the users who gave this feedback to find out more about their interests (because they provided feedback and, therefore, seem to care more about ESERNET than people who do not provide feedback) and their expectations regarding the coverage.
- The results can be used for
  - a revised acquisition strategy or
  - an improved communication regarding what you can expect from ESERNET.

Expected benefits:
- better addressing of the needs of the actual users

Fig. 6. ESERNET maintenance policy derived from Goal 4

The second maintenance policy (Fig. 6) was selected and derived from the feedback channels. Question 2 from Goal 3 "rate of queries where no suitable artifact is found in the query result" is related to the feedback channels with the indicator "not enough useful artifacts in the result of the query" for the generic usage process step "evaluate/examine". In addition, the indicator is related to different causes with different improvement actions each. In particular the causes "coverage too low" and "user overestimates repository system" cannot be reliably identified when the user uses the repository. Therefore, a survey is made among the users that gave this feedback in order to find out more about the users' needs and expectations.

The other ESERNET maintenance policies (10 + 4 optional) can be found in [39].

5.3   Tool Support for Maintenance Decision Making

To allow tool support, the maintenance policies are further formalized as *maintenance guidelines*. The maintenance guidelines have the same basic structure as the maintenance policies. To allow tool support, the following major changes and extensions are made with respect to maintenance policies (see [30] for details).

A partial or complete formalization of the "trigger" is required to allow an automatic tool-based checking of the trigger. The formalized parts of the trigger can refer to items from the standard containers as well as measures, user feedback, periodic events, or events such as the end of a project. For more advanced analyses, the trigger can also refer to results from analysis tools such as data or text mining tools. The parts of the trigger that cannot be formalized are included in the maintenance guideline for manual checks by the role responsible for this. In a case where the actual trigger cannot be formalized at all, then the respective guideline can be triggered periodically as a reminder and the actual condition check is done manually by an ESERNET repository staff member.

The "actions" refer to human-based maintenance processes, automatic maintenance procedures, and the "glue" amongst these. Thus, it is possible to combine automatic procedures with human-based execution of processes. The degree to which the integration is bound together depends on the tools, e.g., one could export cases for analysis with a data mining tool each month (loose integration) or a data mining component could be run automatically (tight integration).

5.4   What Did We Learn about SE Repository Maintenance?

First, we validated the experience base maintenance method, in particular, deriving maintenance policies from GQM plans and using feedback channels.

Second, we developed a set of generic maintenance policies for SE repositories for perceived utility for two viewpoints (user and maintainer). Some of the maintenance policies have variants for the different phases or stages. For the viewpoint user, the maintenance policies are similar to the improvement action-cause-indicator tuples from the feedback channels. However, when there are several causes for an indicator, then this also has to be considered for the maintenance policy.

6   Conclusion

We faced the challenge integrating all the very different opinions from the stakeholders with respect to the granularity of the data to be stored. They vary from very detailed data to allow replication, to the case where only a contact person can be asked for more information. This led us to an incremental implementation, which means that we have started with a web-presentation similar to yellow-pages, this stated what is going on in the field of empirical software engineering and who are the main players (not only in Europe). We also included a seed for the repository in the sense of reported studies available from, e.g., ISERN. These were categorized with respect to ESERNET and made searchable via different mechanisms (plain text search and navigation). During the project it was shown that the effort involved in storing studies in the repository had to be reduced. The only way to do this is to allow the authors to contribute their studies by themselves, which is implemented by online questionnaires. To enable external contributions we also allowed two different levels of detail (Executive Summary Report, and the more detailed ESERNET Planning Phase and Final Report Questionnaires).

The systematic approach described in this chapter led to a repository that matches the users' needs, and this is demonstrated by feedback from users and other stakeholders. A meaningful evaluation based on frequency of usage and utility feedback is not yet possible because the repository is currently at the end of the Phase "version 1" where the initial knowledge acqusition is performed.

The evaluation of ESERNET is similar to the evaluation of CBR-PEB [22] since both are repositories on the web and not in a company intranet. This makes it more difficult to make users contribute and use the repository. For this evaluation program, we used the opportunity to conduct GQM interviews for two new quality foci for repositories in the beginning of the usage and to analyze perceived utility from the maintainers viewpoint in order to have a more maintenance oriented evaluation in addition to the standard viewpoint "users". Furthermore, the feedback channels were validated.

The maintenance is linked to the evaluation in a systematic and traceable manner. The GQM plans were used as starting point to identify the "when" component of maintenance. Based on this, so-called maintenance policies were developed, which describe the "when", "how", and "why" components of maintenance. A set of generic maintenance policies for experience bases and SE repositories for measuring utility could be identified.

Similar to Conradi and Dyba [40] we observed that keeping an EB alive is not only to externalise knowledge, by means of publishing empirical studies, but the hard part is to enable internalisation (for transfer of knowledge see [41]), through transfering experience to other people or even organisations. Hereby, the context is seen as most critical factor for transfering knowledge. Following the arguments described by Brown and Duguid, who argue that the composite concept of "learning-in-doing" best represents the fluid evolution of learning through practice [42], we should emphasize more on informal learning or experience based learning, which is integrated into working processes. We also found that the "real" exchange mostly happens in one-to-one communication, presuming a base of trust [43]. This supports the findings of [40] and [42].

Cross-company exchange of experiences contained within empirical studies often faces the problems of confidentiality. This means that the companies are not willing to contribute detailed information, if it is spread in a more or less uncontrolled way. They prefer exchange of experience in an interpersonal manner, so they know to whom they can provide information. We experienced that having something similar to yellow-pages provides a means of moving towards a more sophisticated solution. The users and operators learn how to deal with the fears of the partners and can adapt the solution incrementally to their needs. This supports the findings of Conradi et al. [20] with respect to web-based repositories.

References

[1] Nick M.; Althoff K.-D.; 2nd German Workshop on Experience Management (GWEM 2003). In Reimer, U. et.al. (ed), Proc. of the 2nd Conf. on Professional Knowledge Management (WM'03). Luzern, Switzerland. Lecture Notes in Informatics, P–28. pp247–306. Apr 2003.

[2] Basili, V.R.; Caldiera, G.; Rombach, H.D., Experience Factory; in: Marciniak JJ (ed.), Encyclopedia of Software Engineering, Vol. 1, pp. 511–519, John Wiley & Sons, 2001.

[3] Basili, V.R. (1985). Quantitative evaluation of software methodology. In Proceedings of the First Pan-Pacific Computer Conf., Melbourne, Australia, September 1985.

[4] Basili, V.R. & Rombach, H.D. (1988). The TAME Project: Towards improvement-oriented software environments. IEEE Transactions on Software Engineering SE–14(6), pp.758–773, June 1988.

[5] Basili V.R.; Lindvall M.; Costa P.; "Implementing the Experience Factory Concepts as a Set of Experience Bases", In Proc.of SEKE 2001 Conf., Buenos Aires, Argentina, June 2001, pp.102–109

[6] Basili, V.R., Daskalantonakis, M.K., and Yacobellis, R.H.. Technology transfer at Motorola. IEEE Software, 11(2): pp. 70–76, March 1994.

[7] Althoff, K.-D.; Müller, W.: Proceedings of the 2nd Workshop on Learning Software Organizations, LSO 2000; Oulu, Finland; Fraunhofer IESE;

[8] Althoff, K.-D.; Feldmann, R.L.; Müller, W. (eds): Advances in Learning Software Organizations. Proc. of the 3rd International Workshop, LSO 2001; Kaiserslautern, Germany, 2001. Springer LNCS 2176.

[9] Althoff, K.-D., Decker, B., Hartkopf, S., Jedlitschka, A., Nick, M. & Rech, J. (2001). Experience Management: The Fraunhofer IESE Experience Factory. In P. Perner (ed.), Proc. Industrial Conf. Data Mining, Leipzig, 24.–25. Juli 2001

[10] Weber R.; Aha D.W.; Beccera-Fernandez I.; "Intelligent Lessons Learned Systems", In. AAAI Press.; Papers from the 2000 Workshop (Technical Report WS–00–008), Menlo Park, CA, 2000

[11] Houdek, F., Schneider, K. & Wieser, E. (1998). Establishing experience factories at Daimler-Benz: An experience report. Proc. 20th Internat. Conf. on Software Engineering (ICSE'98), pp. 443–447

[12] Seaman C.; Mendonca M.; "An Experience Management System for a Software Consulting Organization", In Proc. of the Software Engineering Workshop; NASA/ Goddard Software Engineering Laboratory, Greenbelt, MD, December, 1999

[13] Dingsøyr, T. (2002): Knowledge Management in Medium-Sized Software Consulting Companies. PhD Thesis; Department of Computer and Information Science, Norwegian University of Science and Technology, Trondheim, Norway

[14] Jedlitschka, A. Adaptive Support for IT Security Tasks. In Ricci, F. & Smyth, B. (eds.): Proc.of the AH'2002 Workshop on Recommendation and Personalization in eCommerce, Málaga, Spain, May 28th 2002, pp.70–79.

[15] Brössler P.; "Knowledge Management at a Software House: An Experience Report", In Learning Software Organisations, Methodology and Applications, SEKE '99; Ruhe G.; Bomarius F.; Springer Verlag Berlin Heidelberg, 2000, pp. 163–170

[16] Johansson, C.; Hall, P.; Coquard, M.; " 'Talk to Paula and Peter – They are Experienced' – The Experience Engine in a Nutshell", in [44], pp. 171–185

[17] Hellstroem T.; Malmquist U.; Mikaelsson J.; "Decentralizing Knowledge: Managing Knowledge Work in a Software Engineering Firm", In Journal of High Technology Management Research, vol. 2, No. 3, 2000

[18] Schneider, K.; Experience Magnets, Attracting Experiences, Not just Storing them; In [45], pp126–140

[19] Dingsøyr, T. Moe, N.B., Nytro, O., (2001), Augmenting Experience Reports with Lightweight Postmortem Reviews; In [45], pp.167–181

[20] Conradi R.; Lindvall M.; Seaman C.; "Success Factors for Software Experience Bases: What We Need to Learn from Other Disciplines", In Singer, J. et al., (eds), Proc. ICSE'2000 Workshop on Beg, Borrow or Steal: Using Multidisciplinary Approaches in Empirical Software Engineering Research', Limerick, Ireland, 5 June 2000. 6 p.

[21] Tautz, C.: Customizing Software Engineering Experience Management Systems to Organizational Needs; Ph. D. diss., Dept. of Computer Science, University of Kaiserslautern, Germany; 2000; Stuttgart: Fraunhofer IRB Verlag

[22] Nick, M. and Feldmann, R.: Guidelines for evaluation and improvement of reuse and experience repository systems through measurement programs. In Third European Conf. on Software Measurements (FESMA–AEMES 2000), Madrid, Spain, October 2000.

[23] Dutta, S.; Lee, M.; van Wassenhove, L.: Software Eengineering in Europe: A study of best practices. IEEE Software, May 1999.

[24] Jedlitschka, A.; Nick, M.: Repository validation report. Technical Report Project ESERNET (IST–2000–28754) – Deliverable D.4.4, Fraunhofer IESE, Kaiserslautern, Germany, 2002.

[25] Hartkopf, S.; Feldmann, R.L.; Schmidt-Belz, B.; Wulf V.: Szenarien für die Benutzung des ViSEK Portals. ViSEK-Internal-Report ViSEK/001/D, Kaiserslautern 2001.

[26] Birk A.; "A Knowldege Management Infrastructure for Systematic Improvement in Software Engineering" Ph. D. diss., Dept. of Computer Science, University of Kaiserslautern, Germany; 2000; Stuttgart: Fraunhofer IRB Verlag

[27] Althoff, K.-D., Nick, M.; Tautz, C. (2000). Systematically Diagnosing and Improving the Perceived Usefulness of Organizational Memories. In [44] pp. 72–86

[28] Cooper, W.S.: On selecting a measure of retrieval effectiveness. In Jones, K.S. and Willet, P., editors, Readings in Information Retrieval, Morgan Kaufmann Publishers, 1997. pp 191–204.

[29] Basili, V.R., Caldiera, G., and Rombach, H.D.; Goal Question Metric Paradigm; in: Marciniak JJ (ed.), Encyclopedia of Software Engineering, Vol. 1, pp. 528–532, John Wiley & Sons, 2001.

[30] Nick, M.; Althoff, K.-D. and Tautz, C.: Systematic maintenance of corporate experience repositories. In [36], pp. 364–386.

[31] Althoff, K.-D. & Nick, M.. How To Support Experience Management with Evaluation – Foundations, Evaluation Methods, and Examples for Case-Based Reasoning and Experience Factory. Springer Verlag, 2003. (to appear).

[32] Gresse, C.; Hoisl, B.; Wüst, J.: A process model for GQM-based measurement. Technical Report STTI–95–04–E, Software Technologie Transfer Initiative Kaiserslautern, Fachbereich Informatik, Universität Kaiserslautern, Kaiserslautern, 1995.

[33] Nick M.; Althoff K.-D.;. Acquiring and using maintenance knowledge to support authoring for experience bases. In Weber, R. and Gresse v. Wangenheim, C. (eds), Proc. of the Workshop Program at the Fourth International Conf. on Case-Based Reasoning (ICCBR'01), Washington, DC, 2001. Naval Research Laboratory, Navy Center for Applied Research in Artificial Intelligence, pp. 38–41

[34] Richter, M.M.: Introduction. In Lenz, M.; Bartsch-Spörl, B.; Burkhard, H.-D. and Wess, S., (Eds.), Case-Based Reasoning Technologies: From Foundations to Applications, Springer LNAI 1500, Springer-Verlag, Berlin, Germany, 1998, pp. 1–15.

[35] Bergmann, R., Breen, S.; Göker, M.; Manago, M. and Wess, S.: Developing Industrial Case-Based Reasoning Applications – The INRECA Methodology. Springer Verlag, 1999.

[36] Leake, D.B.; Smyth, B.; Wilson, D.C.; Yang, Q. (eds). Computational Intelligence special issue on maintaining CBR systems, 2001.

[37] Leake, D.B.; Wilson, D.C.: Categorizing case-base maintenance: Dimensions and directions. In Smyth, B. and Cunningham, P. (eds), Advances in Case-Based Reasoning: Proc. of the Fourth European Workshop on Case-Based Reasoning, pp. 196–207, Berlin, Germany, September 1998. Springer-Verlag.

[38] Menzies, T.: Knowledge maintenance: The state of the art. The Knowledge Engineering Review, 14(1): 1998, pp. 1–46.

[39] Jedlitschka, A. Requirements and design of the ESERNET ESE knowledge repository. Technical Report Project ESERNET (IST–2000–28754) – Deliverable D.4.1, Fraunhofer IESE, Kaiserslautern, Germany, 2001.

[40] Conradi, R. and Dyba, T.: An empirical Study on the utility of formaL routines to transfer knowledge and experience; In Gruhn, V. (ed.): Proc. European Software Engineering Conference 2001 (ESEC2001), Vienna, 10.–14.Sept.2001, ACM/IEEE CS Press, p.268–276, 2001

[41] Nonaka, I. and Takeuchi, H.: The Knowledge Creating Company, Oxford University Press, 1995

[42] Brown, J.S. and Duguid, P.: Organizational Learning and Communities of Practice: Toward a Unified View of Working, Learning and Innovation; Organization Science, Vol.2, No.1 (Feb.1991), pp.40–57

[43] Jedlitschka, A. and Pfahl, D.: Experience-Based Model-Driven Improvement Management with Combined Data Sources from Industry and Academia; Submitted to ACM-IEEE International Symposium on Empirical Software Engineering (ISESE 2003);

[44] Ruhe, G. and Bomarius, F.: Learning Software Organizations, Methodology and Applications; Proc. of the 11th International Conference on Software Engineering and Knowledge Engineering, SEKE'99; Springer LNCS 1756; 2000

[45] Bomarius, F.; Komi-Sirviö, S. (eds.): Product Focused Software Process Improvement; Proceedings of the 3rd International Conf., PROFES 2001; Kaiserslautern, Germany; Springer LNCS 2188; 2001.

Using Empirical Studies during Software Courses

Jeffrey Carver[1], Letizia Jaccheri[2], Sandro Morasca[3], and Forrest Shull[4]

[1] Experimental Software Engineering Group, Dept. of Computer Science
A.V. Williams Bldg., University of Maryland, College Park, College Park MD 20742
ph: +1 301 405 2721 fax: +1 301 405-3691
carver@cs.umd.edu
[2] Department of Computer and Information Science, Norwegian University of Science and
Technology, Sem Sælands vei 7-9, 7491 Trondheim, Norway
ph: +47 73593469 fax: +47 73594466
letizia@idi.ntnu.no
[3] Dipartimento di Scienze Chimiche, Fisiche e Matematiche, Università degli Studi
dell'Insubria, Via Valleggio 11, I-22100, Como, Italy
ph: +39 031 2386228 fax: +39 031 2386119
sandro.morasca@uninsubria.it
[4] Fraunhofer USA Center for Experimental Software Engineering Maryland
4321 Hartwick Road, Suite 500, College Park MD 20742, USA
ph.: +1 301 403-8970 fax: +1 301 403-8976
fshull@fc-md.umd.edu

Abstract. A number of empirical studies using students as subjects has been carried out in the last few years. These studies are usually conducted as pilot experiments that allow researchers to fine-tune an experiment before deploying it in an industrial environment. Though one of the issues usually taken into account with these experiments is their external validity, other issues need to be considered, such as the usefulness of these experiments in the context of a software engineering course. This chapter concisely reports on three empirical studies performed at the Università degli Studi dell'Insubria during the ESERNET project and two other empirical studies that we carried out previously, all with students as subjects, so as to provide the context for a discussion on the research and the educational goals that should be taken into account when carrying out an experiment with students to make it successful from both an empirical and an educational viewpoint. Finally, we provide some advice on how to carry out empirical studies with students based on our experiences.

Keywords: Software engineering, software metrics, software engineering measurement, empirical studies, pilot studies, software engineering education

1 Introduction

Quantitative management helps plan, monitor, control, evaluate, and improve software projects based on solid evidence. Measurement-related activities, such as data collection and knowledge extraction from data, should become a part of software engineering practice in software organizations, and so need to be integrated with the other activities of the software development process. Quantitative assessments should

R. Conradi and A.I. Wang (Eds.): ESERNET 2001-2003, LNCS 2765, pp. 81–103, 2003.
© Springer-Verlag Berlin Heidelberg 2003

be applied to the processes, methods, techniques, and tools used by different software organizations. Because of their impact on software quality, costs, and development time, quantitative assessments should be applied to new processes, methods, techniques, and tools that are proposed before they are deployed in industrial software environments.

Even though quantitative information is sorely needed about processes, methods, techniques, and tools, few software organizations use measurement-related activities to obtain solid information. In this context, empirical studies may be used to

- quantitatively assess the specific objects of study (processes, methods, products, etc.) at hand;
- show the advantages of empirical software engineering and open the way for larger-scale data collection activities.

However, empirical studies in industrial settings require a good deal of time, effort, and resources, so they need to be planned and carried out carefully. Before running experiments at software companies, it is therefore advisable to carry out pilot studies with students in academic settings. Pilot studies with students are actually often used with several goals in mind, some are technical, such as obtaining preliminary evidence that supports research hypotheses, while others are organizational, such as fine-tuning the details of the empirical study.

At any rate, carrying out pilot studies should be a two-way street, i.e. both the researchers and the students should obtain something of benefit. The scientific literature has usually examined the advantages of pilot studies only from the researchers' point of view. However, if measurement-related activities are to become a part of accepted practice, it is important that empirical studies are a part of software engineering classes where the students learn how to perform the activities of a software engineering, e.g. program, design, test, specify, etc. By the same token, students should also be introduced to other activities that may be part of their job, such as data collections. Since software development is an inherently creative process, getting used to these activities early may even be more important in software than in other business areas. More importantly, empirical studies should be used as a pedagogical vehicle that helps students have a better understanding of the concepts taught in a software course. It is our belief that empirical studies should provide benefits not only to the researchers, but also to the students.

In this chapter, we report on a set of empirical studies we have carried out using college students as subjects. Based on our experience, we discuss the main benefits to researchers and to students from the execution of empirical studies in software courses. In addition, we offer a number of lessons learned about making empirical studies during software college courses successful. Thus, we view our contribution as a starting point for a much-needed discussion about the relationship between empirical software engineering and software engineering education.

Each of the studies from the set described above will be briefly discussed in Section 2. Three of the studies were carried out at the Università degli Studi dell'Insubria during the ESERNET project on (1) the verification of software programs, (2) software design reading, and (3) the design of web applications. The fourth study was carried out at the University of Maryland, the original study of which the software design reading was a replication. The fifth study was carried out at the IDI NTNU in Trondheim on software process issues. These studies encompass a variety of different software engineering application fields, and allowed us to gather diverse experience on empirical studies with students.

The software engineering education community has been active during the last 30 years striving to provide a pedagogically sound framework for educators [1, 2, 3]. Some of the issues discussed by this community are computing programs and curricula [4], specific courses [5], laboratories, and alternative ways of teaching. Among other proposals, the importance of practice-based software engineering education is well accepted in the community and some good examples are reported in the literature [6, 7]. However, "too few academic programs offer curricula that focus on this type of education. [8]" Therefore, empirical studies may be also seen as a way to promote practice-based software engineering.

This chapter is organized as follows. Section 2 provides a concise description of the five empirical studies with students as subjects used to identify the benefits for the researchers and the students and the lessons learned for carrying out empirical studies with students. Section 3 describes the perspective benefits for the researchers and the students that may be achieved with empirical studies in software college courses. Related works that have appeared in the literature on empirical studies with students are summarized in Section 4. Based on our experiences, we illustrate and discuss a set of lessons learned that may be useful to the researchers carrying out empirical studies with students as subjects in Section 5. The conclusions and an outline of future work are in Section 6.

2 Empirical Studies

Here, we briefly report on a few empirical studies that we have carried out with students as subjects. Three of them have been carried out at the Università degli Studi dell'Insubria in the context of the ESERNET project, while the others are previous studies that give additional support in our discussion on the use and the usage of empirical studies with students. The description of each empirical study will be structured as follows:

- Scope and Basic Ideas
- Main Goals, Assumptions, and Hypotheses
- Experimental Setting
- Steps of the Empirical Study
- Main Results
- Discussion
- Future Work

2.1 A Bayesian Stopping Rule for Testing

2.1.1 Scope and Basic Ideas
This empirical study focused on a stopping rule for testing of both OO and non-OO systems. The basic idea is that the decision on when testing should stop is highly subjective and cannot be based on statistical techniques. This idea is supported by theory (an unwieldy number of inputs would be needed) and common practice

(testing must be an economically viable technique). Thus, the testers need to reach a sufficient degree of confidence that the program will execute correctly on the next input, i.e., they do not deem further testing to be necessary. A more complete description of this study can be found in [9].

2.1.2   Main Goals, Assumptions, and Hypotheses

The main goal of the empirical study was to investigate the changes in the subjective degree of belief in the correctness of a program on a specific input subdomain as testing proceeds. The results obtained on each subdomain can be combined to obtain a result for the program as a whole. Thus, the study can be useful for small, mid-size, and large projects.

Specifically, the goal of the experiment was to study the variations in the degree of belief that the program will execute correctly on the next input, based on the fact that it has executed correctly with the previous inputs. One of the assumptions of the study is that the program under test is of good quality, i.e., it is in its final stages of testing. This assumption is consistent with the final goal of devising a stopping rule for testing.

It seems reasonable to suppose that, with every input (extracted from a subdomain) that does not cause a failure, one gains more confidence in the correct functioning of the program on that subdomain. If this was not the case, then testers would only stop because the time or resources for testing have been consumed, and not because they have good confidence that the program behaves correctly on that subdomain.

A number of hypotheses were tested. Here, we report only on the most important ones, and we only provide the "alternative hypothesis," since the "null hypothesis" is its logical negation:

Hypothesis 1. If a program executes correctly on an input, then the degree of belief that it will execute correctly on the next input increases; if a program executes incorrectly on an input, then the degree of belief that it will execute correctly on the next input decreases.

In addition, we studied whether there was a difference in this "rate of optimism" between test sessions in which the subjects were allowed to create their own test suites and test sessions in which the subjects received the test suites. For instance, given test suites are often used during regression testing.

Hypothesis 2. The "rate of optimism" is greater for test sessions in which the subjects use pre-defined test suites than in sessions in which the subjects create their own test suites.

2.1.3   Experimental Setting

Two groups of subjects participated in the experiment. Both groups were composed of undergraduate students, though the students in one group were more experienced. The subjects were given:

- six Java programs, three of which had faults seeded
- test suites for three programs
- only the specifications and the final product for 2 programs
- the specifications, the final product, and the design for 2 programs
- the specifications, the final product, the design, and the source code for 2 programs

An automated data collection mechanism was in place. The experiment was carried out on Personal Computers.

2.1.4   Steps

- Introduction to testing techniques
- Background explanation to the subjects on the goals of the study
- Experiment execution
- Data analysis

2.1.5   Main Results

The results seem to confirm the initial hypotheses of the study.

- **Hypothesis 1.** On average, the degree of belief changes in the expected direction. It increases after each correct execution of the program, and decreases after each incorrect execution. The data are in Table 1. Column "Sample" describes whether the data in the row are about the entire sample ("Total") or the programs for which the subjects were either allowed to build test suites or they were given test suites. Column "mean (stdDev)" contains the mean value and standard deviation of the percentages of times the change of the degree of belief was in the expected direction. Column "median" contains the median of this percentage. Column "N" contains the sample size.

Table 1. Percentages of success

Sample	N	Median	Mean	stdDev
Total	93	1	0.869	0.18
Built Test Suites	50	0.774	0.774	0.19
Given Test Suites	43	1	0.980	0.06

The data analysis showed that there is a statistically significant (at the 0.05 level) difference between programs with test suites to be built and programs with given test suites:

- **Hypothesis 2.** The functional form adjusts quite well to the data and we used Ordinary Least Squares to estimate the values for coefficient a. The estimated values are
  - -0.0122 for programs with test suites to be built
  - -0.0666 for programs with given test suites.

The difference between these two values is highly statistically significant.

2.1.6   Discussion

In addition to confirming the basic hypotheses, the study also allowed us to acquire preliminary insights into the degree of belief at which testers decide to begin and stop testing a subdomain of a program.

2.1.7   Future Work

These preliminary insights need to be further investigated, since they may depend on
- the time constraints given for allowing testing
- the measurement instruments; for instance, it is possible that the results might change if the subjects are asked to report the degree of belief that the program will fail with the next input
- the experience of the subjects, i.e., professionals may show a different threshold of the degree of belief at which testing should stop

2.2   Web Design

2.2.1   Scope and Basic Ideas

We studied the effort needed for designing Web applications from an empirical point of view. The subjects were asked to use an OO design notation, called W2000, to design web applications. A more complete description of this study can be found in [10]

2.2.2   Main Goals, Assumptions, and Hypotheses

The study had three main goals:

- compare the relative importance of each design activity (specifically, we compared the efforts to build W2000's information and navigation models), to (1) identify possible improvement points in the design process and (2) better plan the design phase
- assess the accuracy of a priori design effort predictions and the influence of some factors on the effort needed for each design activity
- assess the students' perception of the quality of the designs obtained.

Even though this is an exploratory study, we studied the following hypotheses, among others.

Hypothesis 1. The median of the actual effort related to the information model (ActInfoEff) is higher than the median of the actual effort related to the navigation model (ActNavEff).

Hypothesis 2. The median of the actual effort (ActEff) is higher than the median of the estimated effort (EstEff).

Hypothesis 3. There is a positive correlation between the estimated effort and the actual effort.

Hypothesis 4. There is a positive correlation between the students' self-grading of the designs and the grading provided by the instructor.

2.2.3   Experimental Setting

The subjects received

- the specifications of a pilot application (a hypothetical e-commerce application; what changed from project to project was the application domain: books, CDs, groceries, etc.)
- a questionnaire before starting the design, to set their expertise and make them estimate the effort required during the various activities of the design phase
- a questionnaire while completing the model to measure directly the actual effort.

2.2.4   Steps

The subjects were taught to design their applications with W2000 as a part of an advanced web design class:

- The subjects were assigned the applications to design.
- After reading the requirements, which were written in an informal style, the subjects were asked to fill out a questionnaire to
  - acquire information on their general proficiency in computer-science-related college courses

- acquire information on their expertise on Web technologies and design methods, and
- make them estimate the overall design effort, trying to split it according to the main models required by W2000
- While completing their designs, the subjects were asked to fill out a second questionnaire to report the actual effort spent in the different phases/models), list the tools they used, and self-evaluate the quality of their work.
- The data were analyzed.

2.2.5   Main Results

Standard statistical techniques were used, such as Mann-Whitney test, Wilcoxon's test, and Ordinary Least Squares.

Hypothesis 1. Table 2 contains the statistics of our results. We used 49 data points, since we had 49 respondents for both *ActInfoEff* and *ActNavEff*. All the actual and estimated effort data represent work-hours.

Table 2. Descriptive statistics for *ActInfoEff* and *ActNavEff*

Variables	N	Median	Mean	stdDev	p
ActInfoEff	49	15	18.4	10.2	<0.0001
ActNavEff		8	10.4	6.7	

The median of *ActInfoEff* is much greater than the median of *ActNavEff*. The Mann-Whitney test for the medians showed that the probability of the opposite result is less than 0.0001, as shown in the *p* column of Table 2, so we can conclude that our hypothesis is certainly acceptable at the 0.05 level. This is also supported by the fact that 45 out of 49 subjects reported a value of *ActInfoEff* greater than *ActNavEff*. By using Wilcoxon's matched pairs signed rank test we obtained even better significance results.

Hypothesis 2. The statistics for the comparison of *ActEff* and *EstEff* are in Table 3 (here, we had 44 respondents).

Table 3. Descriptive statistics for *EstEff* and *ActEff*

Variables	N	median	Mean	stdDev	p
EstEff	44	15.5	18.1	9.4	0.0006
ActEff		26.75	29.6	15.5	

The median value of *ActEff* is much greater than that of *EstEff*. The statistical Mann-Whitney test shows that the p-value of Hypothesis 2 is 0.0006, so we can conclude at the 0.05 level that the data show that the median of *ActEff* is greater than the median of *EstEff*, i.e., the estimates are overly optimistic. This is also confirmed by the fact that a large majority of subjects (36 out of 44) reported a greater value for *ActEff* than *EstEff*.

Hypothesis 3. Fig. 1 graphically shows the regression line between *EstEff* and *ActEff*, whose equation is

$$ActEff = 2.31 + 1.51\ EstEff$$

and Table 4 summarizes the model statistics. Five outliers were identified during the analysis, so our results and model are based on $N = 39$ data points.

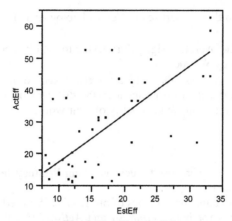

Fig. 1. *EstEff* vs. *ActEff*

Table 4. Model statistics for $X = EstEff$, $Y = ActEff$

Coefficient	N	Estimate	stdDev	P	R^2
Intercept	39	2.31	4.15	0.58	0.54
EstEff		1.51	0.23	<0.0001	

In Table 4, the insufficient statistical significance of the *Intercept* shows that we cannot rule out the (null) hypothesis that *Intercept* = 0, while the statistical signifcance of the coefficient of *EstEff* is very good, i.e., we can safely conclude that *EstEff* can be used to predict *ActEff*. The value of the estimate of the coefficient of *EstEff*, which is greater than 1, confirms that the subjects tended to underestimate the actual effort. At any rate, the estimated effort is useful to predict the actual effort, once one knows about this underestimation problem.

Hypothesis 4. No correlation was found between the students' self-grading and the the grading provided by the instructor.

2.2.6   Discussion
Even though the study was mainly an exploratory one, we have been able to acquire an initial body of evidence on web design effort, which will be useful for future studies.

2.2.7   Future Work
Future research plans include:
- Using measures for internal design attributes; based on the students' projects, i.e., investigating whether internal design attributes (e.g., size, complexity, cohesion, coupling) are related to effort;
- Including an automated measurement tool in the tool that supports the W2000/HDM notation;
- Investigating prediction for other external attributes than effort;
- Investigating the following of web development phases, e.g., implementation and verification;
- Replicating and refining this study, based on the experience we have acquired

2.3   UML Reading at the University of Maryland

2.3.1   Scope and Basic Ideas

The empirical study focused on evaluating the Object Oriented Reading Techniques (OORTs) used to inspect UML design documents. The main idea is that because the multiple UML documents used to describe a system each assume a different perspective, it is not always obvious how these documents should be inspected. Therefore a set of techniques was created to aid inspectors in comparing the various UML artifacts both with themselves and also with artifacts from the requirements phase of the lifecycle.

2.3.2   Main Goals, Assumptions, and Hypotheses

As the OORTs were a relatively immature technology, this study was exploratory in nature rather than confirmatory. The main goals were:

- To get qualitative feedback from the subject as to the feasibility and usefulness of the techniques.
- To understand if different types of techniques led to different types of defects being found.
- To get some idea of the effect different kinds of experience has on the subjects.
- To help the subjects begin to understand the difficulties in evaluating and improving software processes.

Even though this was an exploratory study, we studied the following hypotheses.

Hypothesis 1The horizontal and vertical OORTs would find different defects.

Hypothesis 2 Inspectors who have experience with the associated requirements document will find more defects than those who do not have experience with the associated requirements documents.

Hypothesis 3. Inspectors who are familiar with the application domain of the design will find more defects than those who are not familiar with the domain.

2.3.4   Experimental Setting

The subjects were graduate students in graduate level Software Engineering class. Subjects were given a set of UML documents to inspect. Some of the subject teams had previously inspected the requirements document from which the design was created and the other teams had not inspected those requirements. Subjects worked in teams with one subject performing the inspection while his or her teammate observed and took notes. The reason for the note taking was so that each team would have sufficient information to support conclusions drawn about the OORTs in the analysis report they were required to write after completion of the inspection.

2.3.5   Steps

- Subjects were trained in Inspections and OORTs. Subjects were also trained in how to observe and take notes about their teammate.
- Explanation of inspection assignment and relevance to the material being learned in class.
- Execution of inspection assignment
- Writing of report
- Data analysis

2.3.6   Main Results

In line with our goals, this study provided more qualitative results than quantitative results. The qualitative data showed some potential ways of improving the techniques:

- Order of dealing with information (process steps) must match the subjects' own way of thinking about the problem.
- Amount and type of training needed to be modified
- Differences in design approaches could affect design inspection.

Hypothesis 1. The results showed that different defects were found by the horizontal techniques and the vertical techniques. For one of the designs inspected, of the 25 different defects discovered, only 2 were found by both a vertical and a horizontal technique. The horizontal techniques found 13 unique defects while the vertical techniques found 10 unique defects. For the other design inspected, of the 22 different defects discovered, only 4 defects were found by both horizontal and vertical techniques. The horizontal techniques found 9 unique defects and the vertical techniques also found 9 unique defects.

Hypothesis 2. Inspectors who participated in a requirements inspection of the associated requirements documents did not find more defects than those who had not participated in a requirements inspection of the associated requirements document. Subjects who participated in the requirements inspection found 20.6% of the defects while those that did not participate in the requirements inspection found 17.2%, but this difference was not statistically significant.

Hypothesis 3. Inspectors who were more familiar with the application domain found significantly *fewer* defects than those who were not familiar with the domain. The subjects inspecting the design artifact from the familiar domain found 12.6% of the defects on average, while the subjects inspecting the design from the unfamiliar domain found 25.1% of the defects on average. The p-value for the t-test run between these two groups was .002, showing statistical significance at the 0.05 level.

2.3.7   Discussion

Even though this early experiment on the OORTs did not provide a lot of quantitative data, this study confirmed the basic hypothesis that the OORTs were feasible and useful. Additionally, the qualitative data provided the researches with some clear information about how the techniques should be evolved to be more effective.

A number of replications by other researchers were conducted as a result of this study. After further replications in the university [16] and associated modifications to the experiment, it was successfully run in an industrial setting [19].

2.3.8   Future Work

The qualitative data indicated some specific types of modifications necessary to improve the techniques. The future steps involve making the techniques focus more on the semantic checking during the inspection and less on the syntactical comparison of the artifacts. Also, based on the feedback, the training was modified to ensure that the subjects are trained in the necessary skills.

2.4 UML Reading at Università degli Studi dell'Insubria

2.4.1 Scope and Basic Ideas

The purpose of the experiment was to study reading techniques for detecting faults in UML designs.

2.4.2 Main Goals, Assumptions, and Hypotheses

Even though it originated from previous studies carried out at the University of Maryland, the study was an exploratory rather than a confirmatory one. Therefore, the main goals were to

- acquire evidence on which to base further studies, since the existing body of evidence on the inspection techniques studied still needs to be augmented
- "iron out" the problems related to setting up an empirical study on UML inspections, so as acquire information that can be used in future replications of the study; in particular, problems due to: (1) the fact that students are not used to using inspection techniques for assessing documents; (2) cultural differences between the U.S. and Italy; (3) different ways of carrying out the study (e.g., during classes vs. at home)
- compare two specific types of inspection techniques, horizontal (for ensuring design consistency) and vertical (for verifying the design against system requirements)

An additional goal was the use of the information collected as a part of a model that estimates the number of faults still remaining in a UML artifact after an inspection is carried out.

2.4.3 Experimental Setting

The subjects were undergraduate students. They were given diagrams from a UML case study which had faults seeded. Data were collected by means of paper forms.

2.4.4 Steps

Explanation of UML

- Introduction to the inspection techniques used in the study
- Background explanation to the subjects on the goals of the study
- Experiment execution
- Data analysis

2.4.5 Main Results

The study did not produce a sufficient quantity of data to afford a complete statistical analysis, so more evidence should be gathered on which further hypotheses could be based. A replication has already been planned and will be carried out in 2003.

At any rate, even the limited number of data collected made it possible to estimate the number of remaining faults, by using data analysis techniques borrowed from the software reliability field. During data collection, the students were asked to write the time at which they had found a problem while reading. Thus, each subject that returned the data collection forms also returned a time series for the faults detected, which can be used as the input to a software reliability model.

2.4.6   Discussion

Even though this first empirical study did not provide a sufficient body of evidence, it was nevertheless important to understand the reasons of this outcome, so that the experiment can be more successful in future replications.

The reasons for the limited amount of data were several, starting with the fact that the total number of subjects in the class was fairly small, so any cause of "mortality" could reduce the number of "surviving" subjects below a statistically significant threshold. In our case, insufficient motivation played a key role in the outcome of the empirical study. The reasons for this lack of motivation can be summarized as follows:

- the subjects had already participated in another experiment carried out for ESERNET, so there was a "routine" effect that made the subjects less motivated
- because of the class schedule, the experiment had to be carried out at the end of the semester, when several students were already more prone to study for the exams; when deciding on how to allocate their time, several students chose to study for other exams; that was a rational decision on their side, since it was more "profitable" for them to pass other exams than to devote time and effort for something that would only help them pass one exam.
- the time initially allotted for the study was not sufficient, so the experiment took longer than initially indicated
- the data collection mechanism could not be automated
- the nature of the empirical study was different from the study on testing, which had a "hacking" component to it
- the contribution of the experiment to the learning process was not fully understood.

The last point deserves further attention. Experiments should become an integral part of Software Engineering classes. It is important that an experiment provide the students with a value added in terms of what they learn and that the students understand this value added.

2.4.7   Future Work

The lessons learned in this experiment will allow for

- future replications of the experiment, as already planned
- further studies on how to use experiments in software engineering classes as a part of the teaching/learning processes.

2.5   E3

2.5.1   Scope and Basic Ideas

The empirical study focused on the evaluation of the E3 Process Modeling Language (PML) and tool for the purpose of model creation.

2.5.2   Main Goals, Assumptions, and Hypotheses

The goal was to validate the E3 process modeling language (PML) and associated tool support. The main hypothesis was that the E3 PML and associated tool are easier to use than a standard modeling language and corresponding tool for the creation of software process models.

More specifically, this hypothesis can be set in a quantitative fashion as follows: For the purpose of creating software process models, the average number of problems (P1) that students encounter when using E3 (PML and tool) is less than the average number of problems (P2) they encounter when using IDEF0.

2.5.3   Experimental Setting

This work has been performed in the context of a larger case study in which 40 students (organized into 10 groups) from a software quality and process improvement course interacted with a large telecom company. Among other tasks, the students were asked to model a process fragment from the telecom company, and to report about the problems encountered. Five groups modeled with E3 and five with IDEF0.

Except for one PhD student and three business administration students, all students were majoring in computer science. The groups were hence quite homogenous in age and knowledge.

The experiment was carried out on PCs. Automated data collection mechanisms were not in place.

2.5.4   Steps

Introduction to process modeling as a topic of software process improvement

- Background explanation to the subjects on the goals of the study.
- An external actor from a company introduces the process fragment to be modeled.
- Experiment execution
- Data analysis

2.5.5   Main Results

Based on non-parametric statistical analysis of the data, it is possible to conclude that we are 90% sure that there will be less problems when using E3 PML than when using IDEF0 for the purpose of creating software process models.

Table 5. Raw Data: Number of the problems reported by each of the ten groups

PML	Problems				
Idef0	0	5	1	0	3
E3	0	0	0	2	0

2.5.6   Discussion

There are risks associated with the proposed conclusion:

- The data were collected under the assumption that all the problems are equal. It could be the case that the two problems observed with E3 are extremely serious while the nine problems observed with IDEF0 all are small.
- The use of a normal distribution approximation may not be totally accurate.

We thus have to treat our conclusion "there will be less problems when using E3 PML than when using IDEF0 for the purpose of creating software process models" with some reservation.

2.5.7   Future Work

This experiment is published in [11]. More data are needed to increase our confidence in the conclusion. In addition, we should extend the data collection by letting the subjects:

- Record the time they used to model the process
- Record the criticality of each problem, for example on a three value scale low, medium, high).

3 Discussion

In this section, we first discuss a number of goals that a researcher will want to reach by means of empirical studies with students (Section 3.1). Then, in Section 3.2, we discuss a set of possible benefits for the students.

3.1   Goals for the Researcher

Empirical studies in industrial settings require time, effort, and resources, so they need to be planned and carried out carefully. Empirical studies with students are a way of reducing technical and organizational risks. Therefore, researchers may have a number of goals in mind when carrying out goals with students, including:

- Obtain preliminary evidence to confirm or disconfirm hypotheses. In Software Engineering, as in any other scientific or engineering discipline, new ideas should always undergo an empirical validation before being tried in industrial settings. As a part of the scientific process, the researchers themselves profit from, albeit limited, experiences that can help change or refine the research hypotheses if needed. Obviously, all of the studies we outlined above had this objective.

- Show software companies the relevance of the research and the usefulness of carrying out empirical studies in their own environments. A new idea certainly acquires more strength if it is accompanied by empirical evidence that shows its practical usefulness and an idea of the extent to which its application might contribute to the achievement of a software company's goals. If the evidence gathered via an empirical study with students is positive, software companies are more likely to be willing to participate in further studies in their own environments. The empirical study on testing at the Università dell'Insubria has certainly helped get in touch with a local company to cooperate on the specific empirical study and, furthermore, other testing-related activities. The UML studies resulted in important changes to the processes that were being investigated and accumulated evidence that the processes were feasible, helping to facilitate later studies of the technology in industry. The E3 experiment was itself in fact part of a larger cooperative project with a large Telecom company. This experiment can be seen as a step in gaining mutual respect and comprehension of research and educational activities.

- Show software companies the feasibility of carrying out a full-fledged empirical study in industrial environments, and fine-tune its organization and details before it is carried out in an industrial environment. The experience gathered by means of studies carried out with students is useful to software companies (and the researchers themselves) in assessing the amount of resources needed and the amount of time required for a full-scale empirical study. Planning an empirical study is hardly a simple task. Even when the problem and the hypotheses are well understood and spelled out, many details can hinder the execution of the empirical study. A study with students may be useful to test the experimental design and iron out a number of possible problems before it is actually run in the industry, when the cost of failure would be very high. In addition, researchers would like to avoid problems due to even trivial mistakes because that may make it much more difficult for them to work with an industrial partner in the future. All of the above studies have allowed us to find problems in our empirical studies and remove them. The testing experiment has shown the feasibility of carrying out this empirical study and others. Running the UML studies in student environments did not directly produce changes to the design that was later applied in industry, but led to many associated improvements in conducting the study. For example, it allowed the researchers to give much more reliable time estimates to subjects for the experimental treatments.

- Produce an experimental "kit." The materials, guidelines, and data collection procedures need to be carefully prepared and tested before running an empirical study elsewhere or in the industry. This also helps in future replications of the empirical studies, in both academic and industrial settings. For instance, the UML reading experiment carried out at the University of Maryland resulted in the production of an experimental kit, which was later reused at the Università dell'Insubria and elsewhere. The empirical study on the Bayesian approach to finding a stopping rule for testing has also generated an experimental kit, which will be used in future replications in other academic environments or in the industry.

The scientific literature has often focused on the possible risks associated with drawing general conclusions from empirical studies carried out with students, i.e., on the external validity of the results, and therefore their industrial relevance. While this is certainly an important problem, we would like to point out that:

- External validity is an issue that needs to be taken into account in any empirical study, not only in empirical studies with students; as a matter of fact, there are many different variables (e.g., cultural and technological ones) that are involved in a study, and the subjects' experience is only one of them;

- Obvious as it may be, having an empirical validation with students of some phenomenon of interest is better than no validation at all; too many Software Engineering techniques are introduced in work environments without any kind of preliminary empirical assessment;

- In many contexts, especially in the current US educational climate, the line between students and novice professionals is being blurred. More and more students are working over the summers or as interns in industrial environments, meaning they bring an expanded set of skills to many upper-level courses.

Thus, while one should not unduly overemphasize the general significance of the results obtained via empirical studies with students, those results do have relevance to the progress of the field.

3.2   Goals for the Students

Including experimental activities in software engineering classes also has a number of immediate benefits for the students while they are studying. Here, we list some benefits that students may receive from being involved in empirical studies during their Software Engineering education.

- **Education on state-of-the-art topics:** All of the above empirical studies were carried out on research topics with close connections to the state of the art, since they investigate problems that still need to be solved. In the context of a software quality and software process improvement course, process modelling is an important topic. Though the relevance of a tool like E3 is subjective, E3 includes aspects that are not included in other systems, so participation in the experiment exposes students to a wider range of options and provides them with "food for thought". Even though UML is gaining widespread acceptance in Software Engineering curriculums, inspections are probably less commonly taught than other V&V techniques such as testing. In addition, structured methods for reading and inspections are usually taught with reference to software code—much less common with reference to other software artifacts, such as requirements or designs.
- **Self assessment:** Students can assess for themselves what they know and what they do not know on a specific topic. As long as they attend only lecture classes, students are not forced to think about the various aspects of what the teacher explains. This is what happened with the UML reading studies. Several students had problems reading UML diagrams because they did not understand that there were several aspects in a UML diagram that need to be addressed.
- **Industrial relevance:** Students can get better insights on specific problems, since experiments are usually carried out with an industrial final goal in mind. The testing stopping rule is a well-known problem in software development. The problem of devising a stopping rule for testing is not something that students may have a direct experience on even after they are taught testing techniques. Several proposals exist, but none has gained a universal consensus. Inspections are more and more widely used in the industry, especially for artifacts that are not executable. The idea that one needs to check the consistency across several parts of a document may not be common for students, since they might be more used to and interested in building systems than revising documents. The process modeling experiment clearly is an example of the industrial relevance of empirical studies. The fragment to be modeled was extracted from the process manual of a big software organization. The process was even presented by the process owner of the organization. There is a risk that the complexity of a full-fledged industrial application makes it difficult for the actual educational goals to be achieved.
- **Problem-based software engineering education:** Experimental designs can help teachers design problem-based educational initiatives. Our experience is that a process modelling exercise can easily become an experiment on the same topic. This point makes sense in contexts in which such exercises do not previously exist. In addition, instructors may be willing to change the way they teach a subject only if they can see the advantages from an educational and a research point of view.
- **Empirical methods:** Participating in studies shows students the advantages of using quantitative methods even in a human-intensive business such as software

engineering. The empirical study in Section 2.1 (on a stopping rule for testing) showed the students that decisions are made, even at an implicit level, based on some kind of "gut feeling," which can be quantified via subjective assessment as a degree of belief. The study on web design showed the students that it is important to estimate the effort needed to carry out a software development activity. Paradoxically, the need for sensible effort estimation was highlighted by the empirical study on UML inspections at the Università dell'Insubria. This showed the students that software engineering education should include topics on empirical methods more than it currently does. By involving them in an empirical study, students may realize that there is a need to base the improvement of at least some software development activities on firmer grounds.

• **Third party assessment:** Participation in studies shows students that they should not be afraid of being the subjects of empirical studies and data collection activities in general. Students may believe that during their work life they will not be subject to assessments and they will not have to submit reports. On the contrary, they need to have first-hand experiences that they will be continuously subject to evaluations and that they will have to continuously turn in questionnaires and data for various purposes. The W2000 empirical study forced students to submit estimations on the effort it would take them to complete the various tasks they were required to carry out and then another form in which they summarized the actual values. This kind of data collection is routinely done in many software organizations.

4 Related Work

This chapter investigates the relation between empirical software engineering and software engineering education. An extensive literature exists in both fields; in addition, a number of papers have been published that report on experiments that used students as subjects. So, our review of the literature will not be exhaustive, but we would like to offer an overview of several papers that are closely related to our goals, to illustrate the state of the art. Moreover, there are some works [12, 13, 14] which explicitly address research questions about the relationship between empirical software engineering and software engineering education.

To show how they are related to the research and educational goals we have outlined in Section 3, we have organized the discussion on these works by using those goals, as summarized in tables 6 and 7.

5 Lessons Learned for Classroom Experimenters

Based on the experiences described above, we would like to offer the following concrete advice for researchers running experiments in a classroom environment. Many of them will not be surprising; in fact, they may strike many readers as obvious parts of planning and conducting a university course. However, our experience has been that these areas merit special attention because it is easy for an instructor to believe he or she is adequately prepared, when in actuality much more effort is

Table 6. Goals for the researcher as addressed in the literature

Obtain preliminary evidence to confirm or disconfirm hypotheses	An example is a study on defect detection methods for requirements inspection [15]. Conditions for running experiments with students are identified and described [13]. These are based on generally accepted criteria for internal and external validity evaluation of empirical studies.
Show software companies the relevance and usefulness of the research	Data collected from a series of classroom empirical studies of a new inspection technique for object-oriented designs (described in [16]) were useful not only for helping evolve the techniques themselves, but convinced an industrial company to try them out in a case study in their own environment, with good results [17].
Show software companies the feasibility of carrying out full-fledged empirical studies in industrial environments. Fine-tune the organization and details of an empirical study, before it is carried out in an industrial environments	Studies including both student and industrial data enable researchers to distinguish between expected behaviors for both groups [18]. A study with undergraduates at the University of Trondheim discovered that the time estimates used for the treatment were too short. The student study gave the experimenters a chance to identify and correct this problem without using expensive professional subjects, and later led to a successful industry experiment [19].
Produce an experimental "kit."	The study reported in [20] describes how multiple replications with planned variations are necessary for building a "body of knowledge" about development technologies. The paper also describes how such replications can be facilitated by experimental kits. A format for experimental kits and a system for their maintenance and updating are proposed in [21]. Experiences with experimental kits and replications in general are discussed in [22]. From these experiences, quality goals are elaborated for evaluating the usefulness of kits.

needed to properly deal with the many threats to validity that any study will face. It is our hope that this list can be a useful reminder of things for instructor/experimenters to double-check during course preparation:

- **Make sure the study is well-integrated with the goals and materials covered in the rest of the course. On the assignment sheet, explicitly state the anticipated educational benefits for students.** Instructors are more familiar with the course material than students, and often see the big picture of how the assignment fits into the class but do not communicate that knowledge in sufficient detail. For example, in some of the inspection studies described previously, students have been

Table 7. Goals for the students as addressed in the literature

Education on state-of-the-art topics	The introduction of the Personal Software Process in a software engineering curriculum is discussed in [12]. Moreover, estimation in software development and its relation to education is addressed in [18].
Self assessment	If the output of student assignment is used for research purposes, then the researchers provide good solutions. See for example the solutions published in [23]. These solutions can be used by students for self assessment.
Industrial relevance	Students participate in the same activities as industrial developers [18]. This helps to motivate them that their tasks are of industrial relevance.
Problem based software engineering education	Issues involved with "teaching by doing" are discussed in [24].
Empirical methods	The issues of introducing empirical methods in education are addressed in [2] ("... we should teach students how to use metrics to quantify applicable project and product attributes, to evaluate the claims of methods and tools through objective criteria, and to use quantitative tools as an aid to prediction and assessment ...") In the case study reported in [25], students are asked to analyze and present empirical data.
Third party assessment	Students may learn to see their work as a part of a case study subject to measurements and analysis, as shown in [25].

confused as to why inspection in particular is singled out for special attention, when so many practices are taught during the entire course. We have found that students need help abstracting up the idea that the evaluation methods applied to this particular example practice are generally applicable and can be used for other practices of concern. As a result, the assignment description needs to be written so as to highlight the lessons students will learn about empirical evaluation rather than about the specific practice.

- **Give realistic time estimates. If necessary, run a pilot study or use a few volunteers to test the estimates before giving them to the class.** One of the frustrating things about learning software engineering for students is that there is no definitive right answer to many questions, against which their own answers can be compared. For example, even the best-written requirements documents tend to have ambiguities and make certain assumptions about the outside knowledge required. While it can be instructive to ask students to report defects found in such a document, it is unlikely in the extreme that any student will find all and only the defects intended by the instructor. In such an environment, students seem more willing to compare their performance on a task to subjective evaluations of how long it should take, than to their own gut feelings of when the proper result has been achieved. For this reason, mistaken time estimates cause a great deal of frustration and even anger on the part of students, who might feel less intelligent for not being able to get a task done in an arbitrarily short period of time. If subjects become frustrated, the data provided may be of lower quality because subjects may either quit before completing their task, or may do a poor job once they have exceeded the estimated time. Furthermore, people tend to shy away from processes in general. If students learn a new process and it requires more effort than the estimate they are given, they may become disillusioned with the benefits of software processes and see only that process is overly time-consuming and provides little benefit.

- **Properly motivate the subjects but do not reveal the goals, measures and analysis to them** *prior to executing the study*. **Do make it clear** *after executing the study* **what the study design and analysis are all about.** Although the temptation to explain the specific hypotheses of the study to subjects is fed by good intentions (mainly a desire for students to understand the activity in which they are taking part), doing so can bias the running of the experiment and thus negatively affect the results. Once they are made aware of what measures will be collected and studied, subjects in any study have a propensity to pay more attention to those measures and behave differently than they would in ordinary circumstances. They may also take steps to improve their performance on one treatment but not others; for example, an unconscious desire to please the instructor may make students try to excel at using a new technique that is being introduced. By not making it clear before the study exactly what comparisons will be done, subjects are given less feedback that would permit them to emphasize certain behaviors over others. On the other hand, we have found it very beneficial to give feedback to subjects about the overall design of the study after the data collection has concluded. This benefits the students, as it is a chance to learn about experimental design, how the activities they took part in relate to one another and how to reason about the results of analysis. It is also beneficial to the experimenters, because once the data has been collected students can give objective feedback about what really occurred, for example how closely they conformed to given processes. In some cases, we have even had students suggest new explanations for observed results. (People are often the best explainers of their own behavior!) In general, we have found feedback sessions to be such a mutually beneficial practice that we almost always schedule some time for them in the semester, either in individual office hours or in classroom discussions.

- **Allow students a chance to give feedback. Make their opinions, if clearly based on empirical evidence, count.** An important way to motivate subjects is to make it clear to them that their feedback counts more than their simple ability to follow a process and generate data. Since software processes are interesting only in so far as they are able to be executed by human beings, the responses of subjects as to whether the given process is too onerous, too time-consuming, etc., should be interesting to researchers also. Our experience has been that students seem to do better as subjects when they understand that their role is to undertake an objective evaluation of a new process, which may be either good or bad, and *not* to simply generate data to support a foregone conclusion. The flip side of this is that educators as always must stress that not every opinion is equal; carefully-reasoned opinions supported by the evidence are what is desired. Also, subjects may be more diligent when they know that their feedback, if it is supported by actual data and experiences, will be honestly heard by the researchers.

- **Grade on the quality of the data produced, process conformance or the students' ability to evaluate the technology being studied, not on the results of applying the technique.** In early experiments of this type, we tried to motivate students to perform well by grading them on the number of defects they reported. Our thinking was that higher numbers of defects would correspond to students paying more attention to performing a serious review. However, instead it seemed to motivate students to disregard the process we wanted to study (or at least augment it with additional activities) in order to report as many potential defects as possible. Thus results were unrepresentative of what would have been observed in a normal application of the review technique. We have rectified this mistake on later experiments by grading based on process conformance (as assessed by the creation of intermediate artifacts) as well as on the soundness of the evaluation of the technology done by the subjects after the experiment.

6 Conclusions and Future Work

In this paper, we have reported on a few empirical studies that we have carried out with students. Even though most of these studies were initially conceived for research reasons, we believe that it is important to keep in mind and study the impact of these studies on the students' education.

This paper is a preliminary report in which we have described our experiences and lessons learned, but a lot more work needs to be done. Here, we outline some possible research directions.

Impact of empirical studies on other actors. In this paper, we have focused on the researchers' and the students' viewpoints. However, other actors may play an important role in the process and be affected by it. For one thing, we have assumed throughout the paper that the researcher and the instructor are the same person. This is not necessarily the case, but even so, the same person is playing two different roles, with two different sets of goals and responsibilities. As a researcher, one needs to provide scientifically sound results to the research community and the industry; as an instructor, one needs to provide his or her students with the best education possible for their future activities. The instructor's goals may conflict with the researcher's goals, so a sensible trade-off should be sought. By the same token, when carrying out an empirical study in an industrial environment, one should always try to minimize the risk that the experimental activities disrupt the normal course of business. This minimization of risk can be seen in the examples presented in Sections 2.4 and 2.2. By running and debugging the experiment in the university classroom, researchers were able to have a positive experience when they moved it to and industrial setting.

Costs vs. benefits. The costs and benefits of empirical studies with students need to be investigated more thoroughly. Carrying out empirical studies may entail possible costs for all the actors involved, i.e., the researchers, the students, and the instructors. Thus, we need to clarify the categories of "costs" that will have to be paid for by the actors and quantify their extent.

Ethical issues. Is it ethically correct to "use" students for the researcher's benefit in the context of a college course? For instance, would there be more productive ways for the students to spend the time devoted to participating in an empirical study? Is it right to base some of the final evaluation of a student on his or her degree of participation in a research study? Like in empirical studies in industrial settings, a number of ethical issues need to be investigated in pilot studies with students.

Empirical validation of our goals. Finally, our goals can be regarded as hypotheses that could in principles be empirically validated. The work reported in [10] is a step in that direction as the proposed conditions for running experiments with students are based on empirical methods.

References

[1] Denning, P.: Educating a New Engineer. Communication of the ACM 35 (1992) 83–97
[2] Meyer, B.: Software Engineering in the Academy. IEEE Computer 34 (2001) 28–35
[3] T. B. Hilburn, Humphrey, W. S.: The Impending Changes in Software Engineering Education. IEEE Software 19 (2002) 22/24
[4] Lethbridge, C. T.: On the Relevance of software education: A survey and some Recommendations. Annals of Software Engineering 6 (1998) 91/110
[5] Cannon, R., Diaz-Herrera, J., Hilburn, T. B.: Teaching a Software Project Course Using the Team Software Process. ACM SIGCSE Bulletin, 33rd SIGCSE Technical Symposium on Computer Science Education 34 (2002) 369–370
[6] Melody M. Moore, C. P.: Learning by Doing: Goals & Experience of Two Software Engineering Project Courses. In: Proc. Software Engineering Education, 7th SEI CSEE Conference (1994) 151–164
[7] Rudolf Andersen, R. C., John Krogstie, Guttorm Sindre, Arne Sølvberg: Project Courses at the NTH: 20 Years of Experience. In: Proc. Software Engineering Education, 7th SEI CSEE Conference (1994) 177–188
[8] Bagert, D. J., Hilburn, T. B., Hislop, G., Lutz, M., McCracken, M., Mengel, S.: Guidelines for Software Engineering Education Version 1.0 (1999). CMU/SEI, CMU/SEI–99–TR–032 (1999)
[9] Morasca, S.: A Bayesian Approach to Software Testing Evaluation. Università degli Studi dell'Insubria Dipartimento di Scienze Chimiche, Fisiche e Matematiche, Submitted to pubblication, Como, Italy (2003)
[10] Baresi, L., Morasca S., Paolini, P.: An Empirical Study on the Design Effort of Web Applications. In: Proc. WISE 2002 (2002) 345–354
[11] Jaccheri, L., Stålhane, T.: Evaluation of the E3 Process modelling language and tool for the purpose of model creation. In: Proc. 3rd International Conference on Product Focused Software Process Improvement, Profes (2001)
[12] Runeson, P.: Using Students as Experiment Subjects – An Analysis on Graduate and Freshmen PSP Student Data. In: Proc. 7th International Conference on Evaluation and Assessment in Software Engineering (EASE'2003) (2003)
[13] Höst, M., Regnell, B., Wohlin, C.: Using Students as Subjects – A Comparative Study of Students and Professionals in Lead-Time Impact Assessment. Empirical Software Engineering 5 (2000) 201–214
[14] Höst, M.: Introducing Empirical Software Engineering Methods in Education. In: Proc. Conference on Software Engineering Education and Training CSEE&T (2002)
[15] Porter A., Votta L., V.R., B.: Comparing Detection Methods for Software Requirements Inspection: A Replicated Experiment. IEEE Transactions on Software Engineering 21 (1995) 563–575
[16] Shull F., C. J., and Travassos G. H.: An Empirical Methodology for Introducing Software Processes. In: Proc. European Software Engineering Conference (2001) 288–296

[17] W. Melo, F. Shull, Travassos, G. H.: Software Review Guidelines. Systems Engineering and Computer Science Program, COPPE, Federal University, ES–556/01 Rio de Janeiro (2001)

[18] Jørgensen, M., Teigen, K. H., Mølloken, K.: Better Sure than Safe? Overconfidence in Judgment Based Software Development Effort Prediction Intervals. Journal of Systems and Software (2003)

[19] Reidar Conradi, P. M., Tayyaba Arif, Lars Christian Hegde, Geir Arne Bunde, and Anders Pedersen: Object-Oriented Reading Techniques for Inspection of UML Models – An Industrial Experiment. In: Proc. European Conf. on Object-Oriented Programming (ECOOP'03) (2003) 13 p

[20] Basili, V. R., Shull, F., Lanubile, F.: Building Knowledge through Families of Software Studies: An Experience Report. University of Maryland, CS–TR–3983 (1999)

[21] Conradi R., Basili V. R., Carver J., Shull F., H., T. G.: A Pragmatic Documents Standard for an Experience Library: Roles, Documents, Contents, and Structure. University of Maryland, CS–TR–4235 and UMIACS–TR–2001–24 (2001)

[22] Shull F., Basili V. R., Carver J., Maldonado J. C., Travassos G. H., Mendonca M., S., F.: Replicating Software Engineering Experiments: Addressing the Tacit Knowledge Problem. In: Proc. International Symposium on Empirical Software Engineering, October (2002) 7–16

[23] Prechelt, L., Tichy, W. F.: A controlled experiment to assess the benefits of procedure argument type checking. IEEE Transactions on Software Engineering 24 (1998) 302–312

[24] Schank, R. C.: Revolutionizing the Traditional Classroom Course. COMMUNICATIONS OF THE ACM 44 (2001)

[25] Robbins, K. A., Key, C. S., Dickinson, K.: Integrating a Simulation Case Study into CS2: Developing Design, Empirical and Analysis Skills. In: Proc. SIGCSE (2002)

Practical Experiences in the Design and Conduct of Surveys in Empirical Software Engineering

Marcus Ciolkowski[1], Oliver Laitenberger[2], Sira Vegas[3], and Stefan Biffl[4]

[1] Dept. of Computer Science, Universität Kaiserslautern,
D-67655 Kaiserslautern, Germany
ciolkows@informatik.uni-kl.de
[2] Droege & Comp. GmbH, Internationale Unternehmer-Beratung,
Praterinsel 3-4, 80538 München, Germany
Oliver_Laitenberger@droege.de
[3] Facultad de Informática. Universidad Politécnica de Madrid
Campus de Montegancedo, 28660, Boadilla del Monte, Madrid, Spain
svegas@fi.upm.es
[4] TU Wien, Inst. f. Softwaretechnik und Interaktive Systeme
Favoritenstr. 9/188, A-1040 Wien, Austria
Stefan.Biffl@tuwien.ac.at

Abstract. A survey is an empirical research strategy for the collection of information from heterogeneous sources. In this way, survey results often exhibit a high degree of external validity. It is complementary to other empirical research strategies such as controlled experiments, which usually have their strengths in the high internal validity of the findings. While there is a growing number of (quasi-)controlled experiments reported in the software engineering literature, few results of large scale surveys have been reported there. Hence, there is still a lack of knowledge on how to use surveys in a systematic manner for software engineering empirical research.

This chapter introduces a process for preparing, conducting, and analyzing a software engineering survey. The focus of the work is on questionnaire-based surveys rather than literature surveys. The survey process is driven by practical experiences from two large-scale efforts in the review and inspection area. There are two main results from this work. First, the process itself allows researchers in empirical software engineering to follow a systematic, disciplined approach. Second, the experiences from applying the process help avoid common pitfalls that endanger both the research process and its results. We report on two (descriptive) surveys on software reviews that applied the survey process, and we present our experiences, as well as models for survey effort and duration factors derived from these experiences.

1 Introduction

Although empirical methods have a long history in manufacturing and in traditional areas of science, technology, and medicine, up to now, they have had little impact on software development practices. Fortunately, the situation is constantly improving. An increasing number of researchers (and practitioners) take advantage of empirical research strategies to validate their findings and their work.

R. Conradi and A.I. Wang (Eds.): ESERNET 2001-2003, LNCS 2765, pp. 104–128, 2003.
© Springer-Verlag Berlin Heidelberg 2003

The research strategies primarily employed involve the design and conduct of (quasi-)controlled experiments and cases studies. The results of these studies help researchers gain an understanding of how a technique works and why the technique is useful. Practitioners, on the other hand, benefit from those studies because the results help them assess the leverage they can expect from a particular technique. This may influence their decision as to whether and how to adopt it in their projects.

Any empirical study is, according to Hays [1], a problem in economics. Each choice that a researcher makes for a specific study design has its price. For example, the greater the number of treatments, subjects, and hypotheses considered, the more costly a study is likely to be. This explains why in many cases specific treatment combinations can only be investigated in a single experiment or case study in a specific environment. As a consequence, the possibility for general statements that characterizes the state of the practice in the software industry is limited.

Surveys are an empirical research strategy that helps address this problem. Although this research method allows the creation of a more general picture of technology usage in the software industry, few have been conducted. Hence, there is little experience-based information regarding the details of surveys in a software engineering context. Moreover, the available information focuses mostly on the empirical results, and usually not on the lessons learned while planning, conducting, analyzing and packaging the survey and its results.

This chapter presents practical experiences in the design and conduct of surveys in empirical software engineering to illustrate the usefulness of surveys as an empirical method. It provides some detailed insights into some of the issues. The purpose of this chapter is to describe how surveys can be applied in the software engineering field, not to compare suveys to alternative empirical strategies. The reported experiences were made in a large-scale review survey that was first performed in Germany and then extended worldwide. The goal of this questionnaire-based survey was to characterize the modern review practices as being used in the software industry.

We chose reviews as topic for this survey for several reasons. First, although the software review and inspection methodology has been around for almost 30 years, it is unclear how many organizations practice them on a regular basis. Second, the area is quite well researched. As the basic research questions are well known, reviews and inspections were good topics to gain experiences with how to conduct large-scale surveys.

The rest of this chapter has been organized as follows: Section 2 discusses the state of the practice regarding surveys in empirical software engineering. Section 3 shows the methods and procedures that have been followed to conduct the review survey. Section 4 presents two survey examples and experiences with the survey process, while Section 5 summarizes lessons learned during the two surveys. Finally, Section 6 concludes.

2 State of the Practice

This section details the state of the practice in surveys and reviews. Surveys are a broad investigation where information is collected in a standardized form from a group of people or projects [2]. In section 2.1, we briefly present the state of the practice in lessons learned in software engineering surveys. Section 2.2 details reviews and inspections.

2.1   Lessons Learned in Software Engineering Surveys

There are several types of surveys; Wohlin et al. list in chapter 2 three types of surveys: Descriptive, explanatory, and exploratory surveys. *Descriptive surveys* can enable assertions about some population; for example, determining the distribution of certain characteristics or attributes without explanation for the distribution. *Explanatory surveys* aim at making explanatory claims about the population; for example, explain why developers choose one technique over another. *Explorative surveys* are used as a pre-study to find out opportunities and risks for a more thorough empirical investigation.

Surveys offer a number of advantages [3]: Explanatory surveys can confirm an effect and typically allow the usage of standard statistical techniques. Descriptive (and explanatory) surveys can generalize empirical findings to many projects / organizations and are applicable to real-world projects for research in the large. Exploratory surveys are suitable for early exploratory analysis, can use existing experience, and can help to identify best/worst practices.

Several authors have pointed out the advantages of using surveys in Software Engineering research. Although it is common to find literature surveys in the Software Engineering field, not many efforts are reported in conducting questionnaire-based ones [4]. The main reason for this is that, while the source of information for literature surveys are usually books, technical reports and so on, questionnaire-based surveys deal with people. This, along with the process of conducting the survey itself, makes the success of a questionnaire-based survey more difficult. Whether or not a survey is questionnaire-based, there are two important matters that have to be decided:

- Select the parameters of interest it has to examine.
- Identify the sources of information that are needed (books and/or research papers for literature surveys, and people to be asked for questionnaire based ones).

Regarding the first matter, the set of parameters of interest is usually developed incrementally, which means that several trials are needed in order to get a satisfactory set of the information the survey should request. This is closely related to the second matter. Literature has a greater availability than people. This is probably one of the key issues when asking why questionnaire-based surveys are not common in Software Engineering. Executing Software Engineering surveys require a specific type of person to be available (usually experts) who are usually not readily available, or are expensive to include.

Even though few questionnaire-based surveys have been reported in the Software Engineering area (e.g., [5]; see [3]), the focus of a survey is to get information from the identified sources of information. Thus, surveys and reports on surveys focus on the results obtained during the survey, and not on lessons learned from it.

One of the goals of this paper is to contribute to mitigate the lack of reports on experiences in conducting questionnaire-based surveys in Software Engineering.

2.2   Reviews and Inspections in Software Engineering

In the past two decades, reviews and inspections have emerged as one of most effective quality assurance techniques in software engineering. The primary goal of a review or an inspection is the detection and removal of defects before the testing phase begins. In this way, reviews and inspections strongly contribute to improve the overall quality of software with the corollary budget and time benefits.

In this article, reviews and inspections denote approaches following a process in which qualified personnel analyze a software product for the purpose of detecting defects. The process involves the following six phases in some way or the other: Planning, Overview, Defect Detection, Defect Collection, Defect Correction, and Follow-up. The objective of the planning phase is to organize a particular review or inspection when the materials pass entry criteria, such as when source code successfully compiles without syntax errors. The overview phase consists of a first meeting in which the author explains the product to other participants. The main goal of the defect detection phase is to scrutinize a software artifact to elicit defects. The defects detected by each participant must be collected and documented. Furthermore, a decision must be made whether a defect is really a defect. These are the main objectives of the defect collection phase. Throughout the defect correction phase, the author reworks and resolves defects found. Finally the objective of the follow-up phase is to check whether the author has resolved all defects.

This definition of review and inspection used in this article is broader in scope than the one originally provided by Fagan, which focuses only on inspection technologies. However, after Fagan's seminal introduction of the generic notion of inspection to the software domain at IBM in the early 1970s [6], a large body of contributions in the form of new methodologies and/or incremental improvements has been proposed promising to leverage and amplify the benefits of early quality enhancing activities within software development and even maintenance projects. Many of these contributions have been empirically investigated in the form of (quasi-)controlled experiments. Hence, there are some business cases that demonstrate the pro's and con's of the various approaches.

However, despite the academic work it is often unclear what factors drive the adoption of review and inspection techniques in industry. There is also little understanding of which factors drive their adaptation in practice. Answering these questions is challenging because of the large number of factors that impact a specific review or inspection implementation. For example, when looking at the process described above there are already a large number of decisions and, thus, factors involved in the process design. Hence, any effort to explain the usage of a specific process implementation must look at a large number of factors. Without a comprehensive effort few valid statements can be produced.

Fortunately, there are some literature surveys in the review and inspection area that allow for a collection of possible factors [7, 8, 9, 10, 11, 12]. The literature surveys usually present frameworks to structure the large amount of work in this area. Kim et al. [7] present a framework for software development technical reviews including software inspection [6], Freedman and Weinberg's technical review [13, 14], and Yourdon's structured walkthrough [15]. They segment the framework according to aims and benefits of reviews, human elements, review process, review outputs, and other matters. Macdonald et al. [16] describe the scope of support for the currently available inspection process and review tools. Porter et al. [9] focus their attention on the organizational attributes of the software inspection process, such as the team size or the number of sessions, to understand how these attributes influence the costs and benefits of software inspection. Wheeler et al. [11] discuss the software inspection process as a particular type of peer review process and elaborate the differences between software inspection, walkthroughs, and other peer review processes. Tjahjono [10] presents a framework for formal technical reviews (FTR) including objective, collaboration, roles, synchronicity, technique, and entry/exit-criteria as dimensions. Tjahjono's framework aims at determining the similarities and differences between the review process of different FTR methods, as well as identifying potential review success factors. Laitenberger and Debaud [12] structure the work on inspection technologies around five core dimensions. In addition, they present causal models that allow the explanation of inspection success.

The existing literature surveys were the basis for the elicitation of possible success factors for reviews and inspections. In this way, the literature surveys were the basis for the surveys described later.

3 Method

This section details the most important activities of a survey. The process is based on the framework of the quality improvement paradigm [17], as well as on an empirical study process described in [3]. The section concludes with a model on effort/cost and duration factors for a survey.

3.1   The Survey Process

The process itself consists of six steps: (1) Study definition – determining the goal of the survey; (2) Design – operationalizing the survey goals into a set of questions; (3) Implementation – operationalizing the design to make the survey executable; (4) Execution – the actual data collection and data processing; (5) Analysis – interpretation of the data; and (6) Packaging – reporting the survey results.

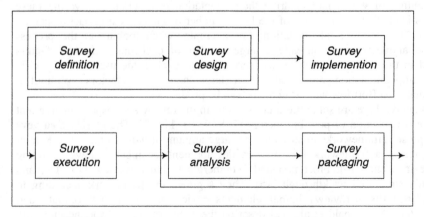

Fig. 1. Survey process steps and typical iterations in the process

These steps are often performed in an iterative fashion. Fig. 1 illustrates the process: the small boxes depict the process steps; larger boxes show typical iterations among activities. Iterations occur on three levels: (a) within a process step, (b) between the steps definition and design, analysis and packaging, (c) when learning from one survey to the next (e.g., pilot survey; replications; similar study designs).

3.2 Survey Definition

The primary objective of the survey definition step is to determine the goal of the survey to be performed; for example, stakeholders' perception of usage and effectiveness of processes before and after adopting a particular technology.

Goal definition is the most important step of a survey [3]: They often start with the awareness that we need further information about a specific topic that we might gain by asking people about it; e.g., that 'little is known about risk management' [18].

The next step is to review the literature to find available information about the specific topic. This helps determine the necessity for doing a survey. The review should result in an inventory of the research that has already been done on the topic; for example, it should produce an overview on risk management literature. Additionally, some exploratory 'in-depth' interviews with stakeholders can be done to get a clearer picture of the problems that should be addressed with the survey.

The review and the additional interviews should result in a statement that denotes the need for the survey and that clearly depicts the topic, population context, and scope. Sometimes research questions are formulated, too; for example, using GQM techniques [19]. Survey definition concerns also the feasibility and usefulness of the survey. For an explanatory survey, for example, it may be necessary to decide whether the necessary number of subjects can be contacted within the survey budget.

3.3 Survey Design

The design of a survey concerns the operationalization of the goal. It demonstrates how data can be collected and interpreted to give an answer to the research questions that are derived from the research goal [3]. The survey project plan records important decisions and activities. The following issues are the most important ones for survey design:
1. Definition of the target population and the survey sample.
2. Conceptual model of the objects and variables of the survey.
3. Approach for data collection.
4. Questionnaire design.
5. Approaches for data analysis.
6. Validity issues: Theoretic validity of the survey design and issues to be dealt with during survey implementation and execution.

Definition of the target population and the survey sample. From the survey goal the target population of the survey can be determined. A sample is a set of respondents selected from the population for the purpose to save time and money. Depending on the type of survey–exploratory, descriptive, or explanatory–the sample can be determined. This is an important step, as surveys are usually dealing with larger populations than case studies or experiments; often, it is not possible to include the whole population into the sample.

Oppenheim [20] states that a representative sample should be drawn such that every member of the population has a statistically equal chance of being selected. The size of the sample depends on several factors: For example, the sampling error (the degree of precision of the sample taken) that can be tolerated, or the population size. Salant and Dillman [21] as well as Oppenheim [20] deal further on this topic.

The characterization of the target population is important when planning a representative sampling for this population. One approach that can be used is the snowballing technique: a few appropriate individuals are located and then asked for the names and addresses of others who fit the sampling requirements. A judgment sample can be taken to conduct a preliminary investigation [20]. Based on the characteristics of the target population, information on the sampling method, and information on the actual subjects of the survey, the bias of the sample can be determined; this bias in turn influences the level of validity of the survey.

The *conceptual model* describes the objects that are investigated, the variables and the expected relationships between them. A survey can focus on objects such as development organizations or projects; see, for example, [22, 23]. The variables that are defined during a survey should be strongly related to the research goal. The conceptual model follows from the definition of goals, questions and hypotheses, according to the GQM approach [17].

Approach for data collection. Depending on the type of data to be collected, the goal has to be expressed in a quantitative manner (including formal hypotheses on what to expect). Wohlin et al. state in chapter 2 that surveys have the ability to provide a large number of variables to evaluate, but that it is necessary to aim at obtaining the largest amount of understanding from the fewest number of variables, because this reduction also eases the analysis work. The two most common means for data collection are questionnaires (paper or electronic) and interviews (telephone or face-to-face) [24], sometimes complemented by literature surveys or project measurement, as appropriate. Questionnaires usually require much less time for the researcher than interviews, especially with mature questions. Interviews, on the other hand, help to reduce uncertainty with exploratory survey questions.

Question (or questionnaire) design is an important aspect of a survey as the clarity of the questions directly influences the quality of responses and thus of the survey data. The questions of the questionnaire should have a strong relation with the survey goal. Exploratory surveys often use open-ended questions that can capture unforeseen answer options, but are harder to analyze. Explanatory and descriptive surveys typically use pre-coded questions matured in pilot studies.

Approaches for data analysis depend on the type of survey and the collected data: For explanatory surveys statistical tests [2] have to be planned, while descriptive and exploratory surveys focus on basic descriptive statistics and aggregation of data for reporting. Typical analyses compare different populations of respondents; analyze associations and trends, or the consistency of scores. Furthermore, the validity of the collected data has to be checked with appropriate context and control questions.

Validity issues. As in every empirical study, surveys are also subject to validity threats. Validity considerations during survey design are a kind of forecast of possible problems and what the survey designer can do to avoid or at least detect them. In principle, similar threats as for experiments and case studies can occur. For an extended description, the lists referenced in the respective chapters; for example, Wohlin et al. in chapter 2 and Robson et al. [2] can be consulted.

Internal validity in surveys concerns the level of controlling the variables, depending on the survey goal and the definition of variables in the study. Variables can be controlled by exclusion, by holding them constant, or by randomization. *External validity* in surveys focuses largely on the representativeness of the sample for the target population. Defining the population as well as taking the final sample determine the external validity. *Experimental validity* deals with the replication of the survey (i.e., 'do we get the same results when the survey is repeated?'). Therefore, it is important to restrict the subjectivity of answers to a minimum level by introducing context and control questions. *Construct validity* deals with the question 'do we measure what is intended to be measured'. A good start is to use similar designs from literature or research communities [3].

Typical survey problems in practice are that (a) they may rely on different projects/organizations keeping comparable data, (b) there is little control over variables, (c) they can at most confirm association but not causality, (d) they can be biased due to differences between respondents and non-respondents (i.e., non-response error), (e) questionnaire design may be tricky (ambiguity, validity, reliability).

3.4   Survey Implementation

The objective of the implementation step is to produce, collect, and prepare all the material that is required to conduct the survey according to the survey plan.

Material to be prepared includes means for data collection (e.g., data collection forms, data collection tools, on-line questionnaires, interview protocols). The effort to implement a complex questionnaire can be considerable, defects in the questionnaire can compromise the validity of the collected data, low usability may annoy prospective respondents and lower the response rate.

For explanatory and descriptive surveys a pilot survey is often performed in order to detect and correct any deficiencies in the prepared products or in the survey design. A goal is often to lower the effort and improve the ease of use for respondents, to improve the likely response rate, especially for large-scale surveys.

3.5   Survey Execution

The objective of the execution step is to run the survey according to the survey plan and collect the required data. The survey project manager has to check the actual execution with the plan and to conduct quality assurance activities that can be audited after the study for anomalies of execution that may impact the survey validity.

3.6   Survey Analysis

The objective of the analysis step is to analyze the collected data according to the data analysis methods selected during the survey definition in order to answer the questions derived from the survey goal. The analysis phase interprets the raw measurement data. In principle several techniques can be used for this, ranging from common sense analysis (using standard descriptive techniques) to sophisticated statistical analysis techniques as appropriate based on the study design. Another issue is to check data validity based on information from design and execution.

3.7   Packaging

The objective of the packaging step is to report the survey and its result so that external parties are able to understand the results and their contexts. Typical target groups are management, quality management, researchers, and those who want to conduct a survey. Packaging survey results should be structured according to target group goals and interests. Examples include writing an executive summary for management, and detailed results for quality management and researchers in empirical software engineering. A standard format to present the survey results should pay attention to issues like: abstract or executive summary, problem statement, methods and procedures, acknowledgement on possible errors, findings, implications and (optional) appendices [21]; see also [25]. Further detail issues on research and analysis are particularly interesting for people who conduct surveys: "How to" steps, tips and tricks for survey conduct and improvement. Explicating the conceptual model as well as the refinement into questions should therefore by mandatory for each document where a survey is presented. However, this is not practice in survey studies, (see e.g. [22, 23]).

3.8   Effort/Cost and Duration Models

For someone planning to conduct a survey, the likely effort/cost and the minimal duration to conduct a survey variant are key information in the face of scare resources for research. Usually, the goal in planning is to optimize the collected information for a given budget or to answer a set of questions with the minimal budget. This subsection lists factors that are likely to have a strong influence on survey effort/cost and/or duration, and it can be used a checklist for the survey planner.

Effort/cost model: Estimate the staff hours needed for each step and role (at least survey planner and respondents) in the survey process. Use a likely cost per staff hour to derive the personnel cost for the survey. Add additional costs for material, tools, documents, travel, communication, and external services for the survey. There are some factors that influence the effort for survey steps (see also Fig. 1 to identify factors and relationships among survey goals, constraints, and solution approaches).

In Section 4.3.3, we detail factors that we found to be relevant in our surveys.

Duration model: Estimate the minimal duration for each step in the survey process based on the activities and size/complexity of results in each step. Further, forecast likely iterations of steps in the process and determine their influence on the overall process duration; for example, with a PERT model.

4 Two Survey Examples: ISERN and ViSEK Review Surveys

In this section, we describe two examples of surveys we conducted. Both studies had many things in common, although they had a slightly different focus. For both studies, the goal was to determine the state of the practice in software reviews and inspections. A sub-goal was to find significant context factors that influence how reviews are conducted.

In the following, we describe the process we followed for the surveys; that is, what the steps were we conducted, where we followed the theory (and where not), and what we learned during conduct.

Thereby, we first describe the ISERN survey [26], a survey we conducted within an international research network. The second survey was conducted within a German network of excellence (ViSEK, see http://www.visek.de). For the ViSEK survey [27], we point out what was different to the first survey. Following that, we present common results for both surveys. It is important to note that we cannot completely present all relevant issues in this section, as this would take too much space. Instead, we present some of the most important excerpts of our work.

4.1 ISERN Survey

The ISERN survey was planned and conducted by members of the *International Software Engineering Research Network* (ISERN; see http://www.iese.fhg.de/ISERN) as a common inter-cultural endeavor.

4.1.1 Survey Definition

We started the survey with the awareness that, although reviews and inspections are well known in practice and frequently examined in empirical research, we still do not know much about how they are applied in practice.

The survey goal was to describe the state of the practice for reviews and inspections. Doing that, we wanted to focus on the process of reviews; that is, how organizations that use reviews actually apply them. For this purpose, we defined "review" as a general term for all kinds of quality assurance activities that

- focus on finding defects,
- are conducted by developers (and not by an external group)
- are conducted as part of the development process, and
- are applied to all kinds of development products, such as requirements or code.

We based our survey, in particular the conceptual model, on existing literature surveys on inspections [7, 8, 9, 10, 11, 12].

A secondary goal of the survey was to find important context factors; for example, whether there is a difference between different types of organizations in the way they apply reviews.

4.1.2 Survey Design

Developing the design of a survey consists of several steps: defining the conceptual model, the population and sample, designing the questionnaire, and formulating validity issues. In the following, we detail each of these steps for the ISERN survey.

Conceptual Model

A conceptual model describes objects, variables and relations of interest for the survey. We identified three areas where we wanted to collect data: organizational context, high-level process, and detail-level process. In addition, we collected information about the person who filled in the questionnaire (the respondent), and about the testing process of the organization (see Table 1).

Table 1. Conceptual model of the ISERN survey

Context	Company
	Typical projects
	Typical products
	General attitude towards QA/maturity
High-level process	Reasons for/against reviews
	Entry/exit criteria for review process
	Metrics collection
	Experience/maturity of reviews
	Estimated effectiveness, effort
	Number of reviewers
Detail-level process	Review process steps and documents
	For each step: entry/exit, goals, effort
	Reading techniques used

The organizational context consists of several dimensions: questions to characterize the organization the respondent is working for, about typical projects and products, and about the general attitude towards quality assurance in the organization or business unit of the respondent. The purpose of the context questions is to classify organizations, to be able to identify factors that have an influence on how reviews are applied.

The high-level process construct describes the review process as a black box. It covers motivation for and against using reviews, entry/exit criteria for the review process, metric collection and estimation of review effectiveness. Further, it covers typical experience of reviewers as well as the typical number of reviewers in a review.

The detail-level construct describes the review process as a white box (or glass box). It covers process steps of reviews and documents reviewed, for each step: entry/exit criteria, goals for the step, and typical effort.

Definition of Target Population / Sampling

In our case, we defined our population as organizations (or business units) worldwide that develop software and that apply reviews.

As sample, we decided to use a convenience sampling. That is, we did not try to compile a representative list of organizations, as this would have required using a more or less complete global list of organizations and randomly selecting organizations from that list. To our knowledge, such a list does not exist. Instead, we decided to use a snowball system through ISERN and related research networks, such as ESERNET. The idea was that researchers in these communities should inform their industry contacts about the survey; these contacts should participate in the survey and, in turn, inform other interested parties. However, such a sample may not be representative, because organizations that are in contact with research organizations may be significantly different from other organizations. Therefore, we decided to also use newsgroups and mailing lists to reach a larger audience, such as comp.software-engineering, or comp.software.testing.

However, the risks of such a convenience sample still exist. For example, it may be biased towards organizations that are interested in quality assurance. That is, we could not expect the results of our survey to be representative for the software industry in general. If at all, it could be representative for the part of the software industry that is interested in quality assurance. Fortunately, we were only interested in organizations that conduct reviews and thus are interested in quality assurance. That is, once the survey was conducted, we had to look at the context data to see how representative the organizations in our sample were for our population.

Questionnaire Design

When we started to develop our questionnaire, we used other questionnaires as a starting point. One was a questionnaire developed by Håkan Petersson, Thomas Thelin, and Katarina Kylvåg from Lund University in Sweden for characterizing inspections in Swedish companies. Further, we used a questionnaire that was developed and applied for improvement of technical reviews at Lucent, Germany [28].

Corresponding to the conceptual model, the questionnaire consisted of three main parts: The first part served to characterize the respondent and his or her organization. The second part asked questions on the high-level process; the third part on the detail-level process. In an additional fourth part, we asked questions on testing and feedback on the survey.

In total, we had about 130 questions in the final questionnaire. Some required just filling in a comment or text, and some were simple multiple-choice questions However, some questions were quite complex and required filling in a matrix, such as rate how relevant potential review goals were for the respondent's context. Table 2 presents an example for such a complex question, taken from the questionnaire design document (i.e., it is not an example of the final questionnaire layout).

In addition to the complexity of the questions, the questionnaire itself was complex, because we had many conditional questions. That is, some questions were only relevant when a previous answer had a specific value. For example, if someone does not collect metrics, it makes no sense to ask how the collected data are analyzed. That is, in some cases, questions can be skipped. In other cases, the question's layout itself changed depending on previous answers. For example, in one question we asked whether a document was produced during development, and in the next question we asked which of those documents were reviewed. Thus, in the second question, we only displayed documents that corresponded to a positive answer in the first question. Altogether, we had 32 conditional jumps in the questionnaire. Further, there were about 10 questions that changed their layout depending on previous answers.

Although the questionnaire was quite complex, the respondents did not have to deal with that complexity, as they just had to answer questions and press the "next question"-button; the tool did the rest. The effort of filling in the questionnaire was still quite high; respondents needed about one hour to answer it, no matter whether we used a paper based (during pilot studies) or web-based version.

Table 2. Example of a more complex matrix question in the final questionnaire

Please rate the importance of the following goals for reviews in your context:	Crucial ⇓	Desir -able	Irrelevant ⇓		
Quality improvement (i.e., find and correct defects)	☐	☐	☐	☐	☐
Enforce the defined standards	☐	☐	☐	☐	☐
...	☐	☐	☐	☐	☐

Validity Considerations

Validity considerations during design are a kind of forecast of possible problems and what we do to avoid them. That is, we compile a plan of possible threats, some of which we can control with our design (e.g., by holding some variables constant), and state how we react to other threats we cannot control when they arise. Here, we present some important validity considerations for our survey.

Internal validity: Internal validity is about whether the design of the study allows us to draw valid conclusions. For example, if the level of control on the study is too low, it is impossible to draw conclusions. For a survey, the control is usually quite low; for example, it is usually impossible to know whether the respondents answer truthfully, or whether other effects bias the results (e.g., history effects—external events that influence someone's view and attitude towards a question). One measure we took to minimize possible threats to internal validity was to use a short time period during which the questionnaire could be answered. Therefore, the risk of external events influencing the result of the study was low. For the ISERN survey, this period was about 8 weeks. Other factors influencing internal validity are, for example:

- *Non-response error*: A significant number of people in the sample do not respond to the questionnaire and are different from those who do. This is relevant in our case, as we were not even able to find out who did not respond to the survey. Even then, due to the design and contents of the questionnaire, there is a tendency that the survey attracted more respondents who have already heard about or used reviews than those who have not, and they may be significantly different from the rest. Thus, it is impossible to draw any conclusions about the software industry in general: The true population of respondents that do not use reviews is probably much larger than the results of our survey indicate. However, this is not a problem, because we were not interested in drawing conclusions about the software industry in general.
- *Measurement error:* A respondent's answer is inaccurate, imprecise, or cannot be compared in any useful way to other respondent's answers. We tried to minimize this error by carefully designing the questionnaire and by making extensive use of pilot studies. In addition, we had the advantage that our conceptual model could be based on a "hard" process description (in contrast to "soft" models like in attitude measurement)

External validity: Another crucial consideration is *external validity*; that is, how representative the results are. For our survey, this is problematic, because we used convenience sampling to draw respondents from the population. That is, we had to carefully check the context data to see whether the participating organizations were representative for that part of the software industry that conducts reviews.

Experimental validity: Further, we have to consider *experimental validity*; that is, whether a repetition will achieve the same results. Experimental validity is highly tied to external validity: If the results are not representative for the population, a different sample might produce completely different results. In our case, from the data we collected, we saw that the external validity was quite high. However, the tricky question here is, whether the same respondents would today still give the same answers as when they originally filled out the questionnaire.

Construct validity: Last but not least, we had to consider *construct validity*; that is, whether we were measuring the right things. Construct validity is especially difficult when dealing with "soft" issues such as attitude measurement or ease of use/usability of products. In that case, it is necessary to very carefully check the construct validity with a series of studies (see, for example, [29]). In our case, we had the advantage that we could refer to a "hard" conceptual model, based upon published descriptions of the review process. The conceptual model could then directly be refined into questions and questionnaire items. Thus, only ambiguity of the questions is a problem, and we conducted several pilot studies to reduce that threat.

4.1.3   Survey Implementation

We had to consider two choices. One was to use questionnaires, the other to conduct interviews. As we wanted to do an descriptive study, interviews would have been an appropriate means, as they allow to clarify open-ended questions, allowing the researcher to gain a better understanding of, for example, how a process is conducted. However, we wanted to cover a large sample; therefore, we decided to go for a questionnaire (see section 4.1.2).

We believe that we avoided typical problems of such studies for several reasons. For one, the area where we wanted to conduct our study (review process) is quite well known, which means that we did not have to explore how the process itself looks like, only on how it is applied in practice. Therefore, we were able to ask closed questions. To avoid problems with the wording of questions and ambiguities, we conducted several pilot studies.

Pilot Studies

As already mentioned, the process for implementing a survey is usually not conducted sequentially. Usually, surveys are designed iteratively, doing pilots as kind of prototyping for the final questionnaire.

First, we conducted an internal pilot by testing and reviewing the questionnaire among the development team. We also conducted an external pilot at an ESERNET workshop on inspections, where we asked about 20 participants from industry and academia to fill in the questionnaire and give us feedback. Further, we conducted in-depth interviews at a large company, and we had an extensive review by experts within ISERN.

However, we still made mistakes during that process. The gravest of them was that, because of time problems, we did not fully analyze data from the ESERNET pilot. Usually, it is recommended to analyze any data from pilot studies, or to invent data if that is not possible. The reasoning behind this is that analyzing data can show flaws and vague formulations in the analysis plan and questions. It turned out that this would have helped us to avoid problems later on.

Questionnaire Tool

The basic decision one has to make is how the survey will be distributed to the respondents; that is, which tool to use for conducting the survey. For several reasons, we decided to use a web-based questionnaire. The main reason was that web-based questionnaires are easy to access, and that everyone in our population should have access to the internet as well as be familiar with web-based questionnaires.

However, the decision on how precisely to implement a web-based questionnaire remains. Several COTS tools for implementing web-based questionnaires exist. Usually, however, this choice is quite expensive, as it is necessary to pay a license fee.

There are several tools available that support the (web-based) execution of surveys, for example WebSurveyor, SurveySaid EE, JMP, GlobalPark, ConfirmIt and others (see also [30]). Instead of using a COTS product, it is also possible to implement an own, customized tool. The cost for that is associated with the effort of implementing it. For companies who have to pay developers, having a highly qualified developer working at implementing a questionnaire may be more expensive than paying for a COTS products. Additionally, the quality of commercial systems can be expected to be higher than that of an own implementation.

In our case, we decided at first to implement our own tool. The main reason was that we were not able to raise funding for using a COTS tool at the beginning. We had a student building an online questionnaire (using PHP), and working prototypes of our tool featured a graphical layout of the questionnaire in a sidebar so that respondents could easily jump back to earlier questions. In addition, we implemented a feature that allowed respondents to temporarily stop answering the questionnaire and continue later at the questions where they had stopped before. However, it turned out that the questionnaire was too complex to be implemented in that way within a reasonable time. Additionally, as we followed an incremental process, we mixed questionnaire design and implementation at that stage. Thus, there were several changes to the questionnaire itself while it was being implemented, in addition to errors that had to be removed from the implementation. These changes turned out to be unmanageable given the student's implementation.

In the end, we decided to give up the tool and instead to use a COTS product, by GlobalPark, for implementing the questionnaire. We had this option now, because we had been able to raise funding in the meantime through the ViSEK survey. In fact, after our own implementation failed, we first translated the questionnaire into German, adapted the design to ViSEK needs, and executed the ViSEK survey. Afterwards, we fed the questionnaire back into the ISERN survey, again slightly adapted the design, and thus extended the survey worldwide.

Implementing our complicated questionnaire with the COTS tool was a much simpler matter than before; the tool was able to handle even conditional questions well. Thus, implementing the questionnaire was a matter of a few days only. Because the tool relieved us of technical implementation details, we were able to focus on the questionnaire design, structure, and content.

While the COTS tool did not have all features that our own tool had had, it offered some support during conducting the survey that turned out to be useful. For example, it was able to give feedback on the survey progress, such as how many respondents had answered, at which questions respondents had stopped answering the questionnaire, or how much time they needed to answer the questionnaire. Additionally, it was possible to perform a simple analysis of the respondents' answers. Further, the tool stored every answer the respondents gave immediately, so questionnaires were stored, even if they were only partially answered. Respondents were able to go back to earlier questions and change their answer; however, they had to use the browser's "back"-button for that. If a questionnaire has many questions, this approach is usually not useful.

Additional advantages in using a COTS tool are that, usually, the company that sells the tool also offers to give feedback on questionnaire design, which can help avoid problems.

4.1.4   Survey Execution

The execution phase was quite simple, at least for the researchers. We placed a call for participation into several mailing lists and newsgroups. All data collection and processing during that phase was done via the tool. All we had to do was to supervise the progress of the execution using GlobalPark's built-in features.

During this phase, the built-in analysis allowed us to react to a pattern, where people stopped immediately after answering the first question. When we looked more in detail, it turned out that the first question asked the respondent's name. Although we had promised anonymity before, we assumed that having to give their name was what stopped people from answering, so we removed that question.

For the ISERN survey, we received 105 responses from companies worldwide. We were able to observe that each new call for participation in a newsgroup was followed by a "peak" of respondents that wore quickly off after a few days. Thus, it seems reasonable for the future to use that pattern to place calls for participation.

We also made an interesting observation: Although answering the questionnaire took about one hour, as we had expected, only around 30% of the people who started responding completed the questionnaire. That is, 325 people started to answer the questionnaire, and only one third completed it. However, if we look closer at the drop-off pattern, we can see that most of those who did not complete the questionnaire did so after the first two pages, where we introduced the purpose and motivation of our study. That is, those people were not interested at participating. After that, only few people stopped answering; that is, if they started to answer questions, they would be likely to finish the questionnaire. That was surprising for us, as we had expected that respondents would gradually stop answering after some time, after getting annoyed or bored.

4.2   ViSEK Survey

The ViSEK survey had the same goals as the ISERN survey. Thus, both surveys were able to profit from each other. However, there were some slight differences between these surveys that we present in this section.

First, the *survey definition* was slightly different in ViSEK. ViSEK is a German project, funded by the German government, so the focus of this survey was mainly the software industry in Germany, and there was stronger additional interest in testing than in the ISERN survey. As a result, the questionnaire had to be translated into German. Usually, such a translation can cause many problems, for example in attitude measurement, as the construct validity is endangered [29].

The *survey design* used the same conceptual model as the ISERN survey, with a slightly higher interest in testing.

The *sampling procedure* was different for the ViSEK survey. Instead of using newsgroups, we used our own industrial contacts—that is, of the Fraunhofer Institute for Experimental Software Engineering—and of industrial contacts of the ViSEK project. Additionally, we used contacts from local quality improvement conferences. In total 865 people were identified to participate in the survey. These were invited to participate.

The *survey implementation* step was the same as in the ISERN survey, except that we immediately tried to use a COTS tool, as the own implementation had failed for the ISERN survey.

During the *survey execution* step, the only difference between the ISERN and ViSEK surveys was that we were able to use a feature of our tool, to send personalized e-mails to contact persons instead of anonymous calls in newsgroups and send up to two reminders to those who had not answered yet. It turned out that this approach resulted in a high response rate of ca. 14%. In our opinion, using personalized e-mails and sending reminders caused this high response rate.

Like in the ISERN survey, we were able to observe a "peak" of respondents each time the tool sent a reminder. Also like in the ISERN survey, about one third of the respondents did not complete the questionnaire; and again, most of them stopped after the introductory pages.

4.3   Considerations for Both Surveys

In this section, we combine our results for the survey steps analysis and packaging. Further, we present our findings concerning effort models from both studies.

4.3.1   Survey Analysis

The goal of this step is to analyze the collected data with respect to the goals of the survey. In the following, we first present some of the results from both surveys (i.e., for ISERN and ViSEK surveys together) and then briefly discuss some validity issues.

Results

Here, we briefly present some excerpts of results from the studies. As the focus of this chapter is to present our experiences, not results of the study, we will only present some results about the high-level and detail-level process constructs. Interested readers should refer to [27].

Regarding the high-level review process, we were most interested in what motivated someone to use reviews, or what stopped them from using reviews. Further, we wanted to know to what extent the review process was conducted; whether it would be applied to all development stages, and what the entry/exit criteria look like.

Considering motivation for reviews, we asked, among others, one question on goals that are associated with reviews. 73% rated quality improvement as a very important goal of reviews, 52% stated that the evaluation of the project status is most important, and 54% see reviews as a means to enforce standards. As reasons against reviews, most respondents mentioned that time pressure prevented the use of reviews (75%), that reviews are too expensive (56%), and that they do not know how to introduce reviews (50%).

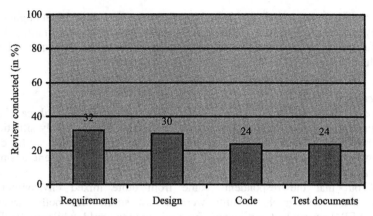

Fig. 2. Review usage: This figure shows the percentage of respondents who usually conduct a review in a specific development phase

Regarding entry/exit criteria of the review process, it seems that almost one third of the participants do not use formal criteria at all to determine when to start a review. For example, concerning how they identified whether a document should be reviewed, 32% stated that they used no criteria at all to select a document for review, and 44% review a document because it is required in the project plan.

Reviews can be conducted at all development stages, from requirements to code, or to check test documents. However, it seems that more than two thirds of the participants do not perform reviews on a regular basis for any development stage (see Fig. 2). Thus, together with other results, we have the impression that reviews are not conducted systematically in practice.

Looking at the detail-level review process, we were, among other things, interested in which review process steps were conducted on a regular basis, and what reading techniques are used. Our data show that many review steps are not conducted on a regular basis. For example, only 20% of the respondents stated that they usually conduct a planning and overview step, and only 40% stated that they usually have a defect detection or defect collection phase, and around 35% usually have a follow-up meeting. Again, this confirms our impression that reviews are not conducted in a systematical way.

Regarding reading techniques used during review, an area where there has been significant research over the last years, we were interested in what reading techniques are applied in practice. Around 55% state they use checklists, and 35% state they use no specific reading technique at all. Only about 10% use more advanced reading techniques, such as scenario-based techniques [31]. However, as many of the respondents have been contacted through our research network, where advanced reading techniques have been promoted for several years, the number of 10% may be a bit higher for our sample than in the rest of the population.

We found a tendency in our data that the use of reviews increased with having certification, with the size of the organization (i.e., large organizations were more likely to apply reviews), with the number of years in business, and with the project size. We conducted chi-square tests to confirm these findings; these tests were significant at the 5% level.

So far, the results seem to indicate that, although reviews are quite often applied in practice, they are not applied in a systematical manner. Moreover, our findings lead us to the assumption that reviews are often introduced because they are required for a certain certification, not because management believes in their usefulness.

Validity Discussion
During survey design, validity discussion is a "forecast" of possible threats and reaction to them. Later, the validity discussion refers to the concrete study situation; that is, we check which threats are really present in the data. In particular, we have to find out how representative our sample is. In the following, we present a small excerpt of available data.

It turned out that the respondents came from quite mixed environments. Interestingly, these demographic results were almost similar for both surveys, although the ISERN survey had participants from all over the world, while the ViSEK participants were from Germany only. Organizations of all sizes participated, from very small (1 – 5 employees) to very large (more than 10000 employees). All in all, about 47% of the respondents were from small and medium enterprises of less than 500 employees.

Further, they were from all kinds of industrial branches, from embedded systems (27%), telecommunication (10%), information systems (30%), web or mobile applications (14%), and others (19%). Concerning important quality aspects, 77% rated security as important, another 77% reliability. 56% of the respondents claim it is crucial that they meet real-time requirements. Concerning safety, the risk of financial loss is major concern for 66% of the respondents, and the risk of life is a concern for 33% of the respondents.

Based on these data, it is hard to conclude whether the sample is representative, as only few studies are available that describe the population (e.g., [32]). However, we believe that there may be a slight bias towards large enterprises and towards embedded/telecommunication organizations compared to the typical software industry. Our population was not the complete software industry, but only the part of it that conducts reviews and is thus more interested in quality assurance. Based on our experience, we believe that our sample may be representative for that part of the software industry. At least, our sample covers a wide range of different types of organizations.

4.3.2   Packaging

The objective of the packaging step is to report the survey and its result so that external parties are able to understand the results and their contexts. So far, we have packaged only parts of the survey results. We wrote several reports on the ViSEK survey ([27, 33]). The first is a technical report on the survey result, while the second one is a short newsletter, an executive summary for interested parties. The first report is in English, the second one was written in German to acknowledge the fact that the survey was conducted within a German project.

Further, this bookchapter is part of the packaging for our surveys, where we document the experiences we made during planning and execution of the surveys.

The ISERN survey has so far not been completely analyzed; first results have been presented at the ISERN workshop 2002 (see http://www.iese.fhg.de/ISERN/ for details).

In addition, we have planned several other publications, among them a German quality conference (SQM). We plan to use conferences to discuss our findings within the community of practitioners to see how well our conclusions meet the practice.

4.3.3   Effort/Cost and Duration Models

Here, we present the experiences we made concerning the models presented in Section 3.8. We provide a short listing and discussion of factors that had important influence on survey cost and duration. We distinguish between "linear" and "exponential" influence. We do not want to imply a mathematical relationship with these expressions; rather, we want to convey a feeling to what extent an increase in a factor influences the effort or time for that step. Please refer to Table 3 for an overview of costs for the ISERN survey. In the following, we present, for each step, the relevant factors and how they influenced the effort for that step.

Table 3. Effort per process step, and role in ISERN and ViSEK surveys

Process step / Role	Experimenter	Subject
Definition	80 to 100 staff hours	-
Design	500 to 600 staff hours	-
Implementation	Own tool: 150 to 200 staff hours COTS: 40 staff hours	-
Execution	25 staff hours	60 to 90 minutes
Analysis	300 to 400 staff hours	-
Packaging	300 to 400 staff hours	-
Sum	*Own tool: 1.350 to 1.725 staff hours* *COTS: 1.200 to 1.550 staff hours*	-

Definition: Time/effort increases if: (a) the research question(s) is/are vague or are numerous, or (b) many stakeholders are involved. In the beginning, we had to put much effort into a clear definition of the research question. The number of research questions also plays a major role; it is important to restrict them to few. Another important influence factor is the number of stakeholders involved. The more stakeholders are involved, the more potential interest conflicts about research questions will arise, which increase the amount of communication involved. Thus, the number of stakeholders is a factor that may contribute exponentially to the total effort.

Design: Time/effort increases basically with (a) the complexity of the conceptual model; (b) the number of contacts based on validity goals and anticipated response rate; and (c) the length of the questionnaire/interview (i.e., number and complexity of questions). The main influence factor for design is the complexity of the conceptual model, which is, in turn, influenced by the number and complexity of research questions. In our experience, the research questions contribute exponentially to the conceptual model; that is, even one additional question can increase the complexity of the conceptual model significantly. In our case, the conceptual model was quite complex, which resulted in a large and complex questionnaire (many conditional questions). This increased the design effort significantly. Therefore, the complexity of the conceptual model has an exponential influence on design effort.

Implementation: Time/effort increases with the complexity of the questionnaire; that is, with the number and complexity of the questions and dependencies (i.e., some questions change or are not relevant dependent on answers given to earlier questions). Further, the tool used plays a major role for implementing the questionnaire structure and phrasing the questions, and for usability testing. When building our own, customized tool, the complexity of the questionnaire had an exponential influence on implementation effort. A COTS tool can significantly lower the effort, and can reduce the influence of the questionnaire's complexity to a linear one.

Execution: Time/effort increases with (a) the number of respondents depending on (b) the data collection approach – questionnaire and/or interviews. During this step, the main influence factor was the number of respondents. As the cost for reaching the respondents was almost zero (in contrast to a traditional sending of paper questionnaires via mail), the only cost from our side was to track the survey status with tool help, and to place calls for participation. Thus, the cost for that step is the cost of having respondents fill in the questionnaire; this amounts to a linear influence.

Analysis: Time/effort increases with the complexity of the conceptual model. If (a) many questions have to be analyzed, and (b) many relations between different variables have to be considered, the analysis is much more complex and time consuming than for a simple model. Depending on the complexity of research questions, this influence may be linear.

Packaging: Time/effort increases with the (a) complexity of the conceptual model; (b) the audiences you want to address: The more diverse audiences you want to address, the more effort you have to put into writing reports. Time/effort can be decreased with (c) a good infrastructure that supports, for example, storing empirical data in a structured way, which makes easier to reuse previously packaged results. The conceptual model has a linear influence here; more important is the number and kind of reports you want to write.

5 Lessons Learned

The examples presented in the previous section demonstrated the usefulness of the survey process. Each of these steps was important for the success of the survey. Overall, the results were helpful to further investigate review and inspection technology. While following the process, there were some lessons learned that may be beneficial for practitioners.

First of all, it is important to follow the recommended survey process. It may be necessary to apply the steps in an iterative manner. The main element of the design phase is the construction of the questionnaire. Typically, after an introduction, which discloses the sponsorship of the survey, the questionnaire begins with non-threatening questions that stimulate interest. The first question should be clearly related to the announced purposes of the survey (not a background question, for instance). Some recommend the second question be open-ended, to allow the respondent to "get into" the subject. Non-threatening background information questions (e.g., demographic information) should be posed early so that these controls will be available if the respondent fatigues and does not answer the later questions. The survey then proceeds to attitude questions, often sequencing from general and less threatening items toward more specific and more sensitive items. Sensitive background questions are usually put at the end. However, the more toward the end of the survey a question is, the lower its response rate is apt to be. For this reason, balancing the foregoing considerations, it is desirable to administer a survey with different question orders to lessen the order/response bias. Modern survey tools usually offer this functionality.

Modern Internet surveys are proliferating. Web surveys clearly work better with software engineering topics, since most respondents are connected to the Internet anyway and it is more attractive, or easier, for them to participate. Yet, this requires more effort regarding the graphical design of the survey. It may also require a higher budget. The question is whether to buy a professional tool. While this is not a yes/no question, the experience of the ViSEK/ISERN-Survey is that it can be time-consuming to build an own, customized, tool. This may be possible for a small number of questions; for example, for less than ten. However, if it is larger and there are conditional responses, one should think about support of a professional tool vendor. In addition, the tool vendor often has experience in questionnaire design and, thus, offers support on questionnaire design. Moreover, these tools often include additional functionality and analysis support; for example, for monitoring at which question participants stop answering the questionnaire. In the context of the ViSEK/ISERN-questionnaire, we used the tool Globalpark. The high response rate of 14% for the ViSEK-Survey indicates that the response rate for online questionnaires can be much higher than for paper-based questionnaires (usually between 1% and 4%). This may be due to the built-in functionality of the tool to remind those that did not complete the questionnaire, and the low effort to answer online questionnaires (you don't have to send mail).

Once the data are collected, they have to be analyzed and the results need to be packaged to develop an interpretation. This effort is often neglected in the design and conduct of the survey. The approach of choice is an iterative approach to analysis: Start with simple analysis questions (e.g., about the demographic information) before going into the details. The documentation adds to the overall packaging effort that needs to be considered in the models.

In both the ViSEK and the ISERN survey, the number of the questions, the clarity of the questions, especially sets of conditional questions, and the tool implementation were major drivers for effort and duration of the survey.

6 Conclusions

Surveys are empirical procedures in qualitative and quantitative research in which researchers administer a questionnaire to a sample or to the entire population in order to describe attitudes, opinions, behaviors, or characteristics of the population. From the results of this survey, the researcher makes claims about trends in the population. Although surveys belong to the set of standard procedures in other disciplines, little has been reported about using this approach to gather data about techniques, methods, and tools in software engineering. In this chapter, we presented practical experiences in the design and conduct of surveys in a software engineering context.

The challenge of a survey derives from the complexity of the investigated topic. In this situation a well-defined survey process is a beacon that can be followed. The process defines the roles, the activities, and the results of each phase. Hence, the complexity can be handled and confusion be avoided. The process is particularly important when researchers from different sites are involved in the survey work. In this situation, the survey process synchronizes the work among participants. The ViSEK/ISERN-survey presented in this paper is an example that illustrates this experience. Finally, deviations from any process are a fact of life. However, to manage a survey effort one needs to know when and why deviations may occur to ensure the successful completion of the whole work.

While using the process in the context of the two inspection surveys, it became obvious that a scientific survey is not a trivial undertaking. It requires careful research and planning, is labor intensive, and can take weeks to implement and analyze. It is not just the development of a questionnaire and the subsequent collection of data. Depending on the complexity of the topic, planning can easily consume up to two months of work; sometimes even more, especially if the questionnaire cannot be taken "off the shelf" but needs to be developed from scratch. Even worse, since there is a clear lack of models in software engineering, one often needs to invest a considerable amount of time to develop the conceptual model. Only the availability of the model ensures that the survey results can be interpreted in an adequate manner.

The process described in this paper has demonstrated its usefulness in the context of two large empirical studies about inspection technologies. This effort itself can be regarded as a kind of empirical study to validate the process. Although some of the experiences presented may sound trivial they are sometimes challenging to fulfill. At least, the work presented in this chapter increases the awareness for practitioners and researchers of the crucial elements involved while planning, designing, conducting and analyzing a survey.

Acknowledgements. Parts of this work have been funded by the ViSEK project, which is in turn funded by the Geman Federal Ministry of Education and Research (BMBF).

The surveys described here have been initiated, planned and conducted by members of the International Software Engineering Research Network (ISERN). We would like to thank all members who have taken part in this endeavour.

Last but not least, we would like to thank the participants of the pilot studies and early interviews for their valuable input, and the participants of the survey for their time and interest.

References

[1] Hays, W. L., Statistics for the social sciences, London: Holt, Rinehart and Winston, 1977.
[2] Robson, C., Real World Research: A Resource for Social Scientists and Practitioners-Researchers, Blackwell, 1993.
[3] Freimut, B., Punter, T., Biffl, S. and Ciolkowski, M., "State-of-the-Art in Empirical Studies," ViSEK Technical Report 007/E, 2002.
[4] Ticehurst, G. and Veal, A., Business Research Methods: A Managerial Approach, Australia: Addison Wesley Longman, 1999.
[5] Dybå, T., "Improvisation in small software organizations," IEEE Software, 17(5), pp. 82–87, September 2000.
[6] Fagan, M. E., "Design and Code Inspections to Reduce Errors in Program Development," IBM Systems Journal, 15(3), pp. 182–211, 1976.

[7]   Kim, L. P. W., Sauer, C. and Jeffery, R., "A Framework for Software Development Technical Reviews," Software Quality and Productivity: Theory, Practice, Education and Training, 1995.

[8]   Macdonald, F., Miller, J., Brooks, A., Roper, M. and Wood, M., "Applying Inspection to Object-Oriented Software," Software Testing, 6, pp. 61–82, 1996.

[9]   Porter, A. A., Votta, L. G. and Basili, V. R., "Comparing Detection Methods for Software Requirements Inspections: A Replicated Experiment," IEEE Transactions on Software Engineering, 21(6), pp. 563–575, 1995.

[10] Tjahjono, D., Exploring the effectiveness of formal technical review factor with CSRS, a collaborative software review system, PhD thesis, Department of Information and Computer Science, 1996.

[11] Wheeler, D. A., Brykczynski, B. J. and Meeson, R. N., "Software Peer Reviews," in R. H. Thayer, ed., Software Engineering Project Management, , IEEE Computer Society, 1997.

[12] Laitenberger, O. and DeBaud, J., "An Encompassing Life-Cycle Centric Survey of Software Inspection," Journal of Systems and Software, 50 (1), 2000.

[13] Freedman, D. P. and Weinberg, G. M., Handbook of Walkthroughs, Inspections, and Technical Reviews, New York: Dorset House Publishing, 1990.

[14] Weinberg, G. M. and Freedman, D. P., "Reviews, Walkthroughs, and Inspections," IEEE Transactions on Software Engineering, 12 (1), pp. 68–72, 1984.

[15] Yourdon, E., Structured Walkthroughs, N.Y.: Prentice Hall, 4th edition, 1989.

[16] Macdonald, F. and Miller, J., Modelling Software Inspection Methods for the Application of Tool Support, Technical Report RR–95–196 [EFoCS–16–95], University of Strathclyde, UK, 1995.

[17] Basili, V. R., Caldiera, G. and Rombach, H. D., "Experience Factory," in J. J. Marciniak, ed., Encyclopedia of Software Engineering , John Wiley & Sons, pp. 469–476, 1994.

[18] Ropponen, J. and Lyytinen, K., "Components of software development risk: how to address them? A project manager survey",IEEE Transactions on Software Engineering", 26(6), 2000.

[19] Basili, V. R., Caldiera, G. and Rombach, H. D., "Measurement," in J. J. Marciniak, ed., Encyclopedia of Software Engineering, John Wiley & Sons, 1994.

[20] Oppenheim, A., Questionnaire design, interviewing and attitude measurement, London: Pinter, 1992.

[21] Salant, P. and Dillman, D. A., How to conduct your own survey?, New York: John Wiley and Sons, 1994.

[22] Paulk, M. C., Goldenson, D. and White, D. M., The 1999 Survey of High Maturity Organizations, Technical Report CMU/SEI–2000–SR–002, SEI, 2000.

[23] European Software Institute, "1995/1996 Software excellence study. Summary of results", 1996.

[24] Babbie, E., Survey Research Methods, Wadsworth, 1990.

[25] Kitchenham, B., Pfleeger, S., Pickard, L., Jones, P., Hoaglin, D., El Emam, K. and Rosenberg, J., "Preliminary guidelines for empirical research in software engineering," IEEE Transactions on Software Engineering, 28(8), pp. 721–734, 2002.

[26] Ciolkowski, M., Shull, F. and Biffl, S., "A Family of Experiments to Investigate the Influence of Context on the Effect of Inspection Techniques," Empirical Assessment of Software Engineering (EASE), Keele, UK, 2002.

[27] Laitenberger, O., Vegas, S. and Ciolkowski, M., The State of the Practice of Review and Inspection Technologies in Germany, Technical Report ViSEK/010/E, ViSEK, 2002.

[28] Laitenberger, O., Leszak, M., Stoll, D. and Emam, K. E., "Evaluating a Model of Review Success Factors in an Industrial Setting," Proceedings of the International Symposium on Software Metrics, 1999.

[29] Davis, F., "Perceived Usefulness, Perceived Ease of Use, and User Acceptance of Information Technology," MIS Quarterly, pp. 319–340, September 1989.

[30] Assmann, D. and Kempkens, R., Tools for Measurement Support, Technical Report No. 97.00/E, Fraunhofer Institute for Experimental Software Engineering, December 2000.

[31] Basili, V. R., Shull, F. and Lanubile, F., "Building Knowledge through Families of Experiments," Transactions on Software Engineering, 25 (4), pp. 456–473, 1999.
[32] GfK; Fraunhofer IESE; Fraunhofer ISI, Analyse und Evaluation der Softwareentwicklung in Deutschland, Eine Studie für das Bundesministerium für Bildung und Forschung (in German), 2000.
[33] Ciolkowski, M. and Kalmar, R., Software-Reviews sind als Instrument zur Qualitätssicherung in der Industrie anerkannt, ViSEK Newsletter, 2002.

Post Mortem – An Assessment of Two Approaches

Tor Stålhane[1], Torgeir Dingsøyr[2], Geir Kjetil Hanssen[2], and Nils Brede Moe[2]

[1] NTNU, Norway
Tor.Stalhane@idi.ntnu.no
[2] SINTEF, Norway
{Torgeir.Dingsoyr,Geir.K.Hanssen,Nils.B.Moe}@sintef.no

Abstract. Learning from experience is the key to successes for all that develop software. Both the successes and the failures in software projects can help us to improve. Here we discuss two versions of Post Mortem Analysis (PMA) as methods for harvesting experience from completed software projects, which can be part of a larger knowledge management program. The two methods are tailored for use in small and medium size companies and are conceptually easy to apply. In addition, they require few resources compared to other methods in the field. We think that the methods are useful for companies when they need to document their knowledge, find improvement actions and as a start of systematic knowledge harvesting.

1 Introduction

An obvious way to improve a software development process is to learn from past mistakes. In practice this has turned out to be easier said than done, but the method of post mortem analysis – also called post mortem reviews or PMA – is one way to achieve it. There are several companies already doing this, such as Apple Computers [1], Rolls Royce [2] and Microsoft [3]. What they all have in common, however, is a rather elaborate and costly process.

We are mostly dealing with small companies, with small projects. The overhead from an approach as ambitious as the one used by, for instance, Apple Computers would be way beyond the reach of most of our customers. We needed something simpler and wanted to try out the two rather simple approaches described in this paper. In order to see if they were useful we tried them out in two companies. Our goals were to see if:

- The approaches worked – i.e. if anything useful came out of them.
- They worked in different ways – i.e. were the information that came out of them different in amount, scope or usefulness.

The research was conducted in close collaboration with industry. We collected experience from real software projects in a real environment, over which we had only limited control. What we present here is thus not a scientific evaluation but a case study of practical improvement work. Thus, what comes out is not hard science in the strict sense but practical experience for practical people working in the area of software process improvement.

R. Conradi and A.I. Wang (Eds.): ESERNET 2001-2003, LNCS 2765, pp. 129–141, 2003.

2 Starting Scenario

To improve software development, it is important to help software developers to learn both from positive and negative experience, i.e. to become what is often termed a "learning organisation" [4]. People usually learn best when they can relate what they learn to their ordinary work. Thus, experience collected from a well-known environment will have a greater learning effect than experience collected from unfamiliar environments.

Learning from your own experience requires that you be allowed to reason about tasks that have been completed to see what went well and what did not and also why things happened the way they did. Thus, it requires observation and reflection [5].

To cover more material, we can learn from other people's experience as well as our own. Thus, it is a goal to transfer experience from one project to another in order to make individual and project-based learning helpful for, say, a whole organisation. An important part of the problem is how this experience can be collected effectively. We will now turn our attention to this question.

3 Method

3.1 Design

As a concept, the PMA is simple – gather all participants from a project that is ongoing or just finished and ask them to identify which aspects of the project worked well and should be repeated, which worked badly and should be avoided, and what was merely "OK" but leave room for improvement. In addition, we need techniques that can be used to elicit experience and document it in such a way that they can be made verifiable and reusable in the most effective way. Reuse of experience is, after all, one of the reasons for doing a PMA.

A PMA can be done in many different ways – varying both in goals and degree of formality. A PMA can be focused on harvesting experience that is available from a single activity or process step or it can try to catch all experience available from a project. Data collection can be done as semi-structured interviews, or as a multi-step defined process, for instance consisting of a group process supported by affinity diagrams, followed by a root cause analysis (RCA), see [6], using an Ishikawa diagram.

Whatever form the PMA might take, one point is important – the consideration of the influence of the project's environment. No experience is reusable without considering these factors. It is often the case that an action undertaken in a project, which led to unfavourable results, was not bad in itself – it was just not a smart thing to do in the current environment.

Given its loose form and lack of formalities, many people find it almost wrong to dignify PMA with the word "analysis", which they think should be reserved for something more scientific. The loose form and simple concept is, however, a strength and not a weakness. It gives us a method that is flexible, easy to learn and apply and containing a minimum of formalities to take care of. In this way everybody in the organisation can participate and not just as information providers. This is crucial in order to support the TQM philosophy – that quality and quality improvement is everybody's responsibility; it is not the domain of the QA department alone.

Thus, we have decided to use just a few simple techniques. One or more of these techniques have been used for all the PMAs that we report from in this paper:

- KJ, which is a structured brainstorming technique [6].
- The Ishikawa diagram – also known as the fishbone diagram [6].
- Structured interviews, where the structuring factors are:
- The purpose of the PMA – for instance causes for underestimation of costs
- The structure of the project – what did we do?
- The structure of the process – how did we do it?

Table 1. The PMA processes used in the two companies

Spacetec	InfoStream
All project members participated	Only those who did the estimation participated
Interview with the PM to get background information (1)	Study project documents to get background information (a)
Introduce the concept of PMA to the participants (2, b)	
Perform a KJ (3)	Perform structured interviews of project participants (c)
Prioritise the items from the KJ (4)	
Prepare the KJ results for an RCA (5)	-
Perform an RCA by using the Ishikawa diagram (6)	Register cause-effect connections during the interviews (d)
Write final report (7, e)	
Present final report and get feedback from participants (8, f)	

The process used in the two projects differed, partly due to company constraints, partly due to each researcher's preferences. The way the PMAs were performed is summed up in Table 1 above.

We start with a short description of the companies (Subjects) before describing how we performed the PMA (Procedure) and present some typical results (Results). In addition to the PMAs we had some activities – called support activities –, which improve on the results from the PMAs by supplying some extra facts. In this way, we are not depending only on the participants' memory.

For Spacetec, we did the interviews before the PMA, while for InfoStream a GQM planning session plus data collection and analysis were done after the PMA. In fact, some of it is still going on.

In order to present the results from the two companies in a uniform way, we have chosen to present the supporting activities after the examples for both companies. In this way, we keep a better focus on the main issues of this presentation, which are the PMAs.

3.2   Subjects/Participants

3.2.1   Spacetec

Spacetec AS is one of the leading producers of receiving stations for data from meteorological and earth observation satellites. They have developed a considerable expertise in delivering turnkey ground station systems, consultancy, feasibility studies, system engineering, training and support.

Spacetec has as an overall goal to increase knowledge transfer between projects, and has chosen estimation of software project costs as its first focus area. The company will build a knowledge repository with cost information on previous projects. One of the goals of the internal improvement project at Spacetec is to improve the estimation accuracy of technical work packages so that the deviation between real and estimated cost will be within 20%.

3.2.2   InfoStream

InfoStream is a medium sized Internet consulting company that recently became part of the international Integra group. Most of the customers are in the financial, energy, media, telecom, and manufacturing sectors. InfoStream has no product line, but develops tailor made solutions for their customers.

Many of the projects of the recent past have missed on the estimates. There have been several delays in delivery and a tendency to overuse resources in the projects. This has serious economic consequences since the estimates are used to set a fixed price. Estimation precision is considered to be an important success factor, and the company is investigating their projects to find what causes these problems.

3.3   Apparatus/Materials

The starting point for the comparisons is the results of the case studies. We wanted answers to two questions:
• Will both PMA approaches work
• Are there situations where one of the approaches will work better than the other one?

In order to find the answers to these questions we performed the two types of PMA on projects of comparable sizes and complexities and evaluated the results. The evaluations were done by two experienced researchers and systems developers. In addition to the two above mentioned questions, we also wanted to increase our general knowledge on how to perform an efficient PMA in an industrial setting.

3.4   Procedure

3.4.1   Spacetec

Two PMAs were carried out for two typical projects. The first projects had lasted for almost a year, and was 75% finished when we did the analysis. The second project was finished less than a year ago. Both projects built software for analysis of image data from satellites. The PMAs were performed as described in the Spacetec-column in Table 1.

Each PMA lasted approximately four hours and we had a feedback session for one hour the following day. Steps 2 and 4 lasted only for one hour each since they were highly creative. In step 3 – see Table 1 – we gave each participant a number of post-it notes and told them to write down an item that was either a problem or a success on each post-it note. We then gathered in a meeting room and asked each participant to attach each post-it note on the whiteboard. In addition, they should explain to the other participants what the issue was and why it was important. Post-it notes that were related should be placed close to each other. We used a tape recorder during steps 2–4, and the results were transcribed and later inserted into the report. Giving the participants quick feedback was of great value both for the participants and for the researcher. The transcribed material, in particular, created important discussions.

We wrote a post mortem report on the project, containing an introduction which described the process, a short description of the project that we analysed, how the analysis was carried out, and the results of the analysis. The result was a prioritised list of problems and successes in the project. We used statements from the meeting to present what was said about the issues with highest priority, together with an Ishikawa diagram to show their root causes. In an appendix, we included everything that was written down on post-it notes during the KJ session, and a transcription of the presentation of the issues that were used on the post-it notes. In total, this report was about 15 pages long.

The total amount of resources needed for a PMA were three persons selected from the project participants. The total work needed was 35 person hours, distributed as follows:

- 4 person hours for the researchers' preparation.
- 20 person hours for the PMA session – researchers and project personnel.
- 6 person hours for writing the report from the interviews – researchers only.
- 5 person hours for feedback and updating – researchers and project personnel.

3.4.2 InfoStream

In order to perform PMAs in this company, we asked our contact person to select three typical projects that had been finished less than a year ago. This limit was imposed in order to make sure that the project experience is still available with a reasonable certainty. The three PMAs were focused on estimation and were performed as described in the InfoStream-column in Table 1.

Each project PMA lasted approximately five hours, including a lunch break in the middle. During the interviews and discussions, we used a whiteboard and a flip-over to document the points as they surfaced. The flip-over was used as a collective short-term memory for the group. Except for the structure imposed by the project's work breakdown structure and the focus provided by the goal of understanding the reasons for incorrect estimates, no further structure was imposed. Thus, the notes from each PMA differs somewhat when it comes to internal structure. For instance: for one project, the participants identified the most important cause for cost overruns for each activity, while this was not done for the other two.

When the interview was finished, the researchers took all the material back to their office and structured and wrote down all the points raised. The points where numbered so that cause-and-effect relationships could be documented. This was done by inserting statements like "The estimate was increased by 40 person hours. This was caused by point 53". See also the chapter "Some Examples" below. The resulting report was sent to the participants for feedback.

The researchers went through all the three PMA summaries and extracted all the registered information that was related to the PMA focus – improving the estimation process. Afterwards we defined a slogan for each information point and wrote them down on post-it notes. This was used as an input to a KJ process undertaken by the two researchers in order to analyse the information. This way to use KJ is in line with the original way to use this method, see [7].

4   Results

4.1   Spacetec

The results from the PMAs at Spacetec are represented as KJ diagrams. One result from one of the KJ sessions was four post-it notes grouped together and named "preparatory work." They are shown in the lower left corner of the results from the KJ process – see Fig. 1. The arrows indicate relationships between the classes and tell which success factors that influence other success factors.

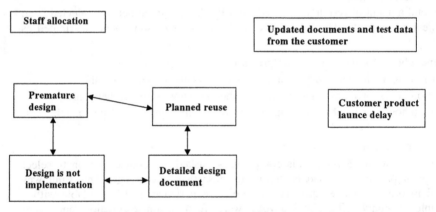

Fig. 1. Post-it notes showing problems in a project

During the PMA meeting, the developers explained the problems related to "preparatory work" in the following way:

- *Design before "full insight". I dare say this as well: It is OK that we are supposed to reuse, but if we had known – now I was not participating in the design, so it is wrong of me to say it – but if we had full control we could have made an architecture that was in fact possible to use later on. ("Premature design")*
- *We put down a lot of effort into the design of the processor [a software module for analysing satellite data], and then it turned out when we were to implement it that we did not at all use the design that we had planned of in the document, so it was maybe a bit stupid to use a lot of time to... and then we don't use it afterwards. ("Design is not implementation")*

When we later tried to find the root causes for the "preparatory work" problem, we ended up with the following Ishikawa diagram:

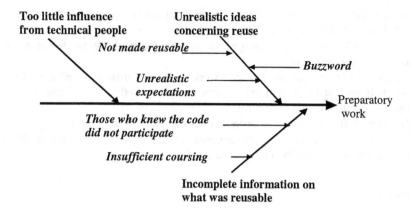

Fig. 2. Ishikawa diagram for "Preparatory work"

The root causes for this problem, as the developers saw it, was that people in the company in general had an idealised conception of reuse. Other root causes were that the company did not have a good enough overview of what was reusable from earlier projects and that the technical personnel did not have influence on the project activities where issues on reuse were discussed.

We then asked people to come up with suggestions for how to reduce this problem:
- Get an overview of reusable components in the company.
- Teach people higher up in the organisation about reusability.
- Update or write a new detailed design document for this project.

These suggestions on short- and long-term improvement actions were documented in the report. At the end of the meeting, we asked people how they felt about the results, and got feedback like: *The issues about contracts with the customer – I think we are too kind. There is so much that is mentioned in the contract that... it is not supposed to be like that.* In general, people said they were made aware of new issues, and were able to see smaller issues more in a larger context.

The next day, we went through the report from the meeting together with the people who attended, as well as the project manager. Some of the participants disliked that we gave a complete transcript of part of the meeting, but after some discussion, they agreed that this is something that could trigger new discussion on relevant topics. We got positive feedback on the way we organised the review, which differed from the project completion reports that the project manager would normally write alone:

One of the problems with the project completion report is that the project manager sits down in the end and sum up what went well and what went badly. And it is one man who remembers what [...] has happened the last two years. Then you have lost a lot. You do not collect a lot of experience. It is the large problems that are already discussed – things that have gone really badly. But if you do this kind of an analysis several times during the project, then we agree – it shows how... you have to think things through!

As a basis for the PMA analysis we first had interviews with another eight persons from the company (developers, project managers, general management, and marketing personnel). Focus in these interviews was the estimation process and how the projects were accomplished compared to the initial plans.

We also conducted an analysis of the project completion report from 12 projects. This resulted in the following improvement suggestions:

- Introduce a 28% contingency budget on each work package to decrease the probability of cost over-runs.
- Do a focused PMA to examine why the work packages "management" and "QA" were strongly underestimated in one project, and why "coding" and "unit testing" are strongly underestimated in general.
- Do PMAs on all future projects in order to increase learning in general.
- Use a standardized structure of work packages to make projects more comparable – thus improving the possibility for comparative data analysis.

4.2   InfoStream

For InfoStream, the researchers constructed the KJ diagram, based on the results from the interviews. Fig. 3 shows all the results from the KJ process. Each box contains several experiences but these are not shown in order to keep the diagram simple. The categories contained in each box are supposed to be the key success factors, and we believe that if the company paid enough attention to them we would not have experienced the poor quality of the estimates that we actually did.

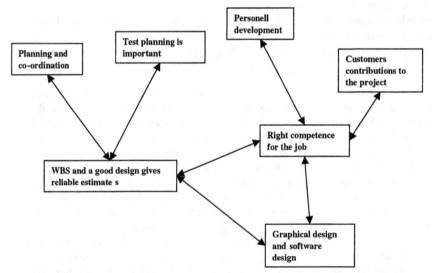

Fig. 3. Post-it notes showing the summary of problems related to estimation

The total effort for each PMA was 45 person hours or approximately one person-week per PMA. This should not frighten anyone if the work results in a substantial improvement in the way the company do their project estimates. The costs were distributed as follows:

- 5 person hours for the researchers' preparation.
- 20 person hours for the interviews – researchers and project personnel.
- 12 person hours for writing the report from the interviews and performing the final KJ – researchers only.

- 8 person hours for commenting and correcting the report – researchers and project personnel.

The following are examples (not a complete list) of the notes taken during two of the PMAs. All items are numbered so that it was possible to cross-reference them and thus to construct cause-and-effect chains.

PMA 1
1. The developers controlled the concept development themselves (because of 2).
2. The ideas for the product were too abstract for the customer (caused 1 and 4).
3. The developers got little feedback from the customers (because of 2).
4. The customers felt that they could change the concept later (caused 3).
5. The customer representatives were few and positive. These were the right people (caused 6 and 7).
6. The customer's participation was controlled by a subsidiary of InfoStream (because of 5).
7. The developers needed few meetings with the customers (because of 5).

PMA 2
15. Too little time was allocated to testing.
16. InfoStream was under heavy pressure from their customer concerning time of delivery (caused 15).
17. The customer was supposed to take full responsibility for the system's test.
18. More errors than expected – confirmed by the test reports.
19. InfoStream has later tried to improve their test planning for this customer (see 17).

Already during the first reading of the PMA reports, the participants were able to identify several improvement possibilities. The following is just a small sample:

- The developers must interact with just a few customer representatives – preferably only one. Otherwise, they will receive a large amount of uncoordinated, often conflicting comments on details in the system under development. To handle this consumes considerable – mostly non-productive – resources.
- Once set, it is next too impossible to change the customer's expectations. Thus, we must be careful when suggesting solutions.
- The graphical designers must co-operate with one or more software developers during the design of all web pages.
- The number of correction / feed back meetings with the customer must be fixed and stated before the estimates are made.

Experience and experiments have shown that most persons have a tendency to be selective in what they remember. The reasons for this are legion and will not be discussed here. An interesting, albeit provocative, discussion on this topic can be found in [8]. In order to have a broader basis for our final conclusion and recommendations, we decided early in the process to collect measurement data for a project that was about to start at that point in time. We ran a GQM (Goal Question Metrics) process [8] in order to develop a measurement plan. Another reason for combining PMA with GQM is that from a data analysis point of view, PMA is mainly a bottom up technique while GQM is a technique that is mainly top-down. Thus, one should expect the two methods to give a more useful and complete picture of the estimation process than either one of them would achieve when applied alone. We discovered later that others have also arrived at this conclusion, albeit via another route – see [10].

5 Discussion

5.1 General PMA Experiences

Our most important experience from doing PMAs is that the participants later told us that it was a highly positive experience. Since the concept of PMA is easy to grasp, everybody could participate. In addition, the developers all felt that they got something back – better insight, ways to improve their job and so on.

It is our experience that PMA is a method that is easy to use. There are no complex routines or tasks that have to be explained in advance, the method relies on the participant's intuitive understanding. A PMA will, however, create a large amount of information. Some of it is important and some is not. The job of separating the two can be both time consuming and challenging.

There are some ground rules that should be applied in order to get a successful PMA:

- The process needs to be structured – it is not a free-for-all happening. On the other hand, too much structuring – for instance extensive use of time boxing – was considered to be negative.
- The PMA will work better with an external facilitator since internal personnel may hesitate to bring up sensitive issues.

Our first question was: Will both PMA approaches work? From what we have seen and done, the answer to this question is definitively "Yes".

5.2 Focused vs. General PMA

Our main question here was: "Are there situations where one of the approaches will work better than the other one?" the answerer to this question is "Yes". Our main experiences are that:

- If we are doing a general, catch-all PMA, people from all parts of the project need to participate. It is for instance not enough to have participants from those who did the coding if someone else did the design.
- If we are doing a focused PMA, the process needs to be steered – sometimes quite strongly – in order not to go astray and wind up as a general PMA or general lamenting over everything that is bad in the company.

Thus, the first decision needed if we want to do a PMA is whether it should be focused or not. Both focused and unfocused PMAs have their strong and weak points that should be considered before we make our choice.

- An unfocused PMA will usually give more surprises since it covers a broader area of experience. Thus, it is always a good idea to do a PMA as a two-stage process – first a general PMA in order to identify all the important issues and then a focused PMA for each issue afterwards.

- A focused PMA is best if we want to understand or improve a single activity. It should be done with just a few participants since the discussion must be steered in order to keep the focus. Few participants will favour structured interviews combined with discussion sessions. A focused PMA will in general require that the facilitator have in-depth knowledge of the field under discussion. This is consistent with the PROFES experience – see [11].

To sum up – both the approaches worked quite well. The approaches were conceptually simple and had a low cost (the participants did for instance not need to prepare themselves) but even so; quite a lot of useful information came out of them. In Spacetec the results from the sessions led to a Contract Change Note to the customer regarding the amount of hours to be used in the project and useful input to the experience database. In InfoStream the results gave important input to a set of checklists that were under development. Thus, at least for SMEs, we do not need the extensive approached used by for instance Microsoft or Apple Computers. The companies involved found it easy to identify improvement opportunities and the participants found the approaches easy to use.

The two approaches differed mainly with respect to the types of information and improvement opportunities identified. We found that semi structured interviews worked well for a focused PMA while the other approach quickly lost focus. The other, open approach – KJ plus RCA – worked well in a catch-all situation and gave more surprises. An optimum solution would be to start out with an open PMA to identify all the issues and then follow up with focused PMAs on the most important ones. This will bring us close to a simplified version of the approach used by Apple Computers.

5.3   Company Benefits

What has been the benefit for the two companies? What have they learned and what will they do different the next time? The feedback after the sessions tells us that the participants felt that they got useful information through the PMA sessions and that they discovered new aspects, or at least was able to express knowledge that earlier had only been tacit.

- *Documenting knowledge* – Documenting a company's knowledge is always a difficult task. By using PMA it became much easier for the companies to document knowledge. The resulting documentation also gave valuable insight into the development process. The knowledge harvested in the process came from several persons in the projects. This made the conclusions more deeply rooted in the organisation than for example an experience report.
- *Source for improvement actions* – The results of the PMA sessions lead to several improvement actions. In Spacetec for example, after discovering in a PMA session that the customer delayed the project, and did not provide test data according to the contract, they sent a Contract Change Note to the customer regarding the amount of hours to be used in the project. Since this method gives fast feedback it is possible to get some "quick wins". You can have a PMA meeting one day and a list of improvement possibilities the following day.

- *A system for harvesting experience* – PMA helped the companies in the process of developing their own system for harvesting experience. Because of the strong involvement from the developers, there was an increasing focus on "learning from experience" in the companies. The motivating factor of the PMA also makes it easier for the companies to implement a system for knowledge management. PMA will be one of the central techniques in such a system.

5.4   Some Final Considerations

We started out by believing that PMAs would work best in a project-oriented organisation without a rigid control structure or an excessive hierarchy. We later learned, however, that the US Army – and maybe other military organisations – uses their own version of the PMA – called After Action Review (AAR) – with great success [12]. These authors have a more narrow definition of a PMA than we do. In their opinion the AAR is not a PMA since it is done on a regular base during the activity's lifetime. Anyhow, the important point is that it seems that the major factor is whether the organisation wants to improve itself by learning from past mistakes, not how it is organised.

For small companies – less than five developers, say – it might be beneficial to let all employees participate actively in the PMA whether they were involved in the project or not. This will make everybody aware of quality problems and the ways to solve them. It will thus strengthen the understanding that quality is everybody's business.

At least two problems are still open:
- The PMA way of learning from experience might not work well when we have several cultures present in the group. A case in point is a PMA where both software developers and graphical designers participate. On the other hand, divergent groups can also be the basis for constructive discussions.
- How can we perform PMAs when the participants are geographically distributed? This can be a problem today and will be even more so as we get more and more distributed or virtual organisations.

6   Lessons Learned

For later PMAs the following points should be taken into consideration:
- *Preparation Work* – If using interviews, it is important to have good knowledge of the project in advance, in order to ask specific and relevant questions. In the KJ phase of the Post Mortem, it is important to be open and leave the word to the participants. Here, being able to moderate discussions is the main virtue.
- *PMA Process* – How the PMA is carried out depends on the number of participants, the complexity of the issues under investigation, and what the focus of the PMA is. Using the KJ method requires at least three participants in order to have enough material to discuss. If the issue under investigation is complex, it might be better to use interviews because it is more difficult to keep people on track using an open process such as the KJ. To get everyone to participate, the KJ method is working very well.

- *Participant Activation* – Some of the developers did not participate much in the RCA phase. It could help people to be more active if one of the participants were moderating this session. Another possibility is to have participants working in groups first, and then present results in a plenary session afterwards.
- *Documentation Techniques* – The techniques we used, KJ and RCA together with detailed minute writing and transcription worked well. The results were easy to understand for people reading the report afterwards, and we got a lot of information in a short time.

Acknowledgement. The authors want to thank the Norwegian research Council that has supported this work through the PROFIT (PROcess Improvement For the IT industry) program and our colleagues at SINTEF and NTNU who, through discussions and comments, have provided many important inputs to this paper.

References

[1] Collier, B. DeMarco, Tom and Fearey, P. A Defined Process For Project Postmortem Review, IEEE Software, July 1996.
[2] Nolan, Andrew J, Learning form Success, IEEE Software, January / February 1999.
[3] Cusumano, Michael A and Selby, Richard W. Microsoft Secrets, The Free Press, 1995, ISBN 0–02–874048–3.
[4] Garvin, David. Building a Learning Organisation, Harvard Business Review, July/ August, 1993
[5] Kolb, David. Management and the learning process, in How Organizations learn (Ed. Starkey, Ken), Thomson Business Press, London, 1996
[6] Straker, David. A Toolbook for Quality Improvement and Problem Solving, Prentice Hall International (UK) Limited, 1995
[7] Scupin, R. (1997) The KJ Method: A Technique for Analyzing Data Derived from Japanese Ethnology, Human Organization, Vol. 56, No. 2, pp. 233–237
[8] Jørgensen, Magne and Sjøberg, Dag. The Importance of NOT Learning from Experience. Proceedings of the EuroSPI 2000 Conference.
[9] van Solingen, Rini, and Berghout, Egon. The Goal/Question/Metric Method, McGraw Hill, 1999. Japanese Ethnology, Human Organization, Vol. 56, No. 2, pp. 233–237
[10] Mendoca, Manoel G. and Basili, Victor, Validation of an Approach for Improving Existing Measurement Frameworks, IEEE Transactions on Software Engineering, vol. 26,no. 6, June 2000.
[11] Oivo, Markku, Andreas Birk, Seija Komi-Sirviö, Pasi Kuvaja and Rini van Solingen: Establishing Product Process Dependencies in SPI, Proceedings of the fourth annual SEPG conference, June 7–10, 1999, Amsterdam, The Netherlands
[12] Baird, L. Holland, P. and Deacon, S. Learning from Action: Imbedding More Learning into the Performance Fast Enough to Make a Difference. Organizational Dynamics, vol. 27, no. 4, 1999.

Evaluating Checklist-Based and Use-Case-Driven Reading Techniques as Applied to Software Analysis and Design UML Artifacts

Giovanni Cantone[1], Luca Colasanti[1], Zeiad A. Abdulnabi[1], Anna Lomartire[2], and Giuseppe Calavaro[3]

[1] Dept. of Informatics, Systems and Production, University of Rome "Tor Vergata"
Via del Politecnico, 1 – I-00133 Rome, Italy
{cantone,zeiad.abdulnabi}@uniroma2.it
luca.colasanti@libero.it
[2] Computing and Documentation Center, University of Rome "Tor Vergata"
Via O. Raimondi, 1 – I-00133 Rome, Italy
annal@ccd.uniroma2.it
[3] Rational Software, via di Torre Spaccata, 172 – I-00169 Rome, Italy
gcalavar@rational.com

Abstract. This chapter discusses the experimental comparison of two reading techniques, comparing their effectiveness and detection rates with respect to inspecting high-level UML diagrams for defects. Artifact-related checklists drive one technique, and application use cases drive the other. Our initial idea was that the latter is more effective than the former. This experiment was developed at the University of Rome "Tor Vergata". It was conducted with junior and senior students of object-oriented analysis and design in the university's Department of Informatics, Systems and Production. The data collected shows that techniques performed differently. Specifically, for effectiveness, CBR in the average performed + 41.6% better than UCDR. CBR detected 15.6% more seeded defects, and +149.3 % more new faults, than UCDR. The latter provided 11.6 % less false positives than CBR. For detection rate, the checklist-based reading technique's peak value occurred 25% later, and was 66.7% greater, than the use-case driven reading's peak value. However, the results were not statistically significant. Because the use-case-driven script turned out to be much more complex than the checklist-driven one, we decided to restructure the former in multiple layers and hence conducted further experiments, the results of which are forthcoming.

1 Introduction

Reading what somebody else has written is part of the everyday job of many people and organizations. There are different types of systematic reading. *Reviews* involve rigorous and punctual reading. *Inspections* are formal, usually professional, reviews.

Reading for software verification [1] has an advantage over program validation by execution-based testing techniques: it applies to software documents of any kind, including analysis and design documents and others that are not machine-

R. Conradi and A.I. Wang (Eds.): ESERNET 2001-2003, LNCS 2765, pp. 142–165, 2003.
© Springer-Verlag Berlin Heidelberg 2003

interpretable, and can be undertaken as soon as these documents have been written, or even while they are being written. Many readers can search for defects in a given document at the same time.

The obvious issues here are how effective and efficient software reading is, and what the costs and risks are for a software company to introduce reading into its software processes. Providing practical solutions related to these issues is the aim of the empirical investigation of software reading. Such investigation includes evaluating the impact of different reading techniques on the quality of software products and processes—for example, evaluating the defect detection rate and effectiveness of the techniques.

This chapter discusses an experimental study of the performance of two techniques for reading high-level software artifacts. Specifically, the two techniques are checklist-based reading and a new use-case-driven reading technique, and the objects of the experiment are made up of software analysis and design Unified Modeling Language (UML) artifacts [2]. The subjects are junior and senior students of object-oriented analysis and design (OOAD) [3] in the Department of Informatics, Systems and Production at the University of Rome "Tor Vergata" (URM2-DISP), and the experiment was conducted using URM2-DISP labs and computing resources.

Before discussing the problem under study in detail, we will give a summary of what happened in the study and why, and briefly discuss the relationship between the experimental hypotheses and the design of the experiment.

Some Rational Software employees, who were formerly students at URM2-DISP, had been voluntarily collaborating with URM2-DISP to offer students parts of OOAD courses, and had been doing UML-related empirical research within the URM2-DISP Experimental Software Engineering Research Group (URM2-DISP-ESEG). Out of this the idea arose of developing a new software reading technique that would meet the following requirements:

1. To perform similarly as, and hopefully better than, other known reading techniques.
2. To be more integrated with the Rational philosophy than other known reading techniques.
3. To improve the process of training domain-expert people who are expert at obsolete development technologies but barely acquainted with OOAD and UML concepts.

The 3rd requirement came out discussing on the difficulties of finding skilled people and the difficulties for domain-expert people, who are expert at obsolete development technologies but barely acquainted with OOAD and UML concepts, to learn UML and OOAD. The idea was that inspections were going to be not only a technique to find defects but also a way to learn OOAD. The inspectors, in fact, where going to look to analysis and design artifacts and learn the characteristics of good and bad work.

A *use-case-driven reading* (UCDR) technique was hence established, and an experiment was launched to compare this new technique with a *checklist-based reading* (CBR) technique. In our view of UML and Rational Unified Process (RUP) [4], Use-cases are more expressive than artifacts that come before in the software process, e.g. formal requirements and key artifacts. Moreover, for artifacts that came later, e.g. View of Participating Classes of use-case realizations and Sequence Diagram scenarios, Use-cases are sufficiently expressive when using the advantage of early verification of software documents. Based on such reasoning, in order to define a UML oriented reading technique, we preferred to deal with Use-cases rather than other UML artifacts.

The expectations for UCDR were to get acceptable results in terms of performance (requirement 1 above) and very positive results in terms of training on the job (requirement 3). (UCDR was to be based on Use-cases, UML and RUP, so requirement 2 would certainly be met.)

Due to the practical and complex nature of these expectations, they had a great impact on the definition and planning of the experiment, as evidenced by the following:

- Realistic rather than "toy" UML artifacts were developed or reworked for use as objects of the experiment.
- Toward the goal of meeting requirement 2, many releases were provided for the experiment object artifacts, in accordance with the Rational Unified Process.
- Related to requirement 3, pre- and post-experiment questionnaires were developed.
- The experiment was technology-based: Rational suites were temporary installed to provide object access; a database was implemented for storing experiment data; PCs from an academic lab were set up with a common hardware and software configuration; and a Web site was eventually set up to provide access from the lab clients and to distribute the remaining experiment documents, including forms, guidelines, training, and, last but not least, the CBR and UCDR procedures.
- Subjects were classified by experience and, because they were students, their locations in the lab were closely studied to prevent exchanges of information between subjects with the same assigned task.

This chapter focuses on the performance of reading UML artifacts (requirement 1). The analysis of results related to requirement 3 (learning by inspections) is forthcoming.

The aims of the experiment can be expressed as in the following:

- To provide empirical evidence of the research hypotheses before moving the experiment to professional environments.
- To test and tune with students an experiment process whose final target is professionals.
- To provide companies and their domain experts with compelling research data, to persuade the former that running an experiment within their organizations will enable them to improve the quality of their products, and to convince the latter that the task of learning professional and evolutionary new analysis and design paradigms, languages, and tools is more feasible than they may have imagined.

A rather strategic implication that could follow from this experiment was that the empirical evidence could support emphasis by Rational Software on the role of inspections in RUP (requirement 2).

In GQM (Goal-Question-Metrics) terms, the goal of our study can be expressed as follows: to analyze a new use-case-driven reading (UCDR) technique and a checklist-based reading (CBR) technique, comparing their effectiveness and defect detection rates with respect to inspecting high-level UML diagrams for defects, in the context of a technology-based academic software lab and with advanced students, from the point of view of a research group aiming to transfer the resulting experiment process and guidelines to industrial settings in the mid-term.

Based on the experiment goal, the research hypotheses of the basic experiment are concerned with whether the Effectiveness and Mean Defect Detection Rate (MDDR) of the reading techniques differ significantly when applied by moderately expert software practitioners to analysis and design UML artifacts, where:

Effectiveness—the number of new positive or seeded defects found, rated to the total number of known defects.

Defect detection rate (Mean) —the number of positive defects found, rated to the total duration time available for the experiment run.

The formal hypotheses of the experiment are:

$H_{0 \text{ (Effectiveness)}}$:	There is no significant difference between CBR and UCDR, for what concerns the effectiveness.
$H_{1 \text{ (Effectiveness)}}$:	There is a significant difference between CBR and UCDR, for what concerns the effectiveness.
$H_{0 \text{ (Defect Detection Rate)}}$:	There is no significant difference between CBR and UCDR, for what concerns the defect detection rate.
$H_{1 \text{ (Defect Detection Rate)}}$:	There is a significant difference between CBR and UCDR, for what concerns the defect detection rate.

In summary, according to these hypotheses, in our experiments, we can identify reading technique as the experiment factor, CBR and UCDR as the treatments, effectiveness and MDDR as the dependent variable that are correlated to the factor. In order to investigate the impact of the treatments on the dependent variable, our experiment controls remaining independent variables at fixed values, including the experience of subjects.

2 Starting Scenario

Many techniques for reading high-level software artifacts have been experimentally studied to date. In February 1995, Oliver Laitenberger of the University of Kaiserslautern, Department of Informatik (UKl-DI), concluded his stage at the University of Maryland, Department of Computer Science (UMDCS), and the Software Engineering Laboratory (SEL) by presenting his study [1] of a new technique, called *perspective-based reading* (PBR), which requires reading a document from the different points of view of the various document stakeholders. The Laitenberger study included results from controlled experiments. Based on empirical evidence, the new technique performed significantly better than those that the participating professional subjects had been using at NASA and Computer Science Corporation. The results were validated, synthesized, and formalized by an extension of the UMDCS Experimental Software Engineering research group, including Laitenberger [5].

Following these pioneering studies, additional research was done to further validate the first empirical results and improve the PBR technique. At Kaiserslautern [6], UKl-DI and Fraunhofer IESE, PBR was experimented and eventually installed (with either minor or major changes) in some German industrial settings, including Daimler-Chrysler and Bosh [7]. Also, in College Park, UMDCS, a replication package was developed and published on the Web [8]. Later, many members of the International Software Engineering Research Network (ISERN) conducted PBR research at their labs [9]. More recently, PBR was investigated with respect to new reusable software artifacts [10], software requirements [11], other high-level software artifacts, and related new methods and technologies [12, 13]. Nowadays, as this book proves, many members of the Empirical Software Engineering Research Network (ESERNET) are conducting European Community funded PBR research.

The experimental study of reading software analysis and design UML artifacts at URM2-DISP included one basic experiment, BE, and two replications, R1 and R2 [14]. This chapter focuses on results from the basic experiment, about which the following can be stated compared to related work:

- The subjects were students only.
- The experiment took place at the very end of the OOAD course, which is when students are graded, so we had to be wary of potential cheating.
- The experiment was not homework; participants were co-located in the same academic lab, and the experiment was run on the laboratory's local network.
- The experiment and training objects were made up of analysis and design UML artifacts, from applications we had previously developed and maintained.

Specifically, the basic experiment took place at the URM2-DISP Laboratory of Informatics, where an Experimental Software Engineering Group has been active for a couple of decades in both research and teaching. External people, including people from Rational Software, are members of URM2-DISP-ESEG, and others participate occasionally. (Details about members and activities of URM2-DISP-ESEG can be found at http://ese.uniroma2.it.)

Regarding related projects:

- The experiment was part of the "Experimental Informatics" project, partially supported by our Ministero dell'Istruzione, dell'Università e della Ricerca Scientifica (MIUR), Grant 020906003 URM2-DISP.
- The experiment aimed to produce results for the EC-funded Empirical Software Engineering Research Network (ESERNET).
- The experimental activities were continually supported by the URM2 project "Cooperation among the ESE groups of URM2-DISP, UMDCS, UKl-DI," Grants 010209013-2001, 010209015-2003 URM2-DISP.
- The experiment aimed to produce results that the Rome branch of Rational Software could potentially show to its customers.

3 Method

To enable interested readers to replicate the experiment, this Section describes in some detail how we conducted the study, the involved roles and people, and the enacted process.

Concerning the roles involved. Right after the initial, broad definition of the research goals, the roles for a research team were defined to be:

- An expert in empirical/experimental software engineering (ESE).
- A beginner software engineer.
- An expert in statistical methods and tools.
- An expert in the UML and Rational Software technologies.
- A system and database administrator and security manager.

Concerning the people involved. Subsequently, the following individuals, who also authored the present Chapter, filled those roles (in the same order as listed above):

- A professor of ESE at URM2-DISP.
- A Diploma Engineer student in Informatics, preparing his final dissertation.[1]
- A PhD student with a Bachelor in Statistical Science.
- A PhD technical group leader at Rational Software
- A Diplomat in Computer Science, actually serving as employee at the URM2 Computing and Documentation Center.
- A Bachelor Engineer student in Informatics, preparing her final project, performed in the additional role of Software engineer Assistant.

Concerning the process enacted. In the role of team leader, the ESE professor arranged a kickoff meeting with the other members of the team. All the students were with URM2-DISP and took classes conducted by the ESE faculty. During the kickoff meeting, after a brief introduction to the experiment, the experiment goals were discussed by the participants and expanded on by the technical expert from Rational. It was proposed that the Diploma student be responsible for the technical support and implementation aspects of the study. Because timing was important to him, in that he intended to get his grade in less than one year, the experiment process was examined and a worst-case analysis (based on the available staff and experience) was conducted for time-to-delivery and risk. Once the team decided on an iterative model for the experiment process, the student agreed to be part of the team. In particular, he negotiated six months full-time collaboration, plus two months for packaging the results from his point of view. He assumed responsibility for technical support and developing the first iteration of the experiment process—that is, delivering the infrastructure necessary to conduct a basic experiment—and possibly the second iteration—that is, collaborating on developing an academic replication.

After the experiment was defined, the planning of the experiment began. An early decision was made to place all the experiment documents and objects on the Internet, and all the collected data in a database. The Diploma student was given the responsibility of developing the experiment electronic material, with minor assistance from the Bachelor student. The Diplomat in Computer Science member of the team assumed the responsibility for electronic intra- and inter-networking, including security.

The objects for the experiment and training were selected. In addition, categories of defects were defined, based on the technical literature [15, 16] and previous works [17, 18]. Eventually, the number of defects to seed for each type and severity level was determined. After the defect seeding was planned, submission forms were designed. Web pages were created in accordance with these forms and placed on the

---

[1] The word Diploma comes from Diploma of Laurea in Engineering and is herein used to denote a 5 years degree in Engineering (7 full-time years, in the average), as provided for centuries by many European Countries, including France, Germany, Italy and Spain. This degree follows an analytical approach and is oriented to both provide fundamentals of engineering, and hence specialized knowledge in some specific field of engineering; it should not be confused both with the 3 years Bachelor Engineer degree, and the post-bachelor 2 years Specialized Engineer degree, which follow quite different approaches.

experiment Web site. Some information, such as subject ID or defect detection timestamp, was designed to be automatically collected. A repository to store defect submissions was created.

Checklists were written (one for each artifact) and validated. The procedures to be enacted by CBR and UCDR subjects were then designed. The UCDR procedure was refined and pseudo-coded. Web pages containing procedures and checklists were added to the experiment firewall- and password-protected Web site. A set of rules was defined to be followed by subjects performing inspections, including the sequence in which object artifacts were to be inspected (version 1 first, then 2 and 3). The Web site was enhanced to provide complete guidelines for subjects, from initial authentication up to defect submission through Web forms. Experiment documents and objects were made available via the network. The Web server performance was tested by a standard package.

The lab was equipped with a dedicated server and a certain number of clients connected to the local network. A couple of weeks before the experiment started, the lab clients were placed under a common hardware and software configuration. Again, this Web server performance was tested by a standard package first, and later through practical use during training sessions.

The training material, originally developed on an Internet-connected server, was also placed on the lab server and was adapted to the new environment. Based on the number of registered subjects and the available resources, subjects were divided into groups and trained.

Two days before the start of the experiment, the lab was closed to students and the experiment material was installed. Access rights to CBR and UCDR materials were installed on alternating workstations, so that no subject could sit next to a subject having the same task assigned. Training material was left on the development server, for access through the Internet.

The experiment was conducted in the lab, lasted one full day, and was split into three consecutive runs. For each run, after an introductory refresh and a questionnaire fill out, the experiment was started, and subjects logged in and accessed their guidelines. The guidelines directed them to carry out their work, which lasted three consecutive hours. When a subject detected a defect, guidelines directed him or her to access and fill out the proper form.

Concerning the language used. Our community is still missing a unified ESE language. However, in order to model our activities and products we used the language implicitly defined by Wohlin e al. [19] (see also Chapter 2 of this book.)

3.1   Design

As noted earlier, the research hypotheses of the basic experiment are concerned with whether the effectiveness and defect detection rates of the reading techniques differ significantly when applied by moderately expert software practitioners to analysis and design UML artifacts. According to the experiment hypotheses, we can identify reading technique as the experiment factor, UCDR and CBR as the treatments, and defect detection rate and effectiveness as dependent variables that are correlated to the factor; in addition, there are independent variables that we controlled at fixed values; furthermore, we should raison about the type of design to adopt. We will now look at each of these identified areas in more detail.

Concerning the factor. A reading technique is step-by-step procedure that guides individual inspectors in uncovering defects in a software artifact. Such a technique is required to provide a systematic and well-defined way of inspecting a document, allowing for feedback and improvement.

Concerning treatments. CBR has been a commonly used technique in inspections since the 1970s. Checklists are based on a set of specific questions that are intended to guide the inspector during inspection. Because the expected answer for each question is of a binary type, {Yes == Checked, Not == Unchecked}, Boolean assertions can replace questions in a checklist. A survey on software inspection [20] presented these weak points of CBR:

- CBR questions are often general and not sufficiently tailored to a particular development environment.
- Concrete instructions on how to use the checklist are often missing—that is, it is often unclear when and based on what information an inspector is to answer a particular checklist question.
- The questions on the checklist are often limited to detection of defects that belong to particular categories (inspectors may hence not focus on previously undetected defect types, and therefore may miss whole classes of defects).

UCDR is a brand new reading technique developed by URM2-DISP-ESEG. The experiment treatments related to UCDR can be synthesized as follows:

- Our checklists for UML object inspections specify what to look for; hence, they are artifact-type-specific. We have four checklists, one for each type of object artifact (Vision Document, Use Case Diagram, View of Participating Classes, and Sequence Diagrams). Each checklist contains from 4 to 12 assertions, which is in line with the recommendation of Gilb and Graham [21] that a checklist should not be longer than a page (approximately 25 items). Our checklists are based on the structure presented by Chernak [22] and take into consideration the weak points of CBR (as mentioned above and discussed in the survey [20]).
- The core philosophy of UCDR is to specify not only what to look for but also how to proceed to find it. The basic idea is to let use cases guide the reading process through the entire document set, from the informal specifications down to use-case realizations and sequence diagrams. The procedure leads the reader to probe deep into the entire set of artifacts, following the software development process steps that produced them. The development process used is RUP, which is heavily use-case-dependent. Starting with the informal specifications, each object artifact is inspected in a fixed sequence according to some artifact-dependent guideline. The final UCDR procedure provided the basic experiment reader with a step-by-step to-do list.

Concerning further independent variables. These are the independent variables, which are controlled at fixed values:

- The subjects' level of knowledge and experience with OOAD concepts, the UML, and Rational Software technology,
- Team size.
- Duration of the experiment runs
- Quality and complexity of guidelines and other material supporting the experiment.
- Reading and form submission technology, including tools and instruments used, screen type and size, and network performance.

- Interaction among subjects and between subjects and observers.
- Other environmental characteristics.

In particular:
- The levels of knowledge and experience of subjects with respect to OOAD and UML concepts and Rational Software technology is fixed at "advanced-not-professional"; Section 3.2 explains how this level was established.
- The subjects will be given the same training. However, although this fixes the training at a common level, it also exposes a threat to validity: because the complexity of the UCDR procedure is greater than that of the sister CBR procedure, the former requires more training. (In fact, applying CBR is an obvious task; the CBR procedure has been formalized only because we have to write a UCDR procedure.)
- The team size is fixed at one person.
- The duration of the experiment runs is fixed at 180 minutes.
- Participants of either CBR or UCDR will use different but similar guidelines, participants assigned to the same technique will use the same guidelines and other supporting materials; all the participants will use the same reading and submission technology, tools and instruments, and network, so the quality, complexity, and performance of these types of support are fixed at a common value.
- The screen type and size is requested to be the same for all participants, as are other environmental characteristics (except time of the day). Interactions will be not allowed among subjects and between subjects and observers.

Since all these variables are independent for each student in the experiment, no further strategy needs to be applied to allocate the subjects into groups.

Table 1 summarizes components of the basic experiment execution, showing the fixed values for both reading techniques.

Table 1. Components of the basic experiment execution

Description	UCDR	CBR
Number of subjects	22	22
Team size	1	1
Experiment-run duration (in minutes)	180	180
Number of experiment objects	1	1
Number of types of UML artifacts per object	7	7
Number of defects seeded	30	30
Number of incremental versions of the UML artifacts	3	3
Number of defects per incremental version of the UML artifacts	10	10

Concerning the type of design. Based on the shown factor and treatments, our experiment design can be a simple type of design having one factor with two treatments. Moreover, the study is designated to be an offline controlled-experiment—specifically, to be conducted under controlled conditions at a university laboratory.

3.2 Subjects/Participants

As already mentioned, the experiment design indicates to select subjects according to convenience sampling technique, and to assign them randomly to treatments in a balanced way. Meanwhile, we invited our students to participate in the experiment during their attendance of the year 2002 OOAD course at URM2-DISP. A few of these students were also taking the Experimental Informatics course (that is, Experimental Software Engineering) in the same department.

In the URM2 present academic organization, OOAD is an intensive course, lasting eight weeks, with three lectures per week, two hours per lecture, plus laboratory and project development. It is directed at graduate students with a Bachelor in Informatic Engineering. Due to the transition from the old to the new academic organization, two additional types of Informatic Engineering students were authorized to attend the OOAD course in 2002: Diploma students at the end of their fifth and last year of study (that is, moderately late students of the old academic organization), and Bachelor students at the end of their third and last year of study. Because the latter students were, in fact, migrating from their previous Diploma course of studies, where they were late, the subjects were around 24 years old. Moreover, all of them had already taken exams in Software Engineering, Operating Systems, and Database. Although Bachelor students were classified as junior and the others as senior, this dimension was not further considered up to now.

By design, the participants are not paid, but they are graded: participation in the experiment would give students the opportunity to improve their exam score by up to 2 points. (Successful scores at URM2 are in the range of 18 to 30 points.) This improvement depends on their performance in detecting actual faults with respect their false positive detections.

Based on design, for all subjects, the training occurs in both class and lab as well as on the Internet. Training can be itemized as in the followings:

- 50 hours of lectures on UML analysis and design.
- 50 hours of lab work for self-practice on the Rational Software suite.
- 10 hours of lab question sessions concerning the use of the Rational Software suite (with each such session lasting 3 hours on average). According to the design, question sessions intertwine with the practical sections listed above.
- Half a day of training on experiment forms, guidelines, data submission through the local network or Internet, and experiment-like objects (restricted to experiment-participating students only).
- 1 week for self-practice with experiment documents in the lab or through the Internet, with 2 additional days for self-practice through the Internet.
- Half an hour training refresh just before the start of an experiment run.

Based on the maximum number of expected subjects (48) and the number of available lab clients (16), lab training groups are arranged for convenience sampling and guided to apply either both techniques, half a day per group, starting from 2 P.M.

Because the experiment is planned to take place during the very end of the OOAD course, subjects would still be expected to expound on the UML and discuss their OOAD project at the final exam within three weeks or more. As a return for subjects, participation in the restricted part of the training would give students an opportunity to improve their knowledge of UML and OOAD concepts; furthermore, participation in the experiment would enable them to test their level of this knowledge before the exam session.

3.3   Apparatus/Materials

Here we will look in more detail at some points made earlier about the objects and seeded faults, infrastructure, and guidelines related to the experiment. Additional information can be found on the URM2-DISP-ESEG Web site, http://eseg.uniroma2.it.

Concerning objects. The objects for the experiment and training are selected from among previously developed applications and are made up of analysis and design UML artifacts. The experiment object is part of an application we had previously developed and maintained for managing employee payroll and vacations in a distributed organization. Table 2 characterizes the original application versus the extended part of it that constituted the experiment object.

Both the basic experiment object and the training object are realistic data management software systems, neither "toy" nor true professional applications.

Defects are categorized in the following specific ways:

- {Omission, Inconsistency, Ambiguity, Incorrectness, Syntax}
- {Severity Class: A, B, and C}.

Based on the experiment design, objects are seeded both with previously detected and already removed defects and with new faults. We seeded CBR and UCDR objects with 30 defects, 10 per each object version.

Concerning infrastructure. The experiment was designed to meet the following requirements as well:

- To be conducted at an academic lab.
- To last one day.
- To run on the Internet. This means that objects, data collection forms, experiment data, procedures, and all other documents were organized to take place on a Web site.
- To be supported by actual, up-to-date Internet and Rational Software information and communication technologies.
- To be based on the assignment of similar workstations to all participants; specifically, the workstations were required to have the same size and the same type of machine, keyboard, and screen (color, 15-inch). Eventually, 16 workstations were designated for set up with the same type and version of OS (Windows NT), Web browser (Internet Explorer 5), and Rational suite (2002.05).

Based on the maximum number of expected subjects, the number of available lab clients, the designed team size (1 subject per team), and the duration in days (1), the experiment is set up to occur in three consecutive runs at the very end of June 2002. Each run is designed to last 180 minutes, plus 15 minutes for filling out pre-experiment questionnaires and another 15 minutes for filling out post-experiment questionnaires.

Concerning guidelines. Beside the training object, detailed guidelines were made available to subjects on the Internet weeks before the experiment date. Guidelines for applying UCDR techniques were written in the form of a pseudo-code. For the basic experiment, they consist of a flat main procedure whose high-level actions are described in natural language, in the imperative form of the Italian language. For reasons of equity, the decision was made of representing the CBR guidelines in a similar form.

Table 2. The original application vs. the experiment object (extended part)

Artifact	Original Application	Extended Part (Object): Additional, {Impacted}, and [Extended] Artifacts		
		Ver. 1	Ver. 2	Ver. 3
Informal specification (number of pages/words)	3/687	1/374		
Features (number of)	15	23	2	
Non-functional requirements (number of)	8			
Constraints (number of)	2	3		
New, {impacted}, [extended] use cases (number of)	6	{3}	{3} [1]	{4} [1]
Actors + specializations (number of)	5 (+3)	1	1	1
Use-case realization 1				
• View of participating classes, VOPC (number of classes)	7			
• Sequence diagrams (no. of)	2			
Use-case realization 2				
• VOPC	7	{7}	{7}	{8}
• Sequence diagrams	3	{3}	{3}	{3}
Use-case realization 3				
• VOPC	8			
• Sequence diagrams	1			
Use-case realization 4				
• VOPC	6			
• Sequence diagrams	3			
Use-case realization 5				
• VOPC	10	{10}	{10}	{10}
• Sequence diagrams	6	{6}	{6}	{6}
Use-case realization 6				
• VOPC	5			
• Sequence diagrams	4			
Use-case realization 7				
• VOPC	N/A	8	{8}	{8}
• Sequence diagrams	N/A	4	{4}	{4}
❖ Use-case extension 7.E1				
• VOPC	N/A	N/A	{4}	{4}
• Sequence diagrams	N/A	N/A	{1}	{1}
Use-case realization 8	N/A	N/A	N/A	
• VOPC	N/A	N/A	N/A	5
• Sequence diagrams	N/A	N/A	N/A	1

Table 3 reports on the cyclomatic complexity and size (number of lines) of UCDR and CDR procedures.

Table 3. Cyclomatic and dimensional complexities of UCDR vs. CBR guidelines

Reading Technique	Cyclomatic Complexity	Size (LOC)
UCDR Just 1 procedure	33	172
CDR (Total I Average) 1 procedure and 1 checklist per type of artifact:	20 I 5	147 I 37
• Use-case diagrams	11	68
• Features	2	15
• Sequence diagrams	3	20
• VOPC	4	44

According to Table 3, the UCDR pseudo-code is much more complex than the CBR pseudo-code. To deal with the problem posed by such a different complexity, the experiment was later conducted using a different organization for the UCDR guidelines, to be described in a forthcoming paper. Specifically, the new UCDR guidelines were structured in a main procedure with a set of nested procedures. We also planned to give more training time to subjects of forthcoming replications of the experiment.

3.4 Procedure

A total of 44 students registered for the basic experiment. Two other students were expected, but they arrived late. They participated but their data was discarded.

According to the experiment design, the procedure began with the training of the subjects who were to participate in the experiment, and each one was uniquely identified by a code. Subjects were assigned at random to techniques and runs, 22 to CBR and 22 to UCDR. They were informed in advance by e-mail about the timing of their run (but not about which technique had been assigned to them).

Based on the technique assigned, a mapping from subjects to particular runs and workstations was established, some by convenience (for example, seats on the aisle were assigned to people with physical disabilities) and the remaining at random. No further counterbalancing or other design control features were applied.

According to design, the experiment occurred in one day, in three consecutive runs, each lasting 180 minutes plus 30 minutes of introductory training refresh, 15 minutes for filling out pre-experiment questionnaires, and an additional 15 minutes for filling out post-experiment questionnaires.

On the experiment day, right before the start of a new run, a list of the involved subject names, codes, and assigned techniques was printed and placed on the lab door. The participating individuals were called by name, told their code, workstation, and technique, and seated. They were told that the session was expected to last up to four hours, that breaks were not allowed, and that interactions of any kind among subjects or with observers were also not permitted.

Not only were the subjects told not to take breaks or interact with each other, but also the use of paper in support of the experiment was also discouraged [23], and eventually was tolerated only for writing brief notes. To prevent interactions among subjects allocated to different runs, subjects of one run entered the lab while the subjects of the previous run were in another room filling out post-experiment questionnaires; for other subjects (neither those just finished with a run nor those about to start one), access to the overall experiment area was forbidden.

These rules were enforced by the continual presence in the lab of at least two observers per run. In total, four different people played the role of observer.

After the introductory refresh and filling out of the pre-experiment questionnaire, the reading experiment was started. Subjects were authorized to access, through the web server, a common UML object, including all the artifacts and versions described in Table 2. Subjects had to start with version 1, and were not allowed to inspect the same artifact in more than one version at a time. One-way access to versions was reinforced by the underlying software support: in other words, rolling back to already answered questions was made impossible, in order to prevent cheating consequential to learning effect.

For the purpose of defect submission, subjects logged in to Rational ClearQuest Web by using their code. Based on this code, ClearQuest identified the assigned reading technique and hence the related defect forms. Subsequently, each subject entered the Web site and displayed the guidelines' procedure script related to the assigned technique. This procedure directed the subject step-by-step to access and search for defects in the experiment object and artifacts, in order starting from version 1.

Having detected a defect, the subject identified it uniquely and submitted related data through ClearQuest.

- For CBR (a checklist assertion failed), the CBR procedure directed the subject to open the associated form and provide the artifact name, its version number, and the incorrect item.
- For UCDR (a step of the UCDR procedure failed), the UCDR procedure directed the subject to open the associated form and provide the current step number and additional step-related data.

Interested readers can find further information, including detailed participant instructions, guidelines, and additional assignment descriptions, on the Web site at http://eseg.uniroma2.it/experiments.

4 Results

For each defect submitted during the basic experiment, the following data was collected:
- Subject ID
- Timestamp
- Reading technique
- UML object artifact
- UCDR procedure step or CBR artifact-related checklist assertion that failed
- Number of artifact's item where failure occurred.

Experiment data was stored in a database at experiment time and processed offline by using first Microsoft Excel 2000 and then some statistical packages.

The rest of this section presents some of the available data for effectiveness and defect detection rate, reports descriptive statistics and inferential statistics, including the value of the test and the probability level, and briefly address questions about the appropriateness of the applied tests.

Concerning Effectiveness. Fig. 1 shows the submissions per subject versus the reading techniques, and the positive detections for both seeded and newly found defects.

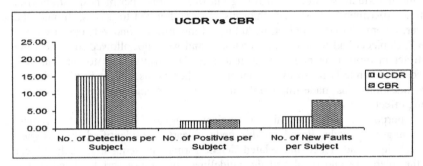

Fig. 1. Summary of results for effectiveness

Pie charts in Fig. 2 extract false positives from the data in Fig. 1 and present an additional view of the same results.

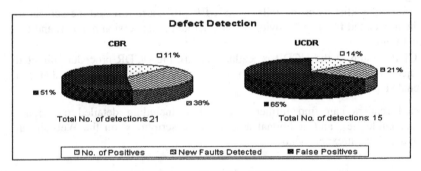

Fig. 2. Comparison between UCDR and CBR for effectiveness

Box-and-whisker plot can be useful for handling and presenting our data values. Box-and-whisker plots allow people to explore data and to draw informal conclusions when two or more variables are present. It shows only certain statistics rather than all the data. These statistics consists of the median, the quartiles, and the smallest and greatest values in the distribution. Immediate visuals of a box-and-whisker plot are the center, the spread, and the overall range of distribution. Fig. 3 represents positively detected defects for both treatments; it shows the Box-and-Whisker plot for means of effectiveness.

We will now consider the final results of the normality testing of the data shown above (see Appendix for further details).

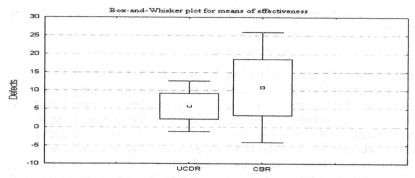

Fig. 3. Box-and-whisker plot for means of effectiveness (positive detections of seeded and new faults)

According to the p-values shown in Table 4, we cannot accept the results of the parametric tests. In fact, the p-value for UCDR effectiveness is greater than 0.05.

Table 4. Test of normality for effectiveness

p-value	W	Shapiro-Wilk
0.0007	0.81047	CBR_Effectiveness
0.0543	0.86136	UCDR_Effectiveness

Because p-value for UCDR effectiveness is insufficient for applying a parametric test, we will have to apply a non-parametric test. Table 5 shows the results of the Mann-Whitney non-parametric test for effectiveness.

Table 5. Test of significance for effectiveness

p-value	Test Type	Test Name
0.0060	Non-parametric	Mann-Whitney

Concerning Defect Detection Rate. In Section 1, we defined the *mean defect detection rate*, MDDR, as the number of positive defects found, rated to the total duration time available for the experiment run—that is:

$$MDDR = D(t_f - t_0) / (t_f - t_0)$$

where D is the total number of positive defects found at the final time t_f, and t_0 is the starting time of the experiment run (thus $t_f - t_0$ is the time elapsed from the beginning of the experiment run). We can hence define the *detection profile,* DP, as the following incremental rate:

$$DP(t) = \Delta D(t) / \Delta t$$

Moreover, we can define the defect *detection distribution,* DD, as the following differential rate:

$$DD(t) = dD(t) / dt$$

where time is theoretically unlimited for both DP(t) and DD(t).

To investigate time needed to detect and submit new defects, efficiency rather than detection rate and distribution could have been used, where efficiency could be measured as the average time between defects detected for each treatment group. Although efficiency and detection rate seem to be the inverse function of each other, efficiency is more appropriate to use with open-ended time, or if much more time is allowed than is needed. Because our subjects had only a limited time (180 minutes) and could not get through the entire review, we are really studying only a subset of the natural defect detection activity, and we are evaluating average time to find defects for an arbitrarily truncated set of defects. In conclusion, while some similarities can be found between the concepts of efficiency and detection rate, we prefer to use the latter, to prevent raising the issue of whether it is realistic to use measures on detection profiles for measuring efficiency.

During our experiment runs, time data was collected directly by the supporting system, which also computed the time-distance between two consecutive submissions. Fig. 4 summarizes the timing of the defect reports by plotting the detection profile, DP(t), for both CBR and UCDR with $\Delta t = 20$ minutes and $t_f - t_0 = 180$ minutes.

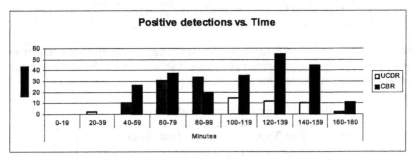

Fig. 4. Summary of results for defect detection rate

According to Fig. 4, UCDR looks like a bell shape; its peak value occurs when the first half (90 minutes) of the investigation time has passed. In contrast, CBR shows two slopes and includes two peaks, which occur when the first third (60 minutes) and second third (120 minutes) of the investigation time have passed, respectively; moreover, the latter CBR peak value is higher than the first one (+48.6%), and much higher than the UCDR peak (+66.7%).

Fig. 5 shows the Box-and-whisker plot for means of defect detection rate for both UCDR and CBR.

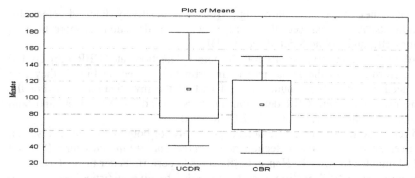

Fig. 5. Box-and-whisker plot for means of defect detection rate

Now we will consider the final results of normality testing of the data above for defect detection rate; see Table 6.

According to the indicated p-values, the test gave us a strongly positive value for applying a parametric test. In fact, both p-values for UCDR defect detection rate are much less than 0.05.

Table 6. Test of normality for defect detection rate

p-value	W	Shapiro-Wilk
0.0066	0.96761	CBR_ Detection Rate
0	0.94145	UCDR_ Detection Rate

Finally, Table 7 shows the results from the parametric t-test for the defect detection rate. Note that the p-value is significantly less than 0.05 at 95% confidence level.

Table 7. Test of significance for defect detection rate, 95% confidence level

p-value	Test Type	Test Name
0.000002	Parametric	t-test

5   Discussion

In this Section, we evaluate the results presented in Section 4 and discuss their implications, especially with respect to the original hypotheses. We also reconsider the threats to validity.

Concerning descriptive results. CBR seems to perform better than UCDR with respect both to effectiveness and defect detection rate. Specifically, for effectiveness, based on Fig. 1, CBR in the average performed + 41.6% better than UCDR. CBR detected 15.6% more seeded defects, and +149.3 % more new faults, than UCDR. We also noticed that UCDR provided 11.6 % less false positives than CBR subjects. The pie charts in Fig. 2 confirm these descriptive results.

As already mentioned, the data in Fig. 3 relates to positively detected defects for both treatments. As we can see, the average number of detections is more than 10 defects for CBR, and around 5 defects for UCDR.

Regarding the descriptive results for the defect detection rate, CBR subjects fall short in performance in the initial part of investigation, based on Fig. 4; they also seem to need a break after around the first half of the investigation time. For the remaining part of the run, CBR detection numbers exceed UCDR values, and both CBR peaks are equal or greater than the UCDR peak.

Fig. 5 relates to rates in detecting defects positively for both treatments. As we can see, the average of this defect detection rate is more than 90 minutes for CBR, and around 110 minutes for UCDR. Hence, CBR seems to perform better than UCDR.

Concerning statistical testing results. In order to give statistical evidence to descriptions above, we need to discuss statistical testing results.

Regarding effectiveness, Table 5 shows that the p-value of our statistical testing is much less than 0.05 at the 95% confidence level. At this level of confidence, the following can be stated regarding effectiveness:

The results provide statistical evidence that there is a significant difference between the two treatments with respect to effectiveness. In particular, the p-value proves that CBR performs better than UCDR in terms of effectiveness.

Regarding the defect detection rate, Table 7 shows the results of the parametric t-test we applied. The p-value is much less than 0.05 at the 95% confidence level. Consequently, the following can be stated regarding the defect detection rate:

The results provide statistical evidence that there is a significant difference between the two treatments with respect to defect detection rate. In particular, the p-value proves that CBR performs better than UCDR in terms of defect detection rate.

The conclusion from the above results of the basic experiment seems to be that there is no hope for UCDR to perform equivalently (or better) compared to CBR, in terms of both effectiveness and defect detection rate. However, we are not fully convinced by these experiment results because of threats to validity. In the following, we will briefly consider the aspects of the study related to validity evaluation and assessment, and hence whether the study can justify the drawn conclusions.

Concerning the construct validity. Conclusion validity is the degree to which conclusions can be drawn about the existence of a statistical relationship between treatments and outcomes. Due to participation on voluntary basis, and because of our small population size, it was not possible for us to plan the selection of a population sample by using one of the common sampling techniques, so we decided to take the whole population of the year-2002 OOAD course as our sample. A limited number of data values were collected during the operation of the experiments, due to the limited duration time and number of objects and subjects. For what concerns the quality of data collecting, conclusion validity is not considered to be critical, because data collection was screen-driven using Rational ClearQuest Web, form fields were checked at run time, and some data (for example, timestamps) were automatically acquired by the system. Finally, the quantity and quality of collected data and data analysis were enough to support our conclusions [19], as described in the previous Sections.

Concerning the internal validity. Internal validity is the degree to which conclusions can be drawn about the causal effect of the treatments on the outcomes.

The experiment was under very strict control and was managed in a way that implicitly kept further independent variables, if any, at as fixed as possible values. Consequently, the observed relationship between the treatments and the outcomes seems to be determined causally rather than the result of a factor that we could not control or had not measured. A threat to internal validity is concerned with the number of participating subjects, which was very less than the minimum needed, in our evaluation. Depending on the number of participating subjects, we could be faced with problems concerning the internal validity. With a suitable sample size (44 subjects, in our evaluation), the internal validity threat would probably be avoided.

Concerning the construct validity. Construct validity is the degree to which the independent variables and dependent variables accurately measure the concepts they purport to measure. In our experiment, measured entities (for example, number of defects) are both well-defined and appropriate measures of the entities we want to measure. Threats to construct validity include following facts:

- The experiment uses one object (project's set of artifacts) for all subjects.
- Our choice of ignoring, in this Chapter, differences between junior and senior subjects.
- The experiment is also part of an academic course in which the students are graded. In fact, based on our organization, students cannot really cheat and bias their data: they are expected to be under the strict continual control with respect to both the system and observers. However, on the one hand, many of them could show abnormally high performance, due to being both younger and more knowledgeable about OOAD and the UML than average practitioners, and to the pressure of being involved with an optional part of an exam; on the other hand, they could try to find as many defects as possible, without placing the necessary attention on categorizing them correctly, in the mistaken belief that the greater the number of defects they find, the greater their exam score.
- Reading procedure for UCDR is much more complex than the CBR procedure. To cope with this threat to validity, we later ran replications with variations of the basic experiment that used a new, structured (rather than flat) UCDR procedure. We are still analyzing the results of those replications.
- The experiment is based on complex objects. However, this point is not considered to be critical, because professional practitioners are the final targets of the study and they are used to dealing with objects of the same type as the experiment objects.

Concerning the external validity. External validity is the degree to which the results of the research can be generalised to the population under study and other research settings. The greater the external validity, the more the results of an empirical study can be generalised with regards to actual software engineering practice. Some threats to validity have been identified which limit the ability to apply generalisation. There is a threat that concerns the experiment duration time. As already mentioned, the experiment was bounded to last 180 minutes. This duration can be considered short with respect to the assigned tasks. We wanted to concentrate all the experiment runs into one day, to prevent the exchange of information among participants. We also wanted to give students no opportunity to conclude their tasks in the assigned time or to help their colleagues, either during or after the experiment run. However, the expected behavior among colleagues is that will help each other, even when they are not supposed to. Consequently, a student who has concluded an exam feels it is morally acceptable (and hence is due if the opportunity arises) to help others obtain the highest possible scores. To deal with this threat to validity, we are planning to run a full-day replication with students at an Internet café that is large enough to host all the participants in one run. To conduct this replication, we only need to train new subjects; in fact, a new OOAD course was recently started, and the experiment material is ready for the Internet. However, this threat should not be considered to be critical; to the best of our knowledge, the inspection activities of our professional practitioners (again, the final target of the study) are not quite standardized, are enacted individually rather than in a group, and take place in sessions lasting no more than half a day. One further threat to external validity concerns objects. Our experiment objects are much more complex than those that are usually used for UML experiments. We do not believe that we should reduce the complexity of objects; we want to work on industry-like objects because we plan to eventually move the experiment from academia to industry. There are additional threats that could affect the external validity of the experiment. The UML knowledge that a student can acquire after two months in an academic course, lab, and training is not equivalent to the knowledge of UML practitioners in the industry. Moreover, during the experiment the students had to work very hard, concentrating on their tasks more than most industry employees would. In conclusion, it is highly probable that results will change when the experiment moves from URM2-DISP students to students of other universities or to professionals, because of their different levels of knowledge and experience. Also, different results could be obtained if the subject students are only experienced in the Bachelor and Specialized Engineer courses (the students we have used to date were either still in the stronger Diploma organization or had previously been there for some years).

6 Lessons Learned

Key lessons that we have learned to date from undertaking this empirical study can be observed from different perspectives. In this section, we assume an internal perspective as the main point of view, so the emphasis will be on lessons learned that concern subjects, process, and materials.

Concerning subjects. Regarding the participation of final engineering students in experiments, we now know that they need to be strongly motivated. Feeling that they are involved in the acquisition of new knowledge motivates them. However, simply obtaining new empirical knowledge is not enough for a deep motivation, because the main goal of these students is to graduate from the university and move on as quickly as possible to working for industries.

Students like to have the opportunity to improve their scores. From the teacher's point of view, the improvement needs to be linked to the student's performance in the experiment; this can lead the research team to show the independent variables of the experiment, hopefully not the experiment goal. Anyway, giving students the opportunity of improving their score is again not enough for obtaining a deep, motivated involvement in experiment tasks; in fact, in our conviction, the additional score that we can give them for the experiment results should not affect more than 5% of the final evaluation, which should indeed depend on their general OOAD preparation.

Furthermore, getting paid for participation seems not to be an additional value. Based on what little money we could offer, students (and their parents, who are paying for their education!) would evaluate their participation from the financial perspective as a loss rather than a good return on time invested.

Three additional items seem to motivate final engineering students, i.e., to learn about OOAD more deeply through training, to verify learning through the experiment and, last but not least, to use the experiment training for getting into contact with industrial people and consultants, who in the future could link them up with potential employers, and could help them someday to understand what parts of their academic knowledge are "really" important from a professional point of view.

Concerning procedure and materials. In our experience, iterative-incremental process models are more convenient than Waterfall and its many variants for modeling experiment processes, especially when the final target of the experiment is made by professional practitioners and the experiment is rather complex.

We cannot anticipate all the experiment requirements at experiment definition time, nor can we predict all the necessary controls during the experiment's planning and design. As a result, we realize only when it is too late to recover—that is, at experiment run time or at data analysis and evaluation time—that some essential aspects have been neglected or misunderstood. These aspects pertain to experiment materials (including objects, guidelines, and forms), subject training, and experiment control. Eventually, overlooked experiment items or misunderstandings adversely affect the overall experiment process. To correct, refine, and tune the experiment process, a certain number of iterations or incremental iterations are necessary.

With regard to the basic experiment described in this chapter, a further iteration of the experiment definition, planning, and design was later enacted. Objects were refined and seeded with some additional defects; minor mistakes were removed from guidelines and forms; and the experiment Web site, database, and data collection process were improved. Two experiment replications were conducted with variations using the updated materials and process.

An additional incremental iteration of the experiment process has also been planned. This updated process will similarly be enacted with students before being moved to industrial subjects. We plan to ensure that subjects will be given a correct and complete interpretation of the role they are asked to perform in the experiment; in other words, we intend to ascertain that use-case-trained CBR subjects will not use some kind of personal UCDR procedure, and vice versa.

As mentioned earlier, we found that the UCDR procedure was more complex than CBR procedure. To deal with this, we are currently working on an incremental version of the experiment material that is expected to include process automation. In other words, we are developing a workflow to lead subjects through all the experiment objects to be read, activities to be performed, and forms to be filled out. This should also reduce the level of general knowledge that is required by participants, eventually decreasing the training time.

Acknowledgements. We thank Caroline Rose for the terrific work and very good results in reviewing the language of the Chapter.

We also thank Sandra Celiberti for the help she gave as observer during the experiment operation and other her contributions to construction of the experiment.

References

[1] Laitenberger O., "Perspective-Based Reading: Technique, Validation and Research in Future", University of Kaiserslautern, Germany, 1995, ISERN-95-01.

[2] Booch G., J. Rumbaugh, and I. Jacobson, "Unified Modeling Language. User Guide", Addison-Wesley, 1999.

[3] Booch G., "Object-oriented analysis and design", Benjamin/Cummings P. C. Inc., 1994.

[4] Kruchten P., "Rational Unified Process. Introduzione", Addison-Wesley Longman Italy, 1999.

[5] Basili V. R., S. Green, O. Laitenberger, F. Lanubile, F. Shull, S. Sorumgard, and M. V. Zelkowitz, "The Empirical Investigation of Perspective-Based Reading", University of Maryland, USA, 1996, ISERN-96-06.

[6] Ciolkowski M., C. Differding, O. Laitenberger, and J. Münch, "Empirical Investigation of Perspective-Based Reading: A Replicated Experiment", Fraunhofer Institute for Experimental Software Engineering, Germany, 1997, ISERN-97-13.

[7] Laitenberger O. and J-M. DeBaud, "Perspective-Based Reading of Code Documents at Robert Bosch GmbH", Fraunhofer Institute for Experimental Software Engineering, Germany, 1997, ISERN-97-14.

[8] UMDCS ESEG, "Lab Package for the Empirical Investigation of Perspective-Based Reading", www.cs.umd.edu/projects/SoftEng/ESEG/manual/pbr_package/manual.html, 18.03.2003.

[9] Laitenberger O., K. El Emam, and T. Harbich, "An Internally Replicated Quasi-Experimental Comparison of Checklist and Perspective-Based Reading of Code Documents", Fraunhofer Institute for Experimental Software Engineering, Germany, 1999, ISERN-99-01.

[10] Shull F., F. Lanubile, and V. R. Basili, "Investigating Reading Techniques for Framework Learning", University of Maryland, USA, 1998 ISERN-98-16.

[11] Lanubile F. and G. Visaggio, "Evaluating Defect Detection Techniques for Software Requirements Inspections", University of Bari, Italy, 2000, ISERN-00-08.

[12] Laitenberger O., C. Atkinson, M. Schlich, and K. El Emam, "Reading Techniques for Defect Detection in UML Design Documents", Fraunhofer Institute for Experimental Software Engineering, Germany, 2000, ISERN-00-01.

[13] Travassos G. H., F. Shull, and J. Carver, "Working with UML: A Software Design Process Based on Inspections for UML", Advances in Computers, Vol. 54, pp. 35–98, 2001.

[14] Cantone G., L. Colasanti, and G. Calavaro, "Evaluating Checklist-Based and Use-Case-Driven Reading Technique of Software Analysis and Design UML Artifacts. Preliminary results from multi-replicated experiments with students of different level of experience", Proceedings of 2002 International Symposium on Empirical Software Engineering, IEEE ISESE, Vol. II—Poster and Demonstration Sessions, 3–4 October 2002, Nara, Japan, pp. 7–8, 2002.

[15] Pfleeger S. L. "Software engineering: Theory and Practice", 2nd edition, Prentice Hall, 2002.

[16] IBM Corp. "S/390 Orthogonal Defect Classification Education". (www-1.ibm.com/servers/eserver/zseries/odc/nonshock/odc8ns.html, 4.04.2003.

[17] Cantone G., and S. Celiberti, "Evaluating efficiency, effectiveness and other indices of code reading and functional testing for concurrent event-driven Java software. Results from a multi-replicated experiment with students of different level of experience", Proceedings of 2002 ISESE, Vol. II—Poster and Research Demonstration Sessions, pp. 23–24, 3–4 October, 2002, Nara, Japan.

[18] Cantone G., Z. A. Abdulnabi, A. Lomartire, and G. Calavaro, "Evaluating efficiency and effectiveness of code reading and functional testing for concurrent event-driven Java software: Preliminary results from a multi-replicated experiment with students of different level of experience", 2003 (see Chapter 10 in this book).

[19] Wohlin C., P. Runeson, M. Horst, M. C. Ohlsson, B. Regnell, and A. Wesslén, "Experimentation in Software Engineering. An Introduction." Kluwer A. P., 2000.

[20] Laitenberger O., and J-M. DeBaud, "An encompassing life cycle centric survey of software inspection", The Journal of Systems and Software, Vol. 50, No. 1, 2000, pp. 5–31.

[21] Gilb T., and D. Graham, Software Inspection, Addison-Wesley, 1993.

[22] Chernak Y., "A Statistical Approach to the Inspection Checklist Formal Synthesis and Improvement", IEEE Transactions on Software Engineering, Vol. 22, No. 12, 1996, pp. 866–874.

[23] Macdonald F., and J. Miller, "A Comparison of Tool-Based and Paper-Based Software Inspection", University of Strathclyde, UK, 1998, ISERN-98-17.

Appendix: Frequencies and Normal Distributions

The following figures show the normality state for the collected data, which have been resulted in Table 4 and 6.

Fig. 6 shows normal distributions for effectiveness along with the available frequencies for both UCDR (left) and CBR (right). Based on this figure, the following summarizes the results with respect to our research hypotheses on the effectiveness: Observations cannot be fitted under the normal curve for all the experiment hypotheses on effectiveness.

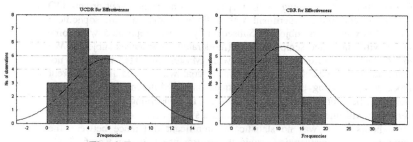

Fig. 6. Testing the normality for fault detection rate

Fig. 7 shows normal distributions for defect detection rates along with the available frequencies for UCDR (left) and CBR (right). Based on this figure, the following summarizes the results with respect to our research hypotheses on the defect detection rates. Observations can be fitted under the normal curve both for $H1_{\text{(UCDR Defect Detection Rate)}}$, and $H_{1\,\text{(CBR Defect Detection Rate)}}$. Observations cannot be fitted under the normal curve both for $H_{0\,\text{(UCDR Defect Detection Rate)}}$ and $H_{0\,\text{(CBR Defect Detection Rate)}}$.

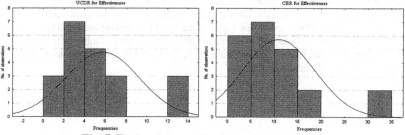

Fig. 7. Testing the normality for defect detection rate

Effectiveness of Code Reading and Functional Testing with Event-Driven Object-Oriented Software

Giovanni Cantone[1], Zeiad A. Abdulnabi[1], Anna Lomartire[2],
and Giuseppe Calavaro[3]

[1] Dept. of Informatics, Systems, and Production, University of Rome "Tor Vergata"
Via del Politecnico, 1 - I-00133 Rome, Italy
cantone@info.uniroma2.it
zeiad.abdulnabi@uniroma2.it
[2] Computation and Documentation Center. University of Rome "Tor Vergata"
Via O. Raimondo, 1 - I-00137 Rome, Italy
annal@ccd.uniroma2.it
[3] Rational Software. Via di Torre Spaccata, 172 – I-00169 Rome, Italy
gcalavar@rational.com

Abstract. This chapter is concerned with experimental comparisons of code reading and functional testing (including fault identification) of concurrent event-driven Java software. Our initial idea was that functional-testing is more effective than code reading with respect to concurrent event-driven OO software. A controlled experiment was initially conducted with sophomore students (inexperienced subjects). Subsequently, it was replicated with some changes with junior and senior students (moderately experienced subjects). We also conducted a further replication with Master students, which is not considered in this Chapter. The experiment goal was studied from different perspectives, including effect of techniques on the different types of faults. Results can be overviewed as the following: 1) Concerning the initial, *basic experiment*: with inexperienced subjects and a strict interval of inspecting time of two hours, there was no statistically significant difference between the techniques under consideration; subjects performance indicator was 62% for code reading and 75% for functional testing. 2) Concerning the (first) *replication*: with moderately expert subjects, again a strict interval of inspecting time of two hours, and more than twice number of seeded faults, there was no statistically significant difference between the techniques; subjects performance indicator was 100% for code reading and 92% for functional testing; subjects performance indicator shows that more experienced subjects were asking for more inspecting time; however, functional testing performed much better than in the basic experiment. Computation faults were the most detectable for code reading while control faults were the most detectable for functional testing. Moreover, moderately expert subjects were more effective than inexperienced ones in detecting interface and event types of faults. Furthermore moderately expert functional testers detected many preexistent (non-seeded) faults, while both inexperienced subjects, and moderately experienced code readers could not detect non-seeded faults.

R. Conradi and A.I. Wang (Eds.): ESERNET 2001-2003, LNCS 2765, pp. 166–192, 2003.
© Springer-Verlag Berlin Heidelberg 2003

1 Introduction

This Chapter presents an empirical study where effectiveness of two logically different fault detection and identification techniques were compared through a controlled experiment in order to address the uncertainty of how to, and when use one technique rather than the other one, or overlap such techniques, in order to test software effectively.

Similarly to other studies known from the literature (see following Section 2 for a brief recall of these studies,) this Chapter analyzes both static and dynamic software-testing techniques. In the followings, two techniques are considered and referred as Code Reading for defect identification, CR, and Functional Testing & fault Identification FTI, where CR is a static testing technique and FTI includes a dynamic black box testing [1]. In particular, we present and discuss results from a couple of experiments, the basic experiment (BE) and the first of its replications (R1), that we conducted at The University of Rome "Tor Vergata", Department of Informatics, Systems and Production, in the Experimental Software Engineering Group (URM2-DISP-ESEG). While both effectiveness and efficiency of software testing techniques were investigated at URM2 [2], this Chapter reasons on effectiveness only. Forthcoming papers will consider efficiency and results from some further replications.

Our experiments show some changes with similar previous research, and we can classify some of these changes as major changes, other ones as minor changes. In fact: 1) Our study emphasizes on specific experiment objects. In particular, our experiment objects are concurrent OO software games; these are realistic software, not "toy" games; they are driven by keyboard and mouse events rather than data. 2) Our subjects are students in Informatics engineering, from sophomores up to seniors. 3) Our experiments are technology-based and run on Internet; documents are in electronic format only, paper supports are not needed, forms are electronically presented, submitted, and database stored; our checklist items are assertions, i.e. Boolean statements to answer by True (Checked) or False (Unchecked) rather than questions to answer by Yes (Checked) or Not (Unchecked).

Based on the specific nature of the software application that we used as objects, the following question arises:

Q: Can results from previous empirical studies, which concerned static and dynamic testing of data-driven programs, be extended to other kinds of software, e.g. concurrent OO event-driven software?

In order to start reasoning about such a question, let us begin by noting that both CT and FTI include code searching for fault identification, but FTI is required to enact one preliminary step: program execution for failure detection. In our reasoning, this does not imply that CR performs better than FTI, at least for some types of faults, with OO event-driven software. In other words, confirmation of previous studies, namely the Basili and Selby empirical study on effectiveness of testing strategies [1], is not quite an obvious conjecture at this point. In fact, checklists only drive CR testers to read code for fault identification, while two items, checklists and detected failures, drive searches of FTI testers; this could help FTI testers to perform better than CR testers, when time necessary to detect a program failure is very small (and, by the way, the program execution is fast enough.)

Based on such initial reasoning, our experiment idea can be derived:

When software user-interfaces are friend and user-interactions is limited to simple actions, e.g. clicking mouse or pressing keys, functional testing performs better than code reading in the average.

Our supposition in this area is hence that FTI would perform better than CR in the average, relying on the following causes:

- Due to the specific type of applications that we are considering, because of their user interfaces and their type of interaction with users, the visibility of failures should be very high and the time strictly necessary to detect such a failure should be very small; consequently, the FTI failure detection phase should have minor impact on the overall testing process.
- The subsequent FTI code-search should perform better than CR with respect to the common task of identifying software defects; in fact, while both techniques use the same static objects and point to get fully identifying faults, the FTI search is driven by known failures and specified assertions, while CR is driven by assertions only. This should make a major difference.

We can now come to define the primary goal of our study. In GQM (Goal-Question-Metrics) terms [3, 4, 5], this can be expressed as in the follows: To analyze checklist-driven Code reading and Functional testing for the purpose of comparing effectiveness and detection rate with respect to testing concurrent event-driven OO software –actually Java games- for defect detection and identification, in the context of advanced software-technology facilities and students of different level of experience, from the point of view of a research group, which also aims to transfer resulting experiment process and guidelines to industrial settings in the mid-term.

As already mentioned in the statement of the primary goal, we aim to move experiment to industry. The strategic goal of our study is thus to learn by a family of experiments how to achieve stability in experiment processes, documents and supporting tools, in the aim of reducing the experiment risk and improving the expected yield on investment. This is considered to be the prerequisite to introduce the techniques into practice.

As the remaining of the Chapter deeply shows, based on the experiment goal, the following items characterize our experiment definition:

- Research hypotheses are concerned with whether performances of two testing techniques differ significantly when applied by inexperienced and moderately expert students of Informatics engineering, respectively. In particular, the null and alternative hypotheses tested by our experiments can be formally stated as in the following:

    $H_{0 \, (Effectiveness)}$: CR and FTI perform insignificantly different in detecting faults.
    $H_{1 \, (Effectiveness)}$: CR and FTI perform significantly different in detecting faults.

- Testing technique is the experiment factor. Experience of subjects is variation, an "inter-experiment" factor.
- CR and FTI are the experiment treatments. Inexperienced or moderately expert subjects are variations, inter-experiment treatments.
- Informatics Engineering sophomores, in the position of inexperienced subjects, and additionally, juniors and seniors, in the position of moderately expert practitioners, are two samples of experiment subjects.

- Concurrent event-driven Java games are the experiment objects.
- Effectiveness is the experiment dependent variable, where:
- *Effectiveness (Mean)*—the number of preexistent or seeded defects found, rated to the total number of known defects.
- The impact of treatments on the dependent variable is observed by the following four perspectives: Inspecting time, Number of seeded faults, Subjects' performance, Types of seeded faults.

In summary, in our experiments, we can identify testing technique as the experiment factor, CR and FTI as the treatments, and effectiveness as the dependent variable that is correlated to the factor. In order to investigate the impact of the treatments on the dependent variable, each our experiment controls remaining independent variables at fixed values, including the experience of subjects. However, in order to evaluate the impact of the latter on the dependent variable, we let it change from the first to the second experiment by fixing it at the level "Basic experienced subjects" in the first case, and at "Moderately experienced subjects", in the second case, hence establishing an "inter-experiment" factor. Moreover, in both cases we use different perspectives to observe the impact of treatments on the dependent variable, namely the number and type of seeded faults, the available inspection time, and the subjects' performance.

2 Starting Scenario

A milestone of empirical research on the effectiveness and efficiency of software testing strategies is the Basili and Selby 1987 IEEE TSE paper [1], and is rooted in the related experimental research that Basili initiated in the 70's and continued to develop in the '80s. This research suggests that experienced subjects are most efficient when using code reading and that experiments involving students confirm the results with minor significance. In particular, for what concerns this Chapter, the major results from the Basili and Selby's study are: 1) With professional programmers, CR detects more software faults than FTI; 2) With advanced students, CR and FTI are not different. 3) Both the number of faults observed, and total effort in detection depend on the type of software tested. 4) CR detects more interface faults than FTI. 5) FTI detects more control faults than CR.

The Basili and Selby study has been replicated a certain number of times with minor or major changes along the last fifteen years, and some supporting tools have also been developed and published. The web sites of the International Software Engineering Research Network, ISERN, and the Empirical Software Engineering Research Network, ESERNET, can reach many of these works. On 1995, Kamsties and Lott conducted quasi-replications of the Basili and Selby study at the University of Kaiserslautern [6]. Results suggested that inexperienced subjects can apply code reading as effectively as an execution-based validation technique, but they are most efficient when using functional testing. Based on such experience, the Basili and Selby study was also replicated in the Strathclyde EFoCS group, where the role of replication in experimental software was investigated in the first part of 90's [7]; in addition; Dunsmore, Roper, and Wood [8] conducted a series of three empirical studies on a rigorous approach to OO code inspection on 2001. More recently, Juristo,

Moreno and Vegas conducted a replication at the Polytechnic of Madrid [9]. Finally, our replications at the URM2 DISP ESEG were conducted with major changes, and further our replications are still ongoing [10].

Regarding projects that relate to this study:

- The experiment is part of the "Experimental Informatics" project, partially supported by our Ministero dell'Istruzione, dell'Università e della Ricerca Scientifica (MIUR), Grant 020906003 URM2-DISP.
- The experiment aims to produce results for the EC-funded Empirical Software Engineering Research Network (ESERNET).
- The experimental activities have been continually supported by the URM2 project "Cooperation among the ESE groups of URM2-DISP, UMDCS, UK1-DI," Grants 010209013-2001, 010209015-2002 URM2-DISP.

3 Method

To enable interested readers to conduct replications, the present Section first describes in some detail how we conducted the study, the roles and people involved, and the process enacted.

Concerning the roles involved. The roles basically involved with this study are:

- An expert in empirical/experimental software engineering (ESE).
- An expert in statistical methods and tools.

Other roles involved are:

- A system and database administrator and security manager.
- A professional, expert in software technology and deeply aware of the state of the art in our software industry.

Concerning the people involved. Subsequently to role definition, the following individuals, who also authored the present Chapter, filled those roles (in the same order as listed above):

- A professor of ESE at URM2-DISP.
- A Research-Doctoral[1] student with a Bachelor in Statistical Science from a foreign university.
- A Diplomat in Computer Science, actually serving as employee at the URM2 Computing and Documentation Center.
- An Informatics engineering PhD, actually with Rational Software.

---

[1] Because the organization of academic degrees changes world wide, in order to prevent misunderstanding, let us explicitly recall the present Italy engineering degrees. Diploma is a five years degree, which ends with a graded, public dissertation of the Laurea Thesis in presence of ten or more local faculties. Bachelor is a three years degree, which ends with a graded, public presentation of a project to five or more local faculties. Specialized Bachelor is a post-bachelor two years degree, which ends similarly to Diploma. Research Doctor is a post-diploma and post-specialized-bachelor three years degree, which needs defense and ends with a public formal dissertation of the Doctoral Thesis in presence of faculties coming from different universities.

A Bachelor Engineer student in Informatics, preparing her final project, performed in the additional role of Software engineer Assistant.

Concerning the process enacted. Let us consider now the process that we enacted in order to develop the basic experiment and its replication. The BE work was started on the very beginning of November 2001 with experiment definition. Based on the time constraints placed by the Bachelor student team-member, in that she intended to get her grade in less than six months, we came to choose for the experiment process an iterative-incremental model, which extends on the process model shown by Wohlin et al. [11]. As deeply explained in the remaining, during the definition of BE, the decision was made to use a balanced multi-test within object study, that is to have the same number of subjects for each testing technique (treatment) and to use one experiment object for multiple subjects. The further decision was made to conduct both the basic experiment and replication in lab through Internet. The development was hence planned of on-line guidelines able to direct subjects to carry out their work, and eventually access and fill out defect forms. The Bachelor student team-member was given the tasks of developing the Web site and the experiment material, with the guide and responsibility of the professor team-member. We selected the experiment and training objects. In addition, based on the technical literature, we categorized defects. Eventually, the number of defects to seed was determined; actual defects were retained or created from the scratch and hence seeded into objects. When the plan for defect seeding was completed, submission forms were designed. Web pages were created in accordance with these forms and placed on the experiment Web site. A repository to store defect submissions was created. The Web site was enhanced to provide complete guidelines for subjects, from initial authentication up to defect submission-through-Web forms. Experiment documents and objects were made available to the research-team via Internet and access-protected by password and through a firewall. The training material was also developed and placed on the same Internet-connected server. The Web server performance was tested by a standard package. A couple of weeks before the start of the experiment, the training material was published on the development server, for access through the Internet, and information was given to registered participants. Finally, both the basic experiment and replication were conducted in lab. On-line guidelines directed subjects to carry out their work, which lasted two consecutive hours. When a subject detected a defect, guidelines directed him or her to access and fill out the proper form.

Concerning the language used. Our community is still missing a unified ESE language. However, in order to model our activities and products we used the language implicitly defined by Wohlin e al. [11] (see also Chapter 2 of this book.)

3.1   Design

As noted earlier, the goal of this study is to carry out comparisons of two testing techniques, focusing on their effectiveness, which is the experiment dependent variable. The research hypotheses of the experiment are hence concerned with whether those two testing techniques differ significantly when applied to concurrent OO event-driven Java software for what concerns their effectiveness. Accordingly, in Section 1, we identified testing technique as the experiment factor, CR and FTI as the treatments, and effectiveness as the dependent variable that is correlated to the factor. In addition, there are independent variables that we are expected to control at fixed values; furthermore, we should raison about the type of design to adopt. We will look now at each of these identified entities in more detail.

Concerning the factor. In order to obtain comparable results, the testing techniques are specified to produce the same type of results, whatever their nature might be. In our case, techniques are required to come to fully identified faults, including the identification of faulted line of code, and fault category. Let us note that, beside the testing technique, our study, which was structured in a basic experiment and a set of replications (with variations!), includes a further "inter-experiment" factor, which is the experience of participating subjects.

Concerning treatments. CR is a step-by-step procedure that guides individual inspectors in uncovering defects in software-coded artifacts. Such a technique is required to provide a systematic and well-defined way of inspecting software code, allowing for feedback and improvement. CR works on the application code as it is; it is hence a static technique. FTI can be seen as organized in two phases: functional testing and fault identification. The former is a dynamic black-box testing technique; it looks for program failures, and requires the execution of the software application. The latter consists in a code search for faults that caused a detected failure. Both our treatments are checklist driven; specifically, they are driven by assertions, i.e. a list of predicates in natural language on the program's specified behavior and non-functional requirements. In particular, for both techniques, testers are given program informal requirements (intended functional behaviors and non-functional requirements) and some construction documents, including source code. Checklists are also given or tester is requested for their development before starting with test. As already mentioned, checklists drive CR testers to read software-code and to compare the asserted requirements with coded ones. A defect is located and identified when an inaccuracy is detected in one of the inspected software document with respect to the asserted requirements. Checklists also drive FTI testers to compare the specified requirements with program actual behave. For functional testing, testers additionally are given the executable version of source code (or the source code interpreter; in our case, the Java machine).   Functional testing only chance is to detect application failures. Subsequently, FTI testers are required an additional step: in order to fully identify faults that caused an observed failure, they access software construction documents, eventually the application code.

Concerning further independent variables. These are the intra-experiment independent variables, which are controlled at fixed values:
- The type of knowledge and experience of subjects.
- The level of knowledge and experience within the same samples of subjects both with concurrent OO event-driven concepts, and Java programming language.
- Team size.
- Duration of the experiment runs.
- Quality and complexity of guidelines and other material supporting the experiment.
- Supporting technologies, including document supports, form-submission technology, tools and instruments used, screen type and size, and network performance.

- Interaction among subjects and between subjects and observers.
- Other environmental characteristics.

Since all these variables are independent for each student in the experiment, no further strategy needs to be applied to allocate the subjects into groups.

Table 1 summarizes components of the basic experiment design and replication design, showing the fixed values for the applied techniques, where N, P, M, and I stand for Not, Practitioner, Inexperienced, and Moderately expert subject, respectively.

Table 1. Components of the BE and R1

Description	BE		R1	
	CR	FTI	CR	FTI
Type and level of knowledge and experience	NPI	NPI	NPM	NPM
Number of subjects	23	22	13	12
Team size	1	1	1	1
Experiment-run duration (in minutes)	120	120	120	120
Number of experiment objects	1	1	1	1
Number of defects seeded	38	38	95	95
Laboratory	L1	L1	L2	L2
Technology	ICT	ICT	ICT	ICT
No. of runs	1	1	1	1

Based on Table 1:

- "Non-practitioner" was the fixed value that we evaluated for the type of knowledge and experience of all our subjects.
- "Inexperienced subject" and "Moderately expert subject" were the fixed values that we evaluated for the level of knowledge and experience of BE subjects (Sophomores) and R1 subjects (advanced students, actually Juniors and Seniors), respectively. See Section 3.3 for further detail about subjects.
- One person was the fixed value that we chose for the experiment-team size.
- We excluded to split an experiment in multiple runs.
- 120 minutes was the fixed valued that we chose for duration of each experiment run.
- Information and communication technology (ICT) was used to support all the experiments. Guidelines with minor treatment-dependencies were also established for all the experiments (as the following Section 3.3 shows). So the quality, complexity, and performance of the supporting materials were fixed at common fixed values.

Concerning the type of design. Since our common aim is to compare two testing techniques, the experimental design for our basic experiment and its replication is the "One factor with two treatments" for comparing the mean of the dependent variable for each treatment [11]. Moreover, the study is an offline, controlled experiment—specifically, to be conducted under controlled conditions at a laboratory. Furthermore, there is an inter-experiment variable, which is the experience of subjects. Indeed, our subjects are assigned to each technique using completely randomized design such that each subject uses only one treatment on one object. Treatments are designed to have the same number of subjects so that design is made balanced. To make sure that subjects will be assigned randomly, their names are designed to be listed with serial number attached; the development of a small application is required for generating random numbers without redraw for each technique. The subsequent step is to assign an experiment code for each subject and technique besides the experiments themselves; as already mentioned, we coded Code reading technique as "CR", Functional testing technique as "FTI", the Basic experiment as "BE", and the (first) replication as "R1". Both in the basic experiment and replication, each subject is treated by his/her experiment code along the experiment process.

3.2   Subjects/Participants

This Chapter reports on a stage of our experimental work on testing techniques, when materials and processes still required for testing, improvement, refinement, and tuning. Too much risk was thus still involved with any tentative of transferring the study to industry. Consequently, we addressed students for the position of experiment subjects. In particular, skilled students of Computer and Information Engineering, including sophomores, juniors and seniors, were involved. Participation was voluntary; we did not pay subjects for participating nor wanted to grade them through the experiment. As a return for participating, subjects were given the opportunity to be trained free on advanced programming topics in class sessions, through Internet and, for R1, through participant-reserved lab training sessions.

Based on convenience sampling, our subjects were defined as the 2002-year population of the URM2-DISP students in three different courses: OOCP, for the basic experiment; Object-oriented analysis and design (OOAD), and Experimental Software Engineering (ESE), for R1.

Eventually, 45 out of 150 sophomores participated on voluntary basis to BE. These subjects had already attended two courses of Computer Science at least, and were in their very end of OOCP. 30 out of 50 advanced students participated on voluntary basis to R1. These were attending OOAD as students in the Bachelor degree (Juniors) or in the Diploma or Specialized-bachelor degrees (Seniors). Additionally, they had already attended courses of Software Engineering, Database, Operating systems, and so on. 10 of those participating seniors were attending ESE; many of these were also attending OOAD.

All subjects were trained. During this stage, the application that subjects applied is a game called "Pinball"; in detail, we released six versions of this application for BE, five versions for R1, each with five types of seeded faults, one version for each game-difficulty level.

For the BE experiment training, we introduced subjects both to CR and FTI techniques, and the "Pinball" game by class lectures. Subsequently, we invited subjects to visit the web site of the experiment, in order to continue the training on personal basis.

For R1 experiment training, we introduced subjects to CR and FTI techniques first in class and then in lab. Subsequently, we invited subjects to continue their visits of the web site of the experiment on personal basis, in order to get further training. For the lab-training sessions, the environment was completely in the control of three observers. The lab had eighteen PC machines available for the experiment training. Subjects were arranged randomly using statistical simple random sample method. Based on the number of subjects and available PCs, subjects were arranged as singles and couples, and the "Pinball" was briefly recalled and shown them in execution. They were hence introduced once more time, for about thirty minutes, to the experiments requirements and both the proposed techniques. Successively, they were randomly assigned to a technique, and started the training session. After one hour of training, they were requested to quit their current technique and switch to the other one. Because FTI and CR commonly share some practical stages, we assumed that the second part of the lab training would not require more than half of an hour.

3.3   Apparatus/Materials

Here we will look in more detail at some points made earlier about the objects and seeded faults, infrastructure, and guidelines related to the experiment. Additional information can be found on the URM2-DISP-ESEG Web site, http://eseg.uniroma2.it.

Concerning objects. As already mentioned, in our experiment definition, games were designated for use as experiment and training objects. Moreover, the decision was also made to select the experiment objects among the games that we had worked with students of previous courses of OOCP. Furthermore, we eventually decided to prefer Solitaire, a game known world wide, as the experiment object, and Pinball, a ball game constructor, as the training object. These objects are based on two Java games that T. Budd had previously authored and published [12], which we had already maintained - by removing some faults, extending some their logic requirements, and improving quality of user interfaces and time performance of user interaction – and reused, in order to produce new games (e.g. Flipper.)

Again during experiment definition, the additional decision was made to further adapt those games according to experiment requirements. Some changes were defined in order to introduce the concept of level of game difficulty, and hence create different versions of objects, one for each level of game difficulty. In fact, Solitaire requires players (and FTI testers in such a role) to spend a certain amount of time for reasoning on what next and what if, with respect to their actual, random selected, case. Vice versa, CR subjects are expected to enact a general reasoning by abstracting on real cases or, in the worst case, working on scenarios. This could penalize FTI subjects with respect to CR ones: in fact, working on abstractions is simpler than working on reality. The organization of the experiment object in multiple levels of difficulty allowed us, on one side, to dividing and managing the game complexity from the player point of view, on the other side, allowed for controlling and limiting the possible interactions between different failures produced by different faults. In order to have different levels of difficulty for the programs, five versions were designated to play the role of the experiment object. Following further decisions were also made: 1) Regarding experiment-game presentation, we decided to introduce a window, where players find buttons to start from level 1, advance in the game difficulty level or eventually quit. (In order to control learning effect, the return to already visited levels was not allowed.) 2) Regarding concurrency, we decided to introduce some new threads for computing and controlling score achieved by a player during the execution of each level. 3) Regarding the object documentation, we decided to improve the in-line code-documentation, and to reverse the code in order to produce class diagrams.

Concerning fault seeding. In order to compare testing techniques, we need to establish a fix point to use as reference. This can be obtained by seeding faults into objects.

Fault seeding is expected to satisfy a realistic categorization of faults. Instances of such categorizations are based on fault-nature, e.g. {Omission, Inconsistency, Ambiguity, Incorrectness, Syntax}, fault-severity, e.g. {Low, Moderate, High}, or fault-type, (see Table 2, for instance). In an experiment, for each selected categorization, faults should be seeded according to a realistic probability of occurrence. S. H. Pfleeger reported on fault classifications and distributions [13].

Table 2 shows our classification of faults for concurrent OO event driven software: it extends on fault definitions of the IBM Orthogonal Defect Classification [14].

Unfortunately, data that concerns distribution of faults in Java event-driven software are still not available, in the best of our knowledge. We hence made the decision to change faults density through the basic experiments and its replications, mainly due to the changes in the number of type D and type H seeded defects.

We seeded our experiment objects with previously detected and already removed faults, and with further faults. Because our objects do not have input data, we did not considered omission or commission faults of type L in Table 2. Moreover, we decided not to seed or consider faults of type M, because our basic experiment was based on sophomores, who are not expected to be aware of design and implementation of relationships between software entities (e.g. classes and objects.).

Table 3 presents the different types of seeded faults for both experiments.

Concerning infrastructure. The experiment was constructed to meet the following low-level design requirements as well:
- To be conducted at an open-workshop laboratory able to guest up to 100 subject at the same time (this is the maximum number of sophomore participants that we estimated during the design of the experiment).
- To use true and up to date IC technology rather than paper and pencil.
- To be easy to replicate in any place, at any time, hence to run on the Internet, so having objects, data collection forms, experiment data, procedures, and all other documents organized to take place on a Web site.
- To run in half of a day.
- To be based on the assignment of similar workstations to all participants, specifically workstations equipped by equal real and virtual machines, keyboards, and screens.

Based on those requirements, the decision was made to run the experiments extra-campus at an Internet Café. We actually conducted the basic experiment at this place as our lab L1 (see Table 1). There were PCs of the same type, ready and connected together to an internal network and via Internet to the experiment Web site (see Section 3.4 in the following, for further detail).

Because in the meantime the Internet Café managers changed their mind and highly raised the half-day rental for a loft-laboratory, we had to reconfigure the experiment design, in order to let the replication be conducted at our academic lab.

Table 2. OO Event-Driven Defect Classification. Extends IBM Orthogonal Defect Classification [14])

Type	Code	Explanation
Assignment Initialization	A	Incorrect implementation or invocation of a constructor, missing or incorrect initialization of data, wrong assignment.
Algorithm: computation Method	B	Faults that lead to incorrect calculations in a given situation or incorrect method.
Algorithm: control	C	Faults that lead the program to follow an incorrect control flow path in a given situation.
Inheritance Reflexivity	D	Faults that relate to static ancestors of a class. Faults that affect the run-time ancestor of a class-object.
Interface Message Polymorphism	E	Faults that affect quality of user interfaces, class definition of behaviors, interface with other subsystems, components or objects or classes or utilities via message exchange or parameters lists, or via calls, macros, or control blocks. Faults related with template instantiations and parameters, or binding a message to the proper port, channel, entry or method of the (variable) destination object.
Function Class Object	F	Faults that affect capability, correctness and completeness of end-user interfaces, product interfaces, interface with hardware architecture, or global data structure, class implementation of specified behaviors.
Event	G	Faults that affect event definition, detection, identification or service activation and completion.
Exception	H	Faults that affect exception raise, detection, identification, or handling activation or completion.
Concurrency	I	Faults that affects synchronization, mutual exclusion, control of non-determinism, and fairness.
Checking	L	Faults in program logic that fails to validate inputted data and value before they are used.
Relationship	M	Faults that relate to problems among objects, procedures, and data structures.

There were 25 PCs of the same type available for the experiment replication, connected together and, via a local network, to the lab server. We adapted those PCs to meet the experiment requirements for apparatuses. We also duplicated our experiment on the Internet-not-connected lab server.

Concerning instruments measurements. Fixed measurement instruments used were as following:

- Detected faults submission electronic forms.
- Detected faults description submission text file.
- Database for storing data submitted by subjects electronically.
- Description electronic forms.

Table 3. Faults seeded per fault-category

Fault Code & Type	BE (# | %)		R1 (# | %)	
A: Initialization	7	18,4	37	38,9
B: Computation	6	15,8	11	11,6
C: Control	5	13,2	8	8,4
D: Polymorphism	5	13,2	0	0,0
E: Interface	6	15,8	19	20,0
F: Function	6	15,8	0	0,0
G: Event	1	2,6	20	21,1
H: Exception	2	5,3	0	0,0
I: Checking	NA	NA	NA	NA
TOTAL	38	100,0	95	100,0

According to fault definitions in Table 2 and the interested types of faults, eight electronic forms were provided with short descriptions. Each provided form was made of two principal parts:

- The first part leads testers to enter their ID Group Number and the relative actual time.
- The second part leads testers to answer some questions, in order to verify whether the detected fault effectively lies on one of the types of faults indicated in this form. Once the tester finds the question that matches the detected fault, the tester enters the class name and line number in which s/he detected that fault, and the detection time (in the current version of the supports, submission time is automatically inserted by the system).

Concerning guidelines. In order to execute uniformly and efficiently the experiment process, it is necessary to define steps for the techniques that testers have to carry out. There are steps that are common to both techniques and steps that are technique specific.

Common steps: subjects have to read carefully documents concerning the software application requirements and hence generate their own assertions, according with those requirements (as already mentioned, the replication package already provides assertions, hence R1 subjects were only asked to read and eventually extend assertion lists). Subjects find assertions in a text file, and write their new assertions in their local copy of this file; (in particular, this file is specified to contain the following descriptions for every assertion: Progressive ID number, Assertion state, and Assertion classification according to the fault type that this assertion addresses.) Subsequently, the subjects view the experiment object class diagrams in order to make an idea of the responsibility given to each class. Finally, the subjects enact the assigned testing technique. The current assertion (state) drives the tester. For each new level of difficulty of the game that a BE tester enters, s/he has to memorize the admission time (during the conduction of BE, we eventually authorized subjects to use paper and pencil for writing down memo for admission time). When a tester detects a fault, s/he classifies this fault according to previously indicated eight categories of faults, and then opens a new form for specific fault type, fills out admission time, current time, and fault description, and eventually submits the form. Thereby a new test-session is defined and so forth, for next fault identification and submission (based on the experience that we gained while conducting BE, our system has been evolved to record admission and submission time automatically). Consecutively, subjects repeat the previous common steps for each further assertion and for each level in the application. Right before the expiration of the time duration assigned to the experiment run, observers require subjects to send the text files that they elaborated to an ad-hoc experiment's e-mail address.

FTI-specific steps: If there are conflicts between the current assertion and the application behavior, then the tester has to describe the wrong behavior in a local text file. Subsequently, FTI tester passes to locate the fault that caused the failure. In order to locate a fault in the application code, the tester is requested to search the software-code of the application classes that caused a failure in her or his conjecture. To have the application class-diagram available for display, can hence help the tester. As already mentioned in the Common steps above, once the tester has identified a faulted line of code, s/he has to fill out the form for this type of defect and submit the related form.

CR-specific steps: CR tester tries to identify the class, which has the responsibility of the current assertion. S/he reads carefully the class code in order to detect faults. If a fault is detected, then tester has to describe the expected wrong behavior from the user point of view in a local text file. S/he hence proceeds to fill out his form for this type defect and to submit the related form, as already mentioned in the Common steps above.

3.4   Procedure

In the BE experiment, subjects were requested to be present at a private Internet Café in Rome downtown in the morning of 2002 February 14, at about 8:30 A.M., where we had reserved an open-workshop for exclusive use. There were 50 PCs of the same type, ready and connected together to an internal network and via Internet to the experiment Web site. A total of 45 individuals participated to the basic experiment as subjects. No. 15 subjects were assigned for individual application of CR, and No. 15 subjects were assigned for individual application of FTI. Moreover, No. 15 subjects were assigned for individual application of FTO, i.e. Functional Testing Only; the task of such subjects was to detect and describe failures only, without entering the code. The experiment was started at 10:30 A.M.; subjects were informed in advance that a very hard deadline of 120 minutes was in place for all the experiment procedures, plus 5 minutes for transferring text files with assertions and error descriptions by e-mail. At 12:30 subjects were requested to exit immediately the experiment web site and start transferring files by e-mail. The Internet café management logged off subjects at 12:40. Because No. 2 CR individuals, and No. 7 FTI individuals were late in their file transfer, we lost their data. In the following, only CR and FTI data will be considered; in fact, we are still working on FTO data.

The R1 experiment is a replication with variations of BE. Subject were on time, in the morning of 2002 March 27, at 9.30, taking their places in the computer lab at the URM2 DISP. There were 25 PCs of the same type, ready and connected together to an internal network and via a local net to the experiment Web mirror on the lab server. No. 13 subjects were assigned for individual application of CR, and No. 12 subjects assigned for individual application of FTI. At 10.00 A.M. they were informed that duration time was two hours, and hence started their task. During the experiment conduction, because one of the FTI subjects did not seem enough trained, observers permitted him to continue his work but also decided to discard his data.

For both experiments, the observers provided all subjects with login name, password and link to electronic documents and instructions to apply the experiment. Common documents included: Solitaire game requirements, Solitaire class diagram, Code of classes for each level of game difficulties, Guidelines for reading and extending assertions, Assertions (for BE, an empty text file). In order to support both the comprehension of the software application, and fault reports, the lines of code of the Solitaire game had been numbered and annotated. FTI-specific documents included both FTI forms, defined according to the classification of faults, and Java Machine executable code of Solitaire (it is present for each level of game difficulty). Functional testers were allowed to access code only after they had detected a program failure. CR-specific documents included CR forms defined according to the classification of faults. CR testers were not allowed to use the Java Machine.

Interested readers can find all the documents and details related to the experiment operation by visiting the web site http://eseg.uniroma2.it/webESEG/esp_cr.htm.

4 Results

In this Section, descriptive statistics and hypothesis testing are presented. First of all, let us present directions that we followed in developing the analysis of quantitative and qualitative data results.

In order to investigate the impact of independent variables on the dependent variables, we evaluated projections of effectiveness with respect to some dimensions (or perspectives); these projections would explain the complete dependent variable when combining them in one. The reason for applying such an approach is to have a full govern of the analysis, and to treat the several independent variables involved with those perspectives in a fair independent way. The perspectives we used, and their explanations are discussed as follows:

- **Inspecting time:** in the present study, based on the definition of effectiveness (see section 1), we are interested in observing the number of faults detected per each technique, and hence, the time available for inspecting is a part of the effectiveness' power of techniques under investigation; that is, one technique could force subjects to invest more inspecting time than another technique in order to detect an equal number of faults in the used objects.
- **Number of seeded faults:** since we are discussing an experiment with one replication, it is significant to describe the effectiveness of the techniques with respect to the number of seeded faults, especially when the number of seeded faults is significantly different in the two experiments. In particular, we are focusing on the number of detected faults out of the seeded ones.
- **Subjects' performance:** again, based on the definition of effectiveness, subjects' performance is one of the indicators of the effectiveness' power of techniques under investigation. In fact, we used two levels of subjects experience; therefore, subjects performance perspective – as we will see later on- effects on the detection process and, as a result, the effectiveness of the techniques.

- **Types of seeded faults:** faults detected by subjects were categorized according to their types; in fact, the type of seeded faults perspective is a sub-case of the number of seeded faults perspective, and hence, we are focusing on the number of detected faults out of the seeded ones for each type.

Thus, the four perspectives are explaining the same object from different points of view, and they also lead, together, to the main goal of this study. We are working for testing how strong the correlation between those perspectives is and, if so, we are going to apply some multivariate analysis [15, 16, 17].

Consider that, in order to give the ability of making comparable decisions between the results from the two experiments (see Section 5), data are normalized to 1 with respect to the number of participants, the number of seeded faults and, in particular, the different types of faults (Fig. 1 excluded, which shows number of detected faults.) Consequently, data are presented in relative values (percentages) rather than absolute values. In particular, percentage data are presented in the range from 0.00 to 1.00 (rather than 0 and 100, respectively, because of their normalization to 1 rather than 100.)

Consider also that, in our definition, total number of *actual faults found* is different from the number of *positive detections*; in fact, many subjects can detect the same actual fault, hence many *positives* can be mapped to the same actual fault. Because it is reasonable to presume that the number of actual faults found tends to reach the number of (seeded or preexistent) faults when search time tends to reach infinite, actual faults found is a proper indicator for demonstrating the effectiveness of testing techniques on the inspection process.

Concerning descriptive statistics. Different types and numbers of faults were seeded in the inspected programs; actually, these faults were seeded with respect to only their different types; however, subjects interacted with these seeded faults and their types with respect to the following four different perspectives.

Inspecting time: Fig. 1 presents inspection process for both techniques with respect to inspecting time. Consider that inspection process for BE and R1 were proceeded within a limited time of two hours.

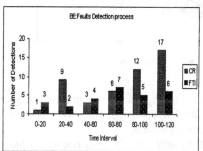 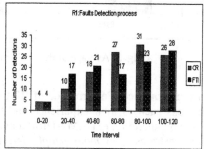

Fig. 1. Inspection Process for CR (left) and FTI (right), BE and R1

Number of seeded faults: For the basic experiment, faults were seeded in an inconsistent way, and inspected faults were really small with respect to the seeded ones. At the beginning, we referred the lack of sufficient data both to subject's inexperience, and the small number of seeded faults, though thirty-eight different types of faults were seeded. Therefore, in the first replication, we seeded ninety-five different types of faults, and selected a higher level of subjects' experience.

In Fig. 2, we present *"how many actual faults out of the total number of the seeded faults were detected"* in BE and R1, respectively.

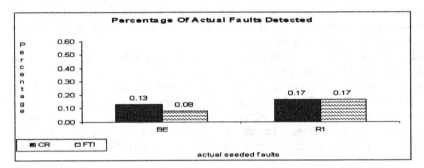

Fig. 2. Percentages of actual faults detected

Fig. 3 demonstrates *"how many positive faults were detected with respect to each testing technique"*. According to our calculations, averages of detections of faults by all subjects were involved, where many subjects can detect the same fault, and this counts for each subject. In other words, percentage of positive fault detection numbers is the overall average of the subjects' fault detection means.

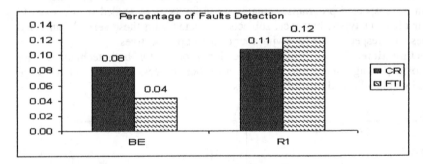

Fig. 3. Average of the total number of detections

Subject performance: Performance of BE and R1 subjects is not equal regarding to many reasons such as their experience and knowledge, though they were chosen from the same population, i.e. URM2-DISP university students.

Fig. 4 demonstrates *"how many people detected positive faults with respect to the technique applied"*.

Types of seeded faults: This is the most important perspective for demonstrating techniques effectiveness. We would like to know *"how many types of faults were detected with respect to techniques under investigation"*.

Let us begin with actual faults. Fig. 5 shows actual faults detected with respect to fault types.

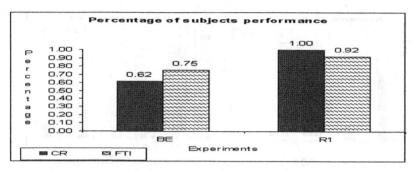

Fig. 4. Percentage of subjects' performance

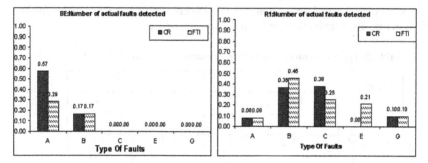

Fig. 5. Actual detected faults classified by their types

Now we would like to know *"which type of actual faults is the most detectable among BE and R1"*. Table 4 shows the detection of actual faults in a descending order.

Let us consider now positives. Fig. 6 shows positive fault detections with respect to fault types.

Table 4. Actual faults detected classified by their types

LEVEL	CR		FTI	
	BE	R1	BE	R1
First	A	C	A	B
Second	B	B	B	C
Third		G		E
Forth				G
Fifth				A

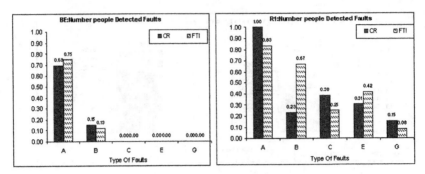

Fig. 6. Positive detections classified by fault types

Now we would like to know *"how many subjects detected each type of faults"*. Table 5 shows positive faults detected in a descending order.

Table 5. Types of faults classified by the number of subject's detections

LEVEL	CR		FTI	
	BE	R1	BE	R1
First	A	A	A	A
Second	B	B	B	C
Third		E		E
Forth		C		B
Fifth		G		G

Concerning hypothesis testing. Let us now present the testing of our hypothesis regarding the effectiveness of CR against FTI. Again, we remind that our main hypothesis' formal state is as the following:

$H_{0 \text{ (Effectiveness)}}$: CR and FTI perform insignificantly different in detecting faults.

$H_{1 \text{ (Effectiveness)}}$: CR and FTI perform significantly different in detecting faults.

Moreover, the research team, according to some initial suppositions and primary analysis, assumes that FTI technique would be more effective in detecting faults than CR technique, with respect to the several perspectives that we previously defined and described in this section.

Notice that, for brevity reasons, we do not consider tests of normality more than presenting the final results from the two experiments. However, we can say briefly that, by applying the test of normality for the basic experiment and its first replication, results are stating that the two reading techniques can be fitted under the normal curve, which means that we can apply a parametric test for testing our hypothesis for each experiment. According with such result, we applied for t-test, which are represented by the p-values shown in Table 6 BE experiment.

The test statistic for the BE experiment shows no significant difference between the two techniques concerning their capabilities of detecting and identifying faults.

Table 6. t-test for effectiveness of CR and FTI for BE experiment

Results	p-value	Test	Alfa
Accept $H_{0 \text{ (BE Effectiveness)}}$	0.08	t- test	0.05

Box-and-whisker plot can be useful for handling and presenting our data values. Box-and-whisker plots allow people to explore data and to draw informal conclusions when two or more variables are present. It shows only certain statistics rather than all the data. These statistics consists of the median, the quartiles, and the smallest and greatest values in the distribution. Immediate visuals of a box-and-whisker plot are the center, the spread, and the overall range of distribution.

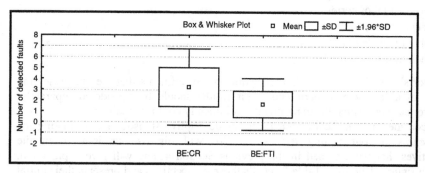

Fig. 7. Box &whiskers plot for effectiveness for BE

For what concerns R1, Table 7 presents the t-test for effectiveness and, again, no significant differences are provided between the techniques with respect to their capabilities of detecting and identifying faults.

Table 7. t-test for effectiveness of CR and FTI for R1 experiment

Results	p-value	Test	Alfa
Accept $H_{0 \text{ (R1 Effectiveness)}}$	0.40	t- test	0.05

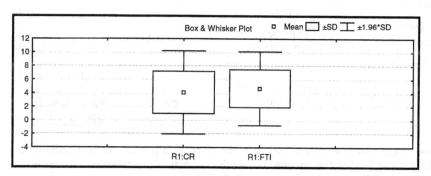

Fig. 8. Box &whiskers plot for effectiveness for R1

5 Discussion

In this Section, we first evaluate the results presented in Section 4, and discuss their implications, especially with respect to the original hypotheses. Then we synthesize and enumerate ten results, whose further investigation is still necessary, with respect to four variables, which should be considered precisely. Finally, we consider threats to validity.

Before we begin analyzing our data, let us point out that when we passed from the basic experiment to its replication, we made some changes, so that the latter faced with noticeable differences, which affected the followings:

- Checklist-construction process
- Experiment laboratories
- Subjects experiences
- Number of seeded faults
- Applied training methods.

Reader should hence consider that, while the experiments that we are presenting are part of a family of experiments, their results should be considered separately, except for cases in which the experiments reciprocally confirm results.

We consider now the extraction from our descriptive statistics for evaluating the effectiveness of our testing techniques. We will discuss our issue from the perspectives that we assumed in the previous Section 4, and will give explanation, based on figures 1 up to 8. Table 8 recalls those perspectives and presents their initial values.

Table 8. Different perspectives for evaluating the effectiveness of CR (left) and FTI (right)

Perspective	Explanation	BE value(s)	R1 value(s)
1st - Inspecting time	Total detection time	120 minutes	120 minutes
2nd - Subjects performance (experience)	Number of subjects detecting faults	0.62 vs. 0.75	1.00 vs. 0.92
3rd - Actual faults detection	Number of detected actual faults	0.13 vs. 0.08	0.17 vs. 0.17
4th - Total of positive fault detections	Frequencies of faults detection	0.08 vs. 0.04	0.11 vs. 0.12
5th - Types of faults	Types of seeded faults found	CR / 1st type: C / 2nd type: B	FTI / 1st types: A, B, G / 2nd type: B

Inspecting time: For each experiment, the inspection process for both techniques was extended to the last few minutes before the inspection's termination. This point is demonstrated by Fig. 1, which implies the following:

1. The assigned testing time was not enough.

    Inspecting time vs. number of seeded faults: Preexistent and seeded detected faults for R1 are around twice higher than BE, in the average. In particular, for actual faults (see Fig. 2), those averages are 10.5% for CR subjects, and 17% for R1 subjects; for positives (see Fig. 3), they are 6%, and 11.5%, respectively. Based on this data, and on the number of seeded faults (see Table 3) it seems that:

2. Inspecting time needed is directly related with the number of actual faults seeded.

    Inspecting time vs. level of experience: Data, which we have considered for the point 2 above, also demonstrates that R1 subjects experience indicator (Moderately expert subjects) was high enough to detect faults more than BE subjects (Inexperienced subjects). Based on this data, it also seems that:

3. Inspecting time needed is directly related with the level of experience of subjects. Concerning again point 3 above, Fig. 4 obviously confirms that R1 subjects could not discharge their capacities within the inspecting time period indicated. In fact, as Table 8 shows, R1 subjects detected an equal number of actual faults for both techniques (3rd perspective), and nearly equal positive faults as well (4th perspective), with maximum subject performance (2nd perspective).

    Subject performance: Actions were done with a very high level of subjects' performances, as shown in Fig. 4, which indicates that, at the end of the experiment duration time, subjects were not yet explaining the difference between effectiveness for both techniques. In particular, for R1, all the CR subjects and almost all the FTI subjects were still positively finding faults. This also explain the high rate of the p-value concerning R1 (see Table 6, 2nd raw). For BE, with less number of seeded faults and less experience for subjects, a small difference (5%) between CR and FTI inspection can be seen (13% for CR against 8% for FTI; see 3rd perspective in Table 8).

4. Moderately expert subjects are more effective than inexperienced ones.

    Types of faults: We can see that types of faults seeded were not all detected, even with different levels of experiences and inspecting time intervals, though the number of actual faults and their detections were higher and significant for CR against FTI in BE (see 3rd perspective in Table 8). In our interpretation, this again confirms point 1 above, by indicating that:

5. More inspecting time period is required with higher expert subjects.

    Let us consider now actual fault detections. Based on Table 4, for the most types of fault detections, it seems that:

6. Inexperienced subjects emphasize on actual faults of the Initialization type.

    Vice versa, moderately experienced subjects place actual Initialization faults at the lowest priority level. In fact:

7. The best performances of moderately experienced subjects relate to Computation and Control actual faults.

    According to Table 4, consider also that moderately experienced subjects were able to pass further levels than inexperienced ones; in fact, they detected actual faults that depend on interaction between different software-coded entities:

8. Moderately experienced subjects were able to detect actual Interface and Event types of fault. Inexperienced subjects weren't.

Let us consider now positive fault detections. Table 5 shows the most common detections.

9. Initialization faults gained the highest score of positive detections by testers for both techniques.
    Meanwhile:

10. For Moderately experienced subjects, Interface and Event faults gained the highest score of positive detections by testers for both techniques (see 3rd and 5th levels in Table 5).

Based on points above, the following main conclusions can be carried out: further investigation is still necessary. In order to see differences in the effectiveness between CR and FTI techniques, the following variables should be considered precisely:

A. Inspecting time. This should be much more than two hours. Since we found that medium expert subjects were still strongly active in applying both techniques after two hours, when there was still no difference between technique effectiveness.

B. Number of seeded faults. Techniques should be tested with a small number of seeded faults, but several types of them. However, faults should be seeded according to the probability of their occurrence.

C. Subject experience. Subjects experience seems to strongly affect on techniques' performances.

D. Types of faults. FTI seems to perform better than CR in detecting interface, event and control faults.

Let us now explore the aspects of the study that related to validity evaluation and assessment, and hence whether our study can justify the drawn conclusions.

Concerning threats to conclusion validity. Conclusion validity is the degree to which conclusions can be drawn about the existence of a statistical relationship between treatments and outcomes. Due to participation on voluntary basis, and because of our small population size, it was not possible for us to plan the selection of a population sample by using one of the common sampling techniques, so we decided to take the whole population of our incoming classes as our target samples, whatever that population would be. A limited number of data values were collected during the operation of the experiments, due to the limited duration time and number of objects and subjects. Regarding the basic experiment, some of the subjects were late in e-mailing their description files, the Internet connection went down before they accomplished their process, and hence we could not give interpretation and use the forms they had submitted. Consequently, the designed balance of subjects using both techniques was lost. For what concerns the quality of data collecting, we had screen-driven automatic data collection; hence data collection in not considered being critical (in addition, starting from R1, some form fields were checked at run time, and some data, e.g. timestamps, was automatically acquired by the system.) Finally, the quantity and quality of collected data and data analysis were enough to support our conclusions, as described in the previous Sections, concerning the existence of a statistical relationship between treatments and outcomes [11].

Concerning threats to Internal validity. Internal validity is the degree to which conclusions can be drawn about the causal effect of the treatments on the outcomes. The experiment was under very strict control and was managed in a way that implicitly kept further independent variables, if any, at as fixed as possible values. Consequently, the observed relationship between the treatments and the outcomes seems to be determined causally rather than the result of a factor that we could not control or had not measured. Some noticeable differences should be noted between the basic experiment and its replications. In particular: Moderately expert subjects were trained both in class, lab and through Internet; inexperienced subjects got class training, did not get lab training, were allowed to get practical training through Internet on personal basis. Moderately expert subjects received checklists as part the experiment package; inexperienced subjects had to produce checklist by themselves. The screen type changed when we passed from the basic experiment to its first replication. The room available for subjects diminished when the experiment passed from a very large Internet Café to a quite small academic lab. A further threat to internal validity is concerned with the number of participating subjects, which was very less than the minimum needed (at least 35 for each technique, in our evaluation) both for BE and R1.

Concerning threats to construct validity. Construct validity is the degree to which the independent variables and dependent variables accurately measure the concepts they purport to measure. We adopted both well-defined and appropriate measures for the attributes of the entities we wanted to measure. Threats to construct validity of our experiments are concerned with following items. Objects: one experiment object was planned for all subjects. Both the experiment and training objects were relatively complex, compared to the time made available for training and experiment (see threats to external validity in the followings.) Subjects: we chose to ignore differences within subjects in the same sample. Moreover, the experiments were planned to be also part of academic courses in which the students are graded. While we informed students that we would not be using the experiment results for grading, we felt that many of them were not quite sure that our mind would not change. Hence, our prediction was that, on one hand, many of them could show abnormally high performance, due to both being younger and more knowledgeable about OO Programming than average practitioners, and to the pressure caused by the wrong believe of being involved with an optional part of an exam; on the other hand, they could try to find as many defects as possible, without placing the necessary attention on categorizing them correctly, in the mistaken belief that the greater the number of defects they find, the greater their exam score. In other words, our subjects could really try to cheat and bias their data. Consequently, our plan for prevention was to keep subjects under the strict continual control with respect to both the system and observers.

Concerning threats to external validity. External validity is the degree to which the results of the research can be generalised to the population under study and other research settings. The greater the external validity, the more the results of an empirical study can be generalised with regards to actual software engineering practice. Some threats to validity have been identified which limit the ability to apply generalisation. There is a threat that concerns the experiment duration time. The duration of both the experiments is short with respect to the assigned tasks. We had foreseen such a threat to validity during the experiment planning. In order to cope with this threat, BE subjects and observers reached the rented lab very early morning; unfortunately, the lab personnel was upgrading the system and, because of some troubles, it was not possible for us to approach the experiment operation before 10 A.M. Moreover, according to our limited budget, it had been impossible for us to plan the basic experiment to last a full day in such a large loft-like rented laboratory. For what concerns the first replication, because we were going to change both the type of laboratory and the level of experience of the participating subjects, we did not want to change the experiment duration time as well. We hence decided to use the same amount of time of 120 minutes. Successively, in order to deal with the threat of time availability, we conducted a further replication with a longer period of duration time; data collected are still under consideration and analysis. Further threats to external validity are concerned with the materials involved. Firstly, fault seeding did not follow distributions known from literature [13]; however, data distributions are not yet quite available, which concern concurrent OO event-driven software. Moreover, we chose an experiment object (Solitaire game, see Section 3.3), which could lead FTI subjects to spend some time with reasoning rather than testing. This object might not be properly representative of event-driven applications. In order to cope with this threat, we organized the experiment objects in multiple versions, one for each level of difficulty. However, in order to investigate this perspective, our plan for future experiments is to extend the set of experiment objects by including a game, namely Flipper game, which requires subjects to reflex, to physical react, rather than to reflect. In conclusion, results could change with students of other universities or professionals, because of their different levels of knowledge and experience.

6   Lessons Learned

We consider now the key lessons that we have learned to date from undertaking this empirical study. We assume an internal perspective as the main point of view, so the emphasis will be on lessons learned that concern subjects, process, and materials.

Concerning training: Training is an essential preparatory phase of any experimentation on software engineering topics. Training enables practicing on the techniques to be compared. To have sufficiently prepared subjects to execute the experiment in the right way is an important aspect for the research team. Let us show now how we trained those subjects through BE and R1, respectively. Training should be conducted both in class and lab. Using Internet only to train subjects usually results into an insufficient training, whatever the level of experience and maturity of the subjects might be.

Concerning experiment objects and other material: Initially, objects, forms, and documentation include many inaccuracies. Hence, they pass through many changes. In order to improve and eventually stabilize the experiment materials, it is very important to conduct a family of experiments rather than a single or few experiments.

Concerning the experiment process: An iterative-incremental experiment process model should take place rather than Waterfall and related variants. In fact, the initial experiment process passes through many modifications, and comes to an acceptable level of stability after that misunderstandings are well explained, mistakes are detected and removed, and essential tacit knowledge is made explicit. Moreover, we cannot discover all the experiment variables and requirements in the first iteration of the experiment planning, because many of them will be seen during the experiment operation.

Concerning experiment replication: In order to make experiments easy to replicate, an appropriate way is to design the experiment for running on an electronic net with the assist of automated data collection.

Concerning capitalization of experiences: In order to manage software experimentations at a reasonable capability and maturity level, software engineering organizational concepts and best practices should be extensively applied. Lessons learned from successful and unsuccessful experiments should be packaged for future reuse. Experiment objects, guidelines and process should be placed under change and version management. Each experiment process should be placed under workflow automation. Eventually the concept of Experience Factory [18, 19] should be specialized [20, 21] to the ESE domain [22, 23].

Acknowledgements. We thank Sandra Celiberti, formerly Bachelor student in the URM2-DISP, for her effort on experiment operation, data management collection, and web site organization. We also thank Luca Colasanti, student in the URM2-DISP, for his participation to the experiment operations in the role of observer. Last but not least, our thanks to Salvatore Nicosia, Chair of the URM2 Informatics engineering faculties, which supported rental of extra campus-wall lab facilities for our experiment with sophomores.

References

[1] Basili V. R., and R. Selby, "Comparing the Effectiveness of Software Testing Strategies", IEEE Transactions on Software Engineering, CS Press, 10(12), pp. 1278–1296, December 1987.

[2] Cantone G., and Z. A. Abdulnabi, "Effectiveness and Fault Detection Rate of Code Reading and Functional Testing with Event-driven OO Java Software: Results from a Multi-replicated Experiment with Students of Different Level of Experience", URM2–DISP–ESEG 01.03 T.R., Rome, April 2003.

[3] Basili V. R., and D. M. Weiss, "A Methodology for Collecting Valid Software Engineering Data", IEEE–TSE, Nov. 1984, pp. 728–738.

[4] Basili V. R., G. Caldiera, and H. D. Rombach, "Goal Question Metric Paradigm", Encyclopedia of Software Engineering, ed. J. J. Marciniak, Vol. I, pp. 528–532, Wiley, 1994.

[5] Solingen (van) R., and E. Berghout, "The Goal/Question/Metric Method: A Practical Guide for Quality Improvement and Software Development", McGraw-Hill Intl. Editions, 1988.

[6] Kamsties E., and C. M. Lott, "An Empirical Evaluation of Three Defect-Detection Techniques", University of Kaiserslautern, ISERN–95–02 T.R., Germany, 1995 (www.iese.fhg.de/cgi-bin/ISERN_bibq ; 4.04.2003)

[7] Brooks A., J. Daly, J. Miller, M. Roper, M. Wood, "Replication's Role in Experimental Computer Science", EfoCS–5–94 (RR/94/171), 1994.

[8] Dunsmore A. M. Roper, and M. Wood, "Practical Code Inspection of Object-Oriented Systems", Proceedings of WISE'01, Paris, 2001. www.cas.mcmaster.ca/wise/

[9]   N. Juristo, and S. Vegas: "Functional Testing, Structural Testing and Code Reading: What Fault Type do they Each Detect?", Universidad Politécnica de Madrid, ESERNET book v3.9, 2003 (see Chapter 12 of this book).

[10] Cantone G., and S. Celiberti: "Evaluating efficiency, effectiveness, and other indices of code reading and functional testing for concurrent event-driven OO Java software: Results from a multi-replicated experiment with students of different level of experience", Proceedings of 2002 IEEE ISESE Symposium, Vol. II, Nara, JP, 3–4 October 2002, Pgs. 23–24.

[11] Wohlin C., P. Runeson, M. Höst, M. C. Ohlsson, B. Regnell, and a. Wesslén, "Experimentation in Software Engineering. An Introduction", Kluwer A. P., 2000.

[12] Budd T. A., Introduction to Object Oriented Programming with Java, Wiley, 2001.

[13] Pfleeger S. L. "Software engineering: Theory and Practice", 2nd edition, Prentice Hall, 2002.

[14] IBM Corp. "S/390 Orthogonal Defect Classification Education". (www-1.ibm.com/servers/eserver/zseries/odc/nonshock/odc8ns.html, 4.04.2003.

[15] Briand and Wüst (2001). Modeling Development Effort in Object-Oriented Systems Using Design Properties. IEEE Transactions on Software Engineering, Vol. 27, N° 11, 963–986.

[16] Genero M., M. Piattini, E. Manso, and G. Cantone, "Building UML Class Diagram Maintainability Prediction Models Based on Early Metrics", Proceedings of the Eighth IEEE Symposium on Software Metrics (METRICS'03), 2003 (to appear.)

[17] Mendes E.I, Watson I., Mosley N. and Counsell S., " A Comparison of Development Effort Estimation Techniques for Web Hypermedia Applications" Proceedings of the Eighth IEEE Symposium on Software Metrics (METRICS'02), 2002.

[18] Basili V. R., Quantitative evaluation of software methodology. (Keynote address). In Proceedings of the First Pan Pacific Computer Conference. Melbourne, Sept. 1985.

[19] Basili V. R., G. Caldiera, and H. D. Rombach, "Experience Factory", Encyclopedia of Software Engineering, ed. J. J. Marciniak, Vol. I, pp. 469–476, Wiley, 1994.

[20] Neighbors J. M., "Draco: A method for engineering reusable software systems", in Software Reusability, Vol. 1: Concepts and Models, pp. 295–319, ACM Press, New York, 1989.

[21] Basili V. R., G. Caldiera G., and G. Cantone, A Reference Architecture for the Component Factory. ACM TOSEM, Vol. 1, No. 1, January 1992.

[22] Cantone G., L. Cantone, and P. Donzelli, "Models, Measures and Learning Organizations for Software Technologies" in Global Semiconductor Technology 2001, published by World Markets Research Centre (WMRC) in association with SIA, SISA, Nepcon WEST, FSA, pp. 136–148, January 2001.

[23] Cantone, G., "Measure-driven Processes and Architecture for the Empirical Evaluation of Software Technology", Journal of Software Maintenance: Research & Practice 12(1): pp. 47–78, 2000.

Experimentation with Usage-Based Reading

Thomas Thelin[1], Magnus Erlansson[1], Martin Höst[1], and Claes Wohlin[2]

[1] Dept. of Communication Systems, Lund University
Box 118, SE-221 00 Lund, Sweden
`{thomas.thelin,martin.host}@telecom.lth.se`
[2] Dept. of Software Engineering and Computer Science Blekinge Institute of Technology
Box 520, SE-372 25 Ronneby, Sweden
`claes.wohlin@bth.se`

Abstract. Software inspections are regarded as an important technique to detect faults throughout the software development process. The individual preparation phase of software inspections has enlarged its focus from only comprehension to also include fault searching. Hence, reading techniques to support the reviewers on fault detection are needed. Usage-based reading (UBR) is a reading technique, which focuses on the important parts from a user's point of view in a software document by using prioritized use cases. UBR has been evaluated in two previously conducted experiments, which investigate the prioritization of UBR and compare UBR against checklist-based reading (CBR). This chapter presents two controlled experiments with UBR on requirements and design specifications. The experiments include individual preparation and inspection meeting, i.e. the first steps of the traditional inspection process. For the requirements inspection, UBR is evaluated against CBR, and for the design inspection, the amount of information needed in the use cases are studied. The studies were conducted in different environments with a total of about 100 students. The result from these experiments shows that UBR is not better than CBR for requirements inspections. Results from the experiment on design inspection indicate that use cases developed in advance are preferable compared to developing them as part of the preparation phase of the inspection.

1 Introduction

Software inspections are regarded as an important technique to detect faults throughout the software development process [1]. The individual preparation phase of software inspections has enlarged its focus from only comprehension to also include fault searching. Hence, reading techniques to support the reviewers on fault detection are needed.

Several reading techniques have been proposed and empirically evaluated for software inspections [2]. The first structured reading technique was checklist-based reading (CBR), suggested by Fagan [1, 3]. CBR provides the individual reviewers with a checklist of the faults that should be looked for. Examples of other reading techniques are defect-based reading [4] and perspective-based reading [5], which both have the goal to minimize the overlap among the faults found and thus increase the

R. Conradi and A.I. Wang (Eds.): ESERNET 2001-2003, LNCS 2765, pp. 193–207, 2003.

effectiveness. In addition, they also force the reviewers to actively design software artifacts during inspections.

1.1   Usage Based Reading

Usage-based reading (UBR) stems from an idea from Wohlin and Ohlsson, which is published in [6]. The purpose was to let the expected usage govern the inspection. The motivation behind the method was that faults that affect the user of the software the most are crucial to find, and hence an inspection method setting the user in focus was needed. Usage-based reading (UBR) is a reading technique, which focuses on the important parts of a software document by using prioritized use cases [7].

Software inspections are carried out in order to find faults at an early stage of the software development process. The general steps of an inspection session are [8]:

1. Presentation of material: The reviewers are presented with the material they should inspect.
2. Individual inspections: All reviewers individually read the material in order to find faults.
3. Meeting: A meeting is held where the reviewers meet and summarize their findings. The result of this step is a compiled list of faults.
4. Update: The inspected material is updated by the author. In some cases a new inspection round is held.

UBR supports mainly step 2 of the process. In UBR, the individual work is guided by a set of prioritized use cases. When the reviewer inspects a document, he/she goes through and manually executes a set of use cases and at the same time checks the document. The use cases are prioritized according to their importance for a user of the system, and the idea is that important faults, from users' point of view, should be found during inspection. UBR is described in more detail in [7, 9].

In this chapter, two experiments on UBR are presented. The experiments evaluate UBR for requirements inspections and design inspections, respectively. The experiments were carried out as two controlled experiments in the ESERNET framework. In both experiments, the subjects were 3rd and 4th year Bachelors and Masters students in courses in software engineering at university level. The results of the experiments could be input to further controlled experiments and industrial experiments.

1.2   Previous Work on UBR

UBR has been evaluated in a series of experiment, where the main purpose is to investigate whether UBR is an efficient and effective reading technique to be used for requirements and design inspections. Before the experiments presented in this chapter, two experiments on UBR have been conducted. In summary, the experiments show positive results in favor for UBR:

- An experiment has been conducted to evaluate the effects of prioritizing use cases. All reviewers used the same use cases, but half of them used a prioritized list and the other half used a non-prioritized list. The reviewers inspected a design document. It was found that the prioritization affected the result of the inspection and that more important faults, from users' point of view, are detected in this way [9].

- An experiment has been conducted to compare UBR against checklist-based reading (CBR) for design specifications. It was found that the UBR technique was more efficient as well as effective than the CBR technique [10].

1.3   Research Questions

The research questions of the two previously conducted experiments were whether prioritization affects the inspection results and which of UBR and CBR is most efficient and effective. The following two research questions are evaluated in this chapter:

- RQ1: Is there a difference in efficiency between UBR and CBR for inspection of requirement specifications? This difference may be in finding faults in general or in detecting the most severe faults.
- RQ2: How much information should be provided in the use cases of UBR when design inspections are performed?

The two research questions are researched in two different studies. RQ1 is investigated in experiment 1, and RQ2 is investigated in experiment 2. Both studies were carried out with students as subjects, and in both studies the inspected material came from the same software system. However, the two experiments were not carried out with the same students.

2 Starting Scenario

Inspection is a structured method to review software documents and is widely accepted as a cost-effective technique to improve the quality of the software. Software inspections are carried out in order to find faults at an early stage of the software development process. The general steps of an inspection process are as described in Section 1.1.

Code and design specifications have, as described above, long been exposed to this kind of review [1], but also requirements specifications have been the object of inspection [4]. As a baseline, it could be said that inspections are carried out in almost all steps of software development and in most kind of projects. In many cases, inspections are carried out as described above.

During the individual inspection, reading techniques have been introduced to guide reviewers. The common purpose of the reading techniques is to help reviewers to detect more faults (effectiveness), and to detect more faults in less time (efficiency). Several reading techniques have been proposed, for example, checklist-based reading [1], defect-based reading [4], perspective-based reading [5] and usage-based reading [9]. The work on these techniques is summarized by Thelin et al. [10]. Checklist-based reading is still regarded as the most commonly used reading technique in industry [11].

3 Method

The two experiments were carried out as *controlled experiments*, i.e. the experimenters had control over the execution of the experiments, for example, they were able to decide which subjects that should use which treatment in the inspections that were carried out.

3.1   Design

3.1.1   Experiment 1: Requirements Inspection
The purpose of experiment 1 is to evaluate UBR versus CBR for requirements inspections. The independent and dependent variables are defined as follows:
- Independent Variable – the reading technique, UBR or CBR.
- Dependent Variables – inspection time, meeting time, and faults. These measurements are used to calculate the effort, efficiency and effectiveness.

In the experiment, the subjects were divided into two groups. One group used UBR in the inspection, and the other group used CBR.

The null and alternative hypotheses were defined as follows:
- H0_eff: There is no difference between UBR and CBR with respect to effectiveness (number of faults found per reviewer)
- Ha_eff: There is a difference between UBR and CBR with respect to effectiveness
- H0_rate: There is no difference between UBR and CBR with respect to efficiency (number of faults found per reviewer and hour)
- Ha_rate: There is a difference between UBR and CBR with respect to efficiency

For statistical comparison of the results, a nonparametric test (Mann-Whitney U-test) was used. P-values less than 0.05 were regarded as significant.

3.1.2   Experiment 2: Design Inspection
The purpose of experiment 2 is to investigate the amount of information needed for UBR inspections. This is evaluated for design inspections. This is conducted by comparing one group of reviewers that utilize developed use cases with another group of reviewers that has to develop use cases during inspection. The latter group was provided with the title and purpose of the use cases but not the tasks. Tasks of a use case are step-by-step instructions for one use case, called task notation in [12]. The independent, controlled and dependent variables are defined for the experiment. These variables are:

- Independent Variable – the reading technique used. The reading technique used was either utilizing (purpose and tasks pre-developed) use cases or developing (only purpose pre-developed) use cases. These treatments were used in two different places, in campus Helsingborg at Lund University and in Ronneby at Blekinge Institute of Technology. The abbreviations used are Util (utilizing use case), Dev (developing use cases), Hbg (Helsingborg), Rb (Ronneby) and the combination of these, i.e. Util-Hbg, Dev-Hbg, Util-Rb and Dev-Rb.
- Controlled Variable – the experience of the reviewers. This is measured on an ordinal scale. The reviewers filled in a questionnaire with seven questions.
- Dependent Variables – preparation time, inspection time and faults. These measurements are used to calculate the effort, efficiency and effectiveness.

The hypotheses of the experiment were set up to evaluate the amount of information needed in order to utilize UBR. The hypotheses are expressed in terms of efficiency and effectiveness of finding critical faults from a user's point of view:

- H0_eff – There is no difference in efficiency (i.e. found faults per hour) between reviewers utilizing pre-developed use cases (Util) and reviewers who develop use cases (Dev).
- Ha_eff – There is a difference in efficiency between reviewers utilizing pre-developed use cases (Util) and reviewers who develop use cases (Dev).
- H0_rate – There is no difference in effectiveness between reviewers utilizing pre-developed use cases (Util) and reviewers who develop use cases (Dev).
- Ha_rate – There is a difference in effectiveness (i.e. rate of faults found) between reviewers utilizing pre-developed use cases (Util) and reviewers who develop use cases (Dev).

For statistical comparison of the results, a nonparametric test (Mann-Whitney U-test) was used. P-values less than 0.05 were regarded as significant.

3.2   Subjects/Participants

In both experiments, students were used as subjects. In experiment 1, the students were in their 3rd or 4th year of a Masters education. In experiment 2, the students were in their 3rd year at a Bachelors education and in their 4:th year at a Masters education.

In study 1, there were 29 subjects, and the prior experience of them is shown in Fig. 1. The dots represent the individual sum of scores within five experience areas (programming, requirement inspections, use cases, taxi systems and using taxis). The horizontal lines represent the median values. There was some difference between the experiences of individuals, but there was no significant difference between the groups. The prior experiences were collected through a questionnaire after the inspection meeting. Hence, no controlled variable was used since the experience of the subjects was checked after the experiment.

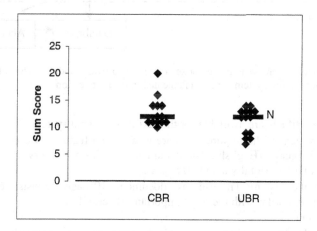

Fig. 1. Previous experience of the students that acted as reviewers in the experiment

In experiment 2, there were 82 subjects, 34 Bachelor students from Lund University (Hbg) and 48 Master students from Blekinge Institute of Technology (Rb). The experiment was a mandatory part of two courses in verification and validation. The courses included lectures and assignments, and both courses were related to verification and validation of software products and evaluation of software processes. Although the courses have the same name, they do not include exactly the same material. The main difference is that the course in Rb is more research oriented and the course in Hbg is more focused on a test project. The main difference between the students in Hbg and Rb can be referred to their education, domain knowledge, and industrial experience.

3.3   Apparatus/Materials

In both experiments, the inspected documents came from the same system, a taxi management system developed by the Department of Communication Systems, Lund University [9]. The system is a simplified version of a system for managing a number of taxi-cars with drivers, and a central node with an operator. The system consists of the following parts (see Fig. 2):
- Taxi-component: a computer and a communication device in every taxi. The taxi drivers operate this component.
- Central node: a central computer, which is operated by an operator.
- Communication link: provides communication between the central system and the taxi-components.

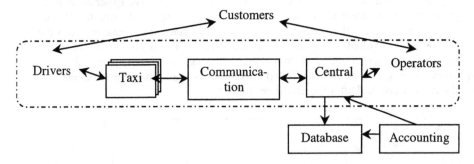

Fig. 2. The taxi management system. The boxes represent software modules. The software for the database and accounting system is not implemented in the first version

The following artifacts are available for the taxi management system:
- Textual requirements: The requirements are written in a feature style notation [12] using natural language (English). The document includes a glossary, a state chart, and a context diagram (totally about 10 pages).
- Use cases for the system: The use case document (10 pages) consists of 24 use cases in prioritized order with the most important use case first.
- Design document
- Checklists for design inspection (not used in the experiments presented here).

- Checklist for requirements inspections: The checklist for requirements inspections is rather short and includes checks for: correctness, completeness, consistency, unambiguous, realistic, and verifiable.
- Code and test cases (not used in the experiments presented here).

3.4   Procedure

In this section, the procedure for both experiments is presented. The following fault classification was used in both experiments:

- A-faults: The most severe faults in critical functions or frequently used functions. Such faults were considered most important for a user of the system.
- B-faults: Moderately severe faults. These faults were found in not so important functions (from a user's point of view) or in not frequently used functions.
- C-faults: Faults that have only a minor impact on the functions.

3.4.1   Experiment 1: Requirements Inspection

Experiment 1 was carried out as shown in Table 1. In step 1, 14 faults were seeded into the requirements document, in which there could be a number of other faults. The seeded faults were mostly faults that previously had been removed from earlier versions of the requirements specification.

Table 1. Summary of experiment 1

Step	Description	Carried out by
1	Fault seeding	Researchers
2	Division into inspection groups	Subjects
3	Start-up meeting	Researchers, subjects
4	Individual inspection	Subjects
5	Inspection meeting	Subjects (inspection groups)
6	Fault classification	Researchers
7	Analysis	Researchers

Two treatments were chosen for the study, UBR and CBR, where CBR was used as a baseline. The students assigned themselves to six inspection groups, i.e. they selected whom to perform the inspection meeting with. Each group consisted of about five people. Hence, randomization was performed on the group level, not on the individual level, i.e. the researchers randomly assigned the treatments to the groups. In step 3 of the experiment the students participated in a start-up meeting. At this meeting they got their individual package of documents to be inspected and forms on paper to fill in. The package included instructions, the requirements specification and use cases or a checklist. They also got detailed instructions for the remaining steps in the process. The two treatments (CBR or UBR) were randomly assigned to three inspection groups. 14 students were assigned to use CBR during inspection and 15 were assigned to use UBR. Then, in step 4, the students inspected the requirements specification individually at home, using the assigned reading techniques. They should use maximally about two hours. In step 5, each inspection group conducted a meeting where they discussed the faults found and produced a common list of faults that they could agree on. After the inspection the students were asked to grade their previous experience (5 areas with 7 questions, each with score 1 to 5) and reveal their educational background. These answers were used during the interpretation of the results of the study. For ethical reasons the students did not write their names on any form. Instead each group got unique identification numbers to distribute within the group in order to connect a form with a group and a treatment.

All documents and forms were written in English. No students have English as their native language.

Before analyzing the result, the issues found by the reviewers were discussed and classified (Step 7). First, a list of all issues found individually was produced. If there were more than one issue referring to the same original fault in the document they were regarded as one fault only. In case the reported faults were not judged as true faults (after precise consideration by the authors of this paper), they were discarded. Finally, all faults in the final list were classified (by the authors of this paper) according to their severity for the function of the final software product. The fault classification was made by the researchers to achieve a common understanding of the faults.

Although the results that are presented in this chapter are derived by the authors, the data produced during the experiment were also analyzed by the students. The objective of this was to teach the students how to carry out empirical studies. This teaching methodology is further presented in [13].

3.4.2   Experiment 2

Prior to experiment 2, the students were asked to fill in an experience questionnaire used for the controlled variable. Using the controlled variable, the students were divided into three groups and then randomized within each group. The three groups consisted of three experience levels (high, medium and low). For each of these levels, the students were randomly assigned to one of the reading techniques, Util or Dev. The division was carried out in Hbg and Rb, separately.

The faults were classified in A, B and C, as in experiment 1. The design document included 38 faults, where 30 were real faults injected during the development of the taxi management system; 8 faults were seeded into the design document by the person who developed the system.

The experiment was conducted during three days, both in Hbg and Rb. However, since the students in Hbg have participated in a course where they developed a requirements document for a taxi management system, they only had a brief introduction. Thus, the general introduction of the taxi management system and the training part were only performed for the students in Rb. The training part included a brief presentation of the reading technique (either Util or Dev) and a small pilot example where the subjects used the reading technique assigned to each group.

The inspection was carried out in a classroom, where at least one of the researchers was present all the time. The subjects received an inspection package containing instructions, a requirements document, a design document, a use case document and an inspection record. During the inspection, the subjects firstly read the documents briefly (about 20 minutes), and then inspected the design document. The inspection was performed individually at maximum 3 hours and 45 minutes.

All documents and forms were written in English. No students have English as their native language.

The analysis was performed by one of the researchers. In this step, false positives were removed and the data were prepared for the statistical analysis. After the first analysis session, another researcher checked the inspection records and the data.

After the experiment had been analyzed, a debriefing session was held with the subjects. The session included a presentation and a discussion of the results of the experiment.

4   Results

4.1   Experiment 1: Requirements Inspections

A first list of 89 possible faults reported individually from reviewers was produced. At the first analysis of this list the numbers of faults were reduced due to one of the following reasons.

- Minor language remarks/criticism. (1 case)
- Duplicates of other faults. (11 cases)
- Conflicts only with use cases and not within the requirement document. (5 cases)
- Not considered as real faults (after careful judgment by the authors of this paper). (25 cases)

47 true faults remained and they were classified in 16 A-faults, 15 B-faults and 16 C-faults.

Below the results from the individual inspections are presented. Since there were so few inspection groups, the results for each group are not presented. Effectiveness refers to the number of faults found independent of the time consumed by the reviewers. Faults that could be most relevant for the user of the final software product were assumed to be A-faults or maybe A- and B-faults together. Fig. 3 shows the effectiveness of the individual inspection considering the different classes of faults and comparing the two different reading techniques, CBR and UBR. There were no significant differences except for B-faults and C-faults. Thus, UBR-reviewers were significantly more effective than CBR-reviewers in finding B-faults but less effective in finding C-faults. No statistical significant differences could be observed in their effectiveness in finding A-faults, both A- and B-faults, or all faults (A+B+C).

The efficiency during fault detection refers to the number of faults found per time unit. Fig. 4 shows the efficiency in terms of number of faults found per hour. The result shows that the CBR approach was significantly more efficient in finding faults than the UBR approach. This can be seen for A- and B-faults, as well as all faults (A+B+C). UBR-reviewers were significantly more efficient in finding B-faults. Interestingly, most UBR-reviewers found no C-faults at all.

4.2   Experiment 2: Design Inspection

There were 38 faults in the design document inspected. No unknown faults were found during the experiment. In this section, the efficiency and effectiveness are evaluated for both places (Hbg and Rb) together and separately.

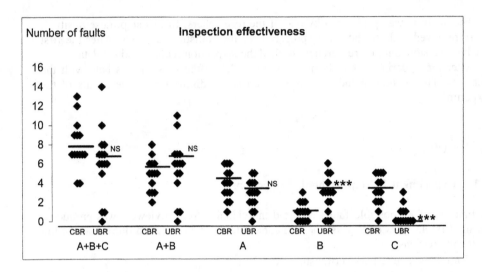

Fig. 3. Individual inspection effectiveness. Individual results are shown as black squares. Horizontal lines represent median values. There were 14 reviewers using CBR and 15 reviewers using UBR (NS= non-significant, * means p<0.05, ** means p <0.01 and *** means p<0.001)

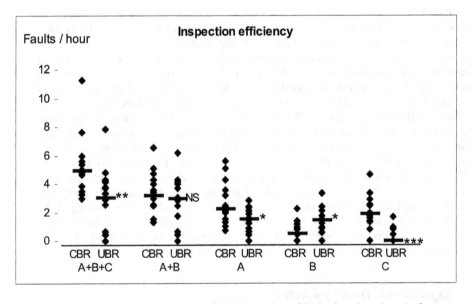

Fig. 4. Individual inspection efficiency. Individual number of faults found per hour is shown as black squares. Horizontal lines represent the median value. There were 14 reviewers using CBR and 15 reviewers using UBR (NS= non-significant, * means p<0.05, ** means p <0.01 and *** means p<0.001)

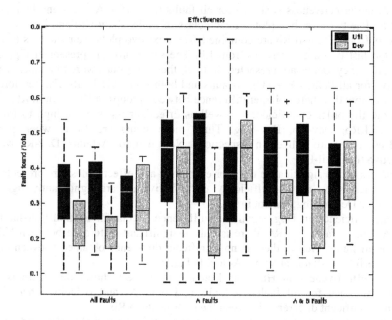

Fig. 5. Individual inspection effectiveness for all faults (A+B+C), A-faults and both A- and B faults. The box plot order for each class of faults is Util (Hbg+Rb), Dev (Hbg+Rb), Util (Hbg), Dev (Hbg), Util (Rb), Dev (Rb)

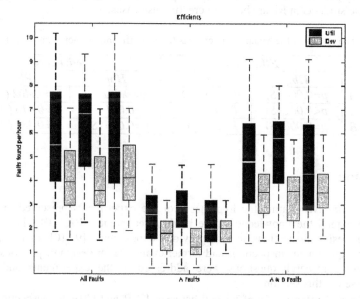

Fig. 6. Individual inspection efficiency for all faults (A+B+C), A-faults and both A- and B-faults. The box plot order for each class of faults is Util (Hbg+Rb), Dev (Hbg+Rb), Util (Hbg), Dev (Hbg), Util (Rb), Dev (Rb)

In Fig. 5, the effectiveness is shown for all faults (A+B+C), A-faults and both A- and B-faults. The two first box plots of each class of faults show Util and Dev when the reviewers from Hbg and Rb are combined. The next two plots are reviewers from Hbg, and the last two are reviewers from Rb. The same order is present in Fig. 6, where the efficiency values are presented. In total, the Util groups were more efficient and effective for all faults (A+B+C), A-faults and both A- and B-faults. Furthermore, the box plots show that there is larger difference between groups in Hbg than in Rb.

In general, the order of efficiency as well as effectiveness is, from high to low, Util-Hbg, Util-Rb, Dev-Rb, Dev-Hbg. Thus, more faults are found when pre-developed use cases are utilized in inspections. Note that for A-faults, Dev-Rb was more effective than Util-Rb.

The p-values of the significance tests for efficiency and effectiveness are presented in Table 2. These show that the efficiency and effectiveness are significantly higher for Util than for Dev in Hbg, but not in Rb.

Regarding efficiency in Hbg, significant differences occur for all faults, A-faults and both A- and B-faults. In Rb, there is only a significant difference between Util and Dev for all faults. Hence, there is no significant difference obtained between the treatments in Rb for A-faults and both A- and B-faults.

Regarding effectiveness in Hbg, the Mann-Whitney test shows that there is a significant difference for all faults, A-faults and both A- and B-faults. There is, however, no significant difference between the treatments in Rb.

Consequently, there is a large difference between Util-Hbg and Dev-Hbg and only a small one between Util-Rb and Dev-Rb. This may depend on two factors; one, more time was used per use case by the reviewers in the Dev-Rb group, and two, there may be a difference between the students' capability in creating use cases between Hbg and Rb, i.e. the students in Rb are better in creating use cases.

Table 2. The results of the Mann-Whitney tests (S = significant, – = non-significant)

	Efficiency		Effectiveness	
	Hbg	**Rb**	**Hbg**	**Rb**
All (A+B+C)	$p=0.006$ (S)	$P=0.043$ (S)	$p=0.002$ (S)	$p=0.462$ (–)
A	$p<0.001$ (S)	$P=0.550$ (–)	$p=0.001$ (S)	$p=0.416$ (–)
A+B	$p=0.008$ (S)	$P=0.097$ (–)	$p=0.006$ (S)	$p=0.582$ (–)

5   Discussion

The rationale for investigating the hypotheses of the experiments presented in this chapter is to extend the knowledge of the reading technique UBR. UBR has been evaluated for design inspections in two previous experiments [9, 10], and is here evaluated for requirements inspections and further evaluated for design inspections.

The following research questions were addressed in the experiments and are further discussed in this section.

- RQ1: Is there a difference in efficiency between UBR and CBR for inspection of requirement specifications?
- RQ2: How much information should be provided in the use cases of UBR when design inspections are performed?

The requirements inspection experiment shows that UBR was neither more efficient nor more effective than using CBR. The purpose of UBR is to get the reviewers better focused on the most important parts of the document, and this to detect the most critical faults from a user's point of view. However, the faults that according to the initial hypothesis were supposed to have the greatest impact on the user were best detected by CBR-reviewers. One explanation could be that the UBR approach was too heavy and exacting for the reviewers when no training session was carried out. Most of the critical faults were missed requirements or conflicts within the requirements document. To detect these kinds of faults the reviewers may need to compare relatively large parts of the document, which requires more domain knowledge. It may be easier when the reviewers just need to read the requirements document. It should be noted that this study is only one single study, and that further experimentation is needed. Opposite to this result, Thelin et al. [10] found that UBR was more efficient and effective than CBR for inspection of design documents. A difference between these studies is that in [10], the subjects were more controlled, i.e. the whole experiment was performed in a classroom.

The conclusion of the design experiment is that it is more efficient to use pre-developed use cases for UBR. However, there is a trade-off of whether the use cases should be developed beforehand or on-the-fly during inspection. The benefit of the latter is that other faults are found, since the reviewers are not that controlled as in the case where they utilize already developed use cases. Hence, there is no clear answer of how much information that is needed for UBR. It depends on the experience of the reviewers, the software organization and effort used for inspections. The purpose of the experiment was to investigate whether UBR can be used without developing the use cases prior to the inspection session. Utilizing pre-developed use cases (Util) leads to reviewers becoming more focused on detecting faults. On the other hand, developing use cases during inspection (Dev) could lead to that other faults are found, since they have to comprehend the document in greater detail to develop the use cases. The data reveal larger differences between the methods in Hbg than in Rb. An explanation of this may be that the Dev-Rb reviewers used more inspection time than the other groups (about 30 minutes more). The reviewers were differently introduced to the methods at the places depending on their experiences and courses taken before the experiment. Another explanation may be that the students in Hbg were less experienced. The students in Hbg were 3rd year Bachelor students and in Rb they were 4th year Master students. Furthermore, the education programme is different and some of the students in Rb have industrial experience. Consequently, less experience may result in less efficiency and effectiveness, especially for the Dev groups, since they had to develop use cases.

In summary, the experimentation with UBR has shown that it is an effective and efficient reading technique for software inspections. However, there still remain questions to be further researched; for example, the experiments need to be replicated, using design and requirements as well as code documents.

It is important to consider the validity of the results of the experiments. The following threats have been found:

- In experiment 1, the randomization of subjects was performed on the group level and not on the individual level. This means that every reviewer of a group used the same treatment (reading technique). The students themselves selected the members of the groups. After the experiment a post-test measuring the experience of the reviewers was performed. The result of this test shows that there was no significant difference between the reviewers of the different treatments. In experiment 2, the experiences of the subjects were measured, on an individual level, prior to the experiments and were used in the controlled variable.

- In experiment 1, the individual inspection was conducted at home. The validity is dependent on that the students honestly report the actual time consumption for the inspection. On the other hand it is assumed that most individual inspections in the industry are conducted very informally, similar to the conditions in the present study. In experiment 2, the individual inspection was carried out in a classroom setting.
- Inspected documents and written instructions are in English, and not in the reviewers' native language. In both experiments, it could have been a burden for some of the students. Though, they could use their own native language when they described the faults in the form. Many Swedish companies write their software documents in English.
- In experiment 1, there was no training period for the students before the real inspection. They might have been too inexperienced to make a real inspection especially using UBR as a reading technique. In experiment 2, there was a training session prior to the experiment session.
- The classification of faults according to their severity is very subjective. However, faults were discussed by all the authors of this paper before the final decision.

These threats should be taken into account when conclusions are drawn. Whether the findings could be generalized to be valid for requirements inspections also in industry is dependent of the generalisability. In this study students were subjects. One can argue that the students' experience is too low compared with practitioners in the industry. However, Porter and Votta [14] reported that although students might have lower performance the result of an experiment with students would be the same as if professionals in the industry have been subjects in the study. In [15], it is also shown that it, under certain conditions, is not a large difference between students and professionals. This threat should also be taken into account when conclusions are drawn based on the result.

6 Lessons Learned

Four experiments on UBR have been conducted, three on design documents and one on requirements document. The three design experiments show positive results in favor for UBR. However, more experiments are needed in order to draw further conclusions about UBR for requirements inspections.

The lesson learned from these studies is that UBR is an efficient and effective reading technique when it is applied to design specifications. Software organizations that utilize use cases during development can preferable prioritize and provide them as input to the reviewers. If use cases not are used, the title and purpose need to be developed before they are used as inspection aid during the individual inspection.

On the other hand, when UBR is used for requirements inspection, it is not possible to conclude whether UBR or CBR should be used. Instead it shows results that are not in line with earlier studies, which makes this study important. The study emphasizes the need for further experimentation in the area.

References

[1] Fagan, M. E., "Design and Code Inspections to Reduce Errors in Program Development", IBM Systems Journal, 15(3):182–211, 1976.

[2] Aurum, A., Petersson, H., Wohlin, C., "State-of-the-Art: Software Inspections after 25 Years", Software Testing, Verification and Reliability, 12(3):133–154, 2002.

[3] Fagan, M. E., "Advances in Software Inspections", IEEE Transactions on Software Engineering, 12(7):744–751, 1986.

[4] Porter, A., Votta, L., Basili, V. R., "Comparing Detection Methods for Software Requirements Inspections: A Replicated Experiment", IEEE Transactions on Software Engineering, 21(6):563–575, 1995.

[5] Basili, V. R., Green, S., Laitenberger, O., Lanubile, F., Shull, F., Sørumgård, S., Zelkowitz, M. V., "The Empirical Investigation of Perspective-Based Reading", Empirical Software Engineering: An International Journal, 1(2):133–164, 1996.

[6] Olofsson, M., Wennberg, M., "Statistical Usage Inspection", Master's Thesis, Department of Communication Systems, Lund University, CODEN:LUTEDX(TETS–5244)1–81/1996&local. 9, 1996.

[7] Thelin, T., Runeson, P. Wohlin, C., "Prioritized Use Cases as a Vehicle for Software Inspections", to appear in IEEE Software.

[8] Ackerman, A. F., Buchwald, L. S. and Lewski, F. H., "Software Inspections: An Effective Verification Process", IEEE Software, 6(3):31–36, 1989.

[9] Thelin, T., Runeson, P. Regnell, B., "Usage-Based Reading – An Experiment to Guide Reviewers with Use Cases", Information and Software Technology, 43(15), pp. 925–938, 2001.

[10] Thelin, T., Runeson, P. Wohlin, C., "An Experimental Comparison of Usage-Based and Checklist-Based Reading", to appear in IEEE Transactions on Software Engineering.

[11] Laitenberger, O., DeBaud, J.M., "An Encompassing Life Cycle Centric Survey of Software Inspection", Journal of Systems and Software, 50(1), pp. 5–31, 2000.

[12] Laueson, S., "Software Requirements – Styles and Techniques" Addison-Wesley, Pearson Education Limited, UK, 2002.

[13] Höst, M., "Introducing Empirical Software Engineering Methods in Education", Proceedings of Conference on Software Engineering Education and Training, pp. 170–179, 2002.

[14] Porter, A, Votta, L., "Comparing Detection Methods for Software Requirements Inspection: A Replication Using Professional Subjects", Empirical Software Engineering, 3(4), pp. 355–380, 1998.

[15] Höst, M., Regnell, B., Wohlin, C. "Using Students as Subjects – A Comparative Study of Students and Professionals in Lead-Time Impact Assessment", Empirical Software Engineering, 5(3), pp. 201–214, 2000.

Functional Testing, Structural Testing, and Code Reading: What Fault Type Do They Each Detect?

Natalia Juristo and Sira Vegas

Facultad de Informática. Universidad Politécnica de Madrid
Campus de Montegancedo, 28660, Boadilla del Monte, Madrid, Spain
{natalia,svegas}@fi.upm.es

Abstract. The origin of the study described here is the experiment performed by Basili and Selby, further replicated by Kamsties and Lott, and once again by Wood *et al.* These experiments investigated the effectiveness and efficiency of different code evaluation techniques (functional and structural testing and code reading). The working hypotheses are the same in all three experiments, although some experimental conditions were changed. The experiments described here use the experiment package elaborated by Kamsties and Lott and examine some of the questions posed as a result of these experiments. Wood *et al.* concluded in their replication of the original study that the relative effectiveness of the techniques depends on the program and fault type. In fact, they suggest formulating a fault taxonomy based on technique sensitivity. Our study intends to compare the relative effectiveness of the testing techniques and to relate the testing techniques to fault types.

1 Introduction

One of the most important activities within software systems development is code evaluation. Code evaluation takes place after coding the system and aims to discover as many defects as possible. There are two complementary forms of evaluating a program: Static analysis and Dynamic analysis.

In static analysis, the code is examined, the aim being to discover as many inaccuracies as possible through observation. Static analysis techniques differ as to the way in which the code is observed or *read*. In dynamic analysis, the code is executed, the aim being to discover code errors by observing system behaviour and trying to deduce whether or not it is satisfactory.

Additionally, whereas static analysis detects the faults the software contains (a fault is an inaccuracy in a software product), all dynamic analysis can do is detect failures (failures occur when a software system does not behave as expected owing to the existence of faults). As the ultimate aim of evaluation is to correct any faults in the software, dynamic analysis calls for a further step to identify faults from the observed failures.

Many static and dynamic techniques for evaluating software system code have been proposed in the literature. Although there are a number of studies where inspections are evaluated, not much work has gone into finding out the strengths and weaknesses of each technique for dynamic techniques. The experiment proposed here

R. Conradi and A.I. Wang (Eds.): ESERNET 2001-2003, LNCS 2765, pp. 208–232, 2003.

aims to contribute to clarifying what differences there between techniques for practical purposes such as how many and what type of errors they detect.

The roots of this study go back to the work of Hetzel [1] and Myers [2]. More precisely, it is the continuation of a line of experiments run by other authors, which have added to the knowledge provided by previous experiments. The original study was conducted by Basili in 1982, 83 and 84 [3]. This experiment studied the effectiveness and efficiency of different code evaluation techniques. Kamsties and Lott first replicated the study in 1995 [4]. This replication assumed the same working hypotheses as in Basili's experiments, but the experiment differed as to the programming language used, as well as the fault detection process. The experiment was replicated again, this time by Wood, Roper, Brooks and Miller, in 1997 [5]. In this case, the experiment followed exactly the same guidelines as the experiment run by Kamsties and Lott (who had built a laboratory package to ease external replication of the experiment[1]), although new analyses were added.

Our experiment follows on from the experiments already performed, although some hypotheses have been altered. For this purpose, we had to modify the laboratory package supplied by Kamsties and Lott. Table 1 gives an overview of the four studies carried out in this series of experiments.

The rest of the chapter has been organised as follows: Section 2 gives an overview of the objectives of the study. Section 3 and Section 4 present each the first and second experiment respectively. Section 5 shows the conclusions obtained in the study.

2 Starting Scenario

One of the findings of the experiment run by Wood et al. toys with the idea that the relative effectiveness of testing techniques depends on the program and fault types. Indeed, they suggest developing a fault taxonomy based on technique sensitivity. The fact, detected in this same experiment by Wood et al., that techniques are much more effective used in combination than used separately backs this hypothesis. On the other hand, however, they also discovered and examined other effects, i.e., subjects applying the same techniques did not generally find the same faults, which have to be taken into account.

The study described here is based on the following recommendation made by Wood *et al.* The relationships between fault type and testing technique effectiveness should be examined in more detail. So, our study aims to **compare the relative effectiveness of different testing techniques and relate the testing techniques to the fault types detected.** For this purpose, the study is composed of two experiments, designed differently to study different factors.

The general hypotheses of the study are:

H_0: Technique effectiveness is independent of the fault type.

H_1: Technique effectiveness is dependent on the fault type.

However, H_1 is decomposed as follows: *technique t_i is the most effective for faults of type f_j,* where there are ixj different subhypotheses.

---

[1] This package is available at: the ESERNET repository.

Table 1. Overview of previous experiments

Author	Techniques	Aspect	Results
Basili & Selby'87	- Boundary value analysis. - Statement coverage. - Stepwise abstraction.	Effectiveness (detection)	- Experienced subjects: Better reading, then functional, and then structural. - Inexperienced subjects: In one case, there is no difference between structural, functional and reading. In the other, functional is equal to reading, and both better than structural. - Depends on software type - Intermediate behave like junior and worse than advanced - Self estimates more accurate for review, then structural. No relationship for structural.
		Effectiveness (observable)	- Functional reveals more observable faults than structural for inexperienced subjects. - Functional technique detects more of these observable faults for experienced subjects.
		Fault detection cost	- Experienced subjects: Equal time and fault rate. - Inexperienced subjects: Structural takes less time than review, which equals to functional - The fault rate with functional and structural is less than with reading for inexperienced - The fault rate depends on the program - Functional testing has more computer costs than structural. - Total effort is the same for all techniques - Fault detection rate is related to experience
		Fault type	- Review is equal to functional and both better than structural for omission and for initialisation faults. - Functional is equal to structural and both better than review for interface faults. - Review is equal to structural and worse than functional for control faults. - Structural is equal to functional and both worse than review for computation faults. - For observable faults, functional and structural behave equal.
Kamsties & Lott'95	- Boundary value analysis. - Branch, multiple condition, loops and relational operators coverage. -Stepwise abstraction.	Effectiveness (detection)	Depends on the program, not the technique
		Effectiveness (isolation)	Depends on the program and subject, not on the technique
		Efficiency (detection)	- Inexperienced subjects: Boundary value analysis takes less time than condition coverage The time spent on finding faults also depends on the subject - Boundary value analysis has a higher fault rate than condition coverage
		Efficiency (isolation)	- Depends on the program and subject, not on the technique - With inexperienced subjects, boundary value analysis takes longer than condition coverage
		Efficiency (total)	- With inexperienced subjects, boundary value analysis takes less time than condition coverage - Time also depends on the subject.
		Fault type	For both detected and isolated: There is no difference between techniques
Wood et al.'97	-Boundary value analysis. - Branch coverage. - Stepwise abstraction.	Effectiveness (detection)	- Depends on the program/technique combination - Depends on nature of faults
		Combination of techniques	Higher number of faults combining techniques
Juristo & Vegas'02	- Equivalence partitiong. - Branch coverage. - Stepwise abstraction.	Effectiveness (detected and observable)	See section 5.

The study presented here consisted of two phases, which took place at the Universidad Politécnica de Madrid in the autumn of 2001 and 2002, and are called Experiment I and Experiment II respectively. The sequential experimentation has enabled the initial hypotheses to be expanded and resolved by further analysis. The hypotheses were further refined by discussions of the preliminary results. For an overview of the experimentation methodology applied in this study see [6].

3   Method for Experiment I

3.1   Design

3.1.1   Hypothesis and Response Variable

To test the hypothesis, that is, whether or not the effectiveness of the testing techniques can be said to be related to the fault types in the program, Experiment I is conceived as follows.

We are going to investigate whether or not technique effectiveness depends on the fault type. Accordingly, the variable we intend to examine is *effectiveness*, which will be the **response variable** and will be measured in terms of the number of subjects who detect a given fault for each fault in the program. As what we intend to test is a relationship (dependency of effectiveness with respect to fault type), the experiment will collect data on the effectiveness for each technique and each fault. We will then examine the statistical significance of the observed differences in effectiveness and, having established significance, we will study whether there is any type of relationship between the techniques and faults in terms of effectiveness.

The *techniques* and *fault type* are the **factors** of this study, whose impact on effectiveness we intend to ascertain. However, if we take into account Wood et al.'s description, which mentions program type, there would appear to be (or at least there is a reasonable doubt about the existence of) another variable (factor) that influences technique effectiveness, which would be *program type*. Hence, we have opted to include this variable in the list of factors.

Therefore, the hypotheses of Experiment I can be detailed as follows:

H_{01}: The *fault detection technique* has no impact on the number of detected faults.
H_{11}: The *fault detection technique* has an impact on the number of detected faults.

H_{02}: The *fault type* has no impact on the number of detected faults.
H_{12}: The *fault type* has an impact on the number of detected faults.

H_{03}: The use of different *fault detection techniques* for different *fault types* has no impact on the number of detected faults.
H_{13}: The use of different *fault detection techniques* for different *fault types* has an impact on the number of detected faults.

H_{04}: The use of different *fault detection techniques* for different *programs* has no impact on the number of detected faults.
H_{14}: The use of different *fault detection techniques* for different *programs* has an impact on the number of detected faults.

H_{05}: Different *fault types* in different *programs* have no impact on the number of detected faults.
H_{15}: Different *fault types* in different *programs* have an impact on the number of detected faults.

3.1.2   Factors and Alternatives

As mentioned above, there are three factors in this experiment: the technique to be used, the fault type and the program. These factors are described below.

Factor 1: Fault Types

We will consider that all the faults cause observable failures and that, therefore, no fault hides another. The faults are selected to assure that the programs fail only for some inputs, where a failure can be a total failure (no output whatsoever), a serious problem (incorrect output) or a minor problem (a wrongly spelt word in the output). The number of faults should be the same for all the programs, and they all have to contain the same fault distribution with respect to fault type.

As the experiment has been conceived, we needed a fault classification. Unfortunately, there are not many classifications in the literature. We have opted to use the classification followed by Basili in the first experiment of the series [3]. In each case, he makes a distinction between something that is **missing** (faults of omission) and something that is **incorrect** (faults of commission):

- **Initialisation (commission and omission):** An initialisation fault is an incorrect initialisation of a data structure. For example, assigning an incorrect value to a variable when entering a module would be an error of commission, whereas failure to initialise when necessary would be an error of omission. Initialisation faults of both commission and omission will be used for the experiment.
- **Control (commission and omission):** A control fault means that the program follows an incorrect control flow path in a given situation. For example, an incorrect predicate in an if-then-else sentence would be a control fault of commission, whereas a missing predicate would be fault of omission. Control faults of both commission and omission will be used for the experiment.
- **Cosmetic (commission and omission):** Cosmetic faults of commission can result, for example, in a spelling mistake in an error message. Faults of omission are faults where an error message should appear and does not. Cosmetic faults of both commission and omission will be used for the experiment.

Note that this study addresses a subset of faults rather than all fault types. This approach was taken for two reasons: first, because two of the fault types are related to integration testing, whereas the study focuses, at least for the time being, on unit testing, and second, because the study is not intended to be exhaustive but rather to test whether the hypothesis is true.

The faults entered in each program for the experiment appear in Table 2. From this table it can be seen that the fault type factor has 9 levels (from F1 to F9).

Table 2. Types of faults used in the programs

	Cosmetic	Initialisation	Control
Omission	F1	F3	F6, F7
Commission	F2	F4, F5	F8, F9

Note that there are three replicated faults: F4 and F5 are the same type of fault, as are F6 and F7 and F8 and F9. The aim here was to introduce replicated fault types, thereby increasing the reliability of the results of the experiment.

Factor 2: Techniques

We have used basically the same fault detection techniques as in the previous experiment [5]: functional testing, structural testing and code reading/review. What we have changed is the criterion of the functional tests, using equivalence class partitioning. This has been done due to time constraints during the operation of the experiment. For the structural technique, the subjects have not used any tool to assure branch coverage, because we wanted to compare the techniques under the same conditions (see [7, 8] for a detailed description of the dynamic analysis techniques used). This will affect the time it will take the subjects to generate the test cases (not the quality of the task performance, as the programs are simple enough for subjects to be able to do without a testing tool). Nevertheless, test case generation time is not relevant, as this experiment will not examine this response variable. All the techniques are applied for failure observation, that is, subjects look for observable differences between the program and the specification. The failure isolation step has been removed during technique application, that is, after finding a failure, subjects proceed to detect the fault that caused it. We did not consider failure isolation to be necessary for technique comparison, because the techniques provide no help for this task.

So, the techniques will be used as follows:

- The technique reading by step-wise abstraction [9] (R) will be used for code review. For this purpose, subjects are supplied with a program listing. They identify subroutines, writing their respective specifications, they group the subroutines and the specifications and repeat the process until they have abstracted the source code, conforming the program specifications. After this, they are given the official specifications and they identify the failures through inconsistencies between the abstracted and supplied specifications.

- The functional tests will be based on the standard techniques of equivalence class partitioning and boundary value analysis (F). Subjects are supplied with an executable version of the program and its specification. The test cases are derived from the specification, they are executed using the executable program and the failures are observed in terms of unexpected results.

- For the structural tests, subjects are expected to get a result as close to sentence coverage and decision coverage as possible (S). Subjects are given the source code without a specification. They store the test data and results. Having completed this step, they are given a specification to test the correctness of the results. The incorrect results represent program failures.

Factor 3: Program

We are going to use four different programs, specifically two very similar programs of each software type, using two software types. We have used the programs created by Kamsties and Lott, also used by Wood et al., plus one that we have developed. The programs used for this experiment were:

- Cmdline (functional): Program that reads the input line and outputs a summary.
- Trade (functional): Program that reads a trade transaction file and outputs statistics about the transactions it contains.
- Nametbl (data): Program that implements the data structure of a symbol table, as well as its operations.

- Ntree (data): Program that implements the data structure of an n-ary tree, as well as its operations.

Therefore, the factor program has four levels, one per program used.

3.1.3   Parameters
The variables used as parameters (that is, whose value has remained unchanged throughout the experiment) are:

- **Program length.** The average program length is similar to the length of the programs suggested by Basili in the first experiment. They contain approximately 200 lines of code, excluding blank lines and comments.
- **Subject type.** Fifth-year students from the School of Computer Science, Universidad Politécnica de Madrid, 1983 syllabus, were used for both experiments. They are subjects with very little experience. During the experiment they will be asked to fill in a self-assessment sheet with regard to their knowledge of the programming language, etc.
- **Programming language used.** The programming language C was used for both experiments so as not to have to recode the programs provided by Woods and, in doing so, involuntarily introduces a fault.
- **Time limit used.** No time limit was imposed in any case.
- **Faults.** Each program has the same number of faults of the same type. There is a total of 9 faults, where 2 are initialisation faults of commission, 1 is a cosmetic fault of commission, 2 are control faults of commission, 1 is an initialisation fault of commission, 2 are control faults of omission and 1 is a cosmetic fault of omission.

3.2   Subjects/Participants

The students are fifth-year computer science students. They are already familiar with the techniques, because they took a related subject in their fourth year, although their practical knowledge will be generally quite limited. Each group represents a set of people who performed the experiment (individually) at the same time (and, therefore, using the same program) applying the same technique. Therefore, we consider that each experimental unit (a program to which a technique is applied) is replicated as many times as subjects there are in the group and as many times as different programs have been used in each experiment (in this case two). The people were assigned to each group depending on the available resources: 25 computers and a classroom with capacity for 40 people.

There are a total of 196 students. Bearing in mind these restrictions, we would have 8 groups of 12 people (four groups will perform structural tests and the other four functional tests) and four groups of 25 people (who will perform code review).

With the aim of maximising experiment randomness, the procedure for assigning groups to days and programs and techniques to groups was as follows: the experiment designer drew slips of paper from a bag that contained the different groups (from 1 to 12). For every three lots drawn, a slip of paper was taken from the bag that contained the days (from 1 to 4) and another from the bag that contained the programs (P1, P2, P3 and P4) until all the lots had been drawn from all three bags.

Table 3. Experiment Design

| | Functional | | | | | | Data | | | | | |
| | Program1 | | | Program2 | | | Program3 | | | Program4 | | |
	R	S	F	R	S	F	R	S	F	R	S	F
Group 1	-	-	-	-	-	-	-	-	X	-	-	-
Group 2	-	-	-	-	-	X	-	-	-	-	-	-
Group 3	-	-	-	-	-	-	X	-	-	-	-	-
Group 4	-	-	-	-	X	-	-	-	-	-	-	-
Group 5	-	-	-	-	-	-	-	-	-	-	-	X
Group 6	-	-	-	-	-	-	-	-	-	X	-	-
Group 7	-	-	X	-	-	-	-	-	-	-	-	-
Group 8	-	-	-	X	-	-	-	-	-	-	-	-
Group 9	-	-	-	-	-	-	-	-	-	-	X	-
Group 10	-	-	-	-	-	-	-	X	-	-	-	-
Group 11	-	X	-	-	-	-	-	-	-	-	-	-
Group 12	X	-	-	-	-	-	-	-	-	-	-	-

After this, a list was drawn up and arranged in increasing order of the groups participating on each day and a slip of paper was drawn from a bag containing three lots (1 per technique) for each group, thus assigning the techniques to each group.
The resulting design is a three-factor design with replication and is shown in Table 3.

3.3   Procedure

The experiment was organised in five different sessions, as shown in Table 4, and the reason for the experiment was explained and the respective documentation delivered in the first session. The students are aware at all times that they are participating in an experiment and that the results will be used for grading (they will be graded using two parameters: technique application and number of faults detected). The students will be asked to study the documentation (they are already familiar with the techniques, as they have studied them earlier in their degree course) and they will have to hand in completed exercise applying the three techniques, obliging them to assimilate the concepts that have been explained.

The students do not know what technique they have been assigned or what program they are going to work on until the experiment starts.

Table 4. Experiment operation

| Day | Day 0 | Day 1 | Day 2 | Day 3 | Day 4 |
Program		cmdline	ntree	nametbl	trade
Group 6 Group 9 Group 5	Learning session and introduction to the experiment	Review Structural Functional			
Group 3 Group 10 Group 1			Review Structural Functional		
Group 8 Group 4 Group 2				Review Structural Functional	
Group 12 Group 11 Group 7					Review Structural Functional

Validity threats like learning have been eliminated, as each individual applies a single technique to just one program. We have also eliminated the influence of individual characteristics, as all the individuals are equally experienced and have fairly homogeneous profiles. The differences with regard to aptitude are eliminated by the random factor of group composition, that is, given the number of subjects and their random assignment to the technique to be applied, it is to be expected that the distribution of more and less able students will be equal for all the techniques.

We have attempted to assure that the faults and program types are representative of reality, that is, we have tried to assure that they simulate the faults programmers would really make during coding.

3.4   Results

For analysis purposes, the SPSS v.10 statistical tool has been used. The data analysis techniques used have been Analysis of Variance (ANOVA) and cluster analysis. For a detailed description of these techniques see [10].

3.4.1   General Analysis

As mentioned earlier, the response variable is the number of people who have detected each fault the program contains. As the number of experiment participants was different for each technique and program combination, we will use the percentage of people who detected the failure rather than the number in absolute terms.

All data resulting from the analysis can be found in [11]. It is important to note that F1 was hidden by another fault in cmdline, and was, therefore, not discovered by the people performing code review.

We have applied analysis of variance to the response variable with respect to the factors program, technique and fault. We have studied both the main effects and the second-order interactions. It is not possible to study the third-order interaction, because there are no response variable replications (this interaction is confused with error). In any case, the experiment was not designed to examine this interaction. Accordingly, we are considering that the third-order interaction is negligible.

As we can draw from the ANOVA, the main effects (program, technique and fault) are all significant, as is the program and fault interaction. With respect to the technique and fault interaction, it could in principle be considered as insignificant, as it is not significant for a confidence interval of 95% (the p-value is greater than 0.05). However, it is significant at 90% (the p-value is less than 0.1). Therefore, we will consider that it is significant.

Hence, we have that **the number of people who will detect a fault depends on the program being tested, the technique being used and the actual fault**. Additionally, **there are faults that behave better for certain programs and faults that are better detected using certain techniques**.

The fact that a fault behaves better with a particular program could be interpreted as meaning that the fault cannot be taken into account separately from the context (for want of a better word) in which it occurs. One possibility is to examine not the actual fault but the failure it causes. Remember that, in the ultimate analysis, structural and functional testing techniques detect failures not faults, whereas review directly detects faults.

Table 5. Results of the four-group cluster analysis

Group	Functional	Structural	Review
Group 1 (well detected)	F3 (I,O) F4 (I,C) F6 (Cn,O) F7 (Cn,O)	F5 (I,C) F9 (Cn,C)	
Group 2 (fairly well detected)	F1 (Cs,O) F5 (I,C) F8 (Cn,C) F9 (Cn,C)	F3 (I,O) F4 (I,C) F6 (Cn,O) F7 (Cn,O) F8 (Cn,C)	F3 (I,O)
Group 3 (poorly detected)		F1(Cs,O)	F1 (Cs,O), F4 (I,C) F5 (I,C), F6 (Cn,O) F7 (Cn,O), F8 (Cn,C) F9 (Cn,C)
Group 4 (very poorly detected)	F2 (Cs,C)	F2 (Cs,C)	F2 (Cs,C)

Additionally, within the dynamic techniques, it is interesting to note that a subject's failure to detect a fault can be due to two very different reasons:

- No test case was generated to show up the fault.
- The test case was generated, but the subject was unable to see the failure on screen.

For this reason, we suggest that *it would be interesting to make a distinction between two separate things in the second-round experimentation (Experiment II): detection of the failures caused by faults (to study visibility) and technique fault detection capability.* As this experiment has been designed, it is impossible to separate one thing from the other.

As interactions between the program and the fault, on the one hand, and the technique and the fault, on the other, have appeared, the factors fault, program and technique cannot be examined separately. Therefore, we will have to study the two interactions that have emerged.

3.4.2 Fault/Technique Interaction

Although we have seen that there is an interaction between technique and fault, we still cannot determine whether or not the difference between technique and fault groups is significant.

We conducted a cluster analysis on the estimated mean for each technique/fault combination to analyse the significance of the fault and technique interaction. Cluster analysis is a data analysis technique used to establish behaviour groups for such an interaction, which means that the technique/fault combinations that behave in the same way will fall into the same group. In this case, four groups were established in the cluster analysis conducted: well detected faults, fairly well detected faults, poorly detected faults and very poorly detected faults. The groups to which each fault/technique combination belongs appear in Table 5:

Four behaviour types can be inferred from the above tables:

1. The three techniques behave equally for a particular fault. This is the case of F2.
2. The three techniques behave differently for a particular fault. This is the case of F4, F5, F6, F7 and F9. Two behaviour types can be established in this case:

- The functional technique behaves better than the structural testing technique and both behave better than review. This is the case of F4, F6 and F7 (F6 and F7 are the same faults, but have nothing in common with F4).
- The structural testing technique behaves better than the functional testing technique, and both behave better than review. This is the case of F5 and F9 (both faults of commission).

3. The structural technique behaves the same as review, and both behave worse than the functional testing technique. This is the case of F1 and F3 (both are faults of omission).

4. The functional technique behaves identically to the structural testing technique, and both behave better than review. This is the case of F8 (control and commission).

The findings from the above are as follows:

- **The cosmetic faults are the most difficult to detect** (F1 and F2 are in groups 3 and 4, except faults of omission using the functional testing technique which are in group 2).
- Generally, it could be said that the fault and technique combination has an impact for the functional and structural testing techniques, as review always behaves worse than the other two, irrespective of the fault type. Note that all the faults fall into group 3 for review, except F2 (cosmetic fault of commission, which belongs to group 4) and F3 (initialisation fault of omission, which belongs to group 2). That is, **the fault type appears to have practically no impact on review effectiveness**, although this technique turns out to be the less effective one in this experiment.
- Given the fault classification used and that, as we have seen from the ANOVA, fault detection depends on the fault and the technique, we would expect the same fault types to behave equally. That is, given that F4 and F5 are faults of the same type (initialisation, commission), they should behave equally, as should F6 and F7 (both control faults of omission) and F8 and F9 (control, commission). However, we find that this only happens in exceptional cases, like F6 and F7 (for all techniques) and F8 and F9 (for functional testing and review). **This makes us think that perhaps the fault classification scheme is not the appropriate one, as it does not allow the detection of the fault type for which the functional and structural techniques are more adequate.**
- The functional testing technique detects faults of omission better than faults of commission (three out of four), whereas the structural testing technique is not very good at detecting faults of omission (they are all in group 2).

Neither can any definitive conclusions be drawn according to each individual classification examined separately.

3.4.3   Fault/Program Interaction

Although we have seen that there is an interaction between program and fault, we still cannot determine whether or not the difference between program and fault groups is significant. Cluster analysis was again applied. This time three groups were established. The results of this analysis are shown in Table 6.

Table 6. Results of the three-group cluster analysis

Group	Data		Functional	
	nametbl	ntree	trade	cmdline
Group 1 (well detected)	F3 (I,O) F5 (I,C) F7 (Cn,O) F8 (Cn,C)	F1 (Cs,O) F4 (I,C) F6 (Cn,O) F9 (Cn,C)		F3 (I,O)
Group 2 (fairly well detected)	F4 (I,C) F9 (Cn,C)	F3 (I,O) F5 (I,C) F7 (Cn,O)	F1 (Cs,O) F3 (I,O) F4 (I,C) F5 (I,C) F6 (Cn,O)	F4 (I,C) F5 (I,C) F6 (Cn,O) F7 (Cn,O)
Group 3 (poorly detected)	F1 (Cs,O) F2 (Cs,C) F6 (Cn,O)	F2 (Cs,C) F8 (Cn,C)	F2 (Cs,C) F7 (Cn,O) F8 (Cn,C) F9 (Cn,C)	F1 (Cs,O) F2 (Cs,C) F8 (Cn,C) F9 (Cn,C)

From the above tables, we can infer the following:

- Fault F2 (cosmetic, commission) behaves identically for all programs and poorly.
- Faults F4, F5, F8 and F9 behave identically for all the processing programs (cmdline and trade): F4 and F5 (both initialisation faults of commission) fairly well and F8 and F9 (both control faults of commission) poorly. It is noteworthy that one and the same fault appears in assorted groups.
- F6 and F7 (both control faults of commission) behave identically for the cmdline program.

Additionally, the data programs behave better than the functional programs.

Generally, there is little more we can say, as we find that the faults behave quite disparately for each program. This suggests that perhaps we used an ineffective program classification.

3.5 Discussion

The results of conducting the ANOVA on the data collected in the experiment revealed that fault detection in a program is influenced by two things: the fault and technique combination and the fault and program combination.

With regard to the first of these combinations, we tried to establish a pattern to predict the fault types that behave better with each technique, although this was not possible. However, we did find that:

- Generally, cosmetic faults are poorly detected, which means that the fault/technique relationship bears no influence on this fault type.
- **Code reading is less sensitive to fault hiding than the other techniques.** The fault detection in code reading does not depend on executing the part of code where the fault is, or on other faults; therefore the detection is less influenced by other factors.
- The fault/technique relationship only occurs for the structural and functional techniques. This led us to look for other factors that may have an impact on one particular fault being detected more often than another in code reviews. For Experiment II, we propose to examine *fault location in the program*.

- Since the subjects executed their own test cases, and the response variable measured the number of people who detected the failure produced by the fault, it was impossible to detect whether the actual technique did not generate a test case to show up the fault or the subject was unable to see the fault uncovered by the technique. This led us to consider examining *actual fault detection capability (generation of test cases which are able to show up the failure) and failure visibility (the subject sees the failure once this is shown up)* in Experiment II. Basili and Selby already studied this.
- Related to the previous bullet, we have also not taken into account the possibility of subject randomisation not working properly (subjects better prepared will find more faults independently of the technique). The previous studies to this one, already discovered that subjects applying the same techniques did not find, generally, the same faults. This led us to consider changing the design of the experiment for Experiment II, where *all subjects will apply all techniques.*
- As far as the functional and structural testing techniques are concerned, it is difficult to establish a behaviour pattern for the different faults. Although the **functional technique behaves better than the structural testing technique** in most cases, the cases in which the two techniques behave identically or better than each other occur indistinctly for each replication of fault type. For example, the functional technique behaves better than the structural technique for F1 (cosmetic, commission), F3 (initialisation, omission), F4 (initialisation, commission) and F6 and F7 (both control faults of omission), the structural technique behaves better than the functional technique for F5 (initialisation, commission) and F9 (control, commission), and both techniques behave identically for F8 (control, commission). On the other hand, the fact that no conclusions can be drawn from the original classification suggests that all the faults should be replicated, and not just some as we did in this experiment (F1, F2 and F3 were not replicated). This led us to consider *creating two versions of each program inserting different faults, albeit of the same type*, for Experiment II. This contrasts with the differences Basili and Selby found for omission faults and for initialisation, interface, control and computation faults, and with the differences that Kamsties and Lott could not find.
- Bearing in mind the fault classification we used, F4 is the same fault as F5 (initialisation, commission), and the same goes for F6-F7 (control, omission) and F8-F9 (control, commission). This means that they should behave identically, but this is only the case for F6 and F7 (control, omission). However, it does appear that **the functional technique behaves better than the structural technique for faults of omission** (all except F4), and **the structural technique behaves better or identically to the functional technique for faults of commission**. This contrasts with what Basili and Selby found about behaving functional technique and code reading equal and better than structural and the no difference found by Kamsties and Lott.

As regards the second relationship, the fault/program combination, our findings were:

- The cosmetic faults of commission are again the ones that behave worst for all programs. This is not true of the cosmetic faults of omission.
- Again, the program classification (data and functions) does not appear to be significant, as no pattern of fault behaviour can be established. This suggests that

we should look for other program classifications, taking into account things like complexity, embedding, etc. This will not be taken into account in Experiment II, and will be left for future research.

- Again, we have encountered problems with the fault classification, as we were unable to establish any fault type pattern with regard to the programs developed. This will be further investigated in Experiment II, *creating two versions of each program*, as mentioned above.

4   Method for Experiment II

We have run another experiment based on the findings of the first, which involved refining the earlier experiment to be able to reach conclusions that could not be drawn from Experiment I due to design limitations.

4.1   Design

4.1.1   Hypothesis, Parameters, and Response Variable

The goal of this second experiment is to investigate three things:

- *Influence of fault visibility.* We were unable to deduce from the earlier experiment whether the fact that a subject does not detect a fault is because the technique does not produce a test case that causes the failure to occur or because the actual subject does not observe the failure when it occurs. This was due to the fact that subjects executed the test cases that they generated to detect the possible program faults. In this experiment, the subjects will be asked to execute a set of test cases that we generate and that detect all the program defects. Accordingly, we will find out how visible the failures caused by the faults are. Additionally, by examining the test cases generated by each individual, we will be able to find out which faults the test cases generated by a given technique potentially detect.
- *Influence of the technique and fault type.* Owing to the above, we cannot be sure that the findings reached in the earlier experiment with regard to the fault/technique interaction are true. Therefore, we want to investigate to what extent the use of one or another testing technique influences fault detection again.
- *Influence of fault position.* In the earlier experiment, we also discovered that there was practically no difference between the number of people who detected each fault for code review. This prompted us to look for another fault characteristic that may influence review effectiveness. It occurred to us that it might perhaps be easier to see certain faults because of their position in the program. This will also be investigated.

Another result of the earlier experiment was that the program classification used was not useful for identifying the behavioural differences between the techniques with regard to programs. However, this is something that has been left for future research and will not be taken into account in this experiment, which will employ a subset of the programs used in Experiment I.

Additionally, the experimental design has been changed, as detailed later in the respective sections.

Accordingly, Experiment II will test the hypotheses investigated in Experiment I (see section 3.1), plus the following:

H_{06}: The *visibility of the failures generated by the faults* has no impact on effectiveness.

H_{16}: The *visibility of the failures generated by the faults* has an impact on effectiveness.

H_{07}: The *position of the faults* has no impact on effectiveness.

H_{17}: The *position of the faults* has an impact on effectiveness.

Both the parameters and the response variable used for this experiment are the same as used in the earlier experiment.

4.1.2   Factors and Alternatives

The earlier experiment was composed of three factors: technique, fault and program. Although we have already mentioned that this experiment will not investigate the impact of the program, this does not mean that it should no longer appear as a factor, since its influence has already been confirmed. Moreover, we found some indications in the earlier experiment that perhaps the fault classification we were using was not suitable. We were, however, unable to confirm this for two reasons. One, which we have already mentioned, is related to the influence of failure visibility on fault detection. The other is that three of the six faults entered in the program occurred only once, whereas the other three were replicated (occurred twice). As the programs are not very long, however, it is not possible to insert a lot of faults, so we opted to implement two versions of each program. This will provide for fault replication in the programs. The version is introduced as a new factor in the experiment.

Factor 1: Fault Types

The same fault types as used for the first experiment will be employed, save that the number of faults will vary as a result of the introduction of the version factor. In this case, the programs will each include 7 faults, these appearing in Table 7:

Table 7. Types of faults used in the programs.

	Cosmetic	Initialisation	Control	Computation
Omission	F1	F3	F5	-
Commission	F2	F4	F6	F7

Clearly, all the fault types are different, which was not the case in Experiment I. We did this because there are two versions for each program in Experiment II, this being how the faults are replicated. Additionally, we have tried to assure, as far as possible, that the same faults generate the same failures. They are shown in Table 8.

Table 8. Failures produced for each fault

Fault	Version	Cmdline	nametbl	ntree
F1	V1	Does not recognise the "top" option.	Does not output error when an unknown resource type is supplied	Does not output error if the first node of the "are siblings" node does not belong to the tree.
	V2	Prints input file names incorrectly.	Does not output error when an unknown object type is supplied	Does not output error if the second node of the "are siblings" node does not belong to the tree.
F2	V1	Use message containing spelling mistake.	Error message containing spelling mistake.[2]	Error message containing spelling mistake.
	V2	Incorrectly written error message.	Message containing spelling mistake.	Error message containing spelling mistake.
F3	V1	Does not output use message when search measure and option is missing.	Correctly assigns the object but outputs an error message saying that the element does not exist.[2]	If the two nodes exist, they are never recognised as siblings.
	V2	Does not output error message when there is no input file.	Correctly assigns the resource but outputs an error message saying that the element does not exist.	Whenever there are two nodes, they are never classed as siblings.
F4	V1	Interprets LKHM as LKOM.	Interchanged DATA and FUNCTION resources, assigns them inversely.	Does not print the far left-hand node.
	V2	Prints the number of input files incorrectly.	Interchanged SYSTEM and RESOURCE objects, assigns them inversely.	Search does not find the far left-hand siblings.
F5	V1	The "minimum" option outputs an error message.	Does not recognise the RESOURCE object	If the second node belongs to the tree, it says it is not there, and if it does not belong, it says nothing.
	V2	Incorrectly interpreted "help" option.	Does not recognise the FUNCTION object.	Search_tree works the wrong way round. If the node does not exist, it outputs strange things.
F6	V1	The "minimum" option with several search options does not output error.[2]	Always assigns the resource irrespective of whether or not the element belongs to the table.	If the node does not belong to the tree, no error message is output during the search.
	V2	Does not output error message when there is an invalid measure option.	Always assigns the object irrespective of whether or not the element belongs to the table.	The tree is not indented when printed.
F7	V1	Prints the names of the input files incorrectly.	Prints the number of table elements incorrectly.	The tree is incorrectly indented when printed.
	V2	Does not recognise the "top" option.	Prints the number of table elements incorrectly.	The tree level is wrong when printed.

Factor 2: Techniques

The same techniques as in the first experiment will be used in this experiment. However, the procedure followed to run the structural and functional tests will differ, because, as already discussed, we intend to separate test case generation and fault detection by the tester from each other.

- The subjects will apply the technique to generate test cases. These test cases will be used in the experimental analysis to determine what faults each technique detects.

- Afterwards, the subjects will execute the test cases we supply, which detect all the program faults. This will enable us to examine whether failure visibility influences failure detection, that is, to check whether the results obtained in Experiment I on the functional and structural techniques are valid and there is no bias.

---

[2] The failures shown on a grey background in this table were hidden in the programs.

Factor 3: Program
Of the four programs used for the first experiment, one will be discarded. Accordingly, for this experiment, we will use the three genuine programs that came with the original experimental package. The reason for this was to balance the experimental design. We found from the previous experiment that randomisation was perhaps not enough to isolate the possible effect of subject capability on whether or not they detect a fault. Therefore, this experiment has been designed differently, and the subject has been introduced as a blocking variable.

Factor 4: Version
We have discussed in Section 3.5 the reason for introducing program versions. The idea is to replicate all the faults under study for each program. As the programs are small in size, we cannot insert as many faults as we would like to without violating the premise of some faults masking others. The solution to this problem is to introduce the concept of version: two versions differ as to the faults they contain, but they always have to contain the same number of faults and the faults have to be of the same type.

4.2   Subjects/Participants

For this experiment, we have 46 subjects. No one of them had participated in, or was aware of the experiment 1. As discussed above, this time each subject will apply all three techniques, leading to the experimental design shown in Table 9 and Table 10. Each group in the experiment will be composed of 7 to 8 people.

Table 9. Experimental design

Program	Cmdline			ntree			Nametbl		
Technique	R	S	F	R	S	F	R	S	F
Group 1	X	-	-	-	X	-	-	-	X
Group 2	X	-	-	-	-	X	-	X	-
Group 3	-	X	-	-	-	X	X	-	-
Group 4	-	X	-	X	-	-	-	-	X
Group 5	-	-	X	X	-	-	-	X	-
Group 6	-	-	X	-	X	-	X	-	-

Table 10. Experiment execution

Day	Day 1	Day 2	Day 3
Program	cmdline	ntree	nametbl
Group 1, Group 2 Group 3, Group 4 Group 5, Group 6	Review Structural Functional		
Group 4, Group 5 Group 1, Group 6 Group 2, Group 3		Review Structural Functional	
Group 3, Group 6 Group 2, Group 5 Group 1, Group 4			Review Structural Functional

4.3   Results

Again, we have used ANOVA and cluster analysis for data analysis. For ease of reading, we have structured the analysis of Experiment II differently to Experiment I. This time we will conduct the analysis on the basis of the findings of Experiment I and discussing the results of Experiment II with respect to the results of Experiment I. The results of each of the three aspects examined during this experiment, which are influence of the testing technique and fault type, failure visibility and fault visibility for code review, are discussed below. More information can be found in [11].

4.4   Discussion

4.4.1   Influence of the Testing Technique

The goal here is to repeat the analysis already conducted during Experiment I that is, we intend to investigate the possible influence of programs, techniques, faults and versions on the response variable. It is important to note that the definition of effectiveness has changed, because the experiment is run differently in this case. Whereas it was defined as the number of students who detect a fault in Experiment I, here it is specified as the number of students who generate a test case capable of detecting the fault. Again we have studied both the main effects and the second- and third-order interactions. Owing to design considerations, it is not possible to study the fourth-order interaction, there being no response variable replications (this interaction is confused with error). We are considering that it is negligible.

As we can draw from the results of the ANOVA, the main effects of technique, version and fault are significant, as are the second-order program/technique, program/fault and technique/fault interactions.

Hence, we have that **the number of people who will generate a test case to detect a fault depends on the version, the technique used and the fault in question.** Additionally, **there are faults that behave better for certain programs, faults that are better detected using certain techniques and programs that behave better for certain techniques.**

As interactions have appeared between the effects of the fault and technique, these factors cannot be studied separately. However, we will not analyse all the interactions that have emerged as significant here. We will concentrate only on the interactions of interest, which are the program/technique and technique/fault interactions. As compared to Experiment I, it is noteworthy that the program effect did not turn out to be significant in this case, whereas the version and the program/technique combination did. We will discuss the influence of the version later in section 4.4.4. The program/fault interaction will be left aside, since we had already planned to research the influence of the program in future experiments.

The ANOVA clearly showed the interaction between technique and fault in this experiment, as it did in Experiment I. We have built the confidence levels of the response variable means for each combination of factor levels to determine how the combinations of the different levels of the two factors are related.

A cluster analysis has been conducted, establishing four groups (as in Experiment I): well detected faults, fairly well detected faults, poorly detected faults and very

Table 11. Cluster analysis results for four groups

Group	Functional	Structural	Review
Group 1 (well detected)	F1 (Cs,O) F2 (Cs,C) F4 (I,C) F5 (Cn,C)	F1 (Cs,O) F2 (Cs,C) F3 (I,O) F4 (I,C) F5 (Cn,C)	--
Group 2 (fairly well detected)	F3 (I,O) F6 (Cn,O) F7 (Cm,C)	F6 (Cn,O) F7 (Cm,C)	--
Group 3 (poorly detected)	--	--	F1 (Cs,O) F3 (I,O) F5 (Cn,C) F6 (Cn,O) F7 (Cm,C)
Group 4 (very poorly detected)	--	--	F2 (Cs,C) F4 (I,C)

poorly detected faults. Table 11 shows the results of this analysis. It is important to note that none of the faults that appear in Table 11 are replicated (F1...F7 are seven different faults), as they were in Experiment I. Replications do not appear here because it is the version that generates the replication, and this does not interact jointly with fault and technique.

As we suspected from Experiment I, although it shows up much more clearly here, **code review always behaves worse than the functional and structural techniques, irrespective of the fault**. As regards the comparison between the functional and the structural techniques, remember that the functional technique behaved better than the structural technique in most cases in Experiment I, although we were unable to establish a behaviour pattern for fault type. In this experiment, we find that **the two techniques behave equally** (which means that they are equally powerful), and the difference there was in Experiment I is no longer there. This can be attributed to the fact that we are now studying whether the technique generates test cases that reveal a given fault type. What Table 11 tells us is that both the functional and the structural techniques are equally effective at generating test cases. Additionally, the behaviour pattern for fault types, which we were unable to establish from Experiment I, can be found here, as we can see that there are faults that behave worse than others (as is the case of F6 and F7).

It is interesting to note that the technique/program interaction turned out to be insignificant in the earlier experiment, whereas it is significant in this one. We conducted a cluster analysis, again establishing four groups. Table 12 shows the results of the analysis.

Unlike Experiment I, where there were no techniques that behaved better for particular programs, here we found that **the program determines technique behaviour**, although generally we can affirm that **the structural and functional testing techniques will behave similarly and always better than review**.

Table 12. Cluster analysis results for four groups

Group	cmdline	nametbl	ntree
Group 1 (well detected)	Structural	Functional Structural	--
Group 2 (fairly well detected)	Functional	--	Functional Structural
Group 3 (poorly detected)	--	--	Review
Group 4 (very poorly detected)	Review	Review	--

4.4.2   Influence of Failure Visibility

The goal pursued by this analysis is to study the visibility of a failure (how many people really observe and, consequently, detect the failure, once it has occurred). While there are currently not many fault classifications, there are even fewer (in fact, there are none) failure classifications, which represents an obstacle to this investigation. Therefore, what we are going to try to do here is to establish a failure classification based on the program, version and fault factors, which are the three parameters that define the behaviour of the failure on the basis of the fault.

During this experiment, as mentioned earlier, the subjects ran test cases with which they were supplied, which means that the technique will not exert any influence whatsoever (the test cases were generated so as to visualise all the program failures without applying any particular technique).

As we can draw from the results of the ANOVA, the main effects version and fault, the second-order interaction between program and fault and the third-order interaction between program, version and fault are significant, which means that **failure visibility** (number of people who detect the failure) **depends on the fault that causes the failure, and the program and version in which the failure occurs**. This is quite logical, as, looking at Table 8, we find that there are different faults and versions that cause one and the same failure (for example, F1 in V1 produces the same failure as F7 in V2). As the third-order interaction is significant, our examination will focus on this interaction, which cancels out the other effects.

Table 13 shows the failure classification developed on the basis of the faults and failures described in Table 8. This is a preliminary classification and has been put together according to two failure parameters:

Failures related to *printing* (P, or the printed contents of the output), *error messages* (E) and *program results* (R).

Failures of omission (O, the program does not do everything it should) or of commission (C, the program does things wrong).

Yet again, we have used cluster analysis as an aid for examining this interaction. Table 14 shows the results of this analysis, establishing five behaviour groups: failures with very good, good, fair, poor and very poor visibility.

Table 13. Program failure classification

Failure	cmdline		nametbl		Ntree	
	V1	**V2**	**V1**	**V2**	**V1**	**V2**
F1	Error Commission	Printing Commission	Error Omission	Error Omission	Printing Commission	Printing Commission
F2	Printing Commission	Printing Commission	Printing[3] Commission	Printing Commission	Printing Commission	Printing Commission
F3	Error Omission	Error Omission	Error Commission	Error Commission	Result Commission	Result Commission
F4	Result Commission	Result Commission	Result Commission	Result Commission	Printing Omission	Result Commission
F5	Error Commission	Result Commission	Result Commission	Result Commission	Result Commission	Result Commission
F6	Error Omission	Error Omission	Result Commission	Result Commission	Error Omission	Printing Commission
F7	Printing Commission	Error Commission	Printing Commission	Printing Commission	Printing Commission	Printing Commission

Table 14. Cluster analysis results for five groups

Group	cmdline		Nametbl		Ntree	
	V1	**V2**	**V1**	**V2**	**V1**	**V2**
Group 1 (Very good visibility)	(P,C) F7	F1 (P,C) F4 (R,C) F5 (R,C)	(E,O) F1 (R;C) F4 (R,C) F5 (R,C) F6 (P,C) F7	(E,O) F1 (E,C) F3 (R,C) F4 (R,C) F5 (R,C) F6 (P,C) F7	(R,C) F3 (P,O) F4 (E,O) F6	(P,C) F1 (R,C) F4 (R,C) F5
Group 2 (Good visibility)	(E,O) F3 (R,C) F4 (E,C) F5	F3 (E,O) F6 (E,O)	--	--	(P,C) F1 (R,C) F5	(R,C) F3 (P,C) F7
Group 3 (Fair visibility)	(E,C)F1	F7 (E,C)	--	--	--	(P,C) F2 (P,C) F6
Group 4 (Poor visibility)	--	F2 (P,C)	--	(P,C) F2	(P,C) F2	--
Group 5 (Very poor visibility)	(P,C) F2	--	--	--	(P,C) F7	--

The suspicion we had in Experiment I that failure visibility has an impact on failure detection appears to be confirmed here. From Table 14, we can deduce that **the errors of omission are very visible,** as they appear in either of the top two visibility groups (good and very good). However, **the visibility of the errors of commission varies,** as they can appear in any of the five groups. On the other hand, **the result failures are the most visible** (together with the failures of omission), as again they always appear in the top two groups. **With regard to error failures, failures of omission appear to behave better than failures of commission,** as the failures of commission tend to appear in group 3 and the failures of omission in groups 1 and 2.

This, together with the earlier result proving that the functional and structural techniques behave equally in terms of fault detection, confirms that **the differences observed in Experiment I depend not on the actual technique, but on how well the failure is visualised.**

---

[3] The failures shown on a grey background in this table were hidden in the programs.

Hence, one wonders whether, owing to its modus operandi, the functional technique may somehow *predispose* subjects to be more sensitive to program failures. Remember that the functional technique is based on the program specifications, which are used to generate the test cases. On the other hand, subjects using the structural technique do not have the program specification until they are about to run the generated test cases, which may mean that they are not as sensitive to the possible failures that may arise.

Another noteworthy point is that there were failures that appeared more than once when the test cases were run during this experiment (there were more than one test case that fired these failures). And some subjects saw these failures every time, other subjects saw them only once and others never saw them at all. For simplicity's sake, we considered for the purposes of this investigation that once a subject had seen a failure (even if only once), it was a detected failure. However, it would also be interesting to explore the question raised by this observation, that is, how many times does a failure need to appear during testing for it to be seen? This could refine the visibility classification.

4.4.3   Influence of Fault Visibility

The goal in this case is to study a possible relationship between the visibility of a fault in the program code using the reading technique and the number of people who detect the fault. For this purpose, fault visibility is defined by its position in the code, which will be determined by three parameters:

Quadrant: The page has been divided into four quadrants so that each fault will have an associated value of 1 to 4 depending on the position it occupies. The quadrants have been numbered from left to right and from top to bottom.

Nesting: Each fault will have an associated number that will indicate its level of nesting within the code.

Place: Page number of the file on which the fault is located.

From the ANOVA, we can deduce that none of the parameters considered and none of their combinations influence the results and, therefore, **the number of subjects who detect a fault using the reading technique does not depend on fault visibility**. This means that code review has no preference for specific fault types. This is the same result as we found for the functional and structural techniques, which behave equally for all faults. At this point, one might wonder what advantages review then has over the dynamic techniques. On the one hand, one of the most valuable features of review is that it is applicable not only to code but also to any software product, which enables earlier fault detection and lowers the cost of correction. On the other hand, we have the point identified in Experiment I that review is not influenced by fault interdependency.

4.4.4   Influence of the Version

This experiment yielded an unexpected result, which was that the version influenced the number of people who detected a fault. This means that, irrespective of the program, technique and fault, more subjects generated test cases that detected faults in version 2 than in version 1. Note that the versions 1 and 2 of each program are identical, the only difference being the faults entered.

This is an interesting result. On the one hand, it ratifies the result obtained in experiment 1, related to the adequacy of the fault classification used, and the need of a fault classification schema sensitive to techniques. On the other, it says that it is the instance of the actual fault and not the program type or form that determines how well a fault will be detected by the testing techniques. This contrasts with the finding from Experiment I that the program was influential.

This raises the ineludible question of which parameters are likely to influence fault detection by a test case. Could it be how well the subject applies the technique? Could it be possible to classify faults so that techniques are sensitive to fault type? These are open questions to be addressed in later studies.

5 Lessons Learned

In this chapter, we presented two successive experiments that aim to clarify the fault detection capability of three code evaluation techniques: two dynamic analysis (functional and structural) and one static analysis (code reading by stepwise abstraction) techniques. The first experiment is based on the earlier findings of the experiment performed by Woods *et al.*, which concluded that the relationship between evaluation techniques and the fault types they detect needed to be investigated.

The design of the first experiment included four programs, four fault types per program (although they contain two faults of three of the types, adding up to a total of nine faults per program) and each subject applied a single technique. From Experiment I, we found that the cosmetic faults showed up worst (irrespective of the technique and the program) and that code review was not affected by the fault type (they were all detected equally). This contrasts with Basili and Selby's findings, of review detecting better certain types of faults, and Kamsties and Loot's finding of no difference between fault type. As regards the actual techniques, the functional technique came out better than the structural technique for faults of omission (the same finding as Basily and Selby) and the structural technique behaved equally or better than the functional technique for faults of commission (Basili and Selby did not find this, but all behaved equally), although, on the whole, the functional technique tended to behave better (as in one of the experiments of Basili). However, we did not manage to discern a clear behaviour pattern as regards what fault types each of the two techniques detects better (contrasting with Basili and Selby's findings).

Some of the findings of Experiment I, however, led to the preparation Experiment II. The fact that not all the faults were replicated in Experiment I led to the creation of two versions of each program in the second experiment. As replicated faults behaved differently (which was strange), we thought that perhaps it could be the failure that caused this variation. Therefore, we examined failure visibility during Experiment II. For this purpose, we generated test cases that detected all the faults and asked the subjects to use these test cases instead of running their own. As the faults did not appear to be having an impact on the static technique, we decided to investigate fault visibility in the static technique in Experiment II. Finally, we also suspected that the subjects might have influenced fault detection in Experiment I, which led us to have all the subjects apply all the techniques rather than just one as in Experiment II.

Experiment II was run on the basis of these premises. The findings from the experiment corroborated some of the suspicions we had had during the first experiment. Firstly, as regards the possible impact of the fault and the technique, we found that the functional and structural techniques behaved identically (this contrasts with Basili and Selby's findings of functional technique behaving better). This refutes the finding from Experiment I that the functional technique behaved better than the structural technique for some fault types. This is because there was a hidden effect in Experiment I, namely, failure type. This was influencing failure detection.

As regards failure visibility, this does indeed have an influence. Hence, we have been able to establish a failure taxonomy, where error messages that do not appear and incorrect results are the most visible. So, the results observed in Experiment I were due to failure visibility not to the power of the techniques. It is not clear, however, whether perhaps the functional technique, owing to its modus operandi, tends to make subjects more sensitive to the detection of certain faults. From this we can deduce that it is not only important to teach subjects the testing techniques, but it would also make sense to teach them to *see* the failures. This would involve training them to use heuristics and checklists concerning the failure types they should look for (for example, *check that all the error messages are output and output at the right time*). However, the failure visibility classification needs to be refined, which leaves room for an extension of this study.

Additionally, a new thing we found was that the program/technique combination has an impact on the number of faults detected (as Wood *et al.* already found), although the functional and structural techniques again behaved equally in all cases for the same program. This means that technique effectiveness (irrespective of whether it is the structural or functional technique) is affected by the program. In other words, whatever the technique (structural or function) we apply, it will always be less effective for a given program type than for another.

Another interesting result was that the position of a fault has no influence on the number of people who see the fault using the reading technique. This suggests that we should look for other factors that may have an impact (perhaps experience, which has been addressed in earlier experiments). Although neither of these experiments has taken this into account, aspects like subject experience have been investigated in earlier experiments examining code review effectiveness.

Finally, another unexpected finding was that the actual version influenced the number of subjects who were able to generate a test case that detected a fault. We have interpreted this as it being the actual fault, that is, the particular instance and not the type of fault, rather than the program type or form that determines whether more or fewer faults are detected. This leaves the field open for further research.

References

[1]   Hetzel, W.C. An experimental Analysis of Program Verification Methods. PhD thesis, University of North Carolina, Chapel Hill, 1976.

[2]   Myers, G.J. 1978. A Controlled Experiment in Program Testing and Code Walkthroughs/Reviews. Communications of the ACM. Vol. 21 (9). Pages 760–768.

[3]   Basili, V.R., and Selby, R.W. 1987. Comparing the Effectiveness of Software Testing Strategies. IEEE Transactions on Software Engineering. Pages 1278-1296. SE-13 (12).

[4]   Kamsties, E., and Lott, C.M. 1995. An Empirical Evaluation of Three Defect-Detection Techniques. Proceedings of the Fifth European Software Engineering Conference. Sitges, Spain.

[5]   Wood, M., Roper, M., Brooks, A., and Miller J. 1997. Comparing and Combining Software Defect Detection Techniques: A Replicated Empirical Study. Proceedings of the 6th European Software Engineering Conference. Zurich, Switzerland.

[6]   Juristo, N and Moreno, A. M. Basics of Software Engineering Experimentation. Kluwer Academic Publishers. 2000.

[7]   Beizer, B. 1990. Software Testing Techniques. International Thomson Computer Press, second edition.

[8]   Sommerville, I. Software Engineering. 6th Edition. Addison-Wesley. 2001.

[9]   Linger, R.C., Mills, H.D, and Witt, B.I. Structured Programming: Theory and Practice. Addison Wesley, 1979.

[10] Norusis, Marija J. SPSS 10.0 Guide to Data Analysis Prentice Hall. 2000.

[11] Juristo, N, Vegas, S. Functional Testing, Structural Testing and Code Reading: What Fault Type do they Each Detect? (extended version). February 2003. Available at http://www.ls.fi.upm.es/udis/miembros/sira/cv_e.html

COTS Products Characterization: Proposal and Empirical Assessment

Alessandro Bianchi[1], Danilo Caivano[1], Reidar Conradi[2], Letizia Jaccheri[2],
Marco Torchiano[3], and Giuseppe Visaggio[1]

[1] Dept. of Informatics – University of Bari - Via Orabona, 4, 70126 Bari – Italy
{bianchi,caivano,visaggio}@di.uniba.it
[2] Dept. of Computer and Information Science, Norwegian University of Science and
Technology, Trondheim Norway
{Reidar.Conradi, letizia}@idi.ntnu.no
[3] Computer Dept – Politecnico of Turin – Corso D. degli Abruzzi, 24, 10129 Turin – Italy
marco.torchiano@polito.it

Abstract. This chapter faces the problem of identifying a set of parameters
characterizing COTS products. The need for this characterization derives from
the problem to identify and select among many available products the ones
which are appropriate for a specific software system. The characterization has
the goal to foresee the integration and maintenance effort in COTS based
systems developed with a COTS-based approach. In our study we propose a set
of COTS product parameters and perform an empirical study in the context of
two industrial software projects to assess these parameters. The assessment
aims at finding any statistically significant correlation among the proposed
parameters and the effectiveness of development and maintenance process. The
obtained results show that our COTS products characterization can be used to
foresee integration and maintenance effort of the COTS based system. The
analysis also shows the need to continue the on-field experimentation, in order
to make the learned lessons effective and applicable.

Keywords: Component-based software engineering, COTS integration,
empirical studies.

1 Introduction

The large availability of previously developed and commercialised software
components enables software organizations to better master the growing complexity
and size of new software systems. In this context, many authors acknowledged the
need to adequately select the proper Commercial Off The Shelf (COTS) product to be
integrated in a COTS based system (CBS): for example, Lawlis et al. [1] analyzed the
difficulty to identify the most appropriate COTS products for specific requirements;

R. Conradi and A.I. Wang (Eds.): ESERNET 2001-2003, LNCS 2765, pp. 233–255, 2003.

Basili and Boehm in Hypothesis 9 in their Top 10 list [2][1] stated the difficulty in learning the features of COTS product necessary for the development of a software system; Boehm and Abts in [3] identified the difficulty to integrate COTS products within the CBS.

More specifically, the choice of the COTS products impacts on both the development of the CBS, and on its maintenance, and it has effects which last for all the lifetime of the CBS. In general, the integration of a COTS product could give rise to problems concerning the individuation of the capabilities (for instance, services, functionality, and so on) the COTS product makes publicly available, so that they could be adequately exploited by the CBS. Further problems derives from the specific mode required by the COTS product to access its capabilities, for instance, through web services, or object request brokers (ORB), or application programming interfaces (API) and so on.

From a maintenance viewpoint, problems derive from the different evolution of the CBS and the COTS products integrated in it, which, in most cases, are asynchronous each other. This feature implies the need to properly manage possible redundancy in the provided capabilities.

In order to face this problem, the authors are performing the PACIE (PArameters for Cots Impact Evaluation) empirical study, which is aimed at identifying the most significant or relevant characteristics to select an appropriate COTS product for a new CBS. In this project, for COTS we mean a software component existing a priori, available to the general public, and which can be bought, or leased or licensed or *freely acquired*. This definition is an extended version of the definition provided by the Software Engineering Institute (SEI) in [4] which considers freely available software products as COTS products.

In the PACIE project, we are interested in understanding how the COTS product characteristics affect integrability and maintainability quality factors of COTS-based software systems. More precisely, PACIE is aimed at:

- identifying the meaningful quality factors and the COTS product characteristics;
- understanding how the COTS product characteristics affect the quality factors of COTS-based software systems;
- evaluating the capability of the COTS product characteristics in identifying the most adequate COTS.

In the current state of the PACIE project, we are pursuing the first two goals. To this end we focalize on quality factors mainly related to integration maintainability of the CBS. The preliminary set of characteristics of COTS products has been identified, according to the authors' experience.

In order to assess the identified characteristics, a post mortem analysis of data concerning two industrial software projects has been executed. Both projects were developed through the integration of a number of COTS products, which were selected making use of specific criteria, depending on both the features of the organizations and of the systems to develop. Moreover both CBSs were maintained, and the maintenance activities impacted the integration of some COTS products.

---

[1] The Top 10 List in [Basili01] includes ten hypotheses which represent different research challenges for "enhancing our empirical understanding of component-based systems". Hypothesis 9 states: "personnel capability and experience remain the dominant factors influencing component-based systems development productivity".

1.1   Related Work

The idea of decomposing the general characteristics of a COTS product into a set of quality attributes has been exploited by several research projects [5], PECA [6], PORE [7]. The fundamental idea of COTS product evaluation is to use the quantitative attributes to measure the conformance of COTS products with a set of requirements [8]. These approaches differ in how attributes are defined and how they can be reused in different projects. For example, [9, 1, 10, 11] propose to redefine attributes based on software system requirements. On the other hand, approaches like [12, 13] and [14] define a set of generic attributes (often inspired by the ISO 9126 standard [15]) that can be reused across projects and possibly organizations.

Our characteristics stem partly from some previous work which has been done by some of the authors ([16, 17]). The proposed characteristics are assessed in [18].

2 Starting Scenario

The current stage of PACIE empirical study has been executed jointly with the development of two different software systems in which some of the authors are involved. The projects are SICOD and DiPNET and they have been developed through a COTS-based approach.

In these projects, the three main reasons for COTS products choice were: the past experience of the working team; the products availability, and the matching of system requirements with COTS products characteristics.

In the following the two projects are outlined.

2.1   SICOD

SICOD (Sistema Informativo per la COnvergenza con i Destinatari, i.e. Information System for Stakeholders Satisfaction) is a software system supporting the qualification of the education and scientific services offered by the University of Bari. It has been developed within the Software Engineering Research Laboratory (SER_Lab) of the same university. The version of SICOD taken into account in the post mortem analysis includes functionality concerning data management, the stakeholder relationship management, the report management and a prototype of a web portal to make the services available through the Internet.

SICOD manages all data in an Oracle 9i database, which has been used because of familiarity reasons of the developers. Since the entire Oracle suite includes a number of COTS, in the context of the present work the following are considered as separated COTS products:

- Oracle 9i, as the database management system for managing data and the environment supporting application development;
- Oracle Internet Application Server 9i, as the application server for managing data through the Internet;
- Oracle Report Builder, as the COTS product for developing reports;

The COTS product for managing the relationship to the stakeholders included into SICOD is Applix iEnterprice. It has been chosen within a set of 31 software systems providing Customer Relationship Management (CRM) functionality after an analysis of the COTS products, which took into account a number of features, as well as, for example, the capability to allow Internet access, the capability to manage the historical data, the availability of tools for managing the workflow and trouble ticketing, the capability to tailor the offer to the needs of a specific customer, the availability of interface allowing integration with other systems, and so on.

The COTS product for the web portal included into SICOD is Plumtree Corporate Portal 4.5. It has been chosen within a set of 15 COTS products providing Portal functionality. The choice of the portal has been driven by the cost-benefits analysis executed by the AMR Research [19].

In SICOD two different COTS products are used for reports production: the reports concerning the data management functionality are managed by Oracle Report Builder, the reports concerning the CRM functionality are managed by Crystal Report. These choices are effects of the previous choices of the COTS products managing the data and the CRM, in that Oracle Report Builder is a COTS integrated within the Oracle environment and Crystal Report is the COTS used by Applix to manage reports.

2.2   DiPNET

The Italian company Network Services with the support of some of the authors developed the DiPNET (DIstributed Production NETwork services) software system, i.e., a web portal supporting different companies cooperating for the development of a project. The portal includes three sub-portals:

- the KnOwledge Factory NETwork Services (KoFNET), which allows distributing knowledge among the cooperating organizations. Moreover, it permits to search the organizations with the most appropriate competences for a specific purpose.
- the PrOduction Lifecycle management – NETwork Services (PoLNET), which distributes products and services required to execute the project among the cooperating organizations.
- the SUpplier Relationship management - NETwork Services (SuRNET), which supports legal and management services

In this context, the main functionality making use of COTS products are the following:
- store and retrieve data;
- manage electronic forum over the Internet;
- manage the knowledge stored in a knowledge base;
- manage the schedule of the activities within the project.

In order to provide the previous functionality, DiPNET integrates a number of COTS products, and more precisely:
- SQL Server 7 as the Database Management System;
- SNITZ Forum, freeware for managing forum over the Internet [20]
- DecisionScript, application server developed by Vanguard Software for browsing knowledge base [21]

- DatePicker, freeware for calendar management [22]
- MS ADO, COM objects for managing access to database, developed by Microsoft [23]
- Internet Information Services (IIS), as the web servers, developed by Microsoft [23]
- MS Index Server (IIXSO) as a full-text indexing and search engine for (IIS) allowing any Web browser to search documents through keywords, phrases, or properties
- MS Collaboration Data Objects for NT (CDONTS) as an interface towards an SMTP server, used as a tool for sending e-mails.

The COTS products have been chosen according to an economical criterion: whenever possible, they have been used the COTS products satisfying any functionality and which have been used in previous projects. If such a COTS product does not exist, then it was searched among the freeware.

2.3 Structure of the Work

In this chapter we report the experience of our post mortem analysis. Section 2 presents the method of the empirical study. Results of the empirical study are summarized on Section 3 and discussed in Section 4. Finally, Section 5 outlines the main conclusions. Appendixes provide details about data and their analysis.

3 Method

The current stage of the PACIE empirical study is based on a post-mortem analysis [24]. The goal of the study is to verify the effectiveness of the proposed set of COTS products characteristics, in the COTS selection of the two projects, with respect to the proposed quality factors. In other words, we are interested in investigating whether the COTS characteristics we propose are meaningful for COTS selection, if they were adopted in those two specific cases.

3.1 Design

The proposed COTS products characteristics are:
- **Adequateness**: it considers the application domain, the functionality provided by the COTS product, its effective usage within the CBS
- **Adoption Costs**: the economical effort required to adopt the COTS product: it includes the costs for its acquisition (e.g., the license) and the costs for properly use it (e.g., the training)
- **COTS Origin**: it includes both the origin of the COTS product (i.e., if it is in-house, existing external, externally developed, specially customized version, independent commercial, ...) and the capability of the organization to affect producer's decisions about new releases

- **Familiarity:** the previous experiences of the developers with the COTS product
- **Integration Technique:** the specific technique provided to integrate the COTS
- **Support**: type and quality of the support the producer provides

The proposed CBS quality factors are:

- **Integration Costs:** The economical effort required to integrate the COTS product within the CBS: it includes the time the effort and the staff required for integration
- **Maintenance of the CBS:** The costs (e.g., time, effort, staff) spent to satisfy maintenance requests in CBS impacting COTS product integration, and its quality degradation after maintenance
- **Issues:** The number and gravity of issues faced during COTS product integration

Both characteristics and quality factors have been detailed in a set of metrics. We expect that a statistically significant relationship exists among the two set of metrics.

3.1.1   Metrics

The COTS products characteristics have been mapped onto a set of metrics, which are reported on Table 1. The quality factors have been mapped onto a set of metrics, which are reported in Table 2. For each metric, we provide a brief description and its scale. Note that all metrics have been collected making use of available documentation or data provided by the software engineers involved in integration and maintenance activities.

For what concerns characterization metrics, it is worth commenting on the two metrics "Functional Coverage" and "Compliance": the former expresses the percentage of

$$Fun\_Cov_i = \frac{Fun_i}{TotFun}$$

capability of each COTS product to support the functionality required by the CBS; the latter expresses the effective usage of each COTS product within the CBS. Both of them refer to the concept of "functionality". In this study, we kept the meaning of the term "functionality" as broad as possible. Examples of functionality are the transactions, packages, methods, etc. the COTS product makes available for public use. In this sense, in Functional Coverage metric, "functionality" is defined in the requirements specification of the CBS; in Compliance metric, "functionality" is provided by each COTS product. The set of functionality provided by each COTS product used in SICOD and DiPNET is summarized Appendix A, in Tables 4 and 5, respectively.

The value of the Functional Coverage metric for the i-th COTS product, Fun_Cov_i, is calculated as follows:
where:

- Fun_i is the number of functionality provided to the CBS by the i-th COTS product,
- TotFun is the total number of functionality provided by all the COTS products to the CBS.

Note that the sum of Functional Coverage values of the COTS products integrated within a CBS can be lower, equals to or greater than 100%. When such a sum is:

Table 1. Metrics for COTS products characteristics

Characteristic	Metric	Meaning	Scale
Adequateness	Application domain	The application domain the COTS has been designed for	Nominal
	Functional Coverage	Percentage of the CBS functionality provided by the COTS	Ratio (percentage)
	Compliance	Percentage of the COTS functionality used into integration	Ratio (percentage)
Adoption costs	License type	What type of license of use has the COTS	Nominal (copyright, free,...)
	Training time	Working time spent for training people involved in the COTS integration	Ratio (working days)
COTS origin	COTS origin	The source of the COTS	Nominal: (In-house, Existing External, Externally Developed, Special Version, ...)
Familiarity	Familiarity	Number of previous projects in which the COTS has been used	Interval (No. of projects)
Integration Technique	Integration technique	The technique used to integrate the COTS into the system	Nominal (wrapper, standard protocol, property protocol, API, ...)
Support	COTS support	Level of support provided by the vendor (through web/discussion groups/news/call service...)	Ordinal (No Support, Low, Medium, High)
	COTS documentation	Quality of available COTS documentation	Ordinal (No Doc, Low, Medium, High)

- lower than 100%, then some functionality required to the CBS are not provided by any COTS product, therefore, they need to be developed by scratch;
- equals to 100%, then there is the optimal coverage of functionality by COTS products;
- greater than 100%, then some functionality required to the CBS are provided by more than one COTS product.

This last case can give rise to problems during maintenance. In fact, when the functionality covered by multiple COTS products has to be maintained, it is necessary to maintain the integration of *all* the COTS products providing it. In order to overcome this problem, it is suggested a deeper analysis of the CBS requirements, in order to better specify the functionality, so that each of them is covered by almost one COTS product.

On the other hand, the value of the Compliance metric for the i-th COTS product, $Compl_i$, expresses its usage within the CBS, as the amount of COTS product functionality employed in the CBS. The value of the Compliance metric for the i-th COTS product, $Compl_i$, is calculated as follows:

$$Compl_i = \frac{Fun_i}{TotFunCOTS_i}$$

where:
- Fun_i is the number of functionality provided to the CBS by the i-th COTS product,
- $TotFunCOTS_i$ is the total number of functionality the i-th COTS product makes publicly available.

It is worth noting that Compliance values for each COTS product can range between 0 and 1. Low values of compliance indicate that the COTS product is poorly used within the CBS; instead, high compliance values imply an intensive usage of the COTS product. Note that, the previous definition is highly impacted by the granularity used for defining the functionality: a coarse granularity implies low compliance, while finer granularity drives to higher values.

Table 2. Metrics for CBS quality factors

Factor	Metric	Meaning	Scale
Integration Costs	Integration time	Elapsed time from the beginning to the end of the integration of the COTS within the CBS	Ratio (working days)
	Integration effort	Effort spent in COTS integration	Ratio (person days)
Maintenance effort of the CBS	Mean Maintenance effort of the CBS	Mean effort spent to satisfy maintenance requests for the CBS	Ratio (person days)
Issues	Number of issues	No. of tickets sent to supplier during COTS integration	Absolute (No. of issues)
	Gravity	Mean gravity of the integration issues	Ordinal (Low, Medium, High)

The effort spent for both integration and maintenance activities are measured in persons days, where each working day is 8 hours long.

"Mean maintenance effort" metric (MME) is used to evaluate the effort of maintenance on the CBS: it is measured by means of the following:

$$MME = \frac{\sum_{i=1}^{n} ME_i}{n}$$

where:
- ME_i is the effort spent for satisfying the i-th maintenance request,
- n is the total number of maintenance requests: note that only request impacting the COTS products integration are considered.

The characteristic dealing with the problems encountered during the COTS products integration has been detailed into two metrics: number of issues and their gravity. An "issue" is defined as every non-routine problem faced by developers with respect to the COTS products integration and which required the help of the COTS product suppliers. These issues are simply counted by the "Number of issues" metric. The issues are then differentiated through their *gravity*, meant as the difficulty in solving them. Both the number of issues and their gravity are subjective metrics, strictly depending on the developer who declared them.

As a final remark, the set of COTS products considered in this study is almost heterogeneous. In general, the values each metric assumes for a specific COTS product is very different from the values for the others. Therefore, all values need to be normalized. The normalization factor NF_i for the i-th quality factors metric is defined as follows

$$NF_i = \sum_{j=1}^{n} (V_i)_j$$

where:

- $(V_i)_j$ is the value the i-th quality factor metric assumes for the j-th COTS product,
- n is the number of COTS products.

In the analysis both absolute and normalized values will be taken into account.

3.1.2   Research Hypotheses

In order to investigate whether the characterization metrics would have been effective if adopted for COTS products selection for SICOD and DiPNET, the values of these metrics will be analyzed. More precisely, the research questions faced by the research are:

- is there any correlation between the characterization and quality factors metrics?
- if so, what is the kind of these correlations?
- what are the effects of the correlations upon the integration and maintenance process?

In order to answer the first question the following hypotheses have been stated:

null hypothesis: there not exists any correlation between the characterization
                            metrics and the quality factors metrics
alternative hypothesis: there exists a correlation between the characterization metrics
                            and the quality factors metrics.

The results of the statistical analysis used to test the research hypotheses will also be used to answer the remaining questions.

Note that, in the current stage of PACIE project, all data have been collected; all of them will be used in discussion, but only data measured on interval, ratio and absolute scales are considered in the statistical analysis: future development will take into account also nominal and ordinal metrics.

Therefore, the independent variables taken into account in this chapter are the characterization metrics and the dependent variables are the quality factors metrics. According to the schema reported in Chapter 2 of the present book, the structure of the investigation is plotted in Fig. 1.

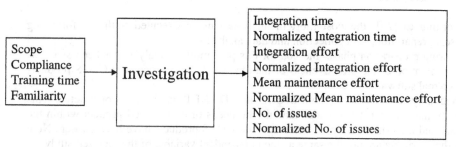

Fig. 1. Variables in the investigation

3.2   Subjects/Participants

The SICOD system has been developed within the Software Engineering Research LABoratory (SER_Lab) of the Informatics Department of University of Bari, by 4 software engineers with the "Laurea" degree in Informatics. Two software engineers have been working in the SER_Lab for three years. The other two subjects have been working in the SER_Lab for one year, and in that period only one of them developed two applications using one of the COTS taken into account in this study.

The DiPNET system has been developed within the company Network Services, by 2 software engineers with the "Laurea" degree in Informatics. All of them have been working in Network Services for 2 years, and they developed at least one project making use of almost of the COTS used in DiPNET.

For both SICOD and DiPNET, the involved software engineers choose the COTS to include in the CBS, according to the specific organization criteria described above. Moreover they integrated the COTS products in the system and tested the resulting system. Finally they also executed the maintenance activities.

In both projects, the teams were managed, coordinated and supported by some of the authors in the execution of the previous activities.

3.3   Apparatus/Materials

The empirical study has been executed on data collected in three different ways:
- The COTS product documentation provided by the suppliers has been used to define the Application domain, License type, Integration technique, and Origin of each COTS product.
- The project managers provided data concerning Functional Coverage, Compliance, Training time, Familiarity, Integration time, Integration effort, and Mean maintenance effort.
- The developers provided data concerning Number and Gravity of issues, Support and Documentation of each COTS product.

Data have been analyzed using Statistica 6.0 developed by StatSoft [25].

3.4   Procedures

According to [26], the post mortem analysis can be executed with the following phases: preparation, data collection and data analysis.

During preparation phase, the goal of this post mortem analysis has been stated as the verification of the effectiveness of the identified characteristics of COTS products in two real software projects.

Secondly, the history of both SICOD and DiPNET has been reconstructed. This activity mainly focused in understanding the needs of each COTS product within the CBSs, and the criteria adopted when specific COTS products have been chosen. Note that these criteria are not the same as the independent variable of the reported study.

Then, data were collected through interviews with the project managers and the developers of both SICOD and DiPNET. Moreover the available documentation of the COTS products adopted in the two projects was studied.

Finally, the collected data were analyzed. In order to verify the research hypotheses, the non-parametric Spearman's regression analysis has been executed. This kind of analysis has been chosen because the assumptions about normality were not always satisfied. However, the scale constraint is satisfied, as all the analyzed data are measured at least on an interval scale [27].

For each pair <v, w>, where v is an independent variable, and w is a dependent variable, this analysis provides a correlation coefficient ρ, ranging from -1 to +1 and the associated p-level, ranging from 0 to 1. The value of ρ establishes the correlation between v and w: the higher is the absolute value of ρ, the higher is the correlation. The value of p-level define the statistically significance of the found correlation: it is conventionally adopted to accept as statistically significant the values of p-level which are lower than 0,05, i.e. they provide a significance greater than the 95%.

4 Results

In this section, we outline the results of the post mortem analysis. For both SICOD and DiPNET, a summary of collected values of metrics are presented the values of characterization metrics, organized according to the characteristics; secondly, there are the values of quality factors metrics. The presentation of the statistical analysis aimed at validating the research hypothesis is summarized at the end of this section.

Detailed collected data and results of statistical analysis are reported in Appendixes B and C, respectively.

4.1 Data Collected in SICOD

4.1.1 Values for Characterization Metrics

Adequateness (Application Domain, Functional Coverage, Compliance)
The COTS products used in SICOD result to be adequate with respect to the specific problem they are called to solve. In fact, each COTS product has been used in the CBS in the same application domain it has been designed for.

Table 4 in Appendix A shows that the number of functionality provided by each COTS product. The total number is 22: four functions are provided by Oracle DB, two by Oracle Internet Application Server, four by Oracle Report Builder, four by Crystal Report, seven by Applix and one by Plumtree. Therefore, the COTS product with highest value of Functional Coverage metric is Applix (with 31,82%), followed by Oracle DB, Oracle Report Builder and Crystal Report (18,18%), while the two remaining COTS products provide less than the 10% of functionality (9,09% is offered by Oracle Internet application Server and 4,55% by Plumtree).

The compliance is in general high: for five COTS products, the percentage of COTS functionality used in SICOD is greater than or equal to 50%; Applix, presents a compliance value of 46%; only Plumtree shows a low value for compliance, which is the 11 %.

Adoption Costs (License Type, Training Time)
All the COTS products used in the SICOD project are software systems licensed in copyright.

In all cases, except of Crystal Report, for which no training was provided, there was a training period ranging from four to fourteen working days.

Familiarity (Number of Previous Projects)
In all cases the developers were little or no familiar to the COTS products: two of them (Crystal Report and Applix) were never been used before SICOD project; one (Oracle Internet Application Server) was used in one past project; one (Plumtree) was

used in two past projects. Only the two remaining COTS products (i.e., Oracle DB and Oracle Report Builder) were used in three past projects.

Integration Technique
The integration techniques provided by the COTS products are spread. In two cases (Oracle Internet Application Server and Oracle Report Builder) the COTS products are integrated through a standard protocol (in both cases through the TCP/IP). Crystal Report and Applix required the application of a specific proprietary protocol, i.e., each of them provides functionality to the CBS only through an exchange of data managed within each COTS product. Plumtree required to be wrapped within the target application. Oracle DB provides white-box integration technique, so that it is possible to directly interact with the whole COTS.

COTS Origin (The Source of the COTS)
All the COTS products used in the SICOD project are software systems produced externally with respect to the CBS and independently from it.

Support (Level of Support Provided by the Vendor)
The support provided by the producer and the quality of the documentation are in general considered good by the developers. In seven cases the COTS products get score "high", and only one COTS product (Crystal Report) gets score "medium".

4.1.2   Values for Quality Factors Metrics
Integration Costs (Integration Time, Integration Effort)
The COTS product which required the lowest integration costs was Crystal Report (ten days spent by one person). Two COTS products (Oracle Internet application Server, and Plumtree) required 50 person days each. One COTS product (Oracle Report Builder) required 70 days spent by one person. The integration of Applix required 210 person days. The highest integration effort was paid for Oracle DB, which required 400 person days (integration time was equal to 200 days for two persons).

Maintenance of the CBS (Mean Maintenance Effort)
The mean effort spent to satisfy maintenance requests impacting integration of
- Crystal Report was four person days;
- Oracle Report Builder was 12 person days;
- Oracle Internet Application Server was 15 person days;
- Applix was 20 person days;
- Oracle DB was 30 person days.

Plumtree did not require any maintenance activity.
The high value of the mean effort spent for maintaining the Oracle DB is mainly due to changing of the adopted version, which was upgraded several times, from the release 7.1 to the release 9.2.0.1.0.
The high value of the mean effort spent for maintaining Applix is due to the execution of only one maintenance request, which required redefinition of the whole user interface.

Issues (Number of Issues, Gravity)
In all cases, the number of issues ranges from two (for Oracle Report Builder) to 50 (for Applix); the mean gravity for all of them was scored as "low", except of Applix

("medium"). The integration of Plumtree presented a different behavior also for what concerns the encountered issues, in that it was the only COTS product which did not give rise to issues during integration.

4.2   Data Collected in DiPNET

4.2.1   Values for Characterization Metrics

Adequateness (Application Domain, Functional Coverage, Compliance)
The Application domain each COTS product has been designed for is the same application domain in which it has been used in DiPNET system.

Table 5 in Appendix A shows that the total number of functionality provided by the COTS products to DiPNET is 20: four functions are provided by SQL Server, two by ADO, eight by SNITZ Forum, one by Decision Script, one by Date Picker, two by IIS and one each by IIXSO and CDONTS. Therefore, the COTS product with highest value of Functional Coverage metric is Snitz Forum (with 40%), followed by SQL Server (20%), then ADO and Internet Information Services (10%) while the four remaining COTS products provide the 5% of functionality

For what concerns the compliance metric, for two COTS products (Date Picker and CDONTS) the percentage of functionality used in DiPNET is the 50%. The remaining COTS products are used in DiPNET with a percentage ranging from 6,67% (Decision Script) to 33,33% (IIXSO).

Adoption Costs (License Type, Training Time)
Two of the COTS products integrated within DiPNET, Snitz Forum and Date Picker, are free software; the other six are licensed in copyright.

For three COTS products (Snitz Forum, Decision Script and Date Picker) no training was provided. For the remaining COTS products there were a period of training ranging from one day (for CDONTS) to five days (SQL Server).

Familiarity (Number of Previous Projects)
In all cases the developers were little or no familiar with the COTS products. Two COTS products (Snitz Forum and Date Picker) were never used before DiPNET project; three COTS products (Internet Information Services, IIXSO and CDONTS) were used in one past project; SQL Server and ADO were used in two past projects; only Decision Script has been used in three past projects.

Integration Technique
The integration technique the COTS products provide is a standard protocol in one case (Decision Script), which can be integrated through the TCP/IP. Three COTS products (SQL Server, Snitz Forum and Date Picker) provides white-box integration technique. The four remaining COTS products require proprietary non-standard protocols.

COTS Origin (The Source of the COTS)
All the COTS products are software systems produced externally with respect to the CBS and independently from it.

Support (Level of Support Provided by the Vendor)
The support provided by the producer and the quality of the documentation are quite spread, ranging from the "low" value for two COTS products (Decision Script and

Date Picker), to "medium" for Snitz Forum, to "high" for the remaining COTS products.

4.2.2   Values for Quality Factors Metrics

Integration Costs (Integration Time, Integration Effort)
The integration of each COTS product within DiPNET required an effort ranging from four person days spent for integrating Decision Script to the 20 person days spent for integrating SQL Server and SNITZ Forum.

Maintenance of the CBS (Mean Maintenance Effort)
The maintenance activities for DiPNET did not impact the integration of Decision Script and Date Picker.

The maintenance activities impacting ADO, Snitz Forum and CDONTS, have been executed with a mean effort equals to one person day. For SQL Server and MS IIXSO, the mean effort spent in maintenance was two person days.

Finally, IIS required six person days for executing maintenance activities.

Issues (Number of Issues, Gravity)
Except of Decision Script, which required to solve eight issues during integration, with a mean gravity scored as "medium", there were not any issue (in five cases) or only three (for SQL Server and ADO, whose gravity scored as "medium" and "low", respectively).

4.3   Statistical Analysis

Table 3 summarizes the correlations between characterization metrics and quality factors metrics. In this table, columns report the quality factors metric, rows report characterization metrics; the generic cell in position (i, j) contains the value of the correlation coefficient between the i-th characterization metric and the j-th quality factors metric, at the conventional 0.05 p level. Otherwise, if such a correlation does not exist, then the cell (i, j) is void.

The complete results of the statistical analysis aimed at investigating the research hypotheses are reported in Table 11 in Appendix C.

Table 3. Map of correlations between characterization metrics and quality factors metrics

	Integration Time	Integration Effort	Mean maintenance effort	No. of issues
Training time	0,691411	0,766341	0,553060	
Familiarity				
Functional Coverage	0,554475	0,538236	0,567733	
Compliance			0,616763	

Results show that among the characterization metrics, only familiarity is not correlated to any quality factors metrics. On the other side, among quality factors metrics, only the number of issues is not correlated to any characterization metrics. In all other cases, each characterization metric is correlated to one or three quality factors metrics, and vice versa, each quality factors metric is correlated to two or three characterization metrics.

Note that all the characterization metrics are independent each other. Table 10 in appendix C reports on the Spearman's analysis aimed at looking for correlations among characterization metrics. In this table no correlations are reported, therefore all the characterization metrics are independent each other.

5 Discussion

The analysis of data concerning the two industrial projects showed that the time spent for training people in SICOD case is significantly correlated to the values of integration time and effort, and to the mean effort spent for maintenance activities. These correlations can be explained considering that the COTS product suppliers propose periods of training depending on the intrinsic difficulty in understanding the COTS products: the more difficult is the comprehension of the COTS product the higher integration and maintenance costs it requires. Therefore, we can argue that the proposed training period is a proper characteristic for COTS products selection, in that it provides an indication of the difficulty in understanding it.

Functional Coverage is statistically correlated to integration and maintenance costs. This can be explained recalling that Functional Coverage is evaluated as the percentage of CBS functionality provided by that COTS product. But this implies that when the COTS product is integrated, all its functionality have to be adequately considered at the same time. This need makes the integration harder. In the same way, the higher Functional Coverage, the higher the probability that maintaining one of the COTS product functions (deployed to the CBS) has consequences on the remaining parts of the CBS which are based on that specific COTS product.

Analogous considerations can be developed with respect to compliance metric, which is statistically correlated to mean maintenance effort. Also compliance definition is affected by the functionality definition, in that it expresses the percentage of COTS product used in the CBS. If such a percentage is high for a COTS product, then each change involving it affects a high number of functionality of the CBS, and therefore the maintenance effort increases.

The absence of correlations concerning the familiarity characterization metric can be explained noting that in all cases the number of projects previously developed making use of the same COTS products is low, ranging from 0 (for four COTS products) to three (for three COTS products). This does not allow to better analyze the effect of familiarity on quality factors metrics.

Finally, the quality factors metric concerning the number of issues faced during COTS products integration resulted to be uncorrelated to any characterization metric. This can be explained with the intrinsic subjectivity of this metric and considering that the effort required to solve issues (i.e., the gravity) has not been taken into account in the present analysis, because it is measured on an ordinal scale. Further studies are needed to better understand the relationship of number and gravity of issues with respect to characterization metrics.

As a final remark, further investigations are needed to validate the cause – effect relationship between characterization metrics and quality factors metrics. These future studies should better take into account the threads which have been ignored in the present post mortem analysis. For example, in this study each COTS product has been used only in one CBS: this implies that we cannot verify whether the same COTS product, used in different projects by different developers, reacts in the same way. In other words, the obtained results can be affected by factors, which have not been adequately taken into account. In future development of our investigation it will be necessary to face the threads to internal validity, in order to remove the suspect that the obtained results are affected by unconsidered factors.

Moreover, in future analysis, it will be worth analyzing both familiarity and issues, despite of the absence of correlations evidenced in the current study. In fact, we can argue that the absence of correlations can be due to the specific projects, in which the values of both familiarity and issues are not meaningful. Further investigations will be based on the statistical analysis results of this preliminary investigation. As an example, we can consider the correlation between the training time of the COTS products and the integration time spent on CBS as a research hypothesis to be further investigated by an industrial case study or a controlled experiment.

6 Lessons Learned

This chapter presented a part of our research aimed at defining a set of COTS products parameters, which should be used when deciding if the adoption of a given COTS product is adequate for a CBS.

A preliminary set of COTS product characteristics has been identified and the post mortem analysis presented above has been executed with the aim to investigate the effectiveness of the identified characteristics with respect to two real projects. The described results are encouraging for our research, in that on one hand they show the effectiveness of a subset of the identified COTS products parameters, and on the other side they provide some suggestions for further studies. In general, this experience suggests that COTS products characteristics can provide information about the integrability and maintainability factors. The characteristics can be evaluated a priori, and in this way it is possible reducing the risk in the adoption of each COTS product.

In more detail, the lesson learned about the Functional Coverage characteristic suggests to adopt COTS products such that each of them provides a few number of functionality to the CBS. In this way, the possible impact of changes on one functionality over the others is reduced. When the available COTS products do not permit to keep Functional Coverage value low, it is suggested to reengineer the CBS. The reengineering should be aimed at a new design in which the number of functionality required to each COTS product is low. Moreover, when a CBS needs to use more than one functionality from a COTS product, it is worth verifying that they are loosely coupled. In other words, the knowledge needed to access each function of the COTS product should be independent from the knowledge needed to access the other functions. If this feature cannot be exploited, then it is worth structuring the CBS so that only one of its functions makes use of the COTS product functions.

A further lesson we learned in this experience is the importance of the training, which affects integration and maintenance. If the producer acknowledges the need of a high training for a COTS product, then it is expected it is difficult to learn and use, therefore its adoption within the CBS can be critical. In this case, the costs overhead due to training integration and maintenance should be counterbalanced by a real effectiveness within the system. Anyway, it is necessary for the organization a deep knowledge of the COTS product before its adoption, therefore, it is advised the trial usage of COTS products for a period of time after the training and before the final decision about their adoption.

Finally, it is worth noting that in this study we referred to projects in which COTS products have been selected making use of specific, organization-driven criteria. This feature suggests that any set of parameters for COTS products identification cannot be generally adopted, but it should include a subset of parameters specified by the organization.

The experience also encourages in executing further empirical studies in order to better face some issues, which have not been deeply taken into account in this analysis. To this end, further studies should better investigate the role of the granularity for an adequate identification of the COTS product functionality. In fact, in this study we considered for all COTS products the functionality as the functions the COTS product allow public access, identified with a coarse granularity. Moreover, it is necessary to investigate whether a weighted approach can be more effective, so that the Functional Coverage of a COTS product is measured through the percentage of the CBS functionality provided by the COTS product, weighted upon the importance of the COTS product within the CBS.

References

[1]   Lawlis, P.K., Mark, K.E., Thomas, D.A., Courtheyn, T.: A Formal Process for Evaluating COTS Software Products, Computer, May (2001), 58–63.

[2]   Basili, V., Boehm, B.: COTS Based Systems Top 10 List. Computer, May (2001), 91–93

[3]   Boehm, B., Abts, C.: COTS Integration: Plug and Pray? Computer, January (1999) 135–138.

[4]   Oberndorf, T.: "COTS and Open Systems: An Overview", CMU-SEI, (2000), available at the url http://www.sei.cmu.edu/str/descriptions/cots.html#110707

[5]   Wallnau, K., Brown, A.: A Framework for Evaluating Software Technology, IEEE Software, 13, 5, (1996) 39–49.

[6]   Comella-Dorda, S., Dean, J., Morris, E., Oberndorf, T.: A Process for COTS Software Product Evaluation, Proc. of 1ˢᵗ International Conference on COTS Based Software Systems (ICCBSS), Orlando (FL), (2002) 86–96.

[7]   Maiden, N., Ncube, C.: Acquiring COTS Software Selection Requirements. IEEE Software, (1998) 46–56.

[8]   Carney, D., Wallnau, K.: A basis for evaluation of commercial software. Information and Software Technology, 40, (1998) 851–860.

[9]   Morisio, M., Tsoukiàs, A.: IusWare: A methodology for the evaluation and selection of software products. IEE Proceedings-Software, 144, 3, (1997), 162–174.

[10] Kitchenham, B.: DESMET: A method for evaluating Software Engineering methods and tools, Keele University, (1996).

[11] Kontio, J.: A Case Study in Applying a Systematic Method for COTS Selection. Proc. of the IEEE-ACM 18th International Conference on Software Engineering (ICSE), Berlin, Germany, (1996), 201–209.

[12] Ochs, M.A., Pfahl, D., Chrobok-Diening, G.: A Method for Efficient Measurement-based COTS Assessment ad Selection - Method Description and Evaluation Results, Proc. of the IEEE 7th International Software Metrics Symposium, London, England, (2001), 285–296.

[13] Boloix, G., Robillard, P.: A Software System Evaluation Framework. Computer, 12, 8, (1995) 17–26.

[14] CLARiFi Consortium (2002).

[15] ISO: Information technology – Software product evaluation – Quality characteristics and guidelines for their use. International Organization for Standardization, International Electrotechnical Commission, Geneva (1991)

[16] Jaccheri, L., Torchiano, M., Classifying COTS Products. Proc. of the 7th European Conference on Software Quality (ECSQ 2002), Helsinki, Finland, (2002), 246–255

[17] Torchiano, M., Jaccheri, L., Sørensens, C.F., Wang, A.I.: COTS Products Characterization, Proc. of the Conference on Software Engineering and Knowledge Engineering (SEKE'02), Ischia, Italy, (2002), 335–338.

[18] Torchiano, M., Jaccheri, L.: Assessment of Reusable COTS Attributes, Proc. of the 2nd Intl. Conference on COTS Based Software Systems (ICCBSS 2003), Ottawa, Canada, (2003).

[19] Murphy, J., Higgs, L., Quirk, C.: The Portal Framework: The New Battle for the Enterprise Desktop, AMR Research Report, March (2002), available on the AMR Research site at the url: http://www.amrresearch.com

[20] SnitzForum, available at the url http://forum.snitz.com/

[21] Decision Script, available at the url http://www.vanguardsw.com/

[22] DatePicker, available at the url http://www.softricks.com/js/

[23] Microsoft, available at the url http://www.microsoft.com/

[24] Wohlin, C., Runeson, P., Höst, M., Ohlsson, M. C., Regnell, B., Wesslén, A.: Experimentation in Software Engineering: An Introduction, Kluwer Academy Publishers, (2000).

[25] Statistica available at the url http://www.statsoft.com/

[26] Birk, A., Dingsor, T., Stalhane, T.: Postmortem: Never Leave a Project without It. IEEE Software, May-June (2002) 43–45.

[27] Conover, W.J.: Practical Nonparametric Statistics, John Wiley and Sons, (1980).

Appendix A: Functionality

The COTS products functionality taken into account in the current stage of the PACIE project has been defined as the functions publicly available. This appendix reports the functionality provided by the COTS products to SICOD and DiPNET, respectively.

Note that both Oracle Report Builder and Crystal Report provides the same functionality. In fact both of them have been used to manage reports: the former manages reports concerning Oracle DB data, the latter manages reports concerning Applix data.

Table 4. Functionality provided by the COTS products used in SICOD.

COTS	Functionality
Oracle DB	1) Data insertion 2) Data modification 3) Data deletion 4) Data browsing
Oracle Internet Application Server	1) visualization of the forms for data management in Internet 2) intercepting of user actions on forms for data management in Internet
Oracle Report Builder	1) Data browsing for report creation 2) Report visualization 3) Report conversion in pdf format 4) Report printing
Crystal Report	1) Data browsing for report creation 2) Report visualization 3) Report conversion in pdf format 4) Report printing
Applix	1) Databanker for interaction with Oracle DB 2) Interface for interaction with Crystal Report 3) Asynchronous exchange of messages among users 4) Escalation agent, which verifies predefined conditions in the DB and consequently performs predefined actions 5) Visualization of the forms for data management in Internet as ASP pages 6) Intercepting of user actions on forms for data management in Internet 7) E-mail sending
Plumtree	1) Hosting of the ASP pages produced by Applix

Table 5. Functionality provided by the COTS products used in DiPNET.

COTS	Functionality
SQL Server	1) Data insertion 2) Data modification 3) Data deletion 4) Data browsing
MS ADO	1) visualization of the forms for data management 2) intercepting of user actions on forms for data management
SNITZ Forum	1) – 2) Post and forum insertion 3) – 4) Post and forum modification 5) – 6) Post and forum deletion 7) – 8) Post and forum browsing
Decision Script	1) Presentation of decisions
Date Picker	1) Presentation of calendar
IIS	1) Page publication over the Internet 2) File upload
IIXSO	1) Text retrieval
CDONTS	1) E-mail sending

Appendix B: Collected Data

In this appendix, all data concerning COTS products taken into account in the study are reported. For each CBS, data are organized in two different tables, one concerning characterization metrics, and the second concerning quality factors metrics.

Table 6. Values of characterization metrics concerning COTS products in SICOD

	Oracle	Oracle Internet Application Server	Oracle Report Builder	Crystal Report	Applix	Plumtree Portal
COTS Application domain	Database	Application Server	Report building	Report building	CRM	Enterprise Portal
Functional Coverage	0,181818	0,090909	0,181818	0,181818	0,318182	0,045455
COTS Compliance	0,80	0,50	0,80	0,571429	0,466667	0,111111
License type	Copyright	Copyright	Copyright	Copyright	Copyright	Copyright
Training time	14	4	4	0	7	8
Familiarity	3	1	3	0	0	2
Integration technique	White box	Standard protocol	Standard protocol	Proprietary protocol	Proprietary protocol	Wrapper
COTS origin	Existing External	Existing External	Existing External	Existing External	Existing External	Existing External
COTS support	High	High	High	Medium	High	High
COTS documentation	High	High	High	Medium	High	High

Table 7. Values of quality factors metrics concerning COTS products in SICOD.

	Oracle	Oracle Internet Application Server	Oracle Report Builder	Crystal Report	Applix	Plumtree Portal
Integration Time	200	50	70	10	105	50
Normalized Integration Time	0,373134	0,093228	0,130597	0,018657	0,195896	0,093284
Integration effort	400	50	70	10	210	50
Normalized Integration Effort	0,458716	0,057339	0,080275	0,011468	0,240826	0,057339
Integration staff	2	1	1	1	2	1
Normalized Integration Staff	0,086956	0,043478	0,043478	0,043478	0,086956	0,043478
Mean maintenance effort	30	15	12	4	20	0
Normalized Mean maintenance effort	0,319149	0,159574	0,127660	0,042553	0,212766	0
No. of issues	39	12	2	3	50	0
Normalized No. of issues	0,325000	0,100000	0,016667	0,025000	0,416667	0
Gravity	Low	Low	Low	Low	Medium	

Table 8. Values of characterization metrics concerning COTS products in DiPNET.

	SQL Server 7	MS ADO	SNITZ Forum	Decision Script	Date Picker	Internet Information Services	MS IIXSO	MS CDONTS
COTS Application domain	Database	DB Interface	Manage Forum	Decision Support	Calendar	Web server	text indexing and browsing	manage e-mail
Functional Coverage	0,20	0,10	0,40	0,05	0,05	0,10	0,05	0,05
COTS Compliance	0,266667	0,142857	0,285714	0,066667	0,50	0,285714	0,333333	0,50
License type	Copyright	Copyright	Free	Copyright	Free	Copyright	Copyright	Copyright
Training time	5	1	0	0	0	4	2	1
Familiarity	2	2	0	3	0	1	1	1
Integration technique	White Box	Proprietary Protocol	White Box	Standard Protocol	White Box	Proprietary Protocol	Proprietary Protocol	Proprietary Protocol
COTS origin	Existing External	Existing External	Existing External	Existing External	Existing External	Existing External	Existing External	Existing External
COTS support	High	High	Medium	Low	Low	High	High	High
COTS documentation	High	High	Medium	Low	Low	High	High	High

Table 9. Values of quality factors metrics concerning COTS products in DiPNET.

	SQL Server 7	MS ADO	SNITZ Forum	Decision Script	Date Picker	Internet Information Services	MS IIXSO	MS CDONTS
Integration time	10	5	20	2	3	6	3	2
Normalized Integration Time	0,018657	0,009328	0,037313	0,003731	0,005597	0,011194	0,005597	0,003731
Integration effort	20	10	20	4	6	12	6	4
Normalized Integration Effort	0,022936	0,011468	0,022936	0,005487	0,006880	0,013761	0,006880	0,004587
Integration staff	2	2	1	2	2	2	2	2
Normalized Integration Staff	0,086956	0,086956	0,043478	0,086956	0,086956	0,086956	0,086956	0,086956
Mean maintenance effort	2	1	1	0	0	6	2	1
Normalized Mean maintenance effort	0,021277	0,010638	0,010638	0	0	0,063830	0,021277	0,010638
No. of issues	3	3	0	8	0	0	0	0
Normalized No. of issues	0,025	0,025	0	0,066667	0	0	0	0
Gravity	Medium	Low		Medium				

Appendix C: Results of Statistical Analysis

In this appendix the results of Statistical analysis are reported.

More precisely, Table 10 presents the results of the Spearman's correlation analysis aimed at verifying that no characterization metric depends on any other characterization metric. In this table, the absence of statistically significant correlation permits to verify that all characterization metrics are independent each other.

Table 11 reports the results of the Spearman's correlation analysis executed for testing the research hypotheses, i.e., it is aimed at looking for correlations between characterization metrics and quality factors metrics.

In both tables, each row is referred to the correlation between a pair of variables. Each pair is associated to the values of the ρ coefficient and the values of the p-level. The pairs of variables for which the correlation exists are highlighted in **bold**.

Table 10. Results of the Spearman's analysis for verifying independence among characterization metrics

Pair of Variables	ρ	p-level
Training Time & Training Time		
Training Time & Familiarity	0,396815	0,160083
Training Time & Functional Coverage	0,125000	0,670270
Training Time & Compliance	0,091118	0,756719
Familiarity & Training Time	0,396815	0,160083
Familiarity & Familiarity		
Familiarity & Functional Coverage	-0,196100	0,501646
Familiarity & Compliance	-0,153016	0,601498
Functional Coverage & Training Time	0,125000	0,670270
Functional Coverage & Familiarity	-0,196100	0,501646
Functional Coverage & Functional Coverage		
Functional Coverage & Compliance	0,248607	0,391418
Compliance & Training Time	0,091118	0,756719
Compliance & Familiarity	-0,153016	0,601498
Compliance & Functional Coverage	0,248607	0,391418
Compliance & Compliance		

Table 11. Results of the Spearman's analysis for COTS products.

Pair of Variables	ρ	p-level
Training Time & Integration Time	**0,691411**	**0,006165**
Training Time & Normalized Integration Time	**0,691411**	**0,006165**
Training Time & Integration effort	**0,766341**	**0,001390**
Training Time & Normalized Integration effort	**0,766341**	**0,001390**
Training Time & Integration staff	0,056408	0,848110
Training Time & Normalized Integration staff	0,056408	0,848110
Training Time & No. of issues	0,328400	0,251649
Training Time & Normalized No. of issues	0,328400	0,251649
Training Time & Mean maintenance effort	**0,553060**	**0,040230**
Training Time & Normalized Mean maintenance effort	**0,553060**	**0,040230**
Familiarity & Integration Time	0,101405	0,730141
Familiarity & Normalized Integration Time	0,101405	0,730141
Familiarity & Integration effort	0,171096	0,558657
Familiarity & Normalized Integration effort	0,171096	0,558657
Familiarity & Integration staff	0,114520	0,696662
Familiarity & Normalized Integration staff	0,114520	0,696662
Familiarity & No. of issues	0,245573	0,397412
Familiarity & Normalized No. of issues	0,245573	0,397412
Familiarity & Mean maintenance effort	0,024061	0,934930
Familiarity & Normalized Mean maintenance effort	0,024061	0,934930
Functional Coverage & Integration Time	**0,554475**	**0,039616**
Functional Coverage & Normalized Integration Time	**0,554475**	**0,039616**
Functional Coverage & Integration effort	**0,538236**	**0,047086**
Functional Coverage & Normalized Integration effort	**0,538236**	**0,047086**
Functional Coverage & Integration staff	-0,131618	0,653782
Functional Coverage & Normalized Integration staff	-0,131618	0,653782
Functional Coverage & No. of issues	0,402027	0,154166
Functional Coverage & Normalized No. of issues	0,402027	0,154166
Functional Coverage & Mean maintenance effort	**0,567733**	**0,034195**
Functional Coverage & Normalized Mean maintenance effort	**0,567733**	**0,034195**
Compliance & Integration Time	0,386668	0,172025
Compliance & Normalized Integration Time	0,386668	0,172025
Compliance & Integration effort	0,317019	0,269427
Compliance & Normalized Integration effort	0,317019	0,269427
Compliance & Integration staff	-0,204745	0,482583
Compliance & Normalized Integration staff	-0,204745	0,482583
Compliance & No. of issues	0,168909	0,563771
Compliance & Normalized No. of issues	0,168909	0,563771
Compliance & Mean maintenance effort	**0,616763**	**0,018806**
Compliance & Normalized Mean maintenance effort	**0,616763**	**0,018806**

Reuse Based Software Factory

Manu Prego

European Software Institute
Bilbao, Spain
Manu.Prego@esi.es

Abstract. This paper reports on an experiment on how is it possible to multiply the efficiency and quality of a software development process by means of industrial manufacturing organizations and methods and state of the art reuse and product-line technology. Of course all methods and technology claim the same objectives, therefore the experiment objective of <u>dramatic</u> improvements. This chapter does not report on toy-demonstrators but on a real application at a large IT development department of a large business user organization using conventional computer technology with high responsibility and reliability requirements. The solutions have since been deployed involving some hundreds of programmers, to the satisfaction of all stockholders in the business: users, developers, management and even owners. The experiment result, in a medium to large development organization, requires a significant investment which produces average Reuse Rates around 70-80%, effectively halves the cost and time-to-market of software development, and reduces the error rates several-fold. The method is compatible and complementary with software development models such as the Capability Maturity Model™, SPICE, ISO9001 or the new Agile software development methodologies.

1 Introduction

Generally speaking, and independently of the industrial sector of application, software development is characterised by problems such as: deadline slips, functional requirements sometimes far from those promised, overrun budgets, bad quality and high error rates. This has been the case since we started to develop software.

An analysis of the current status of software development in the world shows clearly that the quality and productivity of the industry has not been able to keep up with the software needs of Society in general, as shown in the Fig. 1 [1]. Computer science has therefore become an obstacle to progress.

The discipline of Software Engineering has been trying to find a solution to this problem [1] for a long time.

All these problems are only external symptoms of an evil not always evident: software development is a craft; a process that fundamentally depends on the person who carries it out; a process, of course, that uses continually improving tools, but a process in the end in which two developers using the same requirements and the same technology would obtain different results.

---

[1] Source: ITEA - EC Internal Reflection Group on Software Technologies, April 2002

R. Conradi and A.I. Wang (Eds.): ESERNET 2001-2003, LNCS 2765, pp. 256–273, 2003.

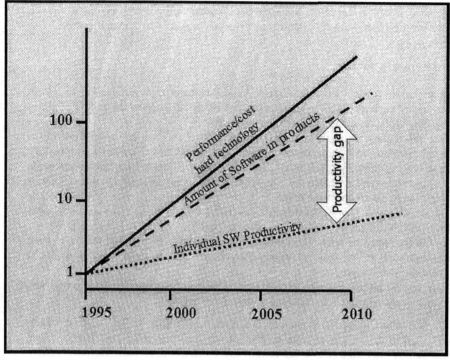

Fig. 1. Software Needs of Society

1.1   The Hypothesis Tested

This situation contrasts heavily with the world of manufacturing, the kingdom of Engineering, where the repeatability of results determines and defines the maturity of the processes.

By means of Engineering, improved processes and capital investment in effective tools, the Manufacturing Industry attain dramatically improved cost reduction, time-to-markets, quality and repeatability.

Therefore, why does not software development apply the concepts and methods of Manufacturing Engineering? In other words, is it possible to apply the concepts and methods of Manufacturing Engineering to software development? And, if it were possible, what results might we expect?

The hypothesis to be demonstrated can be described as follows:

A quantum leap is both needed and possible concerning the cost and time-to-market of software development, as well as to significantly increase quality, by means of the application of techniques mirrored from Manufacturing Engineering.

A corollary is that,

- Such improvements are not to be incremental, but dramatic: say two-fold or larger.
- As in the case of Manufacturing Engineering, such improvements would require large Reuse rates of standard components, and ideas taken from Product-Line theories.

- The success of the enterprise would turn software development from a craft into an Engineering-based industry[2], intensive in capital instead of in human resources.

1.2   Literature Survey

There are a lot of publications on Reuse in the literature [8, 9, 10, 11, 12, 13], from classic papers such as [2] to collections of state of the art such as the Product Family Engineering workshops [3], the [4] or our own [5].

Most researches agree that dramatic reuse rates can only be attained within a Product Line. Yet most publications deal with the Reuse model based on a repository of static objects. The approach in this experiment is different, since the components are flexible and operate before the compilation stage, thus generating source code in the target language an operating domain.

The development team started the experiment by defining the technological strategy. Two basic alternatives were evaluated:

a.   In the first one, the team followed the general trend in the market, that is, to look for solutions to the software problems by means of new tools, in other words, a solution based in products.

b.   The second alternative was to seek innovative solutions, targeting the processes, which could be tried and evaluated within the experiment.

The first alternative, based on products (such as CASE tools), is an approach already tried in the 90's by a large number of organizations [6, 7], but lacking clear success stories providing substantial improvements in the three basic factors (quality, cost, time-to-market). In addition, some of these alternatives had already been tested by the customer organization and are considered a failure.

Thus, the development team chose a strategy based on software process improvement by means of the applications of methods and techniques similar to those used in the manufacturing industry. In this way the team developed a set of instruments, including organization, methods and technology, in order to enable the development of software systems applying concepts of proved success in the industrial manufacturing industry, looking for the transformation of the software development craft into an engineering based industry.

In this context, "component" is a pre-elaborated piece of software designed and tested so that it will be reused (usually in part) for the development of other software.

2   Starting Scenario

The experiment was carried out for an important financial organization with over 25 years of experience in the development of banking software. This organization involves a team of over 100 software development staff and an average of another 200 developers from four external subcontractors. It is, therefore, a company whose systems are developed by own staff and by the external subcontractors, so there are in average 5 independent teams developing software for them.

---

[2] as opposed to the "warehouses of craftmen/women" (often low-wage) frequently so-called Software Factories

The aim of the experiment was to increase the production capacity of the software development department of the customer and its subcontractors, more specifically to improve the quality of the software and simultaneously to build it with less cost and faster time-to-markets.

Moreover, to carry out the experiment it was necessary to take into account the software systems developed by the financial company during the last 25 years. Thus, the experiment had a set of requirements derived from the already existing systems.

The existing software development methodology was traditional and involved three times as many subcontractors as actual staff. The target of the experiment was a new software development method which had to provide a very clear improvement in terms of the following five requirements:

GR[3]-1   the new software development system had to support the existing technological and methodological standards of the customer

GR-2   the customer was not to increase its dependency on suppliers and subcontractors

GR-3   it had to represent a radical and simultaneous change in the three basic factors: quality, cost and time-to-market

GR-4   return-of-Investment (RoI) had to be faster than 18 months

GR-5   should the Pilot Project be satisfactory, it had to escalate to full deployment in the whole of the development organization.

3   Method

3.1   Design

The experiment was conceived as a project with specific deadlines, a specific work team, a structure in phases and activities, and with a set of indicators defined to enable the evaluation of the success or failure of the experiment.

3.1.1   Experiment Indicators

The aforementioned Requirements had to be translated into indicators, since some allowed yes/no evaluation but in other cases they were difficult to measure. Therefore three new indicators were established to determine the success of the experiment.

IS[4]-1   Standards (affects GR-1 and GR-2)

The first indicator, qualitative in nature, refers to the software target[5]. It was defined as: "the new system of software development must produce exactly the code required by each program, fulfilling exactly the coding standards and rules of the company ".

The objective was not only to manufacture working code, but source code which is readable and maintainable, even if for some reason the tools used to develop it eventually become no longer available.

---

[3] GR – General Requirement

[4] IS – Indicator of Success

[5] Target: the software to be developed by means of the RBSF

IS-2   Reuse Rate (affects GR-3, GR-4 and GR-5)
Even though the real target was to <u>reduce cost, time-to-market and increase quality</u>, such objectives were replaced by an indirect indicator which affects directly them all: the Reuse Rate attained. It was defined as

> *One minus the ratio between New SLOC[6] written by the programmer versus New SLOC generated by the system[7] (not taking into account included libraries or subsystems, in order to remain objective).*

That is, the reuse rate

- must be easily and reliably measurable,
- must be real in the sense that it reflects appropriately the software development process and,
- the rate of reused code must be higher than 60 % of the whole produced code, <u>which is dramatically higher than those published in the literature.</u>

This second indicator is not independent at all from the first one. It is easy to increase reuse rates by creating lots of SLOC, but in this case the new system had to produce exactly the code that the system needs (i.e. without any extra line of code, without unnecessary libraries, etc), and at least 60% of this code had to be reused.

IS-3   Number of Components (affects GR-2, GR-3, GR-4 and GR-5)
The last one of the indicators was concerned to the number of the components needed to produce the target applications. Trying to achieve a manageable number of components, the indicator was expressed as: "the new system must not need to use more than 50 components".

Combining this third indicator together with the previous ones, it's clear that the experiment was successful if it was possible to construct a software development system that, supporting all the standards of the financial institution and producing exactly the code needed, it should reach at least 60% of reuse, while using a maximum of 50 previously manufactured components.

3.1.2   Technology

Generic Manufacturing Model

The experiment has been carried out as a pilot project that has used methods, techniques and technologies based on concepts similar to those used in the manufacturing industry.

The general idea of the experiment consisted in the transformation of the organizational model of the customer software department so that they are able to produce software of an industrial fashion, using the models, methods and techniques similar to those used massively by the manufacturing industry. Software is "manufactured" following the manufacturing model of any kind of goods, with the goal to obtain the same consistent quality and effectiveness that any other final product.

---

[6] SLOC: Source Lines Of Code

[7] Would the programmer write 100 LOC in a 1,100 LOC program, Reuse Rate would be 90% (1-100/1000)

The idea is to manufacture software mirroring the series manufacturing of goods such as cars, even though in this case the job does not consist on the manufacture of identical copies, but on the manufacture of *similar* programs; this is not a telecom program today, an accountancy program tomorrow and a Finite Element solver the day after, but all of them in the same class of programs (a Product Line approach).

The experiment emphasizes processes such as the standardization and the normalization of software manufacturing, the development of software by means of components which are specifically customised for the particular customer, the exhaustive management and control of the development, and as much automation as feasible in the software development process.

Three areas were identified in which the experiment would have to act and innovate, since it was clear that improvements targeting any one of them in isolation had no chance to attain the desired improvements:

- the organization of the software development: separate two groups
    o Technical Office: define how software is manufactured, methods, tools, etc
    o Production: manufacture software according to the defined methods
- the method-techniques to use in the new software development system
    o emphasis in Standardisation and
    o Normalisation
- the required technology to support the two previous areas effectively. Yet the automation tools were considered secondary to the issues of organization and methods.

Specific CBSE Technology

From the point of view of the software development model, mirroring the Product Manufacturing industry assembly of parts, the development team defined Component Based Development (CBD) as the model to develop software.

From the technical point of view, the CBD model is supported by a specific technology proprietary to the *European Software Institute (ESI)* called *Flexible Components (FCT)*. This technology facilitates the design, development and test of components to use them in the software development, as well as the production cycle of the programs which make use of such components.

It is a Bottom-Up technique that generates Source Code in the target programming language and for the target architecture.

The FCT technique is designed for the development of components which smartly produce code, therefore supporting a wide degree of variability in the target code.

This technique provides components with the needed flexibility (therefore it's name) to allow the produced code to be adjusted exactly to all the procedures and standards needed; in addition it enables the drastic reduction of the number of components needed to produce code, while remaining widely applicable.

The FCT conceptual base is the design of components by means of the paradigm of *similarity* instead of the paradigm of *equality* widely used in the conventional software development. Thus concepts such as routines, modules, functions, etc., are based in the equality paradigm: it is applicable when two or more programs need to execute the same code. Nevertheless, these techniques cannot be used when the executing code for these programs is similar but not the same. For that reason the use of these techniques to reuse code require a large number of components, a repository to be able to keep track of them, and so on.

For example, we can think of an application to manage information stored in a Relational DataBase (RDB); normally if the application is significant (with several tables and a large number of attributes for table) it will need to code a large number of SELECT instructions, in general all of them different, therefore they would be coded one by one and reuse, handling the equality paradigm, could not be applied.

However, if all these SELECT instructions are analyzed using the similarity paradigm, we will see that all of them are similar, which means (thus it happened in the experiment) that a unique Flexible Component was able to produce all versions of the code associated with the instruction SELECT, to be included in the programs.

Obviously this is only an example, but it shows the idea of the FCT capability.

This technology presents a large number of advantages:

- it lets a component be very flexible yet compact; in spite of the supported flexibility, the resulting programs are not made larger. The resulting programs include just the code required, as developed by the best programmer in the developer's team, so that programs developed through flexible components do not include "any extra line of code".
- it lets a component enforce all the customer regulations and standards for programs, independent of their complexity and no matter their type or nature.
- it enables quality control of the software during the development process, by means of process supervision in order to detect its own inadequate use, which assures a high degree of quality in the final software.
- the target code is readable and maintainable.

The ability of the components created by means of FCT to use the similarity paradigm and combine it with its ability to make decisions and to control all the process of code manufacture, makes this technology the most suitable to be used in situations as those described in the experiment.

3.2 Subjects/Participants

The experiment team was formed by company's technical personnel and the European Software Institute's technical personnel. The Chief Information Officer of the financial institution was nominated as Project Director. The team was made of seven people selected in function of their knowledge and experience in the activities to perform, half from the Technology Provider and half from the User's staff.

- Staff was needed with good knowledge in the Technological Domain (TD) on which the experiment was going to be carried out. Such staff had to show to the rest of the team the procedures and standards to develop software in the company, the requirements derived from the technology of the TD and, definitively, how the software that the new system was going to produce should be.
  Three persons with this profile (from the Customer staff) were included in the experiment team.
- On the other hand, since one of the experiment basic processes was to standardize and normalize the TD software, persons with significant experience in this process

were needed, to detect common and similar software elements in order to apply the Flexible Components technology.

Two persons with this profile were incorporated into the experiment, one from the ESI, the other from the Customer staff, in training.

- Finally, since the experiment aimed to produce a new and real software development system, not a prototype, the team needed to incorporate experts in building, testing and optimizing components. For this reason two more persons joined the team, both experts in component technology, in both cases ESI Consultants.

In terms of experience, there were two persons with over twenty years of experience in software development, three persons with an average experience of ten years and, finally, two with an experience shorter than four years.

The team did develop all the activities at the customer facilities next to the applications development department, who were consulted about specific items during the experiment.

3.3   Apparatus/Materials

As is the case in most large organizations, the software development department of the Customer produced software for its exploitation in multiple technological platforms, from mainframes to ATM[8], and also Windows and UNIX platforms.

It is for this reason that a Technological Domain (TD) had to be selected among those existing in the customer institution. Each Domain was evaluated on the basis of the following variables,

- since standardisation and normalisation are critical,
  - degree of technological stability
  - level of experience and knowledge of the customer in the TD
- volume of annual developments in the TD (measured in number of programs developed the previous year)
- volume of annual investments made by the customer in activities related to the TD (developments and maintenance) during the previous year
- expected future development activities in the TD in the years to come

Once collected and evaluated all the variables for the different existing TD, it was evident that the TD chosen to develop the experiment would be:

- Hardware: IBM Mainframe
- Language: Cobol 85
- Teleprocessing: C.I.C.S.
- Database: DB2/VSAM/QSAM

This TD ensured on the one hand expected high volumes of software development, therefore opportunities for profitability, which was important for the new system deployment throughout the company, would the experiment be successful.

---

[8] Automated Teller Machines

On the other hand, the chosen TD is very stable from technological changes, ensures the availability of customer technical staff expertise in the chosen TD for the experiment. This way it was possible to prevent the lack of technical knowledge on the software to produce that would affect the experiment.

3.4   Procedure

3.4.1   Experiment Phases
Experiment development was organized in four sequential phases.

From the beginning of the project it was decided that all three areas of innovation (organization, methods and tools) would be worked simultaneously along the whole experiment, in order to use the results obtained in each of the innovation areas for stepwise refinement along all phases of the project, as described in Fig. 2.

The whole of the experiment required six months of work.

EXPERIMENT DEVELOPMENT

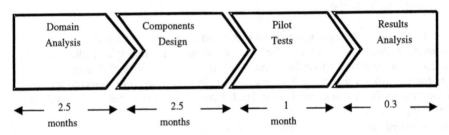

Fig. 2. Experiment Development

Domain Analysis
This first phase of the experiment had to study the domain of application (details in 3.3 Apparatus/Materials) and then design the infrastructure required for the experiment from the already explained three points of view, organization, methods and techniques, and technology to support them all.

From the organizational point of view, the software development team was defined with their responsibilities, as well as the participation of the customer company's departments of exploitation, quality, databases, audit, development, etc. Since the new system was going to affect them all, all the departments had to take part in the experiment. The external companies that at the moment were producing software for the company did not participate in the experiment.

In particular, the Methods (Organization) Group was created within the Customer's IT Department, who in the future would take care of the production facilities, standards and methods.

From the point of view of methods and techniques, during this phase we proceeded to the definition and basic design of the components, using the *Flexible Components* technology. At the end of the phase all the designs were approved by all the previously mentioned departments. This approval marked the end of the first phase and the beginning of the second phase.

Finally, from the technological point of view, the required ESI technology for the design and development of components was installed, in order to be able to train all the experiment team in its use.

Component Design

The second phase of the experiment was to deploy the new system and the realisation of the first tests, evaluating the obtained results.

Again in this phase the three areas of innovation were involved: organization, methods/techniques and technologies.

From the organizational point of view, the team developed the set of procedures required to support the new system for its wide exploitation after the experiment's successful completion. Likewise, the interfaces of the new system with other already existing systems in the company and with which the new system needed to interact, were developed.

From the point of view of methods and techniques, some of the completed activities during this second phase were the development and test of all the components defined in the previous phase, including the redesign and optimisation of some components, as required. Tests of components must be exhaustive

Finally, after the tests and necessary adjustments, the new system began to produce programs that were controlled and accepted by all the departments of the company participating in the experiment.

During this second phase the technology area was also involved in the training of the technical personnel of the company in the design and development of components, as well as in their tests and optimisation.

Finished this second phase, the new system was ready to be trialed by means of the development of pilot application programs.

Standardisation & Normalisation

Throughout the whole experiment the critical element was the definition of standards and procedures defined and used in the software development by the customer development team.

In some cases the standards and procedures were well described and used by the technicians in the correct manner; in other cases in spite of being well defined, they were not used; and in others the programmers used them in spite of not been official. In any case the level of standardization detected during the experiment was low.

For this reason the task of gathering, analysing, verifying and completing the set of procedures and standards for software development was the key of the whole development of the experiment.

In order to identify standards, the program code was classified in four groups: structural code, data access, Input/Output and operations. For all these groups, standards were researched and established according to the following procedure:

a. Definition of a first version
b. Verify the version with existing programs. Obtain the second version
c. Verify with the departments involved
d. Third version of the standard
e. Verification and approval

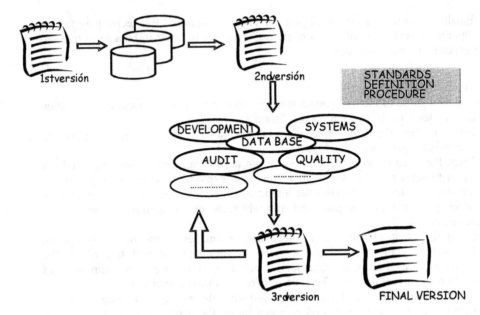

Fig. 3. Definition Procedure

This procedure, reflected in Fig. 3 facilitates the definition of a standard and finally its approval while involving all the affected actors. In this way, all the standards defined in the experiment were the result of a collective work not only of the development team.

A standard defined during the first phase of the experiment, was incorporated to the components during this second phase.

The procedure, as you can see in Fig. 4, was:

a. Code the standard in one or more components, either from scratch or by means of modification of existing ones.
b. Tests of the components that implement the standard.
c. Verification with existing programs using the standard.
d. Update and approve the implementation of the standard

All the customer's existing programs were available during the experiment, so that a representative sample was used to verify the new system before finishing the second phase of the experiment.

Pilot Tests

The customer defined at this stage the application programs to be developed with the new system produced during the experiment. In this context, 'program' is any software code the user wants to develop.

The pilot had to be a real application, so that the results obtained could be compared with the results obtained in the development of similar applications with traditional methods.

The pilot was then the development of a small application made of a set of 60 programs. The objective of this pilot was to produce this set of programs using the new system and then analyze the results obtained.

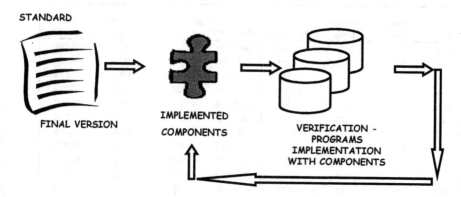

Fig. 4. Implementation of Standards in components

Results Analysis

Once the pilot test was finished we proceeded to evaluate the results, from the perspective of the success indicators of the experiment, as well as the global requirements of the experiment.

4   Results

The evaluation of the experiment results obtained during the pilot was the last phase of the experiment.

Table 1 shows the results obtained during the pilot project. They show the number of lines of code hand written by the programmers (column "Hand written Lines") and the lines of code produced by the new system (column "Generated Lines") and therefore the reuse rate (column "Reuse Rate").

The results obtained were analyzed taking into account the general and technical requirements associated to the experiment. An evaluation team composed of customer staff performed the final result report.

The information contained in the report is abstracted as follows:

- **Representative Sample**

  The software produced during the pilot project (60 programs) was sufficiently representative of the TD on which the experiment was carried out.

  This ensured that the results obtained in the pilot phase were valid, representative and could be extrapolated. The User had great confidence on such results scaling so as to deploy the solution in the whole of the organization.

Table 1. Experiment Results

PROGRAM	Hand written Lines	Generated Lines	Reuse Rate	PROGRAM	Hand written Lines	Generated Lines	Reuse Rate
GSDG001	275	1018	72,99%	GSDG031	149	894	83,33%
GSDG002	266	1286	79,32%	GSDG032	454	2931	84,51%
GSDG003	57	762	92,52%	GSDG033	244	3302	92,61%
GSDG004	2156	4539	52,50%	GSDG034	645	2656	75,72%
GSDG005	110	1281	91,41%	GSDG035	492	4037	87,81%
GSDG006	2739	5152	46,84%	GSDG036	697	3207	78,27%
GSDG007	719	2838	74,67%	GSDG037	182	1114	83,66%
GSDG008	222	1881	88,20%	GSDG038	325	1136	91,23%
GSDG009	394	3027	86,98%	GSDG039	462	2572	82,04%
GSDG010	83	1416	94,14%	GSDG040	306	4221	92,75%
GSDG011	234	1996	88,28%	GSDG041	51	1069	95,23%
GSDG012	129	459	71,90%	GSDG042	310	2574	87,96%
GSDG013	186	750	75,19%	GSDG043	75	1207	93,79%
GSDG014	194	1248	84,45%	GSDG044	83	1266	93,44%
GSDG015	134	295	54,55%	GSDG045	146	1753	91,67%
GSDG016	619	1958	68,39%	GSDG046	44	128	65,75%
GSDG017	160	592	72,96%	GSDG047	133	1681	92,09%
GSDG018	266	2211	87,97%	GSDG048	354	2545	86,09%
GSDG019	825	7689	89,27%	GSDG049	203	656	69,08%
GSDG020	156	690	77,39%	GSDG050	2807	3603	22,09%
GSDG021	356	809	56,01%	GSDG051	842	1469	42,68%
GSDG022	714	5282	86,48%	GSDG052	136	468	70,93%
GSDG023	839	2859	70,65%	GSDG053	131	1025	87,22%
GSDG024	158	456	65,36%	GSDG054	167	441	62,12%
GSDG025	358	1073	66,62%	GSDG055	818	12455	93,43%
GSDG026	794	10490	92,43%	GSDG056	219	780	71,91%
GSDG027	286	2130	86,57%	GSDG057	439	2380	81,55%
GSDG028	168	2134	92,13%	GSDG058	267	2075	87,13%
GSDG029	317	1086	70,81%	GSDG059	327	1305	74,94%
GSDG030	219	986	77,79%	GSDG060	243	776	68,69%

- **Standards Support**

  All customer standards and procedures were supported in the programs developed during the pilot project.

  In other words, the programs produced by the new system followed all the customer standards. The first experiment global requirement GR-1 "the new software development system had to support the current customer technological and methodological standards" was fulfilled.

- **No Overheads**

  Developed software did not include any type of external or undesired code. That is "not any extra line of code".

  Together with the previous result, this meant that the programs made with the new system were constructed as if the best programmer in the company had developed them, while at the same time following all the standards and procedures.

- **Subcontractor Independence**
  The generated source code is very readable. Even more, the code generated by different programmers is much more similar to each other than previous handcrafted code.
  While the tools provided facilitate maintenance, the user could revert to manual maintenance since the source code of the final programs is available.
  Therefore the system fulfilled the second global requirement GR-2 "not to increase its dependency on suppliers and subcontractors".
- **Number of Components**
  The number of components built was 40, of which the programmers that took part in the pilot test made use of only 23; the rest were either hidden components or designed for use by the Technical Office (those developing components; the programmers just use them).
  In this way the new system fulfilled the requirement of "no more than 50 components".
- **Reuse Rate**
  The following criteria was used to calculate de reuse rate: the programs produced by the new system had to be exactly as if developed by the best programmer of the company (without an extra line of code and following all the standards), so the reuse rate is calculated as the ratio between the lines of code handcrafted by the programmers and the total number of lines in that program.
  The average reuse rate was 71.9%; that is, the programmers that took part in the pilot test only had to write 28.1% of the final code.
  The new system fulfilled the condition "minimum real and measurable reuse rate of 60%".
- **Time-to-Market**
  Elapsed development time decreased by 40%, which enables the organization face the development of many more new projects.
- **Error Rate**
  The error rate in both development and testing has decreased in half, dramatically decreasing the expectations for maintenance time.
  All errors detected in the testing phase did correspond to the code handcrafted by the programmers (code not produced by the components), therefore the testing phase was much reduced. The reason is the extensive testing and quality assurance during the Component development phase.

However, not all the global requirements of the experiment could be evaluated at the end of the pilot project. Some requirements, such as the impact of the new system in the basic software factors (quality, cost and time-to-market) GR-3, were extrapolated from the results of the pilot project. It was estimated, for example, that the programming effort had diminished by a factor of three.

Also requirements such as the Return-of-Investment (ROI), GR-4, or time required for the deployment of the new system to the whole organization, GR-5, could not be evaluated at such stage, but only estimated at 12 to 18 months ROI if full deployment could be accomplished within 3 to 5 months.

4.1   Post-experiment Experiences

The customer decided to adopt the new system as its standard system to develop software, both for its development department and for its different subcontractors.

For this reason three years after the experiment it was possible to analyze its impact with the perspective of the time and the experiences with the daily use of the system. A new evaluation confirmed the results obtained during the experiment and complemented them as follows:

- The current number of components used is 31 (from 40).
  The experience of the use of the system allowed the customer to increase the software standardization, so that the number of components needed has decreased.
- RoI
  Payback was achieved in less than two years, although this indicator has a more direct relation with other factors as the cost/hour of programming and (specially) the number of programs produced.
- The level of qualification required by the programmers is now less than at the stage before the launch of the new system.
  This was an unexpected benefit. The fact that the programmer only has to write 30% of the code (the components produce the rest) was expected to facilitate the independence of the software from the programmers. Yet since a lot of the complex technical code was constructed by the component, a side-effect was that the programmers have an easier task because the whole of the code for these functions is handled by the components. Thus, fewer specialists were needed.
- The customer has gained independence (not absolute) from the subcontractors, therefore having more power of negotiation with them.

The customer is currently planning the deployment of the new system in other Technological Domains, using the same procedures developed during the experiment.

To date, nine more large software development organizations are currently exploiting similar approaches, with the average results as shown in Table 2.

Table 2. Average results from similar approaches.

Number of components / domain	38
Number of programs generated	Over 10,000
Reuse Rate	75%
Time-to-market after/before RBSF	3/5
Error rate in development after/before RBSF	50%
Error rate in exploitation after/before RBSF	25%
Largest program developed To Date	Bank Risk Management syst. 1 million SLOC

5   Discussion

The experiment has been useful to test the feasibility of what initially seemed very difficult to achieve. There are a lot of prejudices regarding building software in an 'industrial' (manufacturing) fashion.

Yet the experiment verifies the hypothesis that Software can be developed using techniques mirrored from Manufacturing Engineering, by means of a Reuse Based Software Factory, for quantum leaps in quality, cost, time-to-market, etc.

Other effects are

- Much improved standardization of source code.
- Better programmer independence, since the source code is much more readable and standardized.
- Lower maintenance costs, time-to-markets, etc, due to better quality, better readability and standardization, better support tools, semi-automated program generation, etc.

An unexpected result is the better use of the available human resources, as the experts are employed in the development of the components (at the Technical Office) and less expertise is needed for programming (the "Manufacturing Floor"). Before performing the experiment, resources with a higher profile were performing tasks that are now performed by resources with a lower profile, therefore people and their abilities are better employed.

It is important to highlight that the organization verified that the generated programs included exactly the desired lines of code. This means that the methods/tools used in the experiment did not insert code 'of its own', as existing "code generators" do. The origin of every single line of code can be traced, which lets the programmer know if the line came from any of the components developed by the Technical Office (Domain Engineering) or on the contrary it had been taken as part of the business code and therefore inserted directly by the programmer (Application Engineering).

The complexity of the projects decreased as most technical details are hidden in the components. The effort needed for programming was established in around 40% of that previously needed, which enables the bank to develop more applications than they previously could, due to lack of time and resources, therefore reducing the existing backlog.

The methods are independent of technical domain or programming languages.

The resulting software products attain consistent and repeatable quality and performance.

From the point of view of the lessons learned as a result of the experiment is necessary to emphasize essentially:

a. When the issue is to radically change the results of processes in which an important number of people is involved, the change can not be centered on technology, since the organizational changes and the methods are much more important (change the tactics instead of the players).
b. It is possible to simultaneously innovate in all the areas of the process: organization, methods & techniques and technology.
c. When aiming at very significant quantitative and qualitative improvements in the results and the requirements are strict, generic solutions are not valid.
d. The Flexible Component technology was the basis of the success because it supported all the requirements and objectives of the experiment.

No significant problem has arisen while carrying on the experiment. The lack of existing standards when carrying out the analysis could be mentioned, but this was not a serious problem, as the people involved were highly qualified and experienced, which made decision making fast. Also, the cultural change required by the experiment to be successful was a priori estimated as significant, but the change was quickly assumed after confirmation of the good results obtained.

Treats to the Validity of the Experiment

Significant effort has been dedicated in the experiment to the definition and collection of statistically significant and representative data. Even after its completion, very similar solutions have been applied in different organizations, showing very similar results which show that such results can be generalized. In no case have different results of significance been identified. Whenever problems have appeared they have always been related to issues of leadership and change management within the organization.

Yet a basic assumption for the concept of Software Factory is the existence of a significant amount of software development in a particular technological domain or product line. Should this not be the case, the opportunities for reuse would be much smaller.

On the other hand, the methods are independent on the particular technological domain, yet they have been experimented in only a couple domains, apart from toy prototypes for demonstration purposes. It is possible that currently unexpected problems appear in other domains, yet it seems unlikely; yet the actual metrics might differ from domain to domain.

Of course, if the domain is not reasonably stable, there is no way that the required standardization and normalization can be performed, therefore the methods would not be feasible. Again in this case no product line is possible.

There are currently experiments under development which address the following issues:

- Affordability for small development teams, by means of shared tools and components
- Feasibility of components shared by different organizations, even competitors
- New technological domains, such as those of industrial automation and of PC-oriented services (HTML, Java, VisualBasic).

Results are expected to be available early in 2004 (see http://www.esi.es/).

References

[1] Frederik P. Brooks Jr., "No Silver Bullet – Essence and accidents of Software Engineering", IEEE Computer Magazine, April 1987

[2] Victor R. Basili and H. Dieter Rombach, "Support for comprehensive reuse," IEE Software Engineering Journal, vol. 6, pp. 303–316, Sept. 1991.

[3] IV Product Family Engineering Intl. Workshop, Bilbao Oct. 2001, Spinger

[4] IEEE Software, special issue on Software Product Lines, July/August 2002

[5] Frank van der Linden, "Software Product Families in Europe: the ESAPS & CAFÉ projects", IEEE Software, July/August 2002

[6] Repository of ESPRIT/ESSI Process Improvement Experiments
     http://www.esi.es/VASIE/

[7] IST Advisory Group report on Software technologies, embedded systems and distributed systems, June 2002, page 29 http://www.cordis.lu/ist/istag.htm

[8] Paul G. Basset, "Framing Software Reuse", Prentice Hall, 1997

[9] "European Information Technology Observatory 2001"

[10] Wayne C. Lim, "Managing Software Reuse", Prentice Hall PTR, 1998.

[11] Donald J. Reifer, "Practical Software Reuse", Wiley Computer Publishing, 1997.

[12] Donald J. Reifer, " Strategies for Introducing Reuse Concepts in Your Organization", John Wiley & Sons, 1997.

[13] A.Reppening, Andri Ioannidou, Michele Payton, "Using Components for Rapid Distributed Software Development", IEEE Software, March/April 2001

Appendix – Glossary

Alf Inge Wang and Reidar Conradi (Eds.)

Norwegian University of Science and Technology (NTNU),
NO-7491 Trondheim, Norway
{alfw,conradi}@idi.ntnu.no

Glossary of Common Terminology

Case study is a research technique where you identify key factors that may affect the outcome of an activity and then document the activity, its input constraints, resources and output [1].

Component-based Software Engineering (CBSE) is building and managing large software systems using (reusing) previously developed and offer software components to better master the growing complexity and size of new software systems, resulting in better, cheaper and earlier software systems.

COTS: Commercial off-the-shelf software.

Empirical method is a statistical method used to validate a given hypothesis. Data is collected to verify or falsify the hypothesis [2].

Empirical (experimental) Software Engineering emphasizes the actual study of software engineering using scientific principles for validation.

Empirical study is a systematic, practical test of a hypothesis, e.g. by an experiment, case study, post-mortem analysis, or survey.

ESERNET: Experimental Software EngineeRing NETwork.

Experience: Can be collected raw data (e.g. number of defects) or project summaries (post-mortems). It is also possible to have processed and generalized experience as reusable process models, estimation models, check lists, risk models etc. Experiences can also be realized as reusable software artifacts.

Experience base (EB) is a logical centralized archive where various experiences are stored, for later to be used for other purposes. An experience base can be realized as documents, web, as a database, as a spreadsheet, or/and as a tool that includes rules, algorithms, models, and other resources.

Experience Factory (EF) is a logical and/or physical organization for continuous learning from experience, including an experience base for the storage and reuse of knowledge.

R. Conradi and A.I. Wang (Eds.): ESERNET 2001-2003, LNCS 2765, pp. 274–278, 2003.

Experiment: An act or operation for the purpose of discovering something unknown or of testing the purpose of discovering something unknown or of testing a principle [3].

Experimentation: By using the experimentation engineering method, engineers build and test a system according to a hypothesis. Based upon the result of the test, they improve the solution until it requires no further improvement [2].

Goal Question Metric (GQM) is a method used to define measurement on the software project, process and product. GQM defines a measurement model on three levels: 1) Conceptual level (goal): A goal is defined for an object, for a variety of reasons, with respect to various models of quality, from various points of view, and relative to a particular environment. 2) Operational level (question): A set of questions is used to define models of the object of study and then focuses on that object to characterize the assessment or achievement of a specific goal. 3) Quantitative level (metric): A set of metrics, based on the models, is associated with every question in order to answer it in a measurable way [4].

Hypothesis is a proposition or set of propositions set forth as an explanation for the occurrence of some specified group of phenomena, either asserted merely as a provisional conjecture to guide investigation (working hypothesis) or accepted as highly probable in the light of established facts [3].

Knowledge (operational information): There is no consensus or generally accepted definition of knowledge, but the word can mean information, awareness, knowing, cognition, sapience, cognizance, science, experience, skill, insight, competence, know-how, practical ability, capability, learning, wisdom, certainty etc. [5].

Knowledge base see experience base.

Knowledge management (KM) is the management of the organization towards the continuous renewal of the organizational knowledge base - this means e.g. creation of supportive organizational structures, facilitation of organizational members, putting IT-instruments with emphasis on teamwork and diffusion of knowledge (as e.g. groupware) into place. (Thomas Bertels)

Learning organization is an organization skilled at creating, acquiring and transferring knowledge and at modifying its behavior to reflect new knowledge and insights [6].

Metric is a collection of characteristics (attributes) and their definitions and process for collection, that together characterize a software product and/or software process, for a specific purpose and in a specific context. Typical metrics for software can be lines of code (LOC), defects per LOC etc.

Object-oriented analysis (OOA) is concerned with developing an object-oriented model of the application domain. The identified objects reflect entities and operations that are associated with the problem to be solved [7].

Object-oriented design (OOD) is concerned with developing an object-oriented model of a software system to implement the identified requirements. The objects in an object-oriented design are related to the solution to the problem that is being solved [7].

Object-oriented programming (OOP) is concerned with realizing a software design using an object-oriented programming language. An object-oriented programming language, such as Java, supports the direct implementation of objects and provides facilities to define object classes [7].

Plan-Do-Check-Act (PDCA) is a cycle of actions used to achieve continuous improvement. It is possible to use an external PDCA-cycle for the whole company or several internal PDCA-cycles for specific and project-related initiatives. PDCA is used in TQM.

Post-Mortem Analysis (PMA) is a method used to evaluate some performance after you are finished. PMA can be used to evaluate projects by asking questions, such as what went wrong, what did we do well, what can we do better next time, etc.

Qualitative research is concerned with studying objects in their natural setting. A qualitative researcher attempts to interpret a phenomenon based on explanations that people bring to them [8].

Quality Assurance (QA) is the establishment of a framework of organizational procedures and standards, which lead to high-quality software [7].

Quality Control is the definition and enactment of processes, which ensure that the project quality procedures and standards are followed by the software development team [7].

Quality Improvement Paradigm (QIP) is aimed at building descriptive models of software processes, products, and other forms of experience, experimenting with and analyzing these models, in order to build improvement-oriented, packaged, prescriptive models [9]. QIP uses EF and GQM.

Quality Management involves defining procedures and standards, which should be used during software development and checking that these are followed by all engineers [7].

Quantitative research is initially concerned with quantifying a relationship or to compare two or more groups [10]. The aim is to identify a cause-effect relationship. The quantitative research is often conducted through setting up controlled experiments or collecting data through case studies.

Reuse is further use or repeated use of an artifact. Typically, software artifacts are designed for use outside their original context to create new systems [11].

Software Engineering is an engineering discipline which is concerned with all aspects of software production from the early stages of system specification through to maintaining the system after it has gone into use [7].

Software inspection is a static method to *verify* and *validate* a software artifact manually [12]. Verification means checking whether the product is developed correctly, i.e. fulfils its specification. Validation means checking whether the "correct" product is developed, i.e. to fulfill the customer's needs.

Software measurement is concerned with deriving a (numeric) value for some attribute of a software product or software process [7].

Software process improvement (SPI) is a systematical and focused activity to improve the software quality of the end product and the related software development processes, by using an improvement plan within a software development organization.

Software quality is the totality of features and characteristics of a product or service that bears on its ability to satisfy stated or implied needs (ISO 8402-1986) or software quality is that the developed product should meet its specification [13].

Survey is a retrospective study of a situation to try to document relationships and outcomes. Thus, a survey is always done after an event has occurred [1].

Testing is the process of executing a program (or part of a program) with the intention of finding errors [14].

Total Quality Management (TQM) is *Total* organization using *Quality* principles for the *Management* of its processes [15].

Validation is the process of checking whether entered data meets certain conditions or limitations [16].

References

[1]   N. Fenton and S. L. Pfleeger, "Software Metrics: A Rigorous & Practical Approach", 2nd edition, International Thomson Computer Press, 1996.

[2]   Victor R. Basili, "The experimental paradigm in software engineering". In H. D. Rombach, V. R. Basili, and R. W. Selby, editors, Experimental Software Engineering Issues: A critical assessment and future directions, p. 3–12. Lecture Notes in Computer Science Nr. 706, Springer Verlag, September 1992.

[3]   Webster's Encyclopaedic Unabridged Dictionary of the English Language, Gramercy books 1989.

[4]   The Software Engineering Laboratory, "SEL: Goal-Question-Metric (GQM)", Web: http://sel.gsfc.nasa.gov/website/exp-factory/gqm.htm.

[5]   Karl Erik Sveiby, "The New Organizational Wealth – Managing & measuring knowledge-based assets", Berrett-Koehler Publishers, 1997.

[6]   David A. Garvin, "Building a Learning Organization", Harvard Business Review, July-August 1993.

[7]   Ian Sommerville, "Software Engineering 6th Edition", Addison-Wesley 2001.

[8]   N. K. Denzin and Y. S. Lincoln, "Handbook of Qualitative Research", Sage Publications, London, UK, 1994.

[9]   Experimental Software Engineering Group, "ESEG at UMCP Home Page", Web: http://www.cs.umd.edu/projects/SoftEng/tame/tame.html, 2003.

[10] J. W. Creswell, "Research Design, Qualitative and Quantitative Approaches", Sage Publications, 1994.

[11] Ivar Jacobson, Martin Griss, Patrik Jonsson, "Software Reuse – Architecture, Process and Organization for Business Success", ACM Press book, 1997.

[12] Robert Ebenau and Susan Strauss, "Software Inspection Process", Mc Graw-Hill, 1994, ISBN 0070621667.

[13] Philip B. Crosby, "Quality is Free: The Art of Making Quality Certain", McGraw-Hill, 1979.

[14] G.J. Myers, "Software Reliability, Principles and Practices", New York: Wiley, 1976.

[15] University of Michigan, "Total Quality Management ENG / MFG401", Web: http://www.mazur.net/tqm/default.htm, 2003.

[16] MSDN, "Welcome to the MSDN library", Web: http://msdn.microsoft.com/library/default.asp?url=/library/en-us/off2000/html/defValidation.asp, 2003.

You can also find related terms and definition on the following web sites:

- ESERNET competence center: http://www.esernet.org/
- Software Engineering Institute (SEI): http://www.sei.cmu.edu/
- Software Engineering Laboratory (SEL): http://sel.gsfc.nasa.gov/
- Fraunhofer Center – Maryland: http://fc-md.umd.edu/fcmd/index.html
- Fraunhofer IESE in Kaiserslautern: http://www.iese.fhg.de/

Author Index

Lecture Notes in Computer Science

For information about Vols. 1–2674
please contact your bookseller or Springer-Verlag

Vol. 2715: T. Bilgiç, B. De Baets, O. Kaynak (Eds.), Fuzzy Sets and Systems – IFSA 2003. Proceedings, 2003. XV, 735 pages. 2003. (Subseries LNAI).

Vol. 2716: M.J. Voss (Ed.), OpenMP Shared Memory Parallel Programming. Proceedings, 2003. VIII, 271 pages. 2003.

Vol. 2718: P. W. H. Chung, C. Hinde, M. Ali (Eds.), Developments in Applied Artificial Intelligence. Proceedings, 2003. XIV, 817 pages. 2003. (Subseries LNAI).

Vol. 2719: J.C.M. Baeten, J.K. Lenstra, J. Parrow, G.J. Woeginger (Eds.), Automata, Languages and Programming. Proceedings, 2003. XVIII, 1199 pages. 2003.

Vol. 2720: M. Marques Freire, P. Lorenz, M.M.-O. Lee (Eds.), High-Speed Networks and Multimedia Communications. Proceedings, 2003. XIII, 582 pages. 2003.

Vol. 2721: N.J. Mamede, J. Baptista, I. Trancoso, M. das Graças Volpe Nunes (Eds.), Computational Processing of the Portuguese Language. Proceedings, 2003. XIV, 268 pages. 2003. (Subseries LNAI).

Vol. 2722: J.M. Cueva Lovelle, B.M. González Rodríguez, L. Joyanes Aguilar, J.E. Labra Gayo, M. del Puerto Paule Ruiz (Eds.), Web Engineering. Proceedings, 2003. XIX, 554 pages. 2003.

Vol. 2723: E. Cantú-Paz, J.A. Foster, K. Deb, L.D. Davis, R. Roy, U.-M. O'Reilly, H.-G. Beyer, R. Standish, G. Kendall, S. Wilson, M. Harman, J. Wegener, D. Dasgupta, M.A. Potter, A.C. Schultz, K.A. Dowsland, N. Jonoska, J. Miller (Eds.), Genetic and Evolutionary Computation – GECCO 2003. Proceedings, Part I. 2003. XLVII, 1252 pages. 2003.

Vol. 2724: E. Cantú-Paz, J.A. Foster, K. Deb, L.D. Davis, R. Roy, U.-M. O'Reilly, H.-G. Beyer, R. Standish, G. Kendall, S. Wilson, M. Harman, J. Wegener, D. Dasgupta, M.A. Potter, A.C. Schultz, K.A. Dowsland, N. Jonoska, J. Miller (Eds.), Genetic and Evolutionary Computation – GECCO 2003. Proceedings, Part II. 2003. XLVII, 1274 pages. 2003.

Vol. 2725: W.A. Hunt, Jr., F. Somenzi (Eds.), Computer Aided Verification. Proceedings, 2003. XII, 462 pages. 2003.

Vol. 2726: E. Hancock, M. Vento (Eds.), Graph Based Representations in Pattern Recognition. Proceedings, 2003. VIII, 271 pages. 2003.

Vol. 2727: R. Safavi-Naini, J. Seberry (Eds.), Information Security and Privacy. Proceedings, 2003. XII, 534 pages. 2003.

Vol. 2728: E.M. Bakker, T.S. Huang, M.S. Lew, N. Sebe, X.S. Zhou (Eds.), Image and Video Retrieval. Proceedings, 2003. XIII, 512 pages. 2003.

Vol. 2729: D. Boneh (Ed.), Advances in Cryptology – CRYPTO 2003. Proceedings, 2003. XII, 631 pages. 2003.

Vol. 2731: C.S. Calude, M.J. Dinneen, V. Vajnovszki (Eds.), Discrete Mathematics and Theoretical Computer Science. Proceedings, 2003. VIII, 301 pages. 2003.

Vol. 2732: C. Taylor, J.A. Noble (Eds.), Information Processing in Medical Imaging. Proceedings, 2003. XVI, 698 pages. 2003.

Vol. 2733: A. Butz, A. Krüger, P. Olivier (Eds.), Smart Graphics. Proceedings, 2003. XI, 261 pages. 2003.

Vol. 2734: P. Perner, A. Rosenfeld (Eds.), Machine Learning and Data Mining in Pattern Recognition. Proceedings, 2003. XII, 440 pages. 2003. (Subseries LNAI).

Vol. 2740: E. Burke, P. De Causmaecker (Eds.), Practice and Theory of Automated Timetabling IV. Proceedings, 2002. XII, 361 pages. 2003.

Vol. 2741: F. Baader (Ed.), Automated Deduction – CADE-19. Proceedings, 2003. XII, 503 pages. 2003. (Subseries LNAI).

Vol. 2742: R. N. Wright (Ed.), Financial Cryptography. Proceedings, 2003. VIII, 321 pages. 2003.

Vol. 2743: L. Cardelli (Ed.), ECOOP 2003 – Object-Oriented Programming. Proceedings, 2003. X, 501 pages. 2003.

Vol. 2744: V. Mařík, D. McFarlane, P. Valckenaers (Eds.), Holonic and Multi-Agent Systems for Manufacturing. Proceedings, 2003. XI, 322 pages. 2003. (Subseries LNAI).

Vol. 2745: M. Guo, L.T. Yang (Eds.), Parallel and Distributed Processing and Applications. Proceedings, 2003. XII, 450 pages. 2003.

Vol. 2746: A. de Moor, W. Lex, B. Ganter (Eds.), Conceptual Structures for Knowledge Creation and Communication. Proceedings, 2003. XI, 405 pages. 2003. (Subseries LNAI).

Vol. 2747: B. Rovan, P. Vojtáš (Eds.), Mathematical Foundations of Computer Science 2003. Proceedings, 2003. XIII, 692 pages. 2003.

Vol. 2748: F. Dehne, J.-R. Sack, M. Smid (Eds.), Algorithms and Data Structures. Proceedings, 2003. XII, 522 pages. 2003.

Vol. 2749: J. Bigun, T. Gustavsson (Eds.), Image Analysis. Proceedings, 2003. XXII, 1174 pages. 2003.

Vol. 2750: T. Hadzilacos, Y. Manolopoulos, J.F. Roddick, Y. Theodoridis (Eds.), Advances in Spatial and Temporal Databases. Proceedings, 2003. XIII, 525 pages. 2003.

Vol. 2751: A. Lingas, B.J. Nilsson (Eds.), Fundamentals of Computation Theory. Proceedings, 2003. XII, 433 pages. 2003.

Vol. 2752: G.A. Kaminka, P.U. Lima, R. Rojas (Eds.), RoboCup 2002: Robot Soccer World Cup VI. XVI, 498 pages. 2003. (Subseries LNAI).

Vol. 2753: F. Maurer, D. Wells (Eds.), Extreme Programming and Agile Methods – XP/Agile Universe 2003. Proceedings, 2003. XI, 215 pages. 2003.

Vol. 2754: M. Schumacher, Security Engineering with Patterns. XIV, 208 pages. 2003.

Vol. 2758: D. Basin, B. Wolff (Eds.), Theorem Proving in Higher Order Logics. Proceedings, 2003. X, 367 pages. 2003.

Vol. 2759: O.H. Ibarra, Z. Dang (Eds.), Implementation and Application of Automata. Proceedings, 2003. XI, 312 pages. 2003.

Vol. 2762: G. Dong, C. Tang, W. Wang (Eds.), Advances in Web-Age Information Management. Proceedings, 2003. XIII, 512 pages. 2003.

Vol. 2763: V. Malyshkin (Ed.), Parallel Computing Technologies. Proceedings, 2003. XIII, 570 pages. 2003.

Vol. 2765: R. Conradi, A.I. Wang (Eds.), Empirical Methods and Studies in Software Engineering. VIII, 279 pages. 2003.

Vol. 2766: S. Behnke, Hierarchical Neural Networks for Image Interpretation. XII, 224 pages. 2003.